D0883412

Native Americans

American Political History Series

Native Americans

Edited by Donald A. Grinde Jr.

A Division of Congressional Quarterly Inc.
Washington, D.C.

CQ Press
1255 22nd Street, N.W., Suite 400
Washington, D.C. 20037

202-729-1900; toll free, 1-866-4CQ-PRESS (1-866-427-7737)

www.cqpress.com

Cover design by Naylor Design
Interior design by Auburn Associates, Inc.

Cover photos: *(counterclockwise from left)* Don Wedll (Mille Lacs band of Ojibwe) speaking after the Supreme Court upheld treaty rights in Minnesota (photo by Clint Wood/AP Photo); Earl Old Person (Blackfoot) speaking out against an effort in Montana to allow state sovereignty over reservation lands owned by nontribal members (photo by Bob Zellar/AP Photo); Ramapough Mountain Indians protesting the U.S. government's refusal to recognize their tribe (photo by Charles Tasnadi/AP Photo)

Printed and bound in the United States of America

06 05 04 03 02 5 4 3 2 1

Library of Congress Cataloging-in-Publication Data

Native Americans / edited by Donald A. Grinde, Jr.
p. cm. — (American political history series)
Includes bibliographical references and index.
ISBN 1-56802-683-8 (hardcover : alk. paper)
1. Indians of North America—Government relations. 2. Indians of North America—Politics and government. I. Grinde, Donald A., II. Series.
E93 N32 2002
323.1′197073—dc21

2002014210

F*or my son, Kee Nez Grinde (Navajo), a Native American law student at Arizona State University*

Contents

Part V Recent Movements

Part VI Documents

Part VII Appendices

Preface

In the late eighteenth century, Euro-American settlement of the eastern seaboard extended no more than two hundred miles from the Atlantic coastline. Native Americans were an important part of the multiethnic and multicultural mix that had become the United States of America. The founders had borrowed freely from American Indian ideas on federalism, democracy, individual freedoms, and separation of powers as well as approaches useful in uniting a people across a great geographic expanse. With the ratification of the U.S. Constitution, American Indian tribes seemed to have the same political status as other independent nations and participated significantly in events of historical importance. Over time, however, conquest, subjugation, corruption, genocide, and ethnocide wrought considerable transformations in the lives and governments of Native Americans from coast to coast.

Because many American Indian nations held considerable power and vast lands at the time of U.S. independence, the new republic initially found it necessary to deal amicably with its Native American neighbors; U.S.-tribal treaty relations and federal policies toward the Indians form a significant part of American political history. With the rapid expansion of the United States across the North American continent, however, federal policies and actions eliminated large numbers of Indian nations in the path of conquest; many more were placed on small parcels of land and their members subjected to cultural and religious death through forced conversions to Christianity and attendance at boarding schools where they could not speak native languages or wear traditional dress.

The federal government continued its efforts to wrest the Native American land base in the late nineteenth century with congressional passage of the General Allotment Act, which also represented an attack on American Indian tribalism and governmental autonomy. Federal laws and court decisions destroyed Indian governments and communities with impunity. The white racism and Christian religious arrogance of this time reasoned that American Indians were an inferior people culturally, religiously, and racially. Paternalistic policies applied by a benign superior race would put native peoples on the path toward assimilation and (white) civilization. Paradoxically, whites pursued a concurrent policy of "separate but equal" toward African Americans.

In the 1930s Franklin D. Roosevelt's Indian New Deal introduced a measure of federal tolerance and respect for Indians and their cultures. After World War II, the Eisenhower administration's policy of "termination" posed a renewed challenge to American Indian tribalism, as the United States sought to dissolve tribal governments and end federal assistance to them. Once again, Native Americans survived such efforts, as they had others in the past.

Sorting through Native Americans' individual rights as U.S. citizens—a status that some Indians ignore or downgrade—as well as their collective rights as members of sovereign American Indian nations has informed much of the legislation, executive orders, and court decisions on Indian policy over the years. For example, because Native Americans' status is different from that of other U.S. citizens, Indians tended to be overlooked or alienated during the general push for civil rights in the 1960s and for a period afterward. During the 1960s militant Indians exercised their rights as U.S. citizens and began to demand civil rights for Native Americans and recognition of their treaty rights.

American Indians' legal status, and their overall well-being, continues to be at the mercy of swings in American politics and opinion. Contradictory and confusing changes in federal Indian policy result, dismaying Native Americans and non-Indians dedicated to forging a more consistent and fair path for American Indian people and nations. It is hoped that all the people involved in Native Americans' lives will use the contents of this volume in the spirit of creating a path to the future that is less fraught with confusion, discord, and misunderstandings.

Native Americans represents an attempt to achieve some balance in working toward this goal, by providing students of American political history and Indian policy with insights with which to understand Native Americans and the political and cultural issues concerning them. American Indian self-determination and autonomy—to which the United States agreed centuries ago—will be greatly enhanced when federal and state governments deal openly and honestly with the issues of genocide, ethnocide, American Indian religious freedom, Native American heirship, sovereignty of tribal governments, and the fundamental problems involving the administration of American Indian affairs.

A talented group of Native American and non–Native American scholars from a variety of disciplines wrote the multifaceted essays in this volume, examining these issues in a topical and historical manner while providing innovative and critical analysis of the political history of Native Americans during the past 250 years. Reprints and annotations of letters, legislation, government reports, and judicial decisions, while not exhaustive, complement the topics addressed by the authors in their twenty-two chapters.

I would like to thank acquisitions editor Christopher Anzalone and project editor Robin Surratt of CQ Press for their diligent and patient assistance in bringing this publication to fruition. The University of Vermont must be acknowledged for the 2001–2002 sabbatical that allowed me the opportunity to complete this project. Finally, I would like to express my gratitude to the scholars who contributed to this volume. I have worked with some of them all my professional life and have more recently come to know the other, younger scholars, who are producing notably good work in Native American studies. I hope this collaborative effort provides a useful reference for all people interested in this topic.

Bibliography

Deloria, Vine, Jr., ed. 1985. *American Indian Policy in the Twentieth Century.* Norman: University of Oklahoma Press.

Deloria, Vine, Jr., and David E. Wilkins. 1999. *Tribes, Treaties, and Constitutional Tribulations.* Austin: University of Texas Press.

Lyons, Oren, et al. 1992. *Exiled in the Land of the Free: Democracy, Indian Nations, and the U.S. Constitution.* Santa Fe: Clear Light Publishers.

U.S. — Native American Relations

1

Native Americans and the Founding of the United States

Donald A. Grinde Jr.

As the American Revolution unfolded, intellectual and political leaders in the colonies sought ideas about constructing a new democratic society. Among the Iroquois, there exists an oral tradition that the founders of the United States consulted with them in developing such a government. The evolution of democratic thought and diplomacy in colonial America is a story that includes the presence of Native Americans at the debates on the Declaration of Independence in May and June 1776 in Philadelphia. It is also the story of the extensive experiences of revolutionary leaders, including Benjamin Franklin and Thomas Jefferson, with Native Americans. Both men were influenced by Native American theories of freedom and democracy.

The physical and philosophical presence of Native Americans at the birth of the United States often goes unmentioned although the historical evidence is abundant. Essentially, the United States has been multicultural from its conception due to the contacts between Native Americans and Euro-Americans in interactions that involved more than exchanging corn and other physical items. Many scholars have commented on their exchange of ideas about freedom and democracy, but recognition of this process is far from complete.

The Bicentennial of American Independence

In 1977, the Iroquois (Haudenosaunee) issued a statement acknowledging their nations' role in the development of the U.S. government. Their assertion created a stir among nonnative academics although it had long been a part of the oral history of the Haudenosaunee people. The leadership's statement in part read,

> The Hau de no sau nee is governed by a constitution known among Europeans as the Constitution of the Six Nations and to the Hau de no sau nee as the Gayanashakgoway, or the

> Great Law of Peace. It is the oldest functioning document in the world which has contained a recognition of the freedoms the Western democracies recently claim as their own: the freedom of speech, freedom of religion, and the rights of women to participate in government. The concept of separation of powers in government and of checks and balances of power within governments are traceable to our constitution. They are ideas learned by the colonists as the result of contact with North American Native people, specifically the Hau de no sau nee. (Akwesasne Notes 1991, 80–81)

According to Iroquois tradition and history, the Iroquois Confederacy is the oldest continuously functioning democratic constitution and served as a blueprint for the creation of Western democracies. In 1976 during the U.S. bicentennial, the Sovereign Native Women's Conference declared in a press release, "We, the Indian people, may be the only citizens of this nation who really understand your form of government, and respect that form of government, as this form of government was copied from the Iroquois Confederacy" (Lyons 1992, 228). Among Indian nations across North America, it is common knowledge that the fundamental principles of the U.S. government are reflections of similar concepts in native governments.

Native American Influences on European Ideas of Freedom

The assumption that American democracy evolved from the English parliamentary system or from a perusal of European political thinkers must be tempered with the realization that such writers as John Locke and Jean Jacques Rousseau borrowed some of their ideas about democracy from travelers' accounts of American Indian governmental structures. From the time of their first contacts with Native Americans, many Europeans greatly admired the Indians' working democracies. Baron Lahontan, Voltaire, Rousseau, and Gabriel Sagard compared the Iroquois to the Romans, the Greeks, and the Celts in the areas of natural rights, statecraft, oratory, and public consensus. Hence, the process of colonial democratization that eventually changed the political systems of the world has its roots in Native American democracies.

Locke writes, "the kings of the Indians in America" are not much more than "generals . . . and in time of peace they . . . have . . . moderate sovereignty." He adds that decisions of peace and war were vested "ordinarily either in the people, or in a council" (Grinde and Johansen 1991, 67). Most Europeans, however, viewed Locke's writings as theory, so they did not inspire political change in England or any other country. The first democratic revolution sprang from American unrest because the colonists had partially assimilated the concepts of unity, federalism, and natural rights that they witnessed in American Indian governments. Native American ideas of freedom and limited sovereignty in the executive provided a practical, viable, and workable alternative to the prevailing wisdom of European society.

A decade before the revolution, the famous frontier soldier Robert Rogers told a London audience that among American Indians, "every man is free [and that no one] . . . has any right to deprive him of his freedom" (Lyons 1992, 235). In 1772–1773, another observer, David Jones, wrote that American Indians believed that "God made them free—that no man has the natural right to rule over another" (Grinde and Johansen 1991, 15). Commenting on the Iroquois during the revolutionary era, the English explorer John Long noted that "the Iroquois laugh when you talk to them about obedience to kings [because] . . . they cannot reconcile the idea of submission with the dignity of man" (Lyons 1992, 235). On a very fundamental level, on the eve of U.S. independence Europeans and colonial Americans thought that American Indians represented freedom.

The Iroquois and the Albany Plan of Union

With George Washington's 1754 defeat by the French at Fort Necessity, Pennsylvania, English prestige in North America was shattered, and the storm clouds of the Seven Year's War began to form on the horizon. French expansion into the Ohio country had to be thwarted. Under the sponsorship of the British Crown, colonial delegates assembled at Albany in the summer of 1754 to negotiate a peace with all the Indian tribes (especially the Iroquois) and to win them over before going to war against France.

Among the delegates was Benjamin Franklin, who would later openly acknowledge his indebtedness to the Iroquois for some of his ideas on a governing system for the American Republic. Franklin had made his fortune publishing Indian treaties, and having become knowledgeable of Native American traditions and systems of government, he also published speeches by the Iroquois admonishing the colonies to unify in a similar manner. The Albany Plan of Union called for a "general Government . . . under which Government each colony may retain its present Constitution" (ibid., 245). Basically, the plan provided for Parliament to establish a general government in America that would include the thirteen colonies, each of which would retain its current constitution except for certain powers, mainly concerning mutual defense, which would be given to the general government. The king would appoint a president-general. Each colonial assembly would elect representatives to a grand council. The president-general, with the advice of the grand council, would retain certain powers, such as handling Indian relations, making treaties, deciding upon peace or war, raising troops, building forts, providing warships, and making laws and levying taxes as needed. Franklin's idea embraced a plan for union that the Iroquois leaders Canassateego, Hendrick, and others had urged upon the colonists for a decade or more. Thus, the roots of intercolonial unity grew in Indian-white relations of the early eighteenth century.

In remarks in *Documents of American History* prefacing the Articles of Confederation, historian Henry Steele Commager states that the articles "should be studied in comparison with the Albany Plan of Union and the Constitution" (Grinde and Johansen 1991, 108). According to political scientist Clinton Rossiter, "The Albany Plan is a landmark on the rough road that was to lead through the first Continental Congresses and the Articles of Confederation to the Constitution of 1787" (Lyons 1992, 245). The missing component in this analysis is the role of Iroquois political theory and its influence on the formation of American notions of government. Julian P. Boyd, the leading scholar on the drafting of the Declaration of Independence, noted a generation ago that Franklin "proposed a plan for the union of the colonies and he found his materials in the great confederacy of the Iroquois" (Grinde and Johansen 1991, 108).

The Debates on Colonial Independence

In early 1776 Joseph Galloway, a Franklin ally in the Continental Congress, suggested a plan of colonial union similar to Franklin's Albany

Plan of Union to restore harmony with England. Those who supported Galloway's "olive branch" stalled on the issue of independence at the Second Continental Congress. The supporters of the Galloway Plan feared a lapse in governmental authority and wanted a plan for union before forsaking imperial authority. To salve such fears, Virginia delegate Richard Henry Lee introduced an independence resolution on June 7, 1776, that included a proposed plan of confederation that would be transmitted to the colonies for debate.

In the midst of this debate on government and independence, twenty-one Iroquois leaders arrived to meet with the Second Continental Congress in May 1776. At the Albany conference of 1775 in discussions with the colonists about their plans for government, the Iroquois had expressed concern about the nature of the executive in the Continental Congress. The Iroquois observed the operations of the Continental Congress and its president, John Hancock, for more than a month. Meeting with the Iroquois was so important that the congress ordered General Washington to leave his command in New York and come talk with the Iroquois leaders in Philadelphia. On May 27, 1776, Richard Henry Lee reported that the colonial army had a parade of two thousand to three thousand men to impress the Iroquois with the strength of the American endeavor. On June 11, 1776, while independence was debated, the visiting Iroquois chiefs were invited formally into the hall of the Continental Congress and a speech was delivered calling them "Brothers" and wishing that the "friendship . . . between us . . . will . . . continue as long as the sun shall shine" and the "waters run" (Ford 1904–1937, 5:430–431). The speech also declared that the colonists and the Iroquois are "as one people, and have but one heart" (ibid.). After the speech, an Onondaga chief gave Hancock the Indian name, Karanduawn, or "The Great Tree." On the same day that the Iroquois named Hancock, plans for a confederation based on Franklin's Albany Plan of Union were formulated in committee. That Franklin got his plan from the Great Law of the Iroquois is acknowledged. The question of Iroquois influence on the American governmental system is thus only one of degree.

After the congress voted for independence, John Dickinson of Pennsylvania submitted a rough draft of the Articles of Confederation, or "Our League of Friendship," as it was also called. On July 26, 1776, James Wilson of Pennsylvania argued forcefully for confederation, stating that "Indians know the striking benefits of Confederation" and they "have an example of it in the union of the Six Nations" (ibid., 6:1078). Wilson advocated that a strong union similar to the Iroquois Confederacy would be crucial for the creation of the former colonists' new nation.

Thomas Jefferson and Native American Ideas of Freedom

Historian Richard K. Matthews, discussing Jefferson's interests in American Indians and their relationship to his political ideas, states that the "study of the American Indians . . . helped to convince Jefferson that man was a social, harmonious, cooperative and just creature who . . . could happily live in a community that did not need the presence of the Leviathan." Indeed, Matthews believes that while Alexander Hamilton and James Madison had their ideal of the "market man, Jefferson had the American Indian, who provides the empirical model for his political vision." Matthews concludes that Jefferson's knowledge of American Indians provided his "scientific mind with the concrete evidence that he needed so that he could erect a solid democratic political theory" (Matthews 1984, 17–18, 122).

Historian Julian Boyd also recognizes the enormous impact of Native American people on the Europeans that encountered them:

> In the realm of political thought, the Indian probably had a greater influence over civilized society than any other savage race. . . . Marc Lescarbot, Gabriel Sagard, and the authors of the great Jesuit Relations began in the 16th and 17th centuries by describing Indian society and ended by praising it with a praise that carried an implied criticism of the European political system. From this it was an easy step to put in the mouth of an American savage a blunt criticism of civilized political organization. (Grinde and Johansen 1991, xix)

Boyd believes that Native American influences on colonial and European thought were extensive. He writes that Native American ways inspired Montesquieu's

> *Spirit of Laws* and from the same sources emerged Rousseau's *Social Contract*. . . . [T]he French Revolution was but another link in the chain of influence that has stretched from the western frontiers to the capitals of Europe. . . . The Indian, therefore, was a factor of immense importance in the 18th century, far out of proportion to his actual numbers. (ibid.)

From Jefferson's accounts, we know that his entire life was rich in association with the indigenous peoples of North America. His father, Peter, was an avid naturalist who introduced young Thomas to the Indian *sachems* and visitors who lodged at the family home on their way to and from official business in Williamsburg, Virginia. In a series of published letters toward the end of his life in which he attempted to reconcile the political differences of former presidents Washington and Adams, Jefferson wrote to Adams that he believed his early contacts with Native Americans were an important influence on his development:

> Concerning Indians, in the early part of my life, I was very familiar, and acquired impressions of attachment and commiseration for them which have never been obliterated. Before the Revolution, they were in the habit of coming often and in great numbers to the seat of government *where I was very much with them*. I knew much the great Ontassete, the warrior and orator of the Cherokees; he was always the guest of my father, on his journeys to and from Williamsburg. (Grinde and Johansen 1991, 155, emphasis added)

Certainly, the political concepts of Native Americans held a great fascination for the revolutionary generation. An examination of the papers of Jefferson, Adams, Franklin, and John Rutledge, a South Carolina delegate to the Continental Congress, reveals a free flowing discourse on the nature of American Indian government, including the Iroquois's. Charles Pinckney, a delegate to the Constitutional Convention from South Carolina and Franklin believed that European governments were not applicable to North America. Jefferson summed it up best in his letter in the summer of 1787 to Rutledge as Rutledge was finishing the first draft of the Constitution. Jefferson writes that the "effect of kingly government . . . is to produce the wanton sacrifice . . . of the people" and concludes his analysis by observing that some Americans characterized "our's a bad government. The only condition on earth to be compared with ours, is that of the Indians, where they still have less law than we. The European, are governments of kites over pigeons" (ibid., 216).

Native Americans and the Postcolonial Period

The Declaration of Independence and its administration had little impact on the ideas of eastern Native American tribes because many of them already had functioning confederate and democratic societies. The Indians were outside the purview of U.S. society and its laws about "inalienable rights" and "life, liberty and the pursuit of happiness." Just as these rights were not extended to African Americans because of racism, Native Americans were also ignored by virtue of their race and by being members of nations that had not yet been conquered. From 1776 to 1816 the United States recognized that American Indian nations had the same status as other independent nations. Thus the federal government made every effort to maintain good diplomatic relations with their neighbors to the west. In 1789 the first U.S. Congress ratified the Northwest Ordinance of 1787, asserting that "the utmost good faith shall always be observed towards Indians; their land and property shall never be taken from them without their consent."

Mindful of tendencies in U.S. society to ignore the rights of Native Americans, the first Congress passed several laws to protect American Indians from abuse by non-Indians. The Indian Trade and Intercourse Acts passed in the 1790s stated that people trading with Indians had to possess a federal license, persons committing certain crimes against Indians would be prosecuted by federal authorities, and non-Indians were prohibited from obtaining land from Indians without the consent of the federal government. In 1793 Congress prohibited non-Indians from settling on Indian lands. Federal employees were forbidden to trade with Indians under this legislation, and Native Americans were exempted from state regulations on trade. The attitude of the law toward American Indians during this period was summed up in the Supreme Court's ruling in *Worcester v. Georgia* (1832):

> [t]he early journals of Congress exhibit the most anxious desire to conciliate the Indian nations . . . and everything which might excite hostility was avoided. Sadly, these laws were not enforced, especially those that would retard settlers from advancing the western frontier. Similarly, the government consistently ignored the forcible and illegal taking of American Indian land since it meant to govern and restrain the advance of white settlers—not to prevent it.

While the U.S. government's policies immediately after the revolution were conciliatory, and high-minded rhetoric continued to flow, settler pressure for land forced changes in the American outlook toward native peoples. Attempts to curtail settlers from illegally taking Indian lands were few because the federal government chose to attend to the land interests of white settlers rather than enforce legitimate Native American treaty rights.

Summary

Many of the revolutionaries that declared U.S. independence on July 4, 1776, had some familiarity with Native American ideas of freedom and representative government. References by James Wilson to the advantages of confederation and union like the Iroquois's attests to such knowledge. American Indian governments were often described as having no kings and as being less coercive than European governments, characteristics that fascinated such thinkers as John Locke and Thomas Jefferson.

That American Indians were present at the debates on independence lends even greater credence to the notion that American Indian ideas of government played a key role in the creation of the United States. The British system, the ancient Greeks' order, and the ideas of thinkers such as Locke, of course, are important factors in the grand equation of American democracy and independence, but American Indian ideas and thinkers are also an integral part of what the United States is about. American Indians and their ideas should be recognized as one of the roots of American freedom and democracy.

Despite Native American contributions to the founding of the United States, the promises of freedom and self-expression touted in the Declaration of Independence have often been denied to American Indians. Instead, for some two hundred years, conquest, genocide, ethnocide, and assimilation were the policies of the federal government toward Native Americans. Essentially, the United States was multicultural and multiracial from the start, and it has remained that way, though the sources of freedom and government have been ignored in the case of Native Americans.

Bibliography

Akwesasne Notes, ed. 1991. *Basic Call to Consciousness.* Summertown, Tenn.: Book Publishing Company.

Boyd, Julian. 1981. "Dr. Franklin, Friend of the Indian." In *Meet Dr. Franklin*, edited by Roy Lokken. Philadelphia: Franklin Institute.

Boyd, Julian, et al., eds. 1950– . *The Papers of Thomas Jefferson.* Princeton: Princeton University Press.

Ford, Worthington C., et al., eds. 1904–1937. *Journals of the Continental Congress.* Washington, D.C.: Government Printing Office.

Gilreath, James, ed. 1999. *Thomas Jefferson and the Education of a Citizen.* Washington, D.C.: Library of Congress.

Grinde, Donald A., Jr., and Bruce E. Johansen. 1991. *Exemplar of Liberty: Native America and the Evolution of Democracy.* Los Angeles: American Indian Studies Center, University of California.

Labaree, Leonard W., et al., eds. 1959– . *The Papers of Benjamin Franklin.* New Haven: Yale University Press.

Lyons, Oren, et al. 1992. *Exiled in the Land of the Free: Democracy, Indian Nations, and the U.S. Constitution.* Santa Fe: Clear Light Publishers.

Matthews, Richard K. 1984. *The Radical Politics of Thomas Jefferson.* Lawrence: University Press of Kansas.

Papers of the Continental Congress. National Archives, Washington, D.C. M247, roll 144, item no. 134.

Pevar, Stephen L. 1992. *The Rights of Indians and Tribes.* Carbondale: Southern Illinois University Press.

2 The Enduring Influence of Native American Ideas on American Government

Bruce E. Johansen

Within a few years of the first English landfall on the eastern seaboard of North America, shortly after 1600, Native American governments became part of the European-American calculus for a developing sense of government. Roger Williams, architect of "soul liberty," drew from Native American political and religious conceptions during the first half of the seventeenth century. By the time of the Constitutional Convention in 1787, these Native American political ideas were common currency in the former colonies, as illustrated here by debates between Benjamin Franklin and John Adams at the convention. By the nineteenth century, conceptions of Iroquois society were having an important impact on some of the architects of Anglo-American feminism.

Roger Williams and "Soul Liberty"

The historian Vernon Louis Parrington calls Roger Williams the "first rebel against the divine church-order" (Parrington 1927, 1:6). Max Savelle describes him as the "morning star in the galaxy of the American great" (Savelle 1956, 51). During his life, Williams was excoriated as a spreader of intellectual infections. After his death, he was hailed as the first flower of Enlightenment's spring. Roger Williams was the first North American revolutionary, or at least the first of European extraction.

Although Williams's ideas were couched mainly in a religious context, they also engaged debates on political liberty. Like many of the founders of the United States, Williams often used his perceptions of American Indians and their societies as a reference by which to hone his preexisting desires for an alternative to the European status quo. As the founder of Providence Plantations (later Rhode Island) as a refuge for freethinkers—at least at its inception—Williams tried to implement his ideas of "soul liberty," or political freedom and economic equality. His experiment presaged the later revolution of continental scope.

Educated at London's Charterhouse School and Cambridge University, Williams was one of the Puritans' best and brightest when he emigrated to America. Having asserted the soul liberty among the native peoples of America, as well as dissident colonists, Williams was cast out of Puritania. Like many another Puritans, Williams originally came to America "longing after the natives' soules" (Chupack 1969, 63). More than most, Williams's errand in the wilderness helped shape his predispositions toward freedom. He engendered a passionate debate on both sides of the Atlantic that began to hone the definitions of political and religious liberty that would frame the ideology of the American Revolution.

Within a few months of his arrival in Boston in 1631, Williams was learning the Algonquian language. He would eventually master the dialects of the Narragansett, Nipmuck, Showatuck, and others. Williams's oratorical flourish and compassion won him esteem with congregations at Plymouth and Salem as well as among native peoples of the area, all of whom sought his "love and counsel" (Ernst 1932, 179). Williams's quick mastery of native languages did not alarm the soul soldiers of Puritania. What landed him in hot ecclesiastical water was what he learned from the native peoples as he picked up their languages. Asked by Plymouth leader William Bradford to compose a paper on the compact that established the Puritan colony in America, Williams declared it invalid. How, he asked, could the Puritans claim the land by "right of discovery," when it was already inhabited? Furthermore, Williams argued that the Puritans had no right to deny the Indians their own religions, divine or secular. Soon, the authorities were transferring Williams from pulpit to pulpit, fretting over how easily he won friends not only among colonists but also with the native peoples of the area.

Those friendships would be used to Williams's advantage a few years later when he founded Providence Plantations. Williams became friendly with Massasoit, a *sachem* (chief) among the Wampanoags (also called Pokanokets) and a man described by Bradford in 1621 as "lustie in his best years, an able body grave of countenance, spare of speech, strong [and] tall" (Covey 1966, 125). Williams met Massasoit when the latter was about thirty years of age and, according to Williams, they became close friends. Williams also befriended Canonicus, the elderly leader of the Narragansetts. With both, Williams traveled in the forest for days at a time, learning what he could of their languages, societies, and opinions, drinking in experiences that, along with prior European experience, would provide the intellectual groundwork for the model commonwealth Williams sought to establish in Providence Plantations.

By 1635 Williams was arguing that the Puritans' church had no right to compel membership, or contributions, by force of law, the kernel of church-state separation. With this argument, Williams struck at the assumption that the Puritan church subsumed the state. Taxes were levied to pay ministers; a law passed in 1631 required church membership to hold public office. Magistrates enforced the first four of the Ten Commandments. Williams contended that the church had no such right. Furthermore, he believed that civil authorities could not make an oath of allegiance to the church a part of an oath of citizenship in the colony. He was defending the rights of the area's original inhabitants as well as those of Europeans who did not wish to conform to Puritan doctrine.

"Natural men," as Williams called the native peoples, should not, and could not, be forced "to the exercise of those holy Ordinances of Prayers, Oathes, &c" (Grinde and Johansen 1991, 75). Williams likened society to a ship carrying many kinds of people, each of whom valued his or her own opinions enough to debate, but not to fight. In this spirit, Williams argued against coercion of the soul, for beauty in diversity.

By January 1635 the Puritans' more orthodox magistrates had decided that Williams must be exiled to England, jailed if possible, and shut up. They opposed exiling him in the wilderness, fearing that he would begin his own settlement, from which his "infections" could leak back into Puritania. When a summons was issued for Williams's arrest, he stalled the authorities by contending that he was too ill to withstand an ocean voyage. At the same time, Williams and his associates rushed ahead with plans for their new colony. Williams already had arranged with Canonicus for a tract of land. "It was not price or money that could have purchased Rhode Island," Williams would later write. "Rhode Island was purchased by love" (Winslow 1957, 133). Williams was allowed to remain in Salem until the spring of 1636, provided he refrained from preaching.

Williams held meetings in his home, violating Puritan orders, so the date of his arrest was advanced. Aware of his impending fate, Williams set out three days before magistrates reached his home, during a blinding blizzard, traveling southwest to Massasoit's lodge at Mount Hope. Walking eighty to ninety miles during the worst of a New England winter, Williams suffered immensely and likely would have died without Indian aid.

Week by week, month by month, Williams's family and friends filtered south from Plymouth and Salem. By spring, houses were being erected, and fields were being turned. The growing group also began to erect an experimental government novel by European (or Puritan) standards. For the first time among English-speaking people in America, the colonists attempted to establish a social order based on liberty of conscience and other so-called natural rights.

Beginning about 1640 and continuing for most of his remaining years, Williams engaged major Puritan thinkers (especially John Cotton) in a series of published theological and political sparring matches. In these debates, Williams's image of American Indians and their societies played a provocative intellectual role. To modern eyes, these arguments may seem unceasingly windy and irrelevant, full of the sort of biblical hairsplitting that today eludes all but a covey of religious scholars and a few stump preachers. In the Puritan world of the mid-seventeenth century, however, these debates were vitally important. The same debates also defined the issues of secular and religious authority that would animate the American Revolution.

For much of his adult life, Williams collected material for an Indian grammar, but the press of events left him little time to write. It was not until 1643, on a solitary sea voyage to England, that Williams composed his *Key into the Languages of America*, the first Indian grammar in English, as well as a small encyclopedia of his observations about Native Americans. In the *Key* Williams also began to formulate a critique of European religion and politics that would become a subject of intense debate on both sides of the Atlantic for decades. He offers some of his thoughts on Native Americans in verse:

> I've known them to leave their house and mat
> To lodge a friend or stranger

When Jews and Christians oft have sent
Jesus Christ to the Manger
Oft have I heard these Indians say
These English will deliver us
Of all that's ours, our lands and lives
In the end, they'll bereave us.
(Grinde and Johansen 1991, 83)

In the *Key*, Williams disputes notions that Europeans are intellectually superior to Native Americans: "For the temper of the braine [*sic*] in quick apprehensions and accurate judgements the most high and sovereign God and Creator hath not made them inferior to Europeans. Nature knows no difference between Europeans and Americans in blood, birth, bodies, &c. God having of one blood made all mankind, Acts 17. . . . The same Sun shines on a Wilderness that doth on a garden" (ibid., 84). Thus, by implication, the Puritans had no right to take land and resources from Native Americans by "divine right." Williams's was the first expression in English on American soil of a belief that would power the American Revolution a century and a half later: "All men are created equal, and endowed by their Creator with certain inalienable rights."

In some ways, Williams finds what Europeans called Christian values better embodied in Native American societies than in their own: "There are no beggars amongst them, nor fatherless children unprovided for" (ibid., 84). The *Key* is more than a grammar. It is a lesson in humility directed at the most pompous and ethnocentric of the English:

When Indians heare the horrid filths,
Of Irish, English men
The horrid Oaths and Murthurs late
Thus say these Indians then:
We weare no Cloathes, have many Gods,
And yet our sinnes are lesse:
You are Barbarians, Pagans wild,
Your land's the wildernesse.
Boast not, proud English, of thy birth and blood;
Thy brother Indian is by birth as good.
(ibid., 84)

Orthodox Puritans regarded Williams as a dangerous radical. In addressing Christian hypocrisy and using his image of the Indian as counterpoint, Williams minces no words:

How often have I heard both the English and the Dutch[,] not only the civil, but the most debauched and profane say: "These Heathen Doggs [*sic*], better kill a thousand of them than we Christians should be endangered or troubled with them; they have spilt our Christian blood, the best way to make riddance of them is to cut them all off and make way for Christians. (Brockunier 1940, 141)

In the *Key*, Williams describes the workings of Indian government in ways similar to the structure he was erecting in the new colony: "The sachems will not conclude of ought that concerns all, either Lawes, or Subsidies, or warres [*sic*], unto which people are averse, or by gentle perswasion [*sic*] cannot be brought" (Williams 1963, 1:224). When some Puritans asked whether a society based on individual choice instead of coerced consent would degenerate into anarchy, Williams found the Indians' example instructive: "Although they have not so much to restraine them (both in respect of knowledge of God and lawes of Men) as the English have, yet a man shall never heare of such crimes amongst them [as] robberies, murthurs [*sic*], adultries &c., as among the English" (ibid., 1:225).

Establishing such a utopian society was easier said than done. As Williams watched, some of his co-settlers set up land companies similar to those in other colonies, in an attempt to hoard land set aside for future arrivals. The land had been reserved to prevent the growth of a landless underclass. In 1654 in a letter to the town of Providence, Williams reveals how isolated he sometimes felt in his quest for a new way of life: "I have been charged with folly for that freedom and liberty which have always stood for—I say, liberty and equality in both land and government" (Miller 1953, 221–222).

Where Puritans often saw heathens and devils, Williams saw people, usually friends, with intelligence, a moral sense, and a workable political system based on consensus. Such people had the intelligence and the right, Williams reasoned, to judge Christianity for themselves, and to decide, without coercion, whether they preferred Christian doctrine to their own traditions, making the decision "according to their Indian and American consciences, for other consciences it is not supposed they should have" (Williams 1963, 3:250).

Federalism at the Constitutional Convention

By June 1787 the delegates to the Constitutional Convention were engaged in a debate about the fundamental nature of their new union. Many delegates appeared to agree with James Wilson when he stated, on June 1, that he would not be "governed by the British model which was inapplicable to this country." Wilson believed that America's size was so great, and its ideals so "republican, that nothing but a great confederated republic would do for it" (Grinde and Johansen 1991, 197).

In July 1787, the *American Museum*, a Philadelphia magazine read by most of the members of the Constitutional Convention, reprinted "The Origin of Tobacco," an article by Benjamin Franklin ridiculing European cultural and religious arrogance. In the piece, a Susquehannah Indian and a Swedish minister exchange accounts of the origins of their respective religions. After the Indian recounts his story, the Swedish minister scoffs and calls the Indian's story "fable, fiction, a falsehood" while characterizing the Christian version as "sacred." Replying to the rude minister, the offended Indian asserts that the Indians believed the Europeans' stories, so "Why then do you refuse to believe ours?" The account is an extract from Franklin's earlier "Remarks Concerning the Savages of North-America, 1783." Published four years before the Constitutional Convention while Franklin was in France, "Remarks Concerning the Savages" provides insight into Franklin's knowledge of American Indian polities. In discussing Iroquois government, Franklin asserts the following:

> Having frequent Occasions to hold public Councils, they have acquired great Order and Decency in conducting them. The old Men sit in the foremost ranks, the Warriors in the next, and the Women and Children in the hindmost. The business of the Women is to take exact notice of what passes, imprint it in their Memories, for they have no Writing, and communicate it to their children. They are the Records of the Council, and they preserve Tradition of the Stipulations in Treaties a hundred Years back, which when we compare with our Writings we always find exact. He that would speak rises. The rest observe a profound Silence. When he has finished and sits down, they leave him for five or six Minutes to recollect, that if he has omitted anything he may rise again and deliver it. How different this is from the Conduct of a polite British House of Commons, where scarce a Day passes without some Confusion that makes the Speaker hoarse in calling to order.
> (ibid., 199)

On July 26, the Constitutional Convention adjourned for ten days while the Committee of

Detail—Chairman John Rutledge of South Carolina, Edmund Randolph of Virginia, Nathaniel Gorham of Massachusetts, Oliver Ellsworth of Connecticut, and James Wilson of Pennsylvania—met to arrange and systematize the materials that the convention had collected. For ten days, the committee met, sometimes at Independence Hall or at James Wilson's house and once at the Indian Queen Tavern. At the beginning of the committee's deliberations, Rutledge was reported to have read aloud some Iroquois advice that reflected on the will of "the people," and according to his biographer, Rutledge had been impressed with the government of the Iroquois from the time of the Stamp Act Congress in 1765.

In 1787 on the eve of the Constitutional Convention, John Adams had published *Defence of the Constitutions of Government of the United States of America.* Although Adams was selected as a Massachusetts delegate to the convention, he chose not to attend and instead published his lengthy essay. Charles Francis Adams, Adams's grandson, pointed out that the *Defence* "was much circulated in the convention, and undoubtedly contributed somewhat to give a favorable direction to the opinion of the members" (ibid., 200). On June 6, 1787, James Madison, while reporting the opening of the Constitutional Convention to Thomas Jefferson, wrote that "Mr. Adams' Book . . . has excited a good deal of attention." Madison believed that Adams's *Defence* would be read and "praised, and become a powerful engine in forming the public opinion" (ibid.).

Defence is a critical survey of world governments that includes a description of the Iroquois and other Native American governments as well as historical examples of confederacies in Europe and Asia. In his preface, Adams mentions the Inca, Manco Capac, and the political structure "of the Peruvians." He also notes that tribes in "North America have certain families from which their leaders are always chosen." Adams proffers that American Indian governments assembled their authority in one center, that is, a simple or unicameral model. He also observes that in American Indian governments "the people" believe that "all depended on them." Later in the preface, Adams asserts that Benjamin Franklin, the French philosophes, and other "great philosophers and politicians of the age" were attempting to "set up governments of modern Indians" (Adams 1851, 292).

Adams, an ardent believer in the fundamentals of the British constitution, opposes Franklin's intimation that the new government should resemble the native confederacies, but does believe that it would be productive to have "a more accurate investigation of the form of governments of the Indians." In addition, Adams argues that it would be "well worth the pains to collect the legislation of the Indians" for study while creating a new constitution. In studying American Indian governments, such as that of the Iroquois Confederacy, Americans could observe the best examples of governmental separation of powers. In fact, Adams states that the separation of powers in American Indian governments "is marked with a precision that excludes all controversy." Indeed, Adams points out that American Indian governments were so democratic that the "real sovereignty resided in the body of the people." Personal liberty was so important to American Indians, according to Adams, that Mohawks might be characterized as having "complete individual independence" (ibid., 511).

When discussing the Mohawks, Adams refers to "fifty families governed by all authority in one centre," a statement that reflects the extent of his knowledge of the structure of the Iroquois Confederacy (ibid.). In fact, Adams notes rather casually the number of Iroquois sachemships, which were delineated by Lewis Henry Morgan, the pioneer ethnographer of the confederacy, more than sixty years later. Adams's insight indicates that the founders knew a great deal more about Iroquois governance than has been previously acknowledged. That Morgan arrived at similar conclusions without reference to Adams's and other founders' observations provides independent verification of such knowledge.

Adams further displays his knowledge of Iroquois and other American Indian confederacies in detailed discussion of the sachemship system. He writes that a sachem is elected for life and lesser "sachems are his ordinary council." In this ordinary council, all "national affairs are deliberated and resolved" except declaring war, when the "sachems call a national assembly round a great council fire." At this council, the sachems "communicate to the people their resolution, and sacrifice an animal." No doubt, the animal sacrifice is a reference to the "white dog ceremony" of the Iroquois, also described by Morgan more than six decades after Adams did. Adams goes on to state that "the people who approve the war throw the hatchet into a tree" and then "join in the subsequent war songs and dances." Adams exhibits an understanding of Iroquois warfare's voluntary nature when he asserts that those who do disapprove of the decision to go to war "take no part in the sacrifice, but retire" (ibid., 511, 566–567). The extent of Adams's understanding of the nature of Iroquois government, however, is less important than the awareness that important intellectual connections existed between Native Americans and the founding fathers. Essentially, Adams's insights about Indian governments are personal and cultural manifestations of a lengthy and sustained dialogue between Euro-Americans and Native Americans.

Defence is not an unabashed endorsement of native models for government. Indeed, Adams refutes the arguments of Franklin, who advocated a one-house legislature resembling the Iroquois Grand Council, a model that had been used in the Albany Plan of Union and Articles of Confederation. Adams did not trust the Europeans' use of the consensus model that seemed to work for the Iroquois, instead believing that without the checks and balances built into two houses, the system would succumb to special interests and dissolve into anarchy or despotism. When Adams describes the Mohawks' independence, he exercises criticism, whereas Franklin writes about Indian governments in a much more benign way.

When Adams recommends checks on the caprice of the unthinking heart, he cites the Iroquois Grand Council of the fifty families as a negative example, ignoring the fact, as Franklin had written to his printing partner James Parker in 1751, that it "has subsisted ages" (Grinde and Johansen 1991, 204). Franklin was more of a utopian: he still sought a government based upon the best in human nature, calling its citizens to rise to it. He did not fear unrestrained freedom as did Adams. During the Constitutional Convention, Franklin, according to James Madison's notes, argued, "We shd. not depress the virtue & public spirit of our common people. He did not think the elected had any right in any case to narrow the privileges of the electors" (ibid.). The United States, having tasted revolution and the better part of a decade under the Articles of Confederation, seemed ready in 1787 to agree with

Adams, whose advocacy of two houses prevailed over Franklin's unicameral model. Still, the example of Native American liberty exerted a telling pull on the national soul, and conceptions of Native Americans played an important role in the founders' debates. That Adams in *Defence* repeatedly calls upon native imagery, even when in opposition to its use, is evidence of how widely these ideas were discussed.

The issue of property, and whether government should be constituted to protect it, was a major source of debate at the Constitutional Convention, as it had been during the revolution. Thomas Jefferson had substituted "happiness" for Lockean "property" as a natural right in the Declaration of Independence and invoked Native Americans as examples of it when he wrote to his colleague, Edward Carrington in January 1787. Six months later, at the convention, the native example was invoked negatively by Pennsylvania delegate Gouverneur Morris in a similar argument. According to notes taken July 5 by Rufus King, Morris asserted, "Men do not enter into Society to protect their Lives or Liberty—the Savages possess both in perfection—they unite in Society for the Protection of Property" (ibid., 204–205).

Native American Ideas and the Origins of American Feminism

Early feminists, among others, used the Iroquois as a counterpoint to what they described as European-bred oppressiveness at a time when mainstream America was preoccupied with nineteenth-century westward expansion. No century has been more hostile to America's indigenous peoples, but even in that bleakest of years, impressions of native liberty continued to exert a powerful allure. Prominent U.S. political theorists and politicians felt compelled to use Iroquois examples in their work. John C. Calhoun, in *A Disquisition on Government and a Discourse on the Constitution and Government of the United States*, states that "governments of concurrent majority" are practical because the Iroquois utilized such a system (ibid., 219). Calhoun asserts that the "federal, or general government" of the "Six Nations" constituted a "council of union" in which each member possessed a veto on its decision, "so that nothing could be done without the united consent of all. But this, instead of making the Confederacy weak, or impracticable, had the opposite effect. It secured harmony in council and action, and with them a great increase of power" (ibid.).

During the seventeenth and eighteenth centuries, the role of Indian women was one aspect of Native American life that alternately intrigued, perplexed, and sometimes alarmed known European and European-American observers, nearly all of whom were male. In many cases, Indian women held pivotal positions in native political systems. Iroquois women, for example, nominated men to positions of leadership, and could "dehorn," or impeach, them for misconduct. Women usually approved men's plans for war. In a matrilineal society, and nearly all the confederacies that bordered the colonies were matrilineal, women owned all household goods except for the men's clothes, weapons, and hunting implements. They also were the primary conduits of culture from generation to generation.

The role of women in Iroquois society helped inspire some of the most influential architects of modern feminism in the United States. The Iroquois example also figures importantly in Matilda Joslyn Gage's *Woman, Church and State* ([1893] 1980), a seminal work in what Sally Wagner calls feminism's first wave. Gage acknowledges, according to Wagner's research, that "the modern world [is] indebted for its first conception of inherent rights, natural equality of condition, and the establishment of a civilized government upon this basis," to the Iroquois (ibid., 226–227). Gage was probably one of the three most influential feminist architects of the nineteenth-century women's movement, the others being Elizabeth Cady Stanton and Susan B. Anthony. Gage herself was admitted to the Iroquois Council of Matrons and was adopted into the Wolf Clan with the name Karonienhawi, "she who holds the sky."

The early suffragists developed their work in temporal tandem with Lewis Henry Morgan. According to Wagner, Stanton specifically refers to Morgan's work in "The Matriarchate or Mother-Age," an address she made to the National Council of Women in 1891. Stanton points to the influence of Iroquois women in national councils and to the fact that their society was descended through the female line, and like Gage, she notes the irony that "our barbarian ancestors seem to have had a higher degree of justice to women than American men in the nineteenth century, professing to believe, as they do, in our republican principles of government" (ibid., 227).

Lucretia Mott, who called the Seneca Falls women's conference in 1848, met with the people of the Cattaraugus Seneca reservation days before she met with Stanton and a group of Quaker friends to plan the Seneca Falls event, which became known as the world's first conference explicitly dedicated to women's rights.

The founding mothers of modern feminism in the United States shared their enthusiasm at finding functioning societies that incorporated notions of sexual equality. All seemed to believe that the native model held promise for the future. Gage and Stanton looked to the native model for a design of a "regenerated world." According to Gage, "Never was justice more perfect, never civilization higher than under the Matriarchate." Further, writes Gage, "Under [Iroquois] women the science of government reached the highest form known to the world" (ibid., 226–227). Writing in the *New York Evening Post*, Gage contended that "division of power between the sexes in this Indian republic was nearly equal" (ibid.). In her 1891 speech before the National Council of Women, Stanton said,

> In closing, I would say that every woman present must have a new sense of dignity and self respect, feeling that our mothers, during long periods in the long past, have been the ruling power and that they used that power for the best interests of humanity. As history is said to repeat itself, we have every reason to believe that our turn will come again. It may not be for woman's supremacy, but for the as yet untried experiment of complete equality, when the united thought of man and woman will inaugurate a just government, a pure religion, a happy home, a civilization at last in which ignorance, poverty and crime will exist no more. Those who watch already behold the dawn of the new day.
> (ibid., 89)

Bibliography

Adams, John. 1851. *Defence of the Constitutions of Government of the United States of America.* In *The Works of John Adams*, edited by Charles Francis Adams. Vol. 4. Boston: Little, Brown.

Brockunier, Samuel H. 1940. *The Irrepressible Democrat: Roger Williams.* New York: Ronald Press.

Chupack, Henry. 1969. *Roger Williams.* New York: Twayne Publishers.

Covey, Cyclone. 1966. *The Gentle Radical: A Biography of Roger Williams.* New York: MacMillan.

Ernst, James. 1932. *Roger Williams: New England Firebrand.* New York: MacMillan.

Farrand, Max, ed. 1911. *Records of the Federal Convention.* Vol. 1. New Haven: Yale University Press.

Gage, Matilda Joslyn. [1893] 1980. *Woman, Church and State.* Watertown, Mass.: Peresphone Press.

Grinde, Donald A., Jr. 1977. *The Iroquois and the Founding of the American Nation.* San Francisco: Indian Historian Press.

Grinde, Donald A., Jr., and Bruce E. Johansen. 1991. *Exemplar of Liberty: Native America and the Evolution of Democracy.* Los Angeles: American Indian Studies Center, University of California.

Johansen, Bruce E. 1982. *Forgotten Founders: Benjamin Franklin, the Iroquois, and the Rationale for the American Revolution.* Ipswich, Mass.: Gambit.

Mee, Charles L., Jr. 1987. *The Genius of the People.* New York: Harper and Row, 1987.

Miller, Perry. 1953. *Roger Williams: His Contribution to the American Tradition.* Indianapolis: Bobbs-Merill.

Morgan, Edmund. 1967. *Roger Williams: The Church and State.* New York: Harcourt, Brace and World.

Morgan, Lewis Henry. 1851. Reprint 1962. *League of the Iroquois.* Seacaucus, N.J.: Citadel Press.

Parrington, Vernon L. 1927. *Main Currents in American Thought.* New York: Harcourt, Brace and Co.

Savelle, Max. 1956. "Roger Williams: A Minority of One." In *The American Story.* Great Neck, N.Y.: Channel Press.

Stanton, Elizabeth Cady. 1891. "The Matriarchate or Mother-Age." Address before the National Council of Women, February 1891. *National Bulletin* 1, no. 5 (February).

Wagner, Sally Roesch. 1989. "The Root of Oppression Is the Loss of Memory: The Iroquois and the Early Feminist Vision." *Akwesasne Notes* (late winter): 11.

Williams, Roger. 1963. *The Complete Writings of Roger Williams.* New York: Russell and Russell.

Winslow, Elizabeth Ola. 1957. *Master Roger Williams.* New York: MacMillan.

3

Native American Self-Government and Its Impact on Democracy's Development

Bruce E. Johansen

Native Americans governed themselves for many millennia before their sustained contact with large numbers of Europeans began roughly five centuries ago. During this time, many Native American peoples developed confederate systems of government that would inform the immigrants' philosophies and design of institutions in their adopted land. The Europeans and Euoramericans drew from native peoples, the Iroquois in particular, new definitions of federalism as well as a popular ideology promoting laws that reflected the spirit of "life, liberty, and happiness" that Thomas Jefferson captured in his Declaration of Independence.

During the last two centuries, Native American self-governance has continued to evolve in tandem with the imposition of colonial-style political controls by the immigrants' society. In the last half of the twentieth century, after draconian nineteenth-century repression during the most active decades of the "Indian Wars," Native American tribes and nations sought increasing sovereignty and self-determination, reconciling such structures as the Bureau of Indian Affairs with the development of infrastructures augmenting their economic, political, and social autonomy.

During the 170 years between the first enduring English settlement in North America and the American Revolution, the colonists' perception of their Native American neighbors evolved from the Puritans' "devil-man" to the autonomous Noble Savage to peoples who lived in confederacies governed by natural law so subtle, so nearly invisible, that it was widely believed to be an attractive alternative to monarchy's overbearing hand. The Europeans' view of Indian societies changed as they became more dissatisfied with the European status quo. Increasingly, the native societies came to serve the transplanted Europeans, including some of the United States' most influential founders, as a counterpoint to the Old World order. They found in existing native polities the values that the seminal European documents of the time celebrated in theoretical abstraction—life, liberty, happiness, and government by consensus, under natural rights, with relative equality of property. The fact that native peoples in America were able to govern themselves provided colonial advocates of alternatives to monarchy with practical ammunition for a philosophy of government based on individual rights, which they believed had worked, did work, and would work for them.

This is not to say that the colonists sought to replicate Native American polities. The new Americans were too practical to believe that a society steeped in European cultural traditions could be turned on its head so swiftly and easily. They chose instead to borrow, to shape what they had with what they saw before them, to create a new order that included aspects of both worlds.

The colonists' lives were pervaded by contact with native peoples to a degree that contemporary scholars sometimes find difficult to comprehend. Colonization, especially in its early years, was limited to a few isolated pockets of land, widely dispersed, on a thin ribbon along the eastern seaboard. In the mid-eighteenth century, the frontier ran from a few miles west of Boston through Albany to Lancaster, Pennsylvania, or roughly to the western edges of today's eastern urban areas. The new Americans looked inland, across a continent that they already knew to be many times the size of England, France, and Holland combined. They did not know with any certainty exactly how far their new homeland extended. Maps of the time did not record accurately the distances between the Atlantic and Pacific Oceans. A few Spanish and French trappers and explorers had left their footprints in this vast expanse of land, when at least 90 percent of North America was still the homeland of many hundreds of native tribes.

The American Revolution emerged through events and ideas: life, liberty, happiness; government by reason and consent rather than coercion; religious tolerance (and ultimately religious acceptance) instead of a state church; checks and balances; federalism; relative equality of property; and equal rights before the law. These ideas would be brought to fruition by creating a government suitable for a diverse variety of settlements spread over a broad geographic expanse. Native Americans played a substantial role in shaping all these ideas, as well as the events that turned the colonies into a nation of states.

Native American Confederacies

When European immigrants first encountered Native Americans along the Atlantic seaboard, Indian nations had created numerous confederacies. Among such tribes were the Seminoles in what is now Florida—the French essayist Crèvecoeur called them a "federated republic"—the Cherokees and Choctaws in the Carolinas, the Iroquois and their allies, the Wyandots (Hurons) in the Saint Lawrence Valley, and the Penacook federation of New England. Also similarly governed were the Illinois Confederacy, the Three Fires comprised of the Chippewa, Ottawa, and Potawatomi, the Wapenaki Confederacy, the Powhatan Confederacies, and the tripartite Miami. Each of these native confederacies developed its own variation of counselor democracy, but most were remarkably similar in broad outline. Although consensus seems to have been the model most often used across the continent, some native peoples maintained societies that were strikingly different. For example, the peoples along the northwest coastline paid greater attention to political hierarchy and economic status.

The colonists arriving in eastern North America were at first unfamiliar with government by consensus; after all, they were a people who had been living in societies ruled by queens, princes, and kings. The best known of the consensual governments was the Iroquois Confederacy, which occupied a prominent position in the diplomacy of the early colonies. By the late eighteenth century, as resentment against England's taxation flared into open rebellion along the Atlantic, the colonists displayed widespread knowledge of native governmental systems. Thomas Jefferson, Benjamin Franklin, and others along the length of the coast into the Saint Lawrence Valley all observed confederate governmental systems that shared many traits.

The political system of the Hurons remarkably resembled that of their Iroquois neighbors. According to Bruce J. Trigger's *Children of the Aataentsic: A History of the Huron People* (1976), the Hurons' political system, like that of the Iroquois, was rooted in family structure. Leaders of the various clans used public opinion and consensus in arriving at decisions. Issues were usually discussed until a general consensus was reached and then decided by majority vote. No one was expected to abide by a decision to which he or she had not given conscious consent.

As with the Iroquois, the Huron clans—the Bear, Beaver, Deer, Hawk, Porcupine, Turtle, Snake, and Wolf—created familial affinity across the boundaries of the four confederated Huron nations—the Arendarhonon, Attignawantan, Attigneenongahac, and Tahontaeanrat. Members of each clan traced their ancestries to a common origin through the female line. In each village, clan members elected a civil chief and a war chief. The titles were handed down matrilineally but were bestowed on men, again resembling the Iroquois system. While the titles were hereditary in that sense, they did not pass from one head to another of a particular family as in most European monarchies. In selecting a leader, members of each clan in a particular village chose from several candidates, among whom, according to Trigger, personal qualities counted most heavily, including intelligence, oratorical ability, reputation for generosity, and above all, performance as a warrior. The four Huron nations held a central council, which, Trigger thinks, probably consisted of all village chiefs, representing all the clans. The central council dealt with issues that affected all four nations, such as treaty negotiations and trade with the Europeans.

The Cherokee, who called themselves Ani-Yunwiya (the "Real People," or the "Principal People"), lived in settlements scattered in fertile bottomlands among the craggy peaks of the Great Smokey Mountains. They took public opinion so seriously that they usually split their villages when they became too large to permit each adult a voice in council. In the early eighteenth century the Cherokee nation comprised sixty villages in five regions, with each village controlling its own affairs. Villages sent delegates to a national council only in times of national emergency. The villages averaged three hundred to four hundred persons each. When the population of a village reached close to five hundred people, it usually split.

The Cheyennes maintained a powerful central government that united its various bands and family-based affinities. At the head of this organization sat the Council of Forty-four, on which civil chiefs served ten-year terms. The Cheyenne system closely resembled that of the

Sioux Seven Fires Confederacy, although the Sioux were not as tightly organized. Six Cheyenne military societies served as police as well as organizers of war parties. These voluntary organizations were open to all men of the nation and were similar to the police societies of the Lakota. All of these societies grew out of the horse culture of the Great Plains. The military societies often carried out decisions reached by the council. As the periods of peace dwindled with the onset of the Euro-American invasion, the police societies evolved into war societies that took over much of the authority of the Council of Forty-four.

Cheyenne oral history relates that the Council of Forty-four was started by a woman but its members were male. New chiefs were chosen by the council itself to replace those who left it at the end of their terms. George Bird Grinnell's ([1923] 1962) description of a Cheyenne chief's demeanor sounds remarkably similar to the behavior expected of Iroquois *sachems* (chiefs) under their Great Law of Peace: A chief was expected to be brave in war, generous in disposition, liberal in temper, deliberate in making up his mind, and of good judgment. A good chief directed his whole heart and mind to helping the people to whom he was responsible.

The Iroquois Confederacy

The Iroquois's system was the best known to the colonists in large part because of the confederacy's pivotal position in diplomacy between the English and the French and among other Native American confederacies. Called Iroquois by the French and the Five Nations (later Six) by the English, the Haudenosaunee ("People of the Longhouse") controlled the only relatively level land pass between the English colonies on the Atlantic seaboard and the French settlements in the Saint Lawrence Valley. The Iroquois are linked to each other by their clan system, which ties each person to family members in every other nation of the federation. For example, if a Mohawk of the Turtle clan must travel, he will be hosted by Turtles in each Iroquois nation.

Iroquois and other Native American political leaders did not possess the authority to command, so they honed their persuasive abilities, especially their speaking skills. Cadwallader Colden, in *History of the Five Nations* (1727), attributes the Iroquois's skill at oratory to "a perfect republican government." Colden describes the intense study that the Iroquois applied to the arts of oral persuasion, to acquisition of "grace and manner" before councils of their peers. According to Colden, Iroquois speakers became "very nice in the turn of their expressions. . . . They have, it seems, a certain *urbanitas*, or Atticism, in their language to which the common ears are ever sensible, though only their great speakers ever attain it." Benjamin Franklin compared the decorum of Native American councils to the rowdy nature of debate in British public forums, including the House of Commons. This difference in debating customs persists to this day.

Each Iroquois nation—the Cayugas, Mohawks, Oneidas, Onondagas, and Senecas—has its own council, which sends delegates to the Grand Council, much as each state in the United States has its own legislature in addition to senators and representatives who travel to the central seat of government in Washington, D.C. Sachems of each nation are nominated by the clan mothers of families holding hereditary rights to office titles; the Grand Council also may nominate sachems (to lead a nation, the confederacy, or both) outside the hereditary structure, based on merit alone. These sachems, called "pine tree chiefs," are said to spring from the body of the people as the symbolic Great White Pine springs from the earth.

When representatives of the Iroquois nations meet for the Grand Council, in Onondaga near present-day Syracuse, New York, they form two groups: the Elder Brothers (Mohawks, Onondagas, and Senecas) and the Younger Brothers (Cayugas and Oneidas). The Onondagas are the firekeepers, meaning that they are ever ready to call and host the meetings of the confederacy chiefs. (In the U.S. Congress, a similar position is held by the Speaker of the House.)

The Iroquois built certain ways of doing business into their Great Law of Peace to prevent anger and frayed tempers. For example, an item may not be debated the same day that it is introduced, which allows time for passions to cool. Important decisions must take at least two days, so leaders can "sleep on it" and not react too quickly. The Great Law may be amended just as one adds beams to the rafters of an Iroquois longhouse. The Great Tree of Peace—the physical and organic symbol of the confederacy—is regarded as a living organism. Its roots and branches are said to grow in order to adopt other peoples.

An Iroquois sachem is appointed by clan mothers, who poll for the consensus of their families. The rights, duties, and qualifications of sachems are explicitly outlined. Clan mothers may remove, or impeach, a sachem found guilty of any of a number of abuses of office, from missing meetings to murder. An erring chief is summoned to face charges by the war chiefs, who act in peacetime as the peoples' eyes and ears in the council, somewhat in the way that the press was envisaged by Jefferson and other founders of the United States. A sachem is given three warnings before being removed from the council. A sachem found guilty of murder loses not only his title, but also deprives his entire family of its right to representation. The female relatives holding the rights to the office are "buried," and the title is transferred to a sister family.

A sachem is instructed to always be a mentor for the people. Political leaders must strive at all times to maintain peace within the confederacy. A chief may be "de-horned" (impeached) if he engages in violent behavior. An Iroquois leader's traditional headdress, an emblem of office that includes deer antlers, is said to have been "knocked off" if the sachem is impeached. Chiefs of the Iroquois Confederacy are instructed to take criticism honestly; their skins should be seven spans thick to absorb the criticism of the people they represent in public councils. Political leaders also are to think of the coming generations in all of their actions.

Such a public servant point of view pervades the writings of Jefferson and Franklin. Sachems are not allowed to name their own successors, nor can they carry their titles to the grave. The Great Law of Peace provides a ceremony to remove the "antlers" of authority from a dying chief. The law also includes provisions guaranteeing freedom of religion and the right of redress before the Grand Council; it forbids unauthorized entry of homes, measures familiar to U.S citizens through the Bill of Rights.

In some ways, the Grand Council operates like Congress, with its conference committees. As the council was designed by Deganawidah, the primary founder of the confederacy, protocol demands that debate begin among the Mohawks and Senecas (of the Elder Brothers). After debate by the Keepers of the Eastern Door (Mohawks) and the Keepers of the

Western Door (Senecas), the question is thrown across the fire to the Oneida and Cayuga statesmen (the Younger Brothers) for discussion. Once consensus is achieved among the Oneidas and the Cayugas, the discussion passes back to the Senecas and Mohawks for confirmation. Next, the question is laid before the Onondagas for their decision.

At this stage, the Onondagas exercise a power similar to judicial review in that they can raise objections to the proposed measure if it is believed to be inconsistent with the Great Law of Peace. Essentially, the Grand Council can rewrite the proposed law on the spot to bring it into line with the Iroquois constitution should the original version not meet with Onondaga approval. When the Onondagas reach consensus, Tadadaho, the presiding chief of the Iroquois Confederacy, asks Honowireton, an Onondaga chief who presides over debates between the delegations, to confirm the decision. Finally, Honowireton or Tadadaho gives the decision of the Onondagas to the Mohawks and the Senecas so that the policy may be announced by the Grand Council as its will.

Native American Self-Governance under Colonization

Until about 1800 most Native Americans (with exceptions along the eastern seaboard) managed to retain their political infrastructures. The Iroquois were important powerbrokers until the mid-1760s. While European American settlements were increasing in area and population before 1800, the pace of change did not approach the speed it would in the nineteenth century.

Shortly after 1800 colonization exploded across the Appalachian Mountains, picking up speed until, by the end of the century, the breadth of the continent had been subsumed by the immigrants' cultures. Movement across the continent was propelled by increasing immigration from Europe and the development of the Industrial Revolution in the United States, most notably the laying of the continental network of railroads. During the early 1830s Supreme Court Justice John Marshall struggled with legal definitions of Native Americans' changing relationship with the ever-more dominant European American culture. His definition of native peoples in *Cherokee Nation v. Georgia* (1831) as "dependent domestic nations" was interpreted by the federal government (notably through its Bureau of Indian Affairs) as a license to govern surviving remnants of Native American nations in a colonial manner. Indigenous forms of native governance often were outlawed during this period. Surviving traditional Native American governments usually conducted business in secret because the federal government sought to Christianize and "educate" Native Americans and instill private property ownership upon their communities. These policy objectives largely negated notions of autonomy and freedom of choice for native individuals and governments.

President Franklin D. Roosevelt brought John Collier into his administration as Indian commissioner to construct an "Indian New Deal" during the 1930s. Roosevelt wanted to wrest control of Indian affairs from Christian religious groups bent on proselytizing and place policy in the hands of professional educators and social scientists. While this represented a step toward Native American self-determination, it nonetheless left control of Indian affairs firmly in the hands of non-

Indians. Collier and Roosevelt's policy generally recognized native peoples' right to exist in distinct groups and on their own land under certain governmental controls. The Indian New Deal—legislated as the Indian Reorganization Act (IRA) of 1934—was a new interpretation of Chief Justice Marshall's opinion that the Indians occupied "dependent domestic nations" in that it sought to reverse the erosion of the Indian land base and give people a choice between assimilation and maintaining traditional ways.

Collier's tenure as Indian commissioner lasted close to twelve years, the entire length of Roosevelt's presidency and longer than any other persons' in that post. His policies initiated a slight native resurgence. Some land was added to the native estate, reversing a 150-year trend. The Native American governments created by the Indian Reorganization Act were democratic in function to some degree, but they were still imposed on native peoples in a colonial fashion. During the 1940s and 1950s Native American institutions faced renewed pressure from advocates of "termination," a policy to end all federal services to Indian nations.

During 1961 voices of protest were raised at the American Indian conference in Chicago, which brought together more than five hundred native people from more than sixty groups. At the behest of President John F. Kennedy, the conference was organized by Sol Tax, professor of anthropology at the University of Chicago, as a forum for native people to express views regarding their current state and future.

More politically active Native American organizations emerged during the 1960s. In 1961 a group of young, college-educated American Indians formed the National Indian Youth Council (NIYC), which had deep roots in impoverished, traditional Indian communities. By 1964 the first modern civil disobedience by Native Americans had taken place at Puget Sound salmon streams, as Indian "fish-ins" dramatized native assertions of treaty rights to harvest fish that state authorities had long ignored. American Indian activism and nationalism was transformed by the occupation of the former federal penitentiary at Alcatraz on November 9, 1969. The leaders of the takeover wanted to create a movement for national American Indian autonomy that would resolve the conflicts between multitribal unity and tribal self-determination.

American Indian militant movements were also springing up in other areas of the country. In 1968 the American Indian Movement (AIM) formed in Minneapolis to combat police brutality and the selective law enforcement policies of local police. Initially, they established an "Indian patrol" to follow the police as they traveled through Native American neighborhoods. Arrest rates of Native Americans fell to the citywide average nine months after the patrols were introduced.

Many Native American traditional governments continue to exist, without federal recognition, on reservations around the United States. For example, a traditional Mohawk council is maintained at Akwesasne, a reserve in upstate New York, alongside councils imposed by the governments of the United States and Canada, whose border passes through the reservation. At the same time, many reservation governing councils are working within the framework of their IRA-style governments to develop economic infrastructures (including businesses and taxation) to augment political autonomy and influence.

Bibliography

Boyd, Julian. 1981. "Dr. Franklin, Friend of the Indian." In *Meet Dr. Franklin*, edited by Roy Lokken. Philadelphia: Franklin Institute.

Colden, Cadwallader. [1727, 1747] 1958. *The History of the Five Nations Depending on the Province of New York in America*. Ithaca: Cornell University Press.

Corkran, David H. 1962. *The Cherokee Frontier: Conflict and Survival, 1740–62*. Norman: University of Oklahoma Press.

Franklin, Benjamin. 1868. *The Autobiography of Benjamin Franklin*, edited by John Bigelow. Philadelphia: J. B. Lippincott.

Grinde, Donald A., Jr., and Bruce E. Johansen. 1991. *Exemplar of Liberty: Native America and the Evolution of Democracy*. Los Angeles: American Indian Studies Center, University of California.

Grinnell, George Bird. [1923] 1962. *The Cheyenne Indians: Their History and Ways of Life*. New York: Cooper Square Publishers.

Jefferson, Thomas. [1784] 1955. *Notes on the State of Virginia*, edited by William Peden. Chapel Hill: University of North Carolina Press.

Labaree, Leonard W., et al., eds. 1959– . *The Papers of Benjamin Franklin*. New Haven: Yale University Press.

McKee, Jesse O., and Jon A. Schlenker. 1980. *The Choctaws: Cultural Evolution of a Native American Tribe*. Jackson: University Press of Mississippi.

Morgan, Lewis Henry. [1855] 1962. *League of the Ho-de-no-sau-nee, or Iroquois*. New York: Corinth Books.

Reid, John Phillip. 1976. *A Better Kind of Hatchet: Law, Trade and Diplomacy in the Cherokee Nation during the Early Years of European Contact*. University Park: Pennsylvania State University Press.

Trigger, Bruce G. 1976. *Children of the Aataentsic: A History of the Huron People*. Montreal: McGill-Queen's University Press.

Van Doren, Carl, and Julian P. Boyd, eds. 1938. *Indian Treaties Printed by Benjamin Franklin, 1736–1762*. Philadelphia: Historical Society of Pennsylvania.

Wallace, Paul A. W. [1946] 1994. *The White Roots of Peace*. Santa Fe: Clear Light Publishers.

4 Native American Treaties: Diplomacy and Legality

Vine Deloria Jr.

With the coming of Europeans to the North and South American continents, England, France, and Holland found it necessary to deal with the indigenous peoples in a diplomatic format. They quickly adopted the Indian manner of treaty making, which involved first Wiping Away of the Tears, a ceremonial way of forgiving past transgressions and preparing the parties to negotiate without ill will. Representatives of the parties would then engage in long discussions until all their differences were resolved. The agreement was sealed by the exchange of presents, a marriage, adoption of children of the other nation, and, in the eastern United States, the creation of a wampum belt with symbols of the agreement. Both parties were expected to remember the terms under which the agreements would be enforced. Early on, the French and English made adaptations to the ceremony, featuring a great "covenant chain" and the pledge that their respective kings would align himself with the Indian nation and help to settle their problems or negotiate agreements with their enemies. Sometimes silver chains were made to symbolize the agreement, and from this practice later grew the American custom of presenting "peace medals" to the principal chiefs and headmen.

People appointed by the colonial governors, approved by the Crown, and designated as Crown representatives usually conducted British colonial treaties. The colonies also cooperated with each other when dealing with a particular Indian nation on their frontiers; for example, Virginia and North Carolina would work together, as would Pennsylvania, New York, and Virginia, and so forth. Transcripts of some of the more important treaties, such as the Treaties of Lancaster (1729), Loggstown (1742), and Albany in (1763) sought peace on the frontier as well as cessions of land by different Indian nations. Pressures on the frontier also meant an increase in treaty making between and among the Indian nations. Colonists at interior trading posts recorded some of these agreements. Private individuals invading the frontier made their own treaties with tribes in violation of English imperial rules.

With the outbreak of the American Revolution, treaty making increased substantially. The colonists sought the Indians' neutrality while the English tried to enlist Indian nations, arguing that the Indians had already given their pledge of allegiance to the king through their treaties. Fort Pitt in Pennsylvania was the focal point of revolutionary diplomacy, with four treaties drafted there each year beginning in 1775. The Delawares were considered the most influential group in the Ohio country, and it is in their treaty of 1778 that the United States held out the promise that they could gather other Indian nations as a unified group and send a representative to Congress as a voting delegate. More important, however, was the change in format this treaty represented. Previously, such agreements were negotiated in the Indian way—prolonged discussions to ensure an understanding of the problem and the emergence of an agreement. The Cherokee treaty of 1775, negotiated at Muscle Shoals, Alabama, was recorded in this manner. The 1778 Delaware treaty, however, was written in a formal style, with various articles and provisions that made it appear as a formal legal document. The United States used this format until early in the twentieth century, when gathering a consensus for approval of an allotment agreement was used instead. With this shift, the moral tone of diplomacy changed to a legalistic emphasis on words and phrases, a plague that continues to confuse lawyers and laymen.

During the Revolutionary War, the Continental Congress established basic rules for dealing with Indian nations on the frontier. If a matter involved war and peace, the issue had to be decided by the congress, which would appoint representatives to hold treaty negotiations. If the issue involved the purchase of land, however, it was permissible for a state to inform the congress of its intent to negotiate with an Indian nation and then proceed. When the Constitution was adopted in 1789, Indians were included in the Commerce Clause, thus allowing the U.S. Congress to negotiate with the tribes as sovereign entities as if they had been mentioned in the treaty-making clause as well.

During negotiations in Paris to end the Revolutionary War, the subject of primacy in the old Northwest (that is, Ohio to Wisconsin) arose as a critical issue. England wanted the land set aside as an Indian reserve with political supervision by European nations while the United States insisted that its claims extended from the Appalachian watershed to the Mississippi. Unfortunately for the Indians, the English finally adopted the U.S. point of view thereby abandoning their Indian allies. Following the Treaty of Paris, the United States sought peace treaties with the tribes of the Ohio country in exchange for land cessions north of the Ohio River, a successful ploy because the United States was not in any condition to wage a prolonged war against these Indian nations. Between October 1784 and January 1786 six treaties were signed bringing hostilities with the Indians to an end: October 22, 1784, at Fort Stanwix with the Six Nations (Iroquois Confederacy); January 21, 1785, at Fort McIntosh with the Wyandot, Delaware, Chippewa, and Ottawa; November 28, 1785, at Hopewell with the Cherokees; January 3 and 10 at Hopewell with the Choctaw and Chickasaw; and January 1786 with the Shawnee. Instructions given to U.S. delegates warned that the Indians did not consider themselves conquered and counseled that any mention of the United States assuming the role of conqueror was liable to initiate a frontier war of great proportions.

The Creeks of Georgia, under the leadership of Alexander McGillivray, were meanwhile in the enviable position of receiving diplomatic overtures for alliance from the Spanish government; they finally made a treaty with the United States in 1790 in New York that had far more favorable provisions for them than did the 1784–1786 set of treaties. Spain then became emboldened and made treaties with the Choctaw and Chickasaws, expanding the role they would play in postrevolutionary North America. The southern states, most notably Georgia, continued to (illegally) make treaties with southeastern Indians in an effort to extend their land holdings before they approved the Constitution and would become restricted to smaller boundaries. Refusal to allow the national government to handle all Indian matters would emerge again in the 1820s and 1830s, resulting in the famous Cherokee cases and the eventual removal of the large southeastern tribes to Oklahoma.

With the purchase of Louisiana in 1803, the United States laid claim to the trans-Mississippi interior drainage system and now had to deal with the many Indian nations in this large area. Much of the land was prairie and was considered useless for the commercial agriculture of the new Americans. The idea arose that Indian nations east of the river should be convinced to exchange their lands there for lands with recognized titles in the west. The Ohio country experienced a prolonged war as President George Washington made every effort to extinguish Native American land titles so that land warrants given to soldiers during the Revolutionary War could be used to settle the Midwest. In the Treaty of Greenville (1795), the Miamis and other tribes were forced to cede large portions of what would become the state of Ohio, reserving only small tracts for individual chiefs and headmen and transporting many other tribal members to Illinois, Indiana, and Missouri. Treaties with Indian towns and communities were also negotiated, with Indian nations being fragmented into small bands and removed to Kansas and then to Oklahoma.

In the War of 1812 some Indians allied with Great Britain, and many western Indian nations sent warriors to assist the British in battles in the Great Lakes and Canada. Under the brilliant Tecumseh, the Shawnee warrior, Indians contributed immeasurably to the British resistance but because of supply problems and a lukewarm commitment by England, the cause was lost. Again the British abandoned their Indian allies although a provision in the Treaty of Ghent required the United States and Great Britain to make peace with those Indian nations that had opposed them during the war. This requirement gave the United States the opportunity to negate any loyalty that western Indians had to the British. The government sent a treaty delegation up the Missouri River and made peace treaties with nearly every Indian nation they could entice to meet with them. The series of treaties between 1815 and 1818 reestablished peace with the United States and required the following Indians to acknowledge only the United States as a superior sovereign: Grand Pawnee, the Iowa, Kansa, Kickapoo, Menominee, Noisy Pawnee, Omaha, Osage, Oto, Pawnee Republic, Pawnee Marhar, Ponca, Piankashaw, Potawatomi, Quapaw, Sauk, Sauk and Foxes, Sioux of St. Peter's River, Sioux of the Lakes, Sioux of the Leafs,

Teton, Wyandot and confederated tribes, and Yankton Sioux. For all practical purposes, then, these tribes surrendered their right to negotiate with European (or any other) nations.

With treaty relationships now shifting the focus of Indian policy to the trans-Missouri West, the United States began to exert pressure on the major Indian nations east of the Mississippi to move west and take up lands on the Great Plains. Remaining Indian lands in Ohio, Indiana, and Illinois were ceded by small groups who migrated to Missouri and then to Kansas, often merging again with segments of their nations that had earlier moved west. In the South, the Cherokees and Creeks were forced to give up large portions of their lands with the hope that Georgia and other southern states would refrain from claiming these lands as their own under colonial land grants. It became clear, however, that as the white population surged westward, alternating in the creation of slave and free states, that the Southeast would eventually be cleared of all Indian settlements.

Most of the treaties between 1808 and 1835 involved eastern Indian nations, and thus the federal removal policy, although removal was not formally articulated by Congress until 1830. The removal treaties of the so-called Five Civilized Tribes—Choctaw (1830), the Creeks (1832), the Cherokees (1835), the Chickasaws (1832), and the Seminoles (1833)—were important because of the large populations involved. Although the Seminoles agreed to move in a 1833 treaty, they had been tricked into the treaty; they then fought desperately to remain in Florida. The Seminole War (1835–1842) was the costliest encounter the United States ever had with an Indian nation, but in the end the Indian survivors were rounded up, sent to Oklahoma, and given lands within the Creek nation.

The treaties of the early nineteenth century differed substantially from earlier U.S. treaties with Indian nations. The Five Civilized Tribes were given recognized legal title to their lands, but in other treaties the land remained under federal supervision. Each of the treaties had provisions granting land to individual tribal members who wished to remain on their homeland. These provisions foreshadowed the policy of allotment as a means of settling Indians on restricted tracts of land. Although this same provision appears in the treaties with the Ohio, Indiana, and Illinois Indians, the ability of the Five Civilized Tribes to adjust to U.S. patterns of settlement and commercial agriculture suggested that individual landownership was the proper policy to adopt.

In 1825 a treaty-making expedition led by Gen. Henry Atkinson and Maj. Benjamin O'Fallon ascended the Missouri River to make trade treaties with the Indian nations on the upper Missouri. British traders operating from Hudson Bay posts were in competition with Americans attempting to control the beaver and hide trade in this region, and the United States wanted to gradually bring these Indian nations into the American sphere of commerce. Obvious here is the fine hand of August Choteau, an Indian trader whose trading house in St. Louis was the dominant enterprise in the trans-Mississippi west. Thus, treaties with the Arikaras, Cheyennes, Crow, Hunkpapa Sioux, Kansa, Mandan, Minitaree, Osage, Ponca, Sioune and Oglalas, Teton, and Yankton and Yanktonais Sioux were designed to improve relations with the United States.

After the Mexican revolution against Spain and the establishment of an independent Mexican government in 1821, Americans could be found trading in Santa Fe. Occasionally federal treaties attempted to regulate commerce with

Indian nations in the Southwest. The treaties of 1825 with the Osage and Kansa offered some protection for these nations but they were situated close to American settlements and forts. More critical was the treaty with the Comanches, whose lands were well within the Mexican territory and who resented the intrusions of the Five Civilized Tribes then beginning to settle the lands adjoining them and the Kiowas. The treaty of 1835 with the Comanches guaranteed that the five tribes would submit their grievances against the Comanches to the United States even though the Comanches were regarded as under the protection of the Mexicans.

From the 1820s to the 1840s New York State forced the Six Nations to sell their lands and migrate west. Some went to Oklahoma; the Oneidas moved to Wisconsin. In negotiations with political factions of the Iroquois nations, New York was able to reduce Indian landholdings significantly during this time despite questions over the legality of the process. The state claimed that it had not surrendered its right to negotiate with its Indians over land sales, but it would be made clear in the 1960s that there was always a federal interest in Indian land cessions wherever they might take place. Some of today's land claims stem from New York's forcing land sales by groups of Iroquois without permission from either the Grand Council of the Six Nations or the federal government.

During the 1830s and 1840s the independence movement in Texas, and its successful rebellion against the Mexican government, the Mexican American War, and the fight over the settlement of the Oregon question contributed to the U.S. need to settle Indian land titles in the West. The Texas republic dealt with its Indian nations by treaty during its short political life, but its policy of driving the Indians out of the state meant increasing competition and confrontation with the United States along their border. Texas statehood meant ceding control of the Indians to the United States, and by 1851 Indian parties to Texas treaties came to be regarded as subject to the control of the U.S. government. After the signing of the Treaty of Guadalupe Hidalgo (1849) ending the Mexican American War, U.S. commissioners made treaties with some of the southwestern nations, including the Apaches, Navajos, and Utes for lands in Arizona, Nevada, New Mexico, and Utah. It would later be discovered that these treaties were with bands that happened to be in the vicinity and that there were many smaller groups of Apaches and Utes who acted independently and would need to be dealt with through additional treaties.

The Oregon question arose from the constant settler migrations to the Pacific Northwest beginning in the 1830s. The British had been trading in the Northwest for many decades, going as far east as Fort Hall, Idaho, to establish posts. With American settlers moving into the area and the lack of a clear boundary with Canada, the United States rushed to obtain land titles through treaties with the indigenous nations of the region, thereby preempting potential English claim to these lands. Anson Dart, superintendent of Indian affairs, and later Isaac Stevens and Joel Palmer, Dart's successors, would travel the Northwest making treaties with Indian groups, gaining cessions of their lands and setting aside reservations for them. The Dart treaties were not ratified, but the Stevens treaties attained legal status. Between 1850 and 1856, a substantial amount of land was cleared of its Indian title.

In 1851 the United States conducted two major treaty negotiations further east. A large portion of Minnesota was ceded by the Sioux in treaties at Traverse des Sioux and Mendota. The provisions for paying the Sioux were preempted by manipulating traders and agents, leading to the Minnesota War in 1862. At Fort Laramie, Wyoming, the major Indian nations of the region were brought together to allocate hunting grounds and occupancy areas. Included among these nations were the Arapaho, Arikara, Assiniboines, Cheyenne, Crow, Gros Ventres, Mandan, and Sioux. The Eastern Shoshones arrived at the meeting grounds but because of recent conflicts with the Sioux, they were asked to go home and wait for a visit from a separate treaty commission. In 1854 the altercations surrounding the Mormon cow incident near Laramie broke the peace between Indians and whites, thereafter sparking sporadic fighting between the Sioux and the U.S. Army. In 1856 Gen. William S. Harney called the Sioux together at Fort Pierre in Dakota Territory, issued them medals and certificates recognizing their governments, and thus briefly returned peace to the Northern Plains.

As the Civil War began, conflicts between whites and Indians in Colorado brought about the necessity of new treaties and setting aside a reservation for the Cheyennes and Arapahos. Railroads had by this time approached the frontier in Kansas and Indian territory, so the diplomatic emphasis shifted in this region to treaties and agreements for the benefit of railroad companies seeking rights-of-way for transcontinental lines through the lands of many of the Indian nations that had moved from the East two decades earlier. With Union defeats in important battles in 1862 and 1863, rumors spread across the frontier that the South had made a great alliance with the western Indians with the intent of overrunning all settlements, clearing them of inhabitants. The outbreak of hostilities in Minnesota in 1862 had fueled this belief, and when it reached a fever pitch in Colorado in 1864, the Colorado militia attacked a peaceful Indian camp of Cheyennes and Arapahos near Sand Creek. The grassland Plains exploded in an Indian war of major proportions.

Gold had been discovered in Montana in 1863. Miners traveling there via the Bozeman Trail cut through the best Sioux and Cheyenne hunting grounds, triggering Red Cloud's war with the United States. At the close of the war, a congressional committee headed by Sen. James Doolittle studied the Indian question and issued a report stating that the Indian wars were the result of breaches of the peace by whites and inefficient operation of the frontier posts where the army and civilian appointees seemed to have equal duties and responsibilities. The report led to the creation of a Peace Commission by Congress in 1867. Beginning in October of that year, and continuing until January 1869, the commission negotiated peace treaties with the major Plains Indian nations: the Cheyennes and Arapahos, Comanches, Crow, Eastern Shoshones, Kiowas and Utes, Navajo, Northern Cheyenne and Arapaho, and Sioux.

These treaties recognized the political powers of the Indian nations in providing that jurisdiction over Indians would remain with the tribe concerned. They also provided for a "land book," in which the names of Indians wishing to take allotments would be registered. Most of these treaties also provided that the Indian nations would not be asked to cede lands without the approval of two-thirds or three-fourths of adult males. This provision was respected by Congress when cited in 1882–1883 by the

Sioux but was later voided in *Lone Wolf v. Hitchcock* (1903).

In 1871, as a rider to an appropriation statute, Congress forbid the president from recognizing Indian nations as parties with whom diplomatic relations could be established. Congress could not conceive of a proper way of relating to the Indians thereafter, so "agreements" were made with the Indian nations. They had the same legal status as treaties—and, indeed, were called treaties by federal negotiators—and had to be approved by both houses of Congress. The agreement-making era continued until 1914, when seeking the agreement of a majority of tribal members was made policy, and was revived again in 1950 with the Cheyenne River Sioux.

After 1914 federal agents and negotiators reduced the treaty making function to obtaining a simple agreement by a majority of a tribe at specially called meetings. With the Indian Reorganization Act of 1934, federal officials generally sought the approval of the tribal government before legislation was passed affecting it. Even the policy of "termination," which sought to end all federal services to Indian nations, was subject to this unwritten rule of gaining Indian approval (although it was often a forced approval). With complicated land settlements pending in the 1970s, agreements like the Alaska Native Claims Settlement Act of 1971 (ANCSA) were used by Congress to solve claims problems. The act, an agreement between Indian nations in Alaska and the federal government, covers such topics as water rights, jurisdiction, and land settlements. This procedure was not much different from the old treaty negotiations except that Congress had to approve the final terms. Settlement acts like ANCSA are therefore the modern expression of treaty making as originally practiced.

Much of the important case law that constitutes the body of federal Indian law derives from efforts to interpret treaties in a modern setting. Jurisdictional authority, reservation boundaries, ownership of lakes and rivers, taxation, and other topics relate to treaty provisions. While state and federal courts have frequently dealt with these provisions, little effort has been made by scholars to address treaty relationships. Scholarly historians have written articles from their perspective, and some law reviews have dealt with specific topics derived primarily from case law rather than an analysis of the treaties themselves. Scholars also have tended to examine only the ratified treaties printed in volume two of Charles Kappler's *Indian Affairs: Laws and Treaties*, failing to deal with the great variety of documents available to them in the form of Indian treaties with European nations, with other Indian nations, with railroad companies, and with private groups and individuals. The scholarly community has not yet grasped the full scope of the diplomatic activity engaged in by Indian nations.

Recent scholarship suggests that even executive orders declaring tracts of land as Indian reservations have an implied treaty status since the United States invited the Indians to leave their original homelands and live within a restricted geographical area thereafter. Today considerable time and energy is being spent negotiating agreements with states under Indian gaming laws, which require a state-Indian compact. Since gaming produces large profits that are not taxable by the states, negotiating and finalizing these agreements can be difficult. Nevertheless, the current trend in scholarship places more emphasis on reaching agreements with other political entities than pursuit of litigation or legislative remedies.

Bibliography

Clark, Blue. 1994. *Lone Wolf v. Hitchcock: Treaty Rights and Indian Law at the End of the Nineteenth Century.* Lincoln: University of Nebraska Press.

Kappler, Charles J., comp. 1903. *Indian Affairs: Laws and Treaties.* 2 vols. Washington, D.C.: Government Printing Office.

Williams, Robert A., Jr. 1990. *The American Indian in Western Legal Thought: The Discourses of Conquest.* New York: Oxford University Press.

5

Subverting the Law of Nations: American Indian Rights and U.S. Distortions of International Legality

Ward Churchill

> It's an old story, really. It's
> the story of a strategically
> unchallenged dominion, at
> the apogee of its power and influence,
> rewriting the global rules for how to
> manage its empire.
>
> Bennis 2001

Anyone who has ever debated or negotiated with U.S. officials on matters concerning American Indian land rights can attest that the federal government's first position is invariably that its title to or authority over its territory was acquired incrementally. It obtained its holdings mostly through provisions of cession in some four hundred treaties with Indians ratified by the Senate between 1778 and 1871. When it is pointed out that the United States has violated the terms of every one of the treaties, thus voiding whatever title might otherwise have accrued therefrom, a few moments of thundering silence usually follows. The official U.S. position, publicly framed as recently as 1999 by perennial "federal Indian expert" Leonard Garment, then shifts onto different ground: "If you don't accept the treaties as valid, we'll have to fall back on the Doctrine of Discovery and Rights of Conquest" (Smith and Warrior 1996, 164–165, 174). This rejoinder, to all appearances, is meant to crush, forestalling further discussion of a topic so obviously inconvenient to the status quo.

Although the idea that the United States obtained title to its "domestic sphere" by discovery and conquest has come to hold immense currency among North America's settler population, one finds that the international legal doctrines from which such notions derive are all but unknown except among a few people. This small cadre of arguable exceptions has for the most part, however, not bothered to become acquainted with the relevant doctrines in their original or customary formulations; instead its members content themselves with reviewing the belated and often transparently self-interested "interpretations" produced by nineteenth-century American jurists, most notably Chief Justice John Marshall. Overall, there seems not the least desire—or sense of obligation—to explore the matter further.

This situation is altogether curious, given Marshall's own bedrock enunciation of the United States' self-concept—the hallowed proposition that the United States should be viewed above all else as "a nation governed by laws, not men." Knowledge of or compliance with the law is presupposed, of course, in any such construction of national image. This is especially true with respect to the laws that, like those pertaining to discovery and conquest, form the core of the United States' often and loudly proclaimed contention that the acquisition and consolidation of its transcontinental domain has all along been right, just, and therefore legal. Indeed, there can be no questions of law more basic than those of the integrity of the process by which the United States asserted title to its territory and thereby purports to legitimate jurisdiction over it.

This chapter addresses U.S. performance and the juridical logic attending it through the lens of contemporaneous international legal custom and convention. It concludes with an exploration of the conceptual and material conditions requisite to a reconciliation of rhetoric and reality within the paradigm of explicitly U.S. legal (mis)understandings. Insofar as so much of this discourse devolves upon international law, and given the recent emergence of the United States as "the world's only remaining superpower," the implications are not so much national as global.

The Doctrine of Discovery

The concepts that were eventually systematized as doctrines of discovery primarily originated in a series of bulls promulgated by Pope Innocent IV during the late thirteenth century to elucidate material relations between Christian crusaders and Islamic "infidels." Although the pontiff's primary objective was to establish a legal framework compelling soldiers of the cross to deliver the fruits of their pillage abroad to the Vatican and Church-sanctioned heads of Europe's incipient states, the Innocentian bulls embodied the first formal acknowledgment in Western law that non-Christians as well as Christians enjoyed rights of property ownership. In justice, then, it followed that only those ordained to rule by a Divine Right conferred by the One True God were imbued with the prerogative to rightly dispossess lesser mortals of their lands and other worldly holdings.

The 1492 Columbian "discovery" of what proved to be an entire hemisphere, very much populated but of which most Europeans had been unaware, sparked a renewed focus on questions of whether and to what extent Christian sovereigns might declare proprietary interest in the assets of non-Christians. The first question, however, was whether the inhabitants of the so-called New World were endowed with souls, the criterion necessary for members of humanity to be accorded any legal standing. This issue led to the famous 1550 debate in Valladolid between Frey Bartolomé de las Casas and Juan Ginés de Sepúlveda, the outcome of which was papal recognition that American Indians were human beings and therefore entitled to the exercise of at least rudimentary rights.

Such Spanish legal theorists as Francisco de Vitoria and Juan Matías de Paz were busily revising and expanding upon Innocent's canonical foundation as a means of delineating the property rights vested in those peoples "discovered" by Christian European powers as well as those rights presumably obtained in the process by their "discoverers." In the first instance, Vitoria posited the principle that sovereigns acquired outright title to lands discovered by their subjects only when the territory involved was found to be literally unoccupied (*terra nullius*). Since almost none of the lands European explorers ever came across genuinely met this description, the premise of *territorium res nullius* was essentially moot from the outset. Regardless, the English—and more so their American offshoot—would later twist this concept to their own ends.

For places found to be inhabited, international law, as interpreted by Vitoria, unequivocally acknowledged that native residents held inherent or "aboriginal" title to the land. What the discoverer obtained was a monopolistic right vis-à-vis other powers to acquire the property from its native owners, in the event that they could be persuaded through peaceful means to alienate it. On balance, this formulation seems to have been devised as an attempt to order relations between European states in such a way as to prevent them from shredding one another in a mad scramble to glean the lion's share of the wealth all of them expected to flow from the Americas.

Under the right of discovery, the first European nation to discover a land previously unknown to Europe had what is akin to an exclusive European franchise to negotiate for the indigenous populations' land within that area. International law forbade European nations from interfering with the diplomatic affairs each carried on with the Indian nations within their respective "discovered" territories. The doctrine of discovery thus reduced friction and the possibility of warfare between competing European nations. That this principle of noninterference was well-developed in international law and understood perfectly by the founding fathers of the United States is confirmed in an observation by no less luminous a figure than Thomas Jefferson:

> We consider it as established by the usage of different nations into a kind of *Jus gentium* for America, that a white nation settling down and declaring such and such are their limits, makes an invasion of those limits by any other white nation an act of war, but gives no right of soil against the native possessors. . . . That is to say, [we hold simply] the sole and exclusive right of purchasing land from [indigenous peoples within our ostensible boundaries] whenever they should be willing to sell. (Lipscomb and Bergh 1903–1904, 7:467–469)

The requirement that the consent of indigenous peoples was needed to legitimate cessions of their land was what prompted European states to begin entering into treaties with the "natives" soon after the invasion of North America had commenced in earnest. While treaties between European and indigenous nations comprised the fundamental real estate documents through which the disposition of land title on the continent must be assessed, they also served to convey formal recognition by each party that the other was its coequal in terms of legal stature or sovereignty. To further quote Jefferson, "[T]he Indians [have] full, undivided and independent sovereignty as long as they choose to keep it, and . . . this might be forever" (Prucha 1970, 141). As U.S. attorney general William Wirt would put it in 1828,

> [Be it] once conceded, that the Indians are independent to the purpose of treating, their independence is to that purpose as absolute as any other nation. . . . Nor can it be conceded that their independence as a nation is a

> limited independence. Like all other nations, they have the absolute power of war and peace. Like any other nation, their territories are inviolable by any other sovereignty. . . . They are entirely self-governed, self-directed. They treat, or refuse to treat, at their pleasure; and there is no human power that can rightly control their discretion in this respect. (*Opinions of the Attorney General* 1828, 613–618, 623–633)

From early on, the English had sought to create a loophole by which to exempt themselves in certain instances from the necessity of securing land title by treaty and to undermine the discovery rights of France, whose New World settlement patterns were vastly different from theirs. Termed the Norman Yoke, the theory was that an individual—or an entire people—could rightly claim only such property as they had converted from wilderness to a state of domestication, that is, turned into towns, placed in cultivation, and so forth. Without regard for indigenous methods of land use, it was declared that any area remaining in an "undeveloped" condition could be declared terra nullius by its discoverer and clear title thus claimed. By extension, a discovering power, such as France, that failed to pursue development of the sort evident in the English colonial model forfeited its discovery rights accordingly.

The Puritans of Plymouth Plantation and the Massachusetts Bay Colony experimented with this idea during the early seventeenth century, arguing that although native property rights might well be vested in their towns and fields, the remainder of their territory, since it was uncultivated, should be considered unoccupied, and thus not owned. This precedent, however, never evolved into a more generalized English practice. Indeed, the Puritans abandoned such presumption in 1629.

Whatever theoretical disagreements existed concerning the nature of the respective ownership rights of Indians and Europeans to land in America, practical realities shaped legal relations between the natives and the colonists. The necessity of getting along with powerful Indians, who outnumbered the European settlers for several decades, dictated that as a matter of prudence the settlers buy lands that the Indians were willing to sell, rather than displace them by other methods. The result was that the English and Dutch colonial governments obtained most of their lands by purchase. For all practical purposes, the Indians were treated as sovereigns possessing full ownership of all the land of America.

So true was this that by 1750 England had dispatched a de facto ambassador to conduct diplomatic relations with the Haudenosaunee—the Iroquois Confederacy—and in 1763 King George III issued a proclamation prohibiting English settlement west of the Allegheny Mountains in an effort to quell Indian unrest precipitated by his subjects' encroachments upon unceded lands. This foreclosure of the speculative interests in "western" lands—held by George Washington and other members of the settler elite and coveted in the less grandiose aspirations to landed status by rank-and-file colonials—would prove a major cause of the War of Independence.

Although it is popularly believed in the United States that the 1783 Treaty of Paris, through which England admitted defeat to the colonists, conveyed title to all lands east of the Mississippi River to the victorious insurgents, the reality is rather different. England merely relinquished its claim to the territory at issue. Hence, what the newly established republic actually acquired was title to such property as England owned—that is, the area of the original thirteen colonies situated east of the 1763 demarcation line, plus an exclusive right to acquire such property as native owners might be convinced to cede by treaty as far west as the Mississippi. The same principle pertained to the subsequent territorial acquisitions from European or Euro-derivative countries—for example, the 1803 Louisiana Purchase and the 1848 impoundment of the northern half of Mexico through the Treaty of Guadalupe Hidalgo—from which the forty-eight contiguous states were eventually consolidated.

As a concomitant to independence, moreover, the Continental Congress found itself presiding over a pariah state, defiance (much less forcible revocation) of Crown authority being among the worst offenses imaginable under European law. Unable to obtain recognition of its legitimacy, the federal government was compelled for nearly two decades to seek it through treaties of peace and friendship with indigenous nations—all of them recognized as legitimate sovereigns in prior treaties with the very European powers then shunning the United States—while going to extravagant rhetorical lengths to demonstrate that, far from being an outlaw state, it was really the most legally oriented of all nations.

The fledgling United States could hardly peddle a strictly law-abiding image on the one hand while openly trampling upon the rights of indigenous peoples on the other. As a result, one of the earliest acts of Congress was to pass the Northwest Ordinance although George Washington had secretly and successfully recommended the opposite policy even before being sworn in as president. In the ordinance, the United States solemnly pledged that "the utmost good faith shall always be observed towards the Indians; their lands and property shall never be taken without their consent; and, in their property, rights, and liberty, they shall never be invaded or disturbed." For the most part, then, it was not until the United States had consolidated its diplomatic ties with France, and the demographic and military balance in the West had begun to shift decisively in its favor, that it began to make serious inroads on native lands.

The Marshall Opinions

The preliminary legal pretext for U.S. expansionism, set forth by Chief Justice Marshall in his *Fletcher v. Peck* (1810) opinion, amounted to little more than a recitation of the Norman Yoke theory, which was quite popular at the time with Jefferson and other leaders. The proposition that significant portions of Indian territory amounted to terra nullius, and was thus open to assertion of U.S. title without native agreement, was, however, contradicted by the country's policy of securing by treaty at least an appearance of indigenous consent to the relinquishment of each parcel brought under federal jurisdiction. The presumption of underlying native land title in the doctrine of discovery thus remained the most vexing barrier to the fulfillment of U.S. territorial ambitions.

In the land claim case of *Johnson v. McIntosh* (1823), Marshall therefore proffered a major (re)interpretation of the Norman Yoke doctrine. While demonstrating a thorough mastery of the law as it had been previously articulated, and an undeniable ability to draw all the appropriate conclusions therefrom, the chief justice nonetheless inverted the law completely. Although Marshall readily conceded that title to the territories the United States occupied was vested in indigenous peoples, he denied that this afforded them supremacy within their respective domains. Rather, he argued, the self-assigned authority of discoverers to constrain the ability of indigenous people to alienate their property implied that supremacy inhered in the discovering power, not only with respect to other potential buyers but vis-à-vis the native owners themselves.

Since the sovereign standing of discoverers—or derivatives, such as the United States—could in this sense be said to overarch that of those discovered, Marshall held that discovery also conveyed to the discoverer an absolute title, or eminent domain, underlying the aboriginal title possessed by indigenous peoples. The native right of possession was thereby reduced at the stroke of a pen to something enjoyed at the "sufferance" of the discovering (superior) sovereign:

> The principle was that discovery gave title to the government by whose subjects, or by whose authority, it was made, against all other European governments whose title might be consummated by possession. The exclusion of all other Europeans necessarily gave to the nation making the discovery the sole right of acquiring the soil from the natives, and establishing settlements upon it. . . . In the establishment of these relations, the rights of the original inhabitants were, in no instance, entirely disregarded; but were, to a considerable extent, diminished. . . . [T]heir rights to complete sovereignty, as independent nations, were necessarily diminished, and their power to dispose of the soil, at their own will, to whomever they pleased, was denied by the original fundamental principle, the discovery gave exclusive right to those who made it. . . . [T]he Indian inhabitants are [thus] to be considered merely as occupants.
> (*Johnson v. McIntosh*)

"However extravagant [my logic] might appear," Marshall summed up, "if the principle has been asserted in the first instance, and afterwards, sustained; if a country has been acquired and held under it; if the property of the great mass of the community originates in it, it cannot be questioned." In other words, violations of law themselves become law if committed by those wielding enough power to get away with them. For all the elegant sophistry embodied in *Johnson*, its premise exemplifies the cliche that "might makes right." In this manner, Marshall not only integrated "the legacy of 1,000 years of European racism and colonialism directed against nonwestern peoples" into the canon of American law (Williams 1990, 317), but did so with a virulence unrivaled even by the European jurists upon whose precedents he professed to base his own.

There were, of course, loose ends to be tied, and these Marshall addressed through opinions rendered in the so-called Cherokee cases: *Cherokee v. Georgia* (1981) and *Worcester v. Georgia* (1832). In his *Cherokee* opinion, the chief justice undertook to resolve questions concerning the standing to be accorded indigenous peoples. Since the United States had entered into numerous treaties with native peoples, it was bound by customary international law and Article 1, section 10, of the Constitution to treat them as coequal sovereigns. Marshall's verbiage in *Johnson* had plainly cast them in a very different light. Hence, in *Cherokee*, he conjured a whole new classification of politicolegal entity "marked by peculiar and cardinal distinctions which nowhere else exist." He goes on to state,

> [I]t may well be doubted whether those tribes which reside within the acknowledged boundaries of the United States can, with strict accuracy, be denominated foreign nations. They may, more correctly, perhaps, be denominated domestic dependent nations. They occupy a territory to which we assert a title independent of their will. . . . Their relation to the United States resembles that of a ward to his guardian.

"The Indian territory is admitted to compose a part of the United States," he continues. "In all our maps, geographical treatises, histories, and laws, it is so considered. . . . [T]hey are [therefore] considered to be within the jurisdictional limits of the United States [and] acknowledge themselves to be under the protection of the United States."

What Marshall described is a status virtually identical to that of a protectorate, yet as he himself would observe in *Worcester* a year later, "the settled doctrine of the law of nations is that a weaker power does not surrender its independence—its right of self-government—by associating with a stronger, and taking its protection. A weak state, in order to provide for its safety, may place itself under the protection of one more powerful, without stripping itself of the right of government, and ceasing to be a state." It follows that a protectorate would also retain its land rights, unimpaired by its relationship with a stronger country.

At another level, Marshall was describing a status similar to that of the states of the Union—subordinate to federal authority, while retaining a residue of sovereign prerogative. Yet he, better than most, was aware that if this were the case, the federal government would never have had a basis in either international or constitutional law to enter into treaties with indigenous peoples in the first place, a matter that would have invalidated any U.S. claim to land titles accruing therefrom. Small wonder, trapped as he was in the welter of his own contradictions, that Marshall eventually threw up his hands in frustration, unable or unwilling to further define Indians as either fish or fowl. In the end, he simply repeated his assertion that the U.S.-Indian relationship was "unique . . . perhaps unlike [that of] any two peoples in existence."

Small wonder, too, all things considered, that the chief justice's *Cherokee* opinion was joined by only one other member of the high court. The majority took exception, with Justices Henry Baldwin and William Johnson writing separate opinions and Smith Thompson and Joseph Story entering a strongly worded dissent that laid bare the only reasonable conclusions to be drawn from the (legal and historical) facts.

> It is [the Indians'] political condition which determines their *foreign character*, and in that sense must the term *foreign* be understood as used in the Constitution. It can have no relation to local, geographical, or territorial position. It cannot mean a country beyond the sea. Mexico or Canada is certainly to be considered a foreign country, in reference to the United States. It is the political relation in which one country stands to another, which constitutes it [as] foreign to the other.

Nonetheless, Marshall's views prevailed, a circumstance allowing him to deploy his "domestic dependent nation" thesis against the Cherokees and Georgia in *Worcester*. First, he reserved on constitutional grounds relations with all "other nations" to the federal sphere, thereby dispensing with Georgia's contention that it possessed a state right to exercise jurisdiction over a portion of the Cherokee nation falling within its boundaries. Turning to the Cherokees, he reiterated his premise that they, and by implication all Indians within whatever borders the United States might eventually claim, occupied a nebulous quasi-sovereign status as "distinct, independent political communities" subject to federal authority. In practical effect, Marshall cast indigenous nations as entities inherently endowed with a sufficient measure of sovereignty to alienate their territory by treaty when and wherever the United States desired they do so, but never with enough to refuse.

As legal scholars Vine Deloria Jr. and David E. Wilkins have observed, the cumulative distortions of established law and historical reality in Marshall's Indian opinions created a very steep and slippery slope, with no bottom in sight:

> [T]he original assumption [was] that the federal government is authorized and empowered to protect American Indians in enjoyment of their lands. Once it is implied that this power also involves the ability of the federal government by itself to force a purchase of the lands, there is no way the implied power can be limited. If the government can force the disposal of lands, why can it not determine how the lands are to be used? And if it can determine how the lands are to be used, why can it not tell Indians how to live? And if it can tell Indians how to live, why can it not tell them how to behave and what to believe? (Deloria and Wilkins 1999, 29)

By the end of the nineteenth century, less than seventy years after *Cherokee* and *Worcester*, the U.S. government would, indeed, determine land use, how the Indians would live, how they should behave, and what they should believe. Within such territory as was by then reserved for indigenous use and occupancy, the traditional mode of collective land tenure had been supplanted by federal imposition of an allegedly more civilized form of individual title expressly intended to compel agricultural land usage. Native spiritual practices were prohibited under penalty of law, and entire generations of American Indian children were being shipped off, often forcibly, to boarding schools, where they were held for years on end, forbidden knowledge of their own languages and cultures while they were systematically indoctrinated with Christian beliefs and cultural values. The overall policy of assimilation, under which these measures were implemented, readily conforms to the contemporary legal definition of cultural genocide.

Meanwhile, American Indians had been reduced to utter destitution, dispossessed of approximately 97.5 percent of their original landholdings, and had their remaining assets held in a perpetual and self-assigned trust by federal authorities wielding what Marshall's heirs on the Supreme Court described as an extraconstitutional, or plenary, power—that is, unlimited, absolute, and judicially unchallengeable power over their affairs. Nothing in the doctrine of discovery empowered any country to impose itself on others in this way. On the contrary, the juridical reasoning evident in the Marshall opinions and their successors has much in common with, and in many respects prefigured, the now thoroughly repudiated body of law purported to legitimate the European imperialism of the first half of the twentieth century.

Rights of Conquest

Rights of conquest in the New World accrued under the law of nations as a subset of doctrines of discovery. Under international law, discoverers could acquire land only through a voluntary alienation of title by native owners, with one exception being that those holding discovery rights might seize land and other property through military force. Such instances were restricted, however, to those in which the discovering power was compelled to wage a "just war" against native peoples. The United States clearly acknowledged this exception, in theory, in the Northwest Ordinance, wherein it pledged that indigenous nations would "never be invaded or disturbed, unless in just and lawful wars authorized by Congress."

The criteria for a just war is defined quite narrowly in international law. As early as 1539,

Vitoria and to a lesser degree Matías de Paz asserted that there were only three: the natives had either to have refused to admit Christian missionaries among them, to have arbitrarily refused to engage in commerce with the discovering power, or to have mounted some unprovoked physical assault against the power's representatives or subjects. Absent at least one of these conditions, any war waged by a European state or its derivative would be "unjust"—the term was later changed to "aggressive"—and resulting claims to title illegitimate. One can search in vain for an example in U.S. history in which any of these criteria might actually be viewed as applicable.

A more pragmatic problem confronting those claiming that the United States holds conquest rights to native lands is that although the federal government recognizes the existence of approximately four hundred indigenous groups within its borders, its own count of the number of Indian wars it has fought number about forty. Plainly, the United States cannot exercise conquest rights over the more than three hundred nations against which, by its own admission, it has never fought a war. Yet as is readily evident in *Tee-Hit-Ton v. United States* (1955), the Supreme Court has anchored U.S. land title in a pretense that exactly the opposite is true: "Every American schoolboy knows that the savage tribes of this continent were deprived of their ancestral ranges by force and that, even when the Indians ceded millions of acres by treaty in return for blankets, food and trinkets, it was not a sale but the conquerors' will that deprived them of their land."

Chief Justice Marshall, particularly in his *Johnson v. McIntosh* opinion but also in *Cherokee*, sought to transcend this issue by treating discovery and conquest as if they were synonymous, a conflation evidencing even less legal merit than the flights of fancy discussed above. In fact, the Court was ultimately forced to distinguish between the two, acknowledging that the "English possessions in America were not claimed by right of conquest, but by right of discovery," and, therefore, that the "law which regulates, and ought to regulate in general, the relations between the conqueror and conquered, [is] incapable of application" by the United States to American Indians.

A further complication is that by as early as 1672, such legal philosophers as Samuel Pufendorf had challenged the idea that territory seized in the course of just war might be permanently retained. Although Hugo Grotius, William Edward Hall, Emmerich de Vattel, John Westlake, and other theorists continued to aver the validity of conquest rights through the end of the nineteenth century, by the 1920s a view similar to Pufendorf's had proven ascendant.

Oddly, despite the U.S. stance concerning land cession of American Indians, as well as the government's forcible acquisition of Hawaii, Puerto Rico, and the Philippines, the United States assumed a leading role in championing the inadmissibility of acquiring territory by force. Although the Senate refused to allow the United States to join the League of Nations, President Woodrow Wilson was instrumental in creating the league, an organization intended "to substitute diplomacy for war in the resolution of international disputes" (Boyle 1999, 47–48, 53–54). In some ways, more important was the leadership role the United States assumed in fashioning the 1928 General Treaty on the Renunciation of War, also known as the Kellogg-Briand Pact or Pact of Paris. In this treaty, the Great Powers and other states rejected the use of war as an instrument of national policy:

> By Article 1, "[t]he High Contracting Parties solemnly declare, in the names of their respective peoples, that they condemn war for the solution of international controversies, and renounce it as an instrument of national policy in their relations with one another." By Article 2, the Parties "agree that the settlement or solution of all disputes or conflicts, of whatever nature or of whatever origin they may be, which may arise among them, shall never be sought except by pacific means." (Korman 1996, 192)

In 1932 Secretary of State Henry Stimson announced that the United States would no longer recognize as legitimate the title to territory acquired by force of arms. This new dictum of international law, shortly to be referred to as the Stimson Doctrine, was expressly designed to "effectively bar the legality hereafter of any title or right sought to be obtained by pressure or treaty violation, and which, as shown by history in the past, will eventually lead to the restoration to [vanquished nations] of rights and titles of which [they] have been unjustly deprived" (Briggs 1940, 73).

By the time the Supreme Court penned its opinion in *Tee-Hit-Ton*, the Stimson Doctrine had served as a cornerstone in formulating the charges of planning and waging aggressive war against the primary Nazi defendants at Nuremberg and their Japanese allies in Tokyo in tribunals instigated and organized mainly by the United States. The doctrine had also served as a guiding principle in the (effectively U.S.-instigated) establishment of the United Nations, an entity whose very charter, like that of the ill-fated League of Nations before it, is devoted to the "the progressive codification of [international] law . . . for purposes of preventing war." Correspondingly, Stimson's new dictum found its most refined and affirmative expression in the UN Charter's proviso, reiterated almost as boilerplate in a host of subsequent UN resolutions, declarations, and conventions concerning the "equal rights and self-determination of all peoples."

Contradictory as the *Tee-Hit-Ton* court's blatant conquest rhetoric was to the lofty posturing of the United States in the international arena, its position was even more contradictory with respect to a related subterfuge unfolding on the home front. By 1945 the United States was urgently seeking a means of distinguishing its own record of territorial expansion from that of the Germany whose Nazi leaders it was preparing to hang for having undertaken very much the same course of action. The workhorse employed in this effort was the so-called Indian Claims Commission (ICC), established to make retroactive payment to indigenous peoples whose property had been unlawfully taken over the years. The purpose of the commission was, as President Harry Truman explained upon signing the enabling legislation on August 14, 1946, to foster an impression that the United States had acquired *none* of its land by conquest:

> This bill makes perfectly clear what many men and women, here and abroad, have failed to recognize, that in our transactions with Indian tribes we have . . . set for ourselves the standard of fair and honorable dealings, pledging respect for all Indian property rights. Instead of confiscating Indian lands, we have purchased from the tribes that once owned this continent more than 90 percent of our public domain.

The game was rigged from the outset, to be sure, since the ICC was not empowered to return land to native people even in cases where its review of the manner in which the United States had acquired it revealed the grossest illegalities. The terms of compensatory awards, moreover, were restricted to payment of the estimated value of the land at the time it was taken, often a century or more before, without such considerations as accrued interest or appreciation in land values during the intervening period. Still, despite its self-serving and mostly cosmetic nature, the very existence of the ICC demonstrated quite clearly that, in terms of legality, U.S. assertions of title to or jurisdiction over Indian country could no more be viewed as based in conquest rights than in rights of discovery. All U.S. pretensions to legitimate ownership of property in North America must therefore be seen as treaty based.

Through the Lens of the Law

When Congress established the ICC in 1946, it expected within five years to "resolve" all remaining land rights issues concerning American Indians. The commission was to identify and catalogue the basis in treaties, agreements, and statutes by which the United States had assumed lawful ownership of every disputed land parcel within its purported domain, awarding "just compensation" in each case where the propriety of the transaction(s) documented might otherwise be deemed inadequate. By 1951, however, the 200-odd claims originally anticipated had swelled to 852. The life span of the ICC was extended for five years, and then another five years, a process that was repeated until the third generation of commissioners gave up in exhaustion.

By the time the commission suspended operations on September 30, 1978, it had processed 547 of the 615 dockets into which the 852 claims had been consolidated, none in a manner satisfactory to the native claimants; nearly half the claims were simply dismissed. Title to virtually the entire state of California, for instance, was supposedly "quieted" in the Pit River Land Claims Settlement of the mid-1960s by an award amounting to 47 cents per acre, despite the fact that the treaties by which the territory had ostensibly been ceded to the United States had never been ratified by the Senate.

Most important, the ICC in its final report acknowledged that after three decades of concerted effort, it had been unable to discern any legal basis for U.S. title assertion with respect to what the federal Public Lands Law Review Commission had described as "one third of the nation's land": "The fact is that about half the area of the country was purchased by treaty or agreement at an average price of less than a dollar per acre; another third of a [billion] acres, mainly in the West, was confiscated without compensation; another two-thirds of a [billion] acres was claimed by the United States without pretense of [even] a unilateral action extinguishing native title" (Barsh 1982).

There can be no serious question of the right of indigenous nations to recover property to which their title remains unclouded or that their right to recover lands seized without payment equals or exceeds that of the United States to preserve its territorial integrity by way of paltry and greatly belated compensatory awards. Restitution rather than compensation is, after all, the guiding principle of international tort law. Regarding the treaties or agreements through which the United States ostensibly acquired some areas many of the instruments of cession are known to have been fraudulent or coerced. These must be considered invalid under Articles 48–53 of the Vienna Convention on the Law of Treaties.

A classic illustration of fraud involves the 1861 Treaty of Fort Wise, in which federal commissioners forged the signatures of selected native leaders, several of whom were not even present during the "negotiations," and then the Senate altered many of the treaty's terms and provisions, after it was supposedly signed and ratified, without informing the Indians of the changes. On this basis, the United States claimed to have obtained the "consent" of the Cheyennes and Arapahoes to its acquisition of the eastern half of what is now Colorado. Comparable examples abound, including the treaties ceding California.

Examples of coercion are also legion, but none provides a better illustration than the 1876–1877 proceeding in which federal authorities suspended distribution of rations to the Lakotas—who at the time were directly subjugated by and therefore dependent upon the U.S. military for sustenance—and informed them that they would not be fed until their leaders had signed an agreement relinquishing title to the Black Hills region of present-day South Dakota. Thus did the Congress contend that the 1851 and 1868 Treaties of Fort Laramie, in each of which the Black Hills were recognized as an integral part of the Lakota homeland, had been superseded and U.S. ownership of the area secured.

Without doubt, North America's indigenous nations are entitled to recover lands expropriated through such travesties. Although it is currently impossible to offer a precise estimate of the acreage involved—to do so would require a contextual review of each U.S.-Indian treaty and a parcel-by-parcel delineation of the title transfers accruing from invalid instruments—it is safe to suggest that adding it to the approximately 35 percent of the continental United States that was never ceded would place well more than half the present gross domestic territory of the United States at issue.

The United States holds the power to simply ignore the law in inconvenient situations such as these. Doing so, however, will never legitimate its comportment. It is through this lens that U.S. pronouncements and performance from Nuremberg to Vietnam must inevitably be evaluated, as well as President George Herbert Walker Bush's 1990 rhetoric concerning the United States' moral and legal obligation to end Iraq's forcible annexation of neighboring Kuwait.

On the face of it, the reasonable conclusion to be drawn is that the racial and cultural arrogance, duplicity, and legal cynicism defining U.S. relations with indigenous nations from the outset have come long since to permeate U.S. relations with most other countries. How else to understand Bush's 1991 declaration that the display of U.S. military might he ordered against Iraq was intended more than anything else to put the entire world on notice that, henceforth, "what *we* say, goes" (Chomsky 1992, 49–92)? In what other manner can one explain the fact that although Bush claimed that the so-called New World Order that he was inaugurating would be marked by nothing so much as "the rule of law among nations" (ibid.), the United States was and remains unique in the consistency with which it has rejected the authority of international courts and any body of law other than its own.

For the past fifty years, federal policymakers have been increasingly adamant in their rejection of the proposition that the United States might be bound by customs or conventions that conflict with its sense of self-interest. More recently, U.S. delegates to the United Nations have taken to arguing that new codifications of international law must be written in strict conformity to their country's constitutional requirements and that, for interpretive purposes, the existing law advanced by American jurists be considered preeminent. In effect, the United States casts an aura of legitimacy over its ongoing subjugation of indigenous nations by engineering a normalization of such relations in universal legal terms.

The implications of such maneuvering are by no means constrained to a foreclosure on the rights of native peoples. The broader result of U.S. unilateralism is that the United States is extrapolating its presumptive jurisdictional supremacy to worldwide proportions, just as it did with respect to North American Indian territories. This initiative is especially dangerous, given that the lopsided advantage held by the United States within the present balance of global military power closely resembles that which it enjoyed vis-à-vis American Indians, Hawaiians, and Filipinos during the nineteenth century. The upshot is that if such trends are allowed to continue, the United States will have shortly converted most of the rest of the planet to Indian country.

Bibliography

Barsh, Russel. 1982. "Indian Land Claims Policy in the United States." *North Dakota Law Review*, no. 58: 7–82.

Bennis, Phyllis. 2001. *Calling the Shots: How Washington Dominates Today's UN.* Northampton, Mass.: Interlink Publishing.

Boyle, Francis Anthony. 1999. *Foundations of World Order: The Legalist Approach to International Relations, 1898–1922.* Durham, N.C.: Duke University Press.

Briggs, Henry W. 1940. "Non-Recognition of Title by Conquest and Limitations of the Doctrine." *Papers of the American Society for International Law*, no. 34.

Chomsky, Noam. 1992. "What We Say Goes." In *Col lateral Damage: The New World Order at Home and Abroad*, edited by Cynthia Peters. Boston: South End Press.

Deloria, Vine, Jr., and David E. Wilkins. 1999. *Tribes, Treaties and Constitutional Tribulations.* Austin: University of Texas Press.

Korman, Sharon. 1996. *The Right of Conquest: The Acquisition of Territory by Force in International Law and Practice.* Oxford: Clarendon Press.

Lipscomb, Andrew A., and Albert Ellery Bergh, eds. 1903–1904. *The Writings of Thomas Jefferson.* Washington, D.C.: Thomas Jefferson Memorial Association.

Opinions of the Attorney General. 1828. Washington, D.C.: Government Printing Office.

Prucha, Francis Paul. 1970. *American Indian Policy in the Formative Years: The Trade and Intercourse Acts, 1790–1834.* Lincoln: University of Nebraska Press.

Smith, Paul Chaat, and Robert Allen Warrior. 1996. *Like a Hurricane: The American Indian Movement from Alcatraz to Wounded Knee.* New York: Free Press.

Williams, Robert A., Jr. 1990. *The American Indian in Western Legal Thought: The Discourses of Conquest.* New York: Oxford University Press.

The Courts and Congress

6 Native American Self-Government

Philip L. Fetzer

Well before contact with European explorers, Native Americans had the right to self-government based on tribal sovereignty. Relatively few tribes, however, had organized European-style governments prior to the Revolutionary War. A notable exception was the Iroquois Confederacy, founded in the fourteenth century. The U.S. government explicitly recognized tribal sovereignty for the first time when Chief Justice John Marshall wrote for the Supreme Court in *Worcester v. Georgia* (1832), "The Indian nations [have] always been considered as distinct, independent, political communities." The Court reaffirmed its position on tribal sovereignty in *Oklahoma Tax Commission v. Citizen Band Potawatomi Indian Tribe* (1991). The exercise of federal power through treaties or statutes may limit some of the powers Native Americans' possess, but it is not a source of their powers. Another way to describe tribal power, therefore, is through the concept of limited sovereignty.

Three principles apply to Indian self-government: Indian nations retain all the power of a sovereign state; tribes are subject to congressional authority due to conquest and may not negotiate agreements with other nations; tribal powers can be qualified by treaties or express legislative acts. Selling tribal land without the permission of the federal government, for example, would not be allowed. The fact that tribal power exists, however, does not mean that it is always exercised. Tribal power can be hampered by a lack of economic resources, or federal agencies that take unauthorized actions to impede the application of legitimate tribal authority. Other extralegal limitations on tribal power include abuse of supervisory power by the Bureau of Indian Affairs, the unwillingness of non-Indians in or near a reservation to accept tribal control, and violations of treaty rights by government officials.

Tribal Government and Membership

The ability to create the form of government under which one is ruled is a primary aspect of sovereignty. Established processes for gaining positions of tribal leadership, obtaining duties and responsibilities as officers, and authorizing official acts of the tribe are vital components of tribal government. Historically, most tribal decisions have been made by consensus in open council meetings. In some cases, the chiefs or religious leaders made policy decisions. Traditional leaders were chosen on the basis of their wisdom, courage, generosity, or spirituality. With the passage of the Indian Reorganization Act (IRA) of 1934—the Indian New Deal—the traditional governance of more than a hundred tribes that consented to reorganize under its provisions was replaced by Anglo forms of government. In many cases, attorneys from the Department of the Interior were the primary authors of new tribal constitutions, while in other cases Indian governments submitted every tribal law for review by the secretary of the interior, as required by the act. The Indian Reorganization Act frequently served to reduce tribes' ability to exercise legitimate authority within reservation boundaries. For example, under a typical IRA constitution, the Papago Council, the tribe's governing body, would have to submit for review and approval decisions related to the disbursal of tribal funds, regulation of non-Indian businesses on the reservation, and the administration of justice.

Historically, tribal governments varied considerably, as they do today. While most have written constitutions, some tribes, such as the Navajo and Yakima, do not. The Menominee of Wisconsin have one of the strongest tribal constitutions and one of the most recently written. Some tribes are run as theocracies, while others chose their leaders by heredity. The majority of them elect their leaders. Reflecting the skepticism that many Native Americans have toward Western forms of politics, participation in reservation elections is generally low. Normally, voting rates among eligible members likely fall within the range of 10 to 25 percent. Tribes control all decisions on voting rights in tribal elections.

Indian tribes have full authority to decide all questions of tribal membership absent specific legislative action to the contrary by Congress. This right includes special procedures for recognition or loss of membership, admission of non-Indians or Indians from other tribes, special categories of membership or citizenship as warranted, and exclusion of individuals from the reservation. Tribal powers related to membership, adoption, loss of membership, and readoption were judicially recognized by the District Court of Oregon in *Smith v. Bonifer* (1907) and later by the Supreme Court in *Santa Clara Pueblo v. Martinez* (1978).

Trends in tribal decisions involving membership have tended to move away from traditional notions of rights tied to blood relationships. Recent tribal rulings support the idea of membership more as a political concept than as a matter of race. Congress has granted plenary authority to tribes to make rules governing the domestic relations of its members. State and federal courts provide the same recognition to tribal marriages as that granted to marriages granted under state laws, and both courts recognize tribal jurisdiction over Indian divorces. Indian tribes are fully responsible for identifying and punishing offenses such as adultery.

State laws do not apply to domestic relations of individuals living in a tribal relationship on reservation lands. The Supreme Court recognized tribal rights to regulate relationships regarding marriage, divorce, and adoption in *United States v. Wheeler* (1978). On issues related to inheritance, federal law recognizes traditional Indian marriages; appointment of guardians for minors as well as property relations of spouses, parents, and children are subject to tribal law and custom. Federal statutes do not, however, permit guardians to manage business affairs when federal trust funds are involved.

Regulation of Property

Traditionally, most tribes did not recognize private ownership of land. If the tribe controlled a certain territory, communal use was the rule. The General Allotment Act of 1887, however, changed this by providing for a federal division of communal land into individual plots. Implementation of the act had a grievously negative effect on control of tribal property. During the forty-seven years until the act's repeal in 1934, tribes lost ownership of nearly two-thirds of their communal land.

There are two primary sources of tribal power over property. First, the tribe has rights commonly associated with normal property ownership. Additionally, the tribe has the right to regulate and dispose of the individual property of its members as an aspect of sovereignty. Land owned by the United States but set aside for exclusive use by a tribe is called trust land. Such land may be leased, mortgaged, or sold but only with federal approval. Indian title land is distinguished from trust land in that title land has been occupied as an ancestral home. Tribes have the right to continue to occupy title land absent congressional action to the contrary. While a tribe may grant a right of occupancy of tribal land to members, such action does not generate rights of the occupant against the tribe.

Other tribal property rights include ownership of real and personal property. Real property includes land as well as buildings, minerals, and timber. Automobiles, bank accounts, furniture, and clothing are examples of personal property. The tribal right to regulate tribal property was first recognized by the Supreme Court in *Worcester v. Georgia* (1832) and reaffirmed in *Merrion v. Jicarilla Apache Tribe* (1982). The tribal right to regulate private property is extensive. Federal judges have recognized the authority of tribes to zone land, regulate liquor sales, and exercise the right of eminent domain. Tribal authority to regulate inheritance of private property was recognized by the Court in *Jones v. Meehan* (1889).

Tribes may also limit rights to hunt and fish and to undertake other commercial activities on the reservation. At the same time, in *United States v. Montana* (1981) the Supreme Court limited the right of Native Americans to zone and otherwise regulate non-Indian-owned land on areas of a reservation where non-Indians comprise a majority. The Court later rejected it entirely in *Brendale v. Confederated Tribes and Bands of the Yakima Indian Nation* (1989).

The power to levy taxes is an important aspect of tribal sovereignty that continues, although it can be reduced by an act of Congress, as in *Buster v. Wright* (1905), for example. Taxing authority was affirmed under the terms of the Indian Reorganization Act of 1934. Provisions of the act permit tribal imposition of poll taxes, vehicle, and license taxes on tribal members, and license taxes on nonmembers who occupy tribal property.

Administration of Justice

The right to administer justice is a substantive power of self-government within the scope of tribal sovereignty. Until the nineteenth century, however, Indian reservations were in effect under military supervision. This was the case because the Bureau of Indian Affairs was part of the War Department and the bureau controlled the reservations.

In 1934 as a provision of the Indian Reorganization Act, tribes were expected to organize their own court system. If a tribe has the right to regulate certain activities, it follows that it also has the power to evaluate and make judgments about those activities through institutions created by the tribe. Decisions of Indian tribal courts on civil matters involving traditional laws and customs are entitled to full faith and credit by state and federal courts. Enforcement of contracts and personal injury claims are under tribal jurisdiction, as are regulations on joint business ventures.

In 1953, under a federal policy called termination, Congress adopted Public Law 83-280, transferring complete criminal and some civil jurisdiction from tribal control to state governments in California, Minnesota, Nebraska, Oregon, and Wisconsin as well as the territory of Alaska. Tribal consent was not required. Under provisions of the Indian Civil Rights Act of 1968, however, a tribal consent provision was added to the 1953 law. Since that time, Utah has been the only other state to enact PL 83-280.

In all but the PL 83-280 states, tribes have retained original criminal jurisdiction vis-à-vis states. It is a basic principle that states do not have the general authority to try and punish Native Americans for offenses committed on reservation land. The Supreme Court held in *Oliphant v. Suquamish* (1978), however, that tribes do not have the right to prosecute non-Indians for violations of tribal law on reservation land unless expressly granted by Congress. Off the reservation, state or federal courts may not enforce penal provisions of tribal law against Native Americans. States, however, retain their authority to regulate the conduct of tribal members off-reservation in the same manner as any other individuals residing within the state.

The constitutional authority of the federal government to administer law on reservations is absolute. Legislation specifically authorizing federal power to regulate criminal violations on tribal land has evolved. In 1883, in *Ex Parte Crow Dog*, the Supreme Court held that federal courts were without jurisdiction in a murder case involving two Native Americans on reservation land. The Court concluded that the original sovereignty of the tribe had never been withdrawn and therefore, criminal jurisdiction for all criminal offenses remained with the tribe.

Reacting to *Crow Dog* in 1885, Congress adopted the Major Crimes Act that made seven offenses on Indian reservations subject to federal jurisdiction: murder of a Native American by a Native American, manslaughter, rape, assault with intent to kill, burglary, larceny, and arson. Congress later added robbery, assault with a dangerous weapon, and incest to the list of offenses for which it substituted federal, in place of tribal, jurisdiction. Such traditional federal offenses as counterfeiting and smuggling also remained within the jurisdiction of federal courts.

It is important to remember that a gap in tribal law does not automatically grant jurisdiction to federal courts. An omission in federal law, on the other hand, does mean that jurisdiction remains with tribal courts. Tribes retain authority over such offenses as kidnapping, libel, forgery, bribery, embezzlement, and receiving stolen goods because Congress has not acted to confer federal jurisdiction over them.

In *Talton v. Mayes* (1896), the Supreme Court held that acts of the federal government, but not those of tribal governments, were subject to the provisions of the Bill of Rights. With the adoption of the Indian Civil Rights Act in 1968, however, Congress applied most of the provisions of the Bill of Rights to Indian tribes. Under the act, Congress limits the punishment that tribal courts may apply in criminal cases to six months in prison and a fine of no more than five hundred dollars.

Tribes' additional law enforcement powers include the right to hire and train tribal police forces and establish their own trial courts. The structure and procedures followed by tribal courts differ although most have appellate courts. Qualifications and rules for selection of tribal judges also vary considerably.

Summary

Original tribal sovereignty is the source of self-government for Native Americans. Due to their status as conquered nations, however, tribal power has evolved into what may be more appropriately described as limited sovereignty. The general rule, then, is that tribes may exercise their sovereignty unless or until the federal government has acted to curtail it.

Bibliography

Cohen, Felix S. 1972. *Handbook of Federal Indian Law.* New York: AMS Press.

Pevar, Stephen L. 1992. *The Rights of Indians and Tribes.* Carbondale: Southern Illinois University Press.

Wilkinson, Charles, et al. 1979. *Federal Indian Law.* St. Paul, Minn.: West Publishing.

7

Native Americans and Civil Rights

Donald A. Grinde Jr.

The phrase *civil rights* implies protection from laws and policies that restrict freedom and equality. After white contact with American Indians, colonial, local, state, and federal officials systematically dispossessed, killed, harassed, and subjugated Native Americans through oppressive policies aimed at entire Indian nations as well as individuals within these nations. To many Native Americans, it therefore seems paradoxical to study American Indian civil rights. Native Americans are, however, citizens of the United States, and residents of their respective states, while remaining members of sovereign Indian nations. Like other oppressed groups, American Indians endured the repeated deprivation of their rights by local, state, and federal governments. Central to this process was the ceding of land through treaties in return for retaining certain rights as well as sovereignty and ownership over reservation lands. Throughout U.S. history, Native American people have sought to exercise their religious, treaty, and cultural rights, some of which conflicted with state and federal laws.

Since the creation of the United States, Native Americans, like other people of color, have experienced private and governmental prejudice. American Indians, however, have rights under U.S. law that differ from those of other citizens. Most Native American rights involve a range of preferences, prerogatives, and immunities based on their treaty rights as citizens of American Indian nations, not on their status as members of a "minority" population. Thus, American Indians are treated, under the law, as a "group" with contractual rights (in the form of treaties) with the U.S. government and as individuals of color within the broader American society. These two confusing and sometimes conflicting legal statuses have often worked against Native Americans in the legal system.

The civil rights of American Indians are twofold. The first category involves basic issues of civil rights: freedom of religion and speech, due process, voting, and freedom from racial discrimination. These rights engage not only constitutional limitations on federal and state governments, but also limitations on the prerogatives of Native American governments. The second category involves the rights and disabilities of native peoples as citizens of American Indian nations. Because of Native Americans' duality under the law, the United States has created immunities, disabilities, and legal preferences that apply to American Indian individuals as well as immunities and rights that are a product of the American Indian governmental system. In each of these areas, it is membership in a Native American group that institutes an immunity or a right.

Conquest and U.S. Law

During the conquest of North America, the U.S. government used might, treaties, and the federal laws and executive orders to force American Indian nations onto reservations representing a small portion of their original lands. On March 3, 1871, Congress passed the Indian Appropriations Act, which terminated treaty making between American Indian nations and the federal government and gave the House of Representatives a greater say in the conduct of relations with Native Americans. After 1871, Indian affairs would be carried out through legislation approved in both houses of Congress rather than through treaties ratified only in the Senate. In addition, this new law denied noncitizen Indians and Indian nations the power to make contracts that involved the payment of money for services involving Indian lands or claims against the federal government unless the secretary of the interior and the commissioner of Indian affairs approved the contracts. Since many Indian grievances were against the secretary of the interior and the commissioner of Indian affairs, this statute effectively denied Native Americans a basic right in common law—the right of free choice of counsel for the redress of injuries. Indian rights were further hindered by the Act of May 21, 1872.

This legislation abolished the capacity of American Indian nations to stop federal encroachment into the conduct of tribal affairs. The use of federal power in American Indian affairs became arbitrary. In the early part of the nineteenth century, Chief Justice John Marshall had asserted in *Cherokee Nation v. Georgia* (1831) that U.S.-Indian relations resembled the status of a guardian and a ward. Late in the century, Congress and the courts used Marshall's words to sanction this radical transformation in Indian policy. Basically, tribal-federal relations changed from treaties negotiated between sovereign nations to an oppressive guardianship over a powerless ward that would never be allowed to grow up.

The U.S. government justified its interference in intratribal affairs on the grounds that Indian nations should be protected by the federal government from malevolent local populations. In *United States v. Kagama* (1886), the Supreme Court upheld the validity of the 1885 Major Crimes Act, which imposed certain federal criminal laws on Indians living on federally created reservations. The Court held,

> [T]hey are spoken of as "wards of the nation," "pupils," as local dependent communities. In this spirit the United States has conducted its relations to them from its organization to this time. . . .
>
> These Indian tribes are wards of the nation. They are communities dependent on the United States. . . . From their very weakness

> and helplessness, so largely due to the dealing of the Federal Government with them, and its treaties in which it has been promised, there arises the duty of protection, and with it the power.

In short, the power of the U.S. government is necessary to protect the remnants of a people once powerful, but now weak and diminished in numbers, as well as the safety of those among whom they dwell. In other words, federal policy justified negating treaty rights and stipulations.

Because of the power flowing to the U.S. government from its relationship with Native Americans, the court gave the United States unbridled power not only to determine what was appropriate in the conduct of Indian affairs but also to act on that decision without consulting with American Indian nations. Hence, the federal government, under the guise of "protecting" American Indians, diluted the basic fundamental treaty right of Indian nations—the capacity to remain as distinct cultural and political groups.

The basis for the attack on American Indian rights was the federal government's plan to allot reservation land—which Indians held in common—to adult members of Indian nations and then sell the "surplus" lands to non-Indians. On February 8, 1887, Congress passed the General Allotment Act, which established a commission to survey Indian lands in order to distribute it to individual tribal members. Essentially, the policy reasoned that traditional Native American lifestyles bred indolence and dependency, so to eliminate these undesirable traits, the government should introduce free enterprise in Native American communities to engender independence and initiative. Although holding property was no longer a prerequisite for voting in most states, the General Allotment Act sought to make American Indians voting (as well as tax-paying, church-going) citizens through individual ownership of land.

Most Indian nations vigorously resisted the allotment policies, but the federal government decided to implement them anyway. Although the Bureau of Indian Affairs and the Allotment Commission conducted supposed "negotiations" with Native American governments, the results were debased by coercion, fraud, forgery, and duress. Rather than taking the Indians' objections into consideration, the courts took part in the masquerade on behalf of the government, denying Indian property rights established through treaties. In *Lone Wolf v. Hitchcock* (1903), the Kiowa chief Lone Wolf sought to negate the validity of the "allotment agreement" that sold Comanche, Kiowa, and Kiowa Apache lands to non-Indians. Under the Treaty of Medicine Lodge (1867), no part of the Kiowa-Comanche reservation could be sold to the federal government without the approval of three-fourths of the adult male Indians. Under the General Allotment Act, Congress allotted the reservation and then sold the "surplus" without obtaining the three-fourths approval as stipulated in the 1867 treaty. In upholding the actions of the government, the Supreme Court stated,

> The power exists to abrogate the provisions of an Indian treaty, though presumably such power will be exercised only when circumstances arise which not only justify the government in disregarding the stipulations of the treaty, but may demand, in the interest of the country and the Indians themselves, that it should do so.
>
> In view of the legislative power possessed by Congress over treaties with the Indians, and Indian tribal property, we may not specially consider [the allegations of fraud], since all these matters, in any event, were solely within

> the domain within the legislative authority and its action is conclusive upon the courts.

The justices described this as "plenary authority over the tribal relations of the Indians" and deemed the exercise of these "plenary" powers as being beyond judicial review. Theoretically, Congress could only utilize such powers for the good of Native American nations, but the Court would not second-guess Congress on what was good for them. Hence, *Lone Wolf* held that congressional power was basically unlimited when it involved Indian affairs.

In the early twentieth century, *United States v. Sandoval* (1913) added a racial justification to the government's enormous power over Indians. In this case, the Supreme Court upheld Congress's power to impose "Indian" status on the Pueblo Indians of New Mexico even though they had been regarded as U.S. citizens by the Territory of New Mexico since 1877:

> Always living in separate and isolated communities, adhering to primitive modes of life, largely influenced by superstition and fetishism, and chiefly governed according to crude customs inherited through their ancestors, [Pueblo Indians] are essentially a simple, uninformed and inferior people. . . .
>
> As a superior and civilized nation [the United States has both] the power and the duty of exercising a fostering care and protection over all dependent Indian communities within its borders.

Although the Pueblo had endured hundreds of years of Spanish domination, developed an admirable agricultural system in the desert, and formulated a spirituality that amazed anthropologists, they were, in the eyes of the Court, a simple and superstitious people and thus governable by the "plenary" powers of Congress. Attorney Alvin J. Zionitz opines that the plenary power doctrine "in practice means that Congress has the power to do virtually as it pleases with the Indian tribes. It is an extraordinary doctrine for a democracy to espouse. It would justify abolishing the political existence of the tribes" (Zionitz 1979). Furthermore, Zionitz states, "Short of that, it justifies the imposition of controls over the lives and property of the tribes and their members. Plenary power thus subjects Indians to national powers outside ordinary constitutional limits" (ibid.) Throughout the twentieth century, congressional plenary powers involving Indian affairs would wreak havoc on American Indian governments, lives, and property in spite of progress made in the realm of civil rights for Native American individuals.

The attacks on American Indian people in the late nineteenth century, however, were much broader than simply subverting traditional landholding patterns. Federal agents also sought to discredit tribal governmental practices and leaders by supplanting them with Euro-American modes of governance. To compound matters, the United States actively suppressed tribal religious rituals and beliefs in direct violation of the Bill of Rights. The government encouraged and subsidized Christian missionaries to proselytize among tribal communities. Hence, zealous missionaries and Indian agents legally prohibited American Indian religious rituals and dances in their efforts to convert Indians to Christianity.

These ethnocidal actions did not bring salvation to the Indians or a level of prosperity that white Americans enjoyed. Instead, these policies devastated American Indian individuals and nations. Between 1887 and 1933, Native Americans lost more than half of their land base to thieves, the sale of land to recoup taxes, and governmental sales of "surplus" lands. These policies launched a cycle of poverty that continues to this day, making poor education and ill health hallmarks of tribal societies in America. These policies also strengthened the resolve of many Native American peoples to nurture and cleave to their old ways.

American Indian civil rights suffered the most from 1887 to 1933, a period of forced assimilation, or ethnocide. In spite of constitutional affirmations, the government denied American Indian property rights, free speech, and free exercise of religion. On a more fundamental level, the rights of Native American tribes to their distinct status were violated systematically. This damage to American Indian communities and the civil rights of individual Native Americans has not been mended.

After World War I, some enlightened individuals decided to overturn oppressive "assimilationist" policies toward American Indians with new legislation, such as the American Indian Citizenship Act of 1924. Many Native Americans had become U.S. citizens through "competency commissions" and treaties, but many others had been wary of citizenship through "competency" because it often meant that their federal land allotments would no longer be protected. In fact, thousands of newly created Native American citizens saw their lands removed from federal protection and sold from under them. In 1924 Congress unilaterally granted citizenship to all American Indians.

Many Native American leaders asserted that the American Indian Citizenship Act was a mischief maker in American Indian policy. They did not like the way it was imposed—without consultation and without consent from American Indian communities. Tuscarora chief Clinton Rickard summarized the views of many American Indians, when he stated in 1973 in his autobiography,

> The Citizenship Act did pass in 1924 despite our strong opposition. By its provisions all Indians were automatically made United States citizens whether they wanted to do so or not. This was a violation of our sovereignty. Our citizenship was in our own nations. We had a great attachment to our style of government. We wished to remain treaty Indians and preserve our ancient rights. There was no great rush among my people to go out and vote in the white man's elections. Anyone who did so was denied the privilege of becoming a chief or clan mother in our nations. (Graymont 1973, 55)

Although the 1924 act granted Indians citizenship, it did not end federal protection of Indian lands and government entities. Hence, American Indians acquired a new status as American citizens while maintaining their privileges and rights as members of distinct Native American political units. Indian policymakers in 1924 had assumed that tribal governments would wither away when American Indians became U.S. citizens, but most did not disappear, so today American Indians enjoy a special dual citizenship.

Indian Affairs in the 1920s

As already noted, poverty, poor education, and ill health characterized the existence of most Native Americans in the 1920s. When American Indian lands were allotted, the federal government assured communities that they would be supported during the transition from communal ways to the individualistic mores of Euro-American society, but these promises were not kept. In some cases, Indian communities were devoured by their more greedy and competitive neighbors. In other cases American Indians continued to reject this government-sanctioned individualism and cling to traditional values.

In 1928 the federal government commissioned a study of Indian policy. The resulting Meriam Report catalogues the woeful condition of American Indians at that time (Institute for Government Research 1928). Researchers found them to be without rudimentary health care services, to have infant mortality rates twice the national average, and to be seven times more likely to die of tuberculosis than the general population. Sanitary conditions were awful, and many Indians were disease-ridden. The report characterized Indian boarding schools as "grossly inadequate." From 1800 to 1926, the Bureau of Indian Affairs had separated Indian children from their parents in an attempt to Christianize and "civilize" them. (Male survivors of this period joked that upon arriving at these boarding schools a missionary or teacher would point to a picture of Jesus Christ with long flowing hair and state that they were to become like this man; they would then order that the boys' long hair be cut.) The Meriam Report documented the harsh discipline heaped on Indian children and such practices as forbidding them to speak their native languages, practice their religion, or wear traditional clothing. Those who violated these rules were subject to physical abuse. Most boarding schools relied on the children for labor to keep the schools going. The schools were overcrowded and staffed with unqualified personnel that provided poor medical care and an unhealthy diet. Not surprisingly, Indian literacy rates remained low.

Economic and legal structures to protect the rights of Native Americans were nonexistent. According to the Meriam Report, only 2 percent of all American Indians earned in excess of $500 per annum, and 96 percent of all Native Americans made less that $200 per year. Almost half of all Native Americans had lost their land through unscrupulous people manipulating the law to take advantage of allotted Native American lands. Legal authorities were unsure who held jurisdiction to hear cases involving Indians and non-Indians as defendants and victims or whether they should be held on reservations or off reservations. When such cases were actually adjudicated, justice was not often the result.

The Meriam Report recommended an infusion of funds to correct the ills of the system pertaining to Native Americans, calling for a new office in the Bureau of Indian Affairs to institute new programs and monitor existing ones. It faulted the government, especially the Bureau of Indian Affairs, for exhibiting an extremely hostile attitude toward Indian families and cultures. The allotment system, the cornerstone of Indian policy after 1887, was found to be the major cause of American Indian poverty. Basically, the Meriam Report documented a national scandal; the deplorable conditions on reservations were a byproduct of governmental policies and neglect. By the 1930s American Indian policy was taken out of the hands of missionaries and transferred to social scientists. Meanwhile, Indian leaders knew that the persistence of American Indian ways depended on their maintaining their land base and traditional identities, so they looked to the Bill of Rights for the legal machinery to facilitate this survival process.

The Indian New Deal

The reforms that emerged in the 1930s were based on the idea that American Indian culture and nations had a place in twentieth-century America. President Franklin D. Roosevelt's commissioner of Indian affairs, John Collier, instituted a policy to restore the vitality of

Native American governments through the Indian Reorganization Act (IRA) of 1934. The IRA encouraged tribes to promulgate their own constitutions and eliminated allotment policies. In addition, empowering American Indian governments was recognized as the basic way to approach federal Indian policies. For the first time in fifty years, the right of Native Americans to maintain distinct tribal communities was reasserted. The idea that tribes would eventually disappear was no longer the underlying assumption behind U.S. Indian policy.

Paradoxically, federal officials during the 1930s often pursued goals of American Indian autonomy with an enthusiasm that limited the Indians' right of choice. In the zeal for social change, Collier pushed for the adoption of Native American constitutions, but in his mind they should convert old tribal structures to reflect contemporary constitutional structures. As a result, IRA constitutions were forced upon many tribes although they opposed such measures. During this period, most Native Americans continued to be suspicious of governmental programs to aid them. Despite Indian apprehension, the reforms of the 1930s continued. Tribal governments were revitalized, and their authority over reservation life was reinvigorated. Gradually, American Indians started to recover from the devastation of the allotment policy, and health and education programs improved. These reforms, however, proved short-lived.

World War II and the Rise of Termination Policies

As the Great Depression ended and World War II began, the United States turned away from Native American issues. The budget for the Bureau of Indians Affairs decreased, and conservative politicians attacked Collier's policies of empowering Native American societies. Racism played an important role in this backlash, as did non-Indian businessmen who had lost their ability to plunder American Indian resources and lands. The cost of reforming the administration of Indian affairs was also a source of friction. Then, out of the anticommunist hysteria of the day, a strange ideological attack against American Indians emerged, painting American Indian ways as un-American and communist. These ideological critiques paved the way for another attack on American Indian societies in the late 1940s and early 1950s.

The ethnocidal criticisms of American Indian ways sounded familiar, with people in government arguing once again that Native Americans should be brought into the mainstream of white society. Right-wing policymakers contended that American Indians should be entitled to the same privileges and rights and subject to the same laws as everyone else. As before, these policies purported to be in the best interest of Native Americans despite nearly universal opposition among American Indian people. The new federal policy of termination in the late 1940s came to be called "liquidation," which for many Native Americans conjured up images of the Nazi's "Final Solution" during World War II.

In response to Indian fears, U.S. officials changed the name of the new policy to "termination." Because the policy stressed the abrogation of treaty rights, it involved the dismantling of Indian governments, the distribution of tribal estates to tribal members, and the termination of federal services aimed at individual Indians. Advocates of this policy stated that they were freeing native peoples from federal control. Unfortunately, the wisdom of destroying tribal governments to emancipate American Indians from federal control went unexamined. The group, or treaty, rights of American Indians were to be sacrificed for integration into the dominant society.

Termination represented a philosophical and legal assault on Native Americans. Philosophically, the termination movement forced the assimilation of individual American Indians into mainstream American life, thus espousing an end to the federal government's treaty obligations. To achieve termination's goals, legislation was implemented in four distinct areas: ending federal trust responsibilities and treaty relations with American Indian nations; repealing legislation that set Native Americans apart from other citizens; removing supervision over certain individual American Indians and restrictions relating to federal guardianship; and shifting services historically provided by the Bureau of Indian Affairs to local, state, or other federal agencies.

In 1950 Dillon S. Myer became the new commissioner of Indian affairs and a principal architect of termination policies. From 1942 to 1944 Myer, a career bureaucrat, had headed the War Relocation Authority, which had supervised the removal of ten of thousands of Japanese Americans and Japanese aliens and their detention in concentration camps. Oscar Chapman, secretary of the interior during the Truman administration, observed that Myer had done "an outstanding job in the maintenance and relocation of the Japanese evacuated from the Pacific Coast region" (Fixico 1986, 64). Furthermore, it was felt that Myer's War Relocation Authority experience would make him a good commissioner of Indian affairs. Thus, a man who had created concentration camps for Japanese Americans during World War II was judged worthy and experienced in the affairs of nonwhite people, particularly American Indians. Myer seemed to think that the federal government had herded Native Americans onto reservations—which he viewed as concentration camps—a hundred years prior but had then failed to relocate and integrate them into American society.

In the late 1940s and early 1950s American Indian policy appeared an arcane backwater to most politicians in Washington. Thus, a few conservatives operating in the House and Senate Interior and Insular Affairs committees as well as in the Senate Public Lands Committee shaped laws and policies for Native Americans. Liberals in Congress opposed to the conservatives' agenda were persuaded by their conservative comrades of inefficiency in the Bureau of Indian Affairs and a desperate need to impart civil liberties to another persecuted minority group. These motivations were coupled, in the post-World War II years, with a bipartisan consensus to promote dams, parks, and various development projects that often conflicted with American Indian landholdings and rights. The confluence of these bipartisan interests in the Congress provided the broad-based impetus for many termination policies.

In August 1953, House Concurrent Resolution 108, the cornerstone of termination policies, was passed. It asserted,

> [I]t is the policy of Congress, as rapidly as possible, to make the Indians within the territorial limits of the United States subject to the same laws and entitled to the same privileges and responsibilities as are applicable to other citizens of the United States, to end their status as wards of the United States, to grant them all the rights and prerogatives pertaining to American citizenship.

In addition, the resolution provided that certain Native Americans "be freed from federal supervision and control and from all disabilities and limitations specifically applicable to Indians." In 1957 Sen. Arthur Watkins, a Republican from Utah, praised what he interpreted as the virtues of this policy:

> With the aim of "equality before the law" in mind, our course should rightly be no other. Firm and constant consideration for those of Indian ancestry should lead us all to work diligently and carefully for the full realization of their national citizenship with all other Americans. Following in the footsteps of the Emancipation Proclamation of ninety-four years ago, I see the following words emblazoned in letters of fire above the heads of the Indians—THESE PEOPLE SHALL BE FREE! (Hurtado and Iverson 1994, 492)

This new assimilationist policy took on other trappings as well. The BIA enticed Indian families to move to cities, where they were placed in substandard housing, given menial jobs, and forsaken. This policy created poor American Indian communities in such urban areas as Chicago, Los Angeles, and New York. Senator Watkins characterized the relocation program as "the Indian freedom program." Even though the overwhelming majority of Native Americans opposed termination, policymakers stated that it "would still have to be accepted as a controlling policy" (ibid.). The results of the relocation program are incalculable. Gerald One Feather (Oglala Sioux) observed, "The relocation program had an impact on our . . . government at Pine Ridge. Many people who could have provided [our] leadership were lost because they had motivation to go off the reservation to find employment or obtain an education. Relocation drained off a lot of our potential leadership" (Grinde 1998, 229).

Federal responsibilities and tribal power were further eroded by the passage of Public Law 83-280, a statute that shifted federal, civil, and criminal jurisdiction in Indian country to states. Some states were offered the option of taking jurisdiction over federal Indian reservations when they felt the need. Slowly, the federal government shifted education and health programs to the states through more legislation. In the Truman and Eisenhower administrations, 109 American Indian groups lost their status as federally recognized tribes. In human terms, 13,263 individuals owning 1,365,801 acres of land were unilaterally denied their treaty rights as Native Americans.

During the era of termination, the doctrine of plenary powers was used to condemn thousands of acres of American Indian lands protected by treaty. With judicial acquiescence, Congress permitted the Army Corps of Engineers and the Bureau of Reclamation in the Department of the Interior to seize significant portions of Chemehuevi, Fort Mohave, the Colorado River, and the Yuma and Gila Bend reservations in Arizona to manage the power and watershed of the Colorado River basin. The Pick-Sloan Plan for the Missouri River basin condemned Arapaho, Chippewa, Hidatsa, and Mandan land in Wyoming; Assiniboine, Blackfoot, Cree, and Crow land in Montana, and 200,000 acres of Sioux land in North and South Dakota. All of this land was flooded when the Big Bend, Fort Randal, and Oahe dams were completed.

In western New York, the U.S. government built the Kinzua dam, which violated the Pickering Treaty of 1794, flooded more than 9,000 acres of excellent farm land, ruined the Cold Spring longhouse, the spiritual center of the Allegany Seneca reservation, and caused the removal of 130 families from the rural area adjacent to the dam and their relocation to suburban-style housing several miles away at Steamboat and Jimersontown. In ensuing legal battles, government attorneys argued that based on *Lone Wolf v. Hitchcock* and other cases, "treaty rights do not forbid the taking, by the United States, of lands within the Allegany Reservation" (ibid., 230). In all of these land confiscations, the federal government exercised its plenary powers over Native Americans by uprooting them from their homelands, disturbing sacred sites, and altering significantly the ecology of their regions.

Essentially, the federal government's flood control projects of the 1940s and 1950s showed little concern for the treaty and civil rights of American Indians. Without a doubt, the federal government was seeking to abrogate its treaty responsibilities during the 1950s with a vengeance, but it did so for reasons other than civil rights.

The 1960s

Paradoxically, the campaign to destroy American Indian tribal governments led to a movement in the courts to shore up the rights of American Indians as individual citizens. Although the Indian Citizenship Act of 1924 had granted citizenship to Native Americans, states with significant Indian populations had developed laws and procedures severely limiting or prohibiting American Indians from exercising their right to vote, provide testimony in court, and serve on juries. During the 1950s the courts struck down these discriminatory practices through reinterpretations of the rights of American Indians under the Fourteenth and Fifteenth Amendments. While in the East the National Association for the Advancement of Colored People (NAACP) and other civil rights groups argued test cases that ended the separate but equal doctrine of *Plessy v. Ferguson* (1896), civil rights lawyers in the West whittled away at the discriminatory laws that deprived American Indians of their rights on the basis of race.

American Indians, like African Americans, often had civil rights in theory but not in practice. Racist practices toward Native Americans in the communities where they lived were as flagrant and widespread as those experienced by African Americans. Discrimination in public accommodations and racial epithets were an integral part of American Indian life into the 1950s. Consequently, Native Americans became one of the prime beneficiaries of the 1960s civil rights movement.

Termination had been discredited by 1960. All the American Indian nations that had their treaty obligations terminated descended into poverty and ruin; many of the members of the newly terminated tribes joined the state welfare rolls, and the wealth of terminated tribes was raided by non-Indians intent on quick profits. Eventually, even sincere supporters of termination policies became discouraged by their efforts at reform. The termination era was a tragedy for all Native Americans. The Seminole historian Donald Fixico characterized termination as threatening "the very core of American Indian existence—its culture" (Fixico 1986, 183).

When the civil rights movement gained momentum in the 1960s, American Indian activists joined the struggle. Although the Native American agenda was similar to other minorities in terms of citizenship rights, American Indians also wanted to protect their other rights, including treaty rights and their special and separate cultural and political communities. In essence, Indians wanted to retain their right to be different.

Although many Americans failed to appreciate the diverse aspirations of Native Americans in the 1960s, American Indians did manage to regain some civil rights as well as group rights. The civil rights legislation and judicial decisions of the 1960s and early 1970s, such as the Voting Rights Act, the Fair Housing Act, and the Equal Employment Opportunity Act, routinely included American Indians as a people that could not be discriminated against. For instance, the Voting Rights Act not only bans discrimination against American Indians, it also gives them special protection as a people since their primary language may not be English.

Because of American Indians treaty rights, some of the new civil rights legislation contained stipulations regarding them. For example, the Equal Employment Opportunity Act allows employers on or near reservations to grant Indians employment preferences. This right was attacked on the grounds of reverse discrimination, but in *Morton v. Mancari* (1974) the Supreme Court held that a law granting Indians employment preference in the Indian Health Service and the Bureau of Indian Affairs was constitutional. The decision stated that the preference was based on the treaty status that Indian *nations* had with the United States, not on race. Social legislation passed in the 1960s also acknowledged Indian tribes as unique and distinct political communities. Many Great Society programs—for example, Headstart, Community Action, the Comprehensive Older Americans Act, and the Elementary and Secondary Education Act—allowed Indian tribal governments to participate.

The civil rights movement had an enormous impact on American Indian people and their governments. With newly defined legal rights and economic resources flowing to their communities, American Indians experienced a renewed dignity and determination. Federal termination policies had made Indian leaders more cautious. If a tribe enjoyed even moderate economic gains then it could be subjected to the termination process, because wealthier tribes were judged fit to carry on without treaty rights. Termination had kept tribes impoverished and pliant, but the civil rights movement swept away these fears, as American Indians learned that they could push for their rights without fear of losing their treaty status.

American Indian Religious Freedom

One major area of civil rights for American Indians continued to be neglected until the late 1970s—religious freedom. In 1978 Congress passed the American Indian Religious Freedom Act, which declared that the federal government would seek to preserve and protect the exercise of traditional spiritualities and gave American Indians access to sacred sites on federal lands for religious rituals. In the past, the courts had not been sympathetic to American Indian site-based religious activities. Unfortunately, the law proved to be ineffective and did not give the tribes judicial redress for arbitrary federal actions.

A decade after its passage, the Supreme Court struck down the heart of the law in *Lyng v. Northwest Indian Cemetery Protective Association* (1988). Basically, the Court found that the National Forest Service had the right to construct a road through sacred Indian sites even though such a road would destroy the ability of Native Americans to conduct rituals that they had practiced in the area from time immemorial. Justice Sandra Day O'Connor, in the majority opinion, admitted that "the government does not dispute, and we have no reason to doubt, that the logging and road-building projects at issue in this case could have devastating effects on traditional Indian religious practices." The Court found that government activities could not be disrupted by the religious claims of its citizens since there was a wide array of religious beliefs in American society. O'Connor stated that a "sudden revelation" of sacredness to an individual at the Lincoln Memorial ought not constrain visitation to this federal landmark. Essentially, O'Connor and the majority of the Court dismissed the notion of American Indian religious freedom, thus denying American Indians their rights to practice traditional tribal spirituality.

With the federal government excluding itself from enforcing American Indian religious freedom, it was not long before the states were emboldened to pursue a similar course in *Employment Division, Department of Human Resources of Oregon v. Smith* (1990). Alfred Smith and Galen Black, two Native Americans living in Portland, Oregon, were fired as drug counselors at a private drug rehabilitation program when it was discovered that they had used peyote during a ritual at a Native American Church ceremony. They applied for unemployment compensation but were denied benefits because Oregon claimed that the two men had been dismissed for misconduct. When the Supreme Court heard the case, it ruled against Smith and Black and upheld all of Oregon state court decisions. This Court decision was not only a major blow to Native American religious freedom, it also invited state agencies to launch an assault on the Native American Church.

Five justices, led by Antonin Scalia, accepted the idea that the sacramental use of peyote could be prohibited under a state criminal statute even though Oregon did not enforce the law. According to Scalia's majority opinion, the Oregon statute did not violate the free exercise provisions of the First Amendment or the American Indian Religious Freedom Act. The Court found that no person could assert his or her religious rights above a state's right to regulate the use of drugs. Under U.S. law, the use of peyote is a legally sanctioned sacrament in the Native American Church, but the Court seemed unconcerned about this. Incredibly, the Court appeared to contradict itself, and discriminate against Native Americans, in its observation that the physical act of drinking wine during Christian communion rituals—even by minors, which is a direct violation of state alcohol statutes—was acceptable.

Essentially, the majority of the Court dismissed all previous tests that had delineated the limits of the Free Exercise Clause. The justices in the minority wrote a scathing dissent that accused the majority of not knowing what it was doing. The minority described the majority opinion as follows:

> The Court today—interprets the [Free Exercise] Clause to permit the government to prohibit, without justification, conduct mandated by an individual's religious beliefs, so long as the prohibition is generally applicable. But a law that prohibits certain conduct—conduct that happens to be an act of worship for someone—manifestly does prohibit that person's free exercise of his religion. A person who is barred from engaging in religiously motivated conduct is barred from freely exercising his religion. Moreover that person is barred from freely exercising his religion regardless of whether the law prohibits the conduct when engaged in for religious reasons, only by members of that religion, or by all persons.

Basically, the high court voided long-held interpretations of the constitutional protections extended to the free exercise of religion, and it struck down these protections not only for Native Americans but for everyone else. For the first time since the inception of the U.S. federal government, the Supreme Court allowed state laws and "community standards" to influence the free exercise of religion. It is too early to determine whether this decision will become the prevailing statement on American Indian religious freedom. In 1994 Congress passed a second American Indian Religious Freedom Act, but its scope was quite narrow and had little impact. If the *Smith* decision is allowed to stand, there can be no Native American religious freedom in the United States. The ruling essentially implies that Native Americans and other people have the right to be Presbyterians, Catholic, or members of some other mainstream religion and little else.

Reburial Rights and Native American Human Remains

During the 1980s debate swirled around the reburial of American Indian human remains deposited in federal agencies. After a thorough investigation in academic circles, it was widely observed by Native American leaders that the federal government had an established policy that encouraged the collection of American Indian human remains. Native American spiritual leaders, however, argued that these remains should be returned to Mother Earth. Many other American Indians also disliked the retention of their ancestors' remains in such places as the Smithsonian Institution, which claimed that the remains were part of its research collection and database. Since no other ethnic groups had been submitted to such practices with regard to burials, many Native American leaders termed this practice "conquest archaeology."

After a concerted effort by Native American organizations to have Indian human remains returned to their tribes, Congress enacted the Native American Graves Protection and Repatriation Act (NAGPRA) of 1990. It required that federal agencies and private museums holding federal grants inventory their collections of Native American human remains and funerary objects associated with them and notify tribal governments that they would be returned to them upon request. The act affirmed that cultural artifacts and human remains excavated or found on federal and tribal lands belong to the respective tribes, and trafficking in Native American cultural objects and human remains acquired in violation of NAGPRA was banned. Federal agencies and private museums receiving federal monies had to prepare an itemized catalogue of Native American sacred and funerary artifacts in their possession and return the objects to Native American communities in cases where the right of possession could be determined. Many legal scholars have characterized this law as the most significant piece of human rights legislation for Native American people since the enactment of the American Indian Freedom of Religion Act of 1978.

Many cases relating to American Indian freedom of religion have also arisen in state prisons, where regulations have prohibited Native American religious practices, such as sweat lodges, the wearing of long hair, and pipe ceremonies. Some Native Americans have also had to use the courts to uphold their right to hold public office, to receive public assistance, and to enroll their children in public schools. These legal problems arose because many states claimed that Native Americans should not be given the rights that other citizens enjoy because they are exempt from certain state taxes.

Some state officials and members of the public assert that granting American Indians certain exemptions from state law is unfair on the basis of equal protection. This argument has been the grounds for contemporary state refusals to uphold Native American fishing and hunting rights delineated by treaty. In such cases, state officials often disregard long-standing federal law upholding the rights guaranteed in Native American treaties over state laws. The contractual rights granted in American Indian treaties, however, do not deny equal protection to non-Indians, who are not entitled to treaty benefits.

Although it is, theoretically, well established that American Indians have enforceable civil rights, such as the right to seek and hold public office, to vote, and to be free from discriminatory practices, there is still much conflict in the application of these laws at the federal, state, and local levels. As demonstrated here, legal enforcement of these rights has been problematic throughout U.S. history.

Contemporary Issues

Today, there are more than a million Native Americans residing on almost three hundred federal and state Indian reservations. Usually, tribal members share a similar historical and racial background. They identify strongly with the experiences of their kin and the common bonds that unite them. Most Native Americans are keenly aware of ethnocidal federal policies that have sought to rob them of their culture, and they are dedicated to the continued survival of their people and culture. The distinctive group values held by Native Americans are often characterized as tribalism. When tribalism clashes with the rights of individuals, there is a resulting stress between Native American people that believe in the primacy of tribal rights and other people who claim that Native American governments are violating their rights as individuals.

Although almost half of the three hundred tribal governments have constitutions with some bill of rights provisions, the Supreme Court ruled in *Talton v. Mayes* (1896) that the federal Bill of Rights does not apply to American Indian courts or governments. Furthermore, the Court held that the Bill of Rights only restricts the powers of state and federal governments. In theory, American Indian tribal governments are not subordinate to either state or federal governments. Since these tribal governments obtain their sovereignty from their indigenous self-governing status, the U.S. Constitution does not pertain to them.

This treaty right seemed of little importance until the advent of the civil rights movement in the 1960s. In 1961 two special committees—one federal and one private—began studying civil rights on American Indian reservations. Subsequently, the Special Task Force on Indian Affairs recommended to the Department of the Interior that tribal governments secure civil liberties on reservations by enacting and enforcing new legislation. Paradoxically, the Commission on the Rights, Liberties, and Responsibilities of the American Indian (financed by the Fund for the Republic, a Washington think tank) argued that Native American governments should be accountable under the Bill of Rights since the current system of tribal courts and governments put in jeopardy "the very assumptions on which our free society was established" (Wunder 1994, 133). These advocates of termination reasoned that if they could not abolish Native American governments, they would impose on them standard constitutional practices. These conflicting viewpoints led to hearings before Sen. Sam Ervin's (D-N.C.) Subcommittee on Constitutional Rights relating to Native Americans and the Bill of Rights.

Ervin heard testimony from American Indians and other interested parties for seven years. People related stories about violations of their personal liberties and religious freedoms by American Indian governments. Improper court practices by tribal courts were documented along with injustices on reservations caused by poor legal training of tribal lawyers and justices, a lack of resources, and various states' failure to enforce laws on reservations covered by Public Law 83-280. In the end, the subcommittee recorded more than a thousand pages of testimony.

The hearings confirmed that American Indians were also being deprived of their civil rights through improper state and federal actions. In South Dakota, Native Americans were often treated as virtual slaves, and the police in Gallup, New Mexico, and Pocatello, Idaho, denied medical services to Navajos and Shoshones, sometimes letting them die in jails. Reservation courts of Indian offenses cooperated with local police to abduct Native Americans on their reservations and take them off the reservations to expedite arrests. Often, state courts denied rights to counsel, and not guilty pleas were prohibited. Such states as California, with powers under Public Law 83-280, refused to budget enough funds for policing reservations.

Although the civil rights issues of the 1960s brought significant social change for individuals of color, the major difficulty for many Native Americans during this time was interpreting the movement in a manner that supported their unique status. After much deliberation, Congress passed the Indian Civil Rights Act in 1968, which essentially ordered tribal governments to give people under its authority the basic civil rights that they enjoy under the U.S. Constitution. The legislation was, however, flexible with regard to tribal prerogatives. For instance, the free exercise of religion was incorporated, but restrictions on the establishment of a state religion were not, in order to protect tribal theocratic governments. The act also differed from the Bill of Rights on the right to counsel in criminal cases. The Supreme Court, by 1968, had mandated state and federal governments to pay for counsel in proceedings involving poor criminal defendants. Tribal governments, however, did not have the funds for such a right, so the law stated that in tribal courts defendants had a right to counsel but only if they paid for it.

Unlike the U.S. Constitution, the Indian Civil Rights Act set limits on punishments issued by tribal courts. The maximum punishments allowed in criminal cases before tribal courts were $500 and six months in jail. Under the Major Crimes Act of 1885, the federal government held the power to prosecute almost all felonies on Indian reservations. This provision caused many problems because federal officials were slow to act on crimes on reservations, which could result in a tribal judge meting out minimal sentences for serious crimes. Furthermore, the act failed to address tribal concerns about the possibility of an abundance of federal lawsuits lodged against tribal officials. Since the act did not specify which suits might be appropriate, for more than a decade the federal courts heard a wide array of cases. Essentially, federal courts overruled tribal claims of sovereign immunity as well as challenges to the jurisdiction of tribal courts. Until 1978 federal courts had unchallenged jurisdiction over suits against tribes.

In 1978 the Supreme Court reexamined the right of federal courts to hear cases under the Indian Civil Rights Act in *Santa Clara Pueblo v.*

Martinez (1978). In a 7-1 decision, the high court found that since the act did not surrender the tribal governments' sovereign immunity, Native American nations remained immune to suits under the law. Tribal officials were also protected because the Court held that the act did not grant tribal members the right to file suit. In effect, the Court struck down ten years of suits against tribal governments.

Martinez basically denied federal judicial redress to persons who could sue Native American nations under the Indian Civil Rights Act. The Court held out one exception to its ruling; it continued to uphold the right of habeas corpus to persons held in tribal custody. As a result of *Martinez*, students of Native American law and civil libertarians expressed concerns about the absence of federal judicial review of tribal court decisions. Who would defend American Indians from caprice by their own tribal governments? In response, the high court stated that tribal governments or tribal courts would protect Native American civil rights under the Indian Civil Rights Act, a deliberate but tentative step forward for American Indian self-determination.

In the wake of the *Martinez* decision, tribal courts have performed a critical judicial role in the lives of American Indian people. Initially, many people were skeptical that the tribal courts would uphold Native American civil rights, but a survey of the situation in the 1990s, after *Martinez*, indicates that such misapprehensions were unfounded. Judges in tribal courts created a national association in 1970 to further judicial education programs for its members. Subsequently, this organization and similar ones have offered seminars and training programs around the country for interested tribal judges. Basically, tribal courts have steadily enhanced their abilities to deal with civil rights issues on their reservations. Some of the larger Native American nations created courts of appeal, while smaller tribes established intertribal courts. Increasingly, tribal courts are staffed by judges with law degrees, and non-Indian as well as Indian lawyers practice before them.

Although the tribal courts still have their critics, the Supreme Court continues to uphold their jurisdiction. In *National Farmers Union Insurance Company v. Crow Tribe* (1985) and *Iowa Mutual Insurance Company v. LaPlante* (1987), the high court affirmed the right of tribal courts to adjudicate personal injury cases involving non-Indians. Both decisions found that federal courts could not assume jurisdiction in personal injury cases until a tribal court had heard the cases and determined its own jurisdiction. By the 1990s tribal courts had become an integral part of tribal government. In 1991 the Supreme Court asserted in *Oklahoma Tax Commission v. Citizen Band Potawatomi Indian Tribe* (1991) that "[Native American tribes] exercise inherent sovereign authority over their members and their territory. Suits against Indian tribes are thus barred by sovereign immunity absent a clear waiver by the tribe or congressional abrogation." Since *Martinez*, tribal courts are the only courts with clear jurisdiction to hear cases against tribal governments and officials involving civil rights violations.

As the civil rights struggles of the 1960s subsided, treaty rights and self-determination became the focus of Native American efforts. With their individual rights as American citizens now formally codified into law (although not always affirmed in fact), American Indians started to assert their rights as tribal citizens. Hundreds of treaties upheld these rights as well.

Native American fishing rights guaranteed through treaties were one of the primary battlegrounds for Native American civil rights. The Native American right to fish on the Nisqually River in Washington State was one of the early focal points of the struggle. The Treaty of Point Elliott, signed by Native American nations and ratified by the U.S. Senate in the 1850s, stated that American Indians could reserve the right to take "fish at usual and accustomed grounds . . . in common with all citizens of the territory." Native Americans in Washington utilized this right for more than a hundred years before the state began to infringe on them. Although a 1963 federal court decision upheld the fishing rights of American Indians, Washington state courts continued to forbid Native Americans from net fishing. In a series of protests, Native American fishermen were cited, arrested, and incarcerated for violating state fishing laws. In response, Indians lodged complaints of police brutality but to no avail. In spite of their victories in federal court, Native American fishermen continued to be mistreated, threatened, and in one instance shot by non-Indian vigilantes. In this case, federal authorities in the Nixon administration reacted very slowly.

Undaunted by their odds, the Indians of Washington persisted in their struggle until 1974, when Judge George H. Boldt, in *United States v. Washington* (Phase I) (1974), found that American Indians were entitled to almost one-half of the salmon catch in the state. Although many non-Indians were infuriated, the decision was sustained through judicial review and reaffirmed by the Supreme Court in *United States v. Washington* (1979). American Indians thus succeeded in the fight to keep their century-old treaty rights to fish and demonstrated that treaty rights do not alter with the passage of time. Moreover, the allocation of fishing resources bargained in such treaties was declared binding on the descendants of the treaty parties in spite of changes in non-Indian and American Indian communities.

Tribal attorneys in the eastern United States discovered that many of the treaties used to take lands from Native American nations had not been ratified by Congress although the Indian Trade and Intercourse Acts enacted at the end of the eighteenth and early nineteenth centuries required it. Hence, the intercourse acts voided many old land transactions. The Indian land cases brought forward challenged the U.S. commitment to the rule of law. Despite intense pressure from state governments and residents, however, federal courts ruled favorably for American Indians in these cases. The rules of law in force some two hundred years ago remained valid. For example, in *County of Oneida v. Oneida Indian Nation* (1985), the Supreme Court upheld Oneida Indian land claims and found that abuses done two centuries prior could be redressed in the courts and the rights of American Indians upheld. Many cases were settled out of court, with the settlements subsequently approved by Congress.

Native American rights to self-government and self-determination were also regained through congressional acts. Termination policies were formally rejected when the Menominee Tribe of Wisconsin recovered its tribal status in 1973 by an act of Congress. In 1975 the Indian Self-Determination and Education Assistance Act granted tribes the right to administer federal assistance programs, ending the control of such programs by non-Indian administrators, who had dominated reservation life for more than a century. In 1978 the Indian Child Welfare Act put the well-being of American Indian children firmly in the hands of the tribes and curtailed the powers of the states in this area. Previously, American Indian children had been taken arbitrarily from their tribal setting and placed in non-Indian environments. The child welfare act curbed the power of non-Indians in the affairs of American Indian families. In 1978 the American Indian Religious Freedom Act sought (though not necessarily successfully) to honor and nurture traditional Native American religious rituals and practices.

Despite such advancements, American Indian group rights remain largely misunderstood by the non-Indian population, which is a continuing dilemma for Indians and their governments and a challenge for the court system. Although it is difficult to analyze the impact of militant groups like the American Indian Movement (AIM) on the political landscape, the frustrations and aspirations of AIM echo much of the anger and despair of many Native Americans in regard to government policies. American Indian activists, tired of having their rights denied, staged the occupation of Alcatraz Island in 1969, the seizure of the Bureau of Indian Affairs headquarters in 1972, and the confrontations at Wounded Knee, South Dakota, in 1973 to dramatically highlight the injustices and lack of sovereignty in contemporary American Indian life. Young American Indians took militant actions in the late 1960s and early 1970s because they felt that the government and the legal system were incapable of reforming themselves.

Although AIM was adroit at focused media attention on the deplorable conditions that Native Americans lived under, its agenda often differed from the objectives of tribal governments. Its activities also heightened tensions between Indians and non-Indians. AIM's actions at Wounded Knee on the Pine Ridge reservation incited excessive force by federal authorities that created a climate of systematic abuse of the civil rights of Native American persons affiliated and not affiliated with AIM. In the final analysis, the impact of AIM was mostly positive because it solidified the determination of Native Americans to advance their rights and confirmed the lengths to which some people were prepared to go in the absence of justice. Since the 1970s the influence and power of AIM has decreased because of harassment by the Federal Bureau of Investigation and its COINTELPRO programs, which sought to disrupt and neutralize activist minority organizations like the American Indian Movement, and other systematic campaigns to defame its membership and purposes.

Summary

The advancement of the rights of American Indians in the 1960s and 1970s fueled an ominous counterattack by groups wanting to eliminate Native American government rights and treaty rights. Utilizing the rhetoric of reverse discrimination, this movement claims that contemporary Euro-Americans should not be held accountable for historical policies that discriminated against and violated the rights of people of color. This ideology also contends that the white majority should not be made to suffer as a result of remedies for past inequities. Although this argument may have some merit in some historical situations, it completely overlooks the context of American Indian treaty rights.

The U.S. government did not grant treaty rights to Native American tribes to be altruistic. These treaties were legal agreements for the conveyance of huge amounts of American Indian real estate. The Indian concessions thus allowed whites to "settle" these lands "legitimately." Despite historical and continued mistreatment, American Indian nations have not demanded that all of these lands be returned to their aboriginal owners. Furthermore, Native Americans have not demanded that non-Indian rights under these treaties be rescinded. Thus, the demands by non-Indians that Native Americans give up their rights are inconsistent with the historical record and difficult to understand. Although anti-Indian backlash was worrisome throughout the 1980s, it failed to attain any significant legislative victories at the federal level. Tensions between Native Americans and state governments over treaty rights and religious freedom remain.

Any analysis of the civil rights of Native Americans within a tribal context is fraught with tension and contention between the individualistic values of the dominant society and the more collectivistic morays of tribalism. Today's Native American communities are spirited democratic societies. Although tribal courts are relatively new additions, the strides that they have made in furthering justice are remarkable. A growing awareness exists that tribal courts are a significant and integral part of tribal governance. There is also a feeling that they will safeguard the civil rights of tribal members.

Civil rights means many things to many people, and the Bill of Rights is often regarded as the foundation of individual freedom and liberty in the United States. History shows that individuals and groups hold basic, fundamental rights that they may use to check the caprice of government. Certainly, liberty and freedom involve the balancing of coercive state power against the collective and individual rights guaranteed in the Bill of Rights. The Bill of Rights, however, does not grant protection for Native Americans from the abuses of tribal, local, state, and federal governments, thus denying Native Americans the basic rights that other inhabitants of the United States take for granted. Contemporary legal decisions have deemed American Indian sovereignty incompatible with the Bill of Rights. Only Congress can therefore end the denial of American Indian rights by the non-Indian majority in the courts.

While many American Indian people and nations today are better off than their predecessors, many areas of their lives could be improved. In the late twentieth century American Indians suffered from the highest unemployment rate, lowest per capita income, and worst housing and health conditions of any ethnic group in America. Without a doubt, American Indians suffer injustices that are a product of historically discriminatory policies toward them as individuals and as members of tribal political entities. The sensitivity or insensitivity in different historical periods to the rights of American Indians marks the ebb and flow of the United States' faith in democratic principles. Indeed, Felix Cohen once characterized the rights of American Indians in our society as the "miner's canary," holding that if American Indian legal rights suffered, the fundamental freedoms in U.S. democracy are endangered for everyone.

Every generation of American Indian wonders if the dominant society will continue to acknowledge the special rights granted to them by previous generations. In the final analysis, the solution to this rights dilemma will demand significant progress in comprehending and adapting the legal systems of the larger American society so that Native American demands for the recognition and nurturing of their treaty rights and civil rights can be accommodated.

Bibliography

Barsh, Russel Lawrence, and James Youngblood Henderson. 1980. *The Road: Indian Tribes and Political Liberty.* Berkeley: University of California Press.

Canby, William C. 1981. *American Indian Law.* St. Paul, Minn.: West Publishing.

Cohen, Felix S. 1982. *Felix S. Cohen's Handbook of Federal Indian Law.* Charlottesville, Va.: Mitchie/Bobbs-Merrill.

Cornell, Stephen. 1988. *The Return of the Native: American Indian Political Resurgence.* New York: Oxford University Press.

Fixico, Donald L. 1986. *Termination and Relocation: Federal Indian Policy, 1945–1960.* Albuquerque: University of New Mexico Press.

Getches, David H., and Charles F. Wilkinson. 1986. *Federal Indian Law: Cases and Materials.* St. Paul, Minn.: West Publishing.

Graymont, Barbara. 1973. *The Fighting Tuscarora: The Autobiography of Chief Clinton Rickard.* Syracuse: Syracuse University Press.

Grinde, Donald A., Jr. 1998. "Native American Civil Rights." In *Civil Rights in America, 1500 to the Present,* by Jay Sigler. Detroit: Gale Research.

Hurtado, Albert L., and Peter Iverson. 1994. *Major Problems in American Indian History.* Lexington, Mass.: D. C. Heath.

Institute for Government Research. 1928. *The Problem of Indian Administration.* Baltimore: Johns Hopkins University Press. Also available at http://www.alaskool.org/native_ed/research_reports/IndianAdmin/Indian_Admin_Problms.html.

Jaimes, M. Annette, ed. 1992. *The State of Native America: Genocide, Colonization, and Resistance.* Boston: South End Press.

Lyons, Oren, et al. 1992. *Exiled in the Land of the Free: Democracy, Indian Nations, and the U.S. Constitution.* Santa Fe: Clear Light Publishers.

Pevar, Stephen L. 1992. *The Rights of Indians and Tribes.* Carbondale: Southern Illinois University Press.

Price, Monroe E., and Robert Clinton. 1983. *Law and the American Indian.* Charlottesville, Va.: Mitchie/Bobbs-Merrill.

Shattuck, Petra H., and Jill Norgren. 1991. *Partial Justice: Federal Indian Law in a Liberal Constitutional System.* New York: Berg.

U.S. Commission on Civil Rights. 1980. *American Indian Civil Rights Handbook.* Washington, D.C.: Government Printing Office.

West, W. Richard, Jr., and Kevin Gover. 1988. "The Struggle for Indian Civil Rights." In *Indians in American History,* edited by Frederick E. Hoxie. Arlington Heights, Ill.: Harlan Davidson.

Wunder, John R. 1994. *"Retained by the People": A History of American Indians and the Bill of Rights.* New York: Oxford University Press.

Zionitz, Alvin J. 1979. "After *Martinez*: Indian Civil Rights under Tribal Government." *University of California, Davis, Law Review* 12, no. 1.

Native Americans and Judicial Review

Philip L. Fetzer

In its early days, the Supreme Court claimed for itself a power nowhere to be found in the Constitution—judicial review. Speaking for the Court in *Marbury v. Madison* (1803), Chief Justice John Marshall asserted that the Court had the authority to declare federal laws unconstitutional or beyond the scope of authorized power. Several years after *Marbury*, the Court extended its power to address state laws as well. When issues arise that indicate a possible violation of tribal rights, Native Americans, like other litigants, face two hurdles to their legal challenges. First, courts may hear only those cases that they have the authority to consider. Jurisdictional restrictions thus affect the potential vindication of valid rights. Second, governments are protected from suits through the doctrine of sovereign immunity. Under this rule, a government—whether tribal, state, or federal—may not be sued without its consent. Courts are bound to dismiss cases within their jurisdiction if and when a government claims such immunity.

Judicial Review and State Government

Although treaties, the U.S. Constitution, and numerous federal laws may protect tribal rights, state governments are often charged with enforcing these protections. States, however, frequently act to undermine these rights. Local biases or raw economic or political power sometimes affect the willingness of state courts to fairly administer laws pertaining to Native Americans. Consequently, tribes usually prefer to go into federal courts when a legal ruling is needed to support their claims. If a tribe or a tribal member believes that a state or state official has violated federal law, four provisions of Title 28 of the United States Code may apply—sections 1331, 1343(3), 1353, and 1362.

Section 1331 addresses civil actions covered by the Constitution, treaties, or federal laws. This is an important statute for Native Americans because its provisions grant federal courts authority to protect rights secured through federal laws and treaties. In *County of Oneida v. Oneida Indian Nation* (1985), for example, the Supreme Court held that a federal court could require non-Indians to be excluded from federally secured tribal land.

Under 42 United States Code 1983, Congress adopted civil rights legislation proscribing state officials from denying an individual "any right, privilege or immunity secured by the Constitution of the United States or by an Act of Congress providing equal rights of citizens." Section 1343(3) of Title 28 grants federal courts jurisdiction for enforcing these rights on behalf of tribes or tribal members. State officials or municipal governments that violate these rights may be sued in federal court.

The General Allotment Act of 1887 provides for individual allocations of land that had previously been held in common among Native Americans. Section 1353 of Title 28 of the United States Code protects Native American rights to this land. In 1986 in *United States v. Mottaz*, the Supreme Court found that Indians could bring lawsuits that would require the federal government to issue an allotment. Additionally, the Court held that Native Americans could sue to protect allotments that had already been granted.

Section 1362 of Title 28 provides federal courts with the authority to hear civil cases brought by tribes seeking to enforce provisions of the Constitution, treaties, or federal law. The section stands out in that it permits tribes to bring suits themselves rather than having to depend on the federal government for protection. Under section 1362, for example, Native Americans filed suit against the collection of a state sales tax on tribal land in *Moe v. Confederated Salish and Kootenai Tribes* (1976). Enforcement of private contracts (as opposed to federal rights) is not covered by sections 1362 or 1331.

Finally, it should be noted that states do not have sovereign immunity against federal suits. The federal government may (but is not obliged to) sue a state to protect tribal rights. Tribal consent for such federal suits is not required. If, however, a tribe requests such assistance, the federal government is required to provide it. In order to protect tribal rights, state officials may even be directed by the federal courts to take actions inconsistent with state law.

Judicial Review and the Federal Government

Tribal rights have been extensively recognized through treaties, executive orders, agency rulings, and federal law, but federal officials and Congress have violated nearly every one of these rights. At the same time, Congress has provided for enforcement of tribal rights through passage of legislation waiving the federal government's sovereign immunity in certain instances. Congress has also authorized suits by Native Americans for monetary damages against the federal government. One of the most important laws in this area is the Federal Tort Claims Act, which provides for compensation in cases where federal officials, acting within their authority, cause injury through wrongful or negligent action. For example, *Hatahley v. United States* (1956), a suit against federal agents who improperly removed property, falls within the scope of the act.

Indians can also pursue monetary remuneration through the Court of Claims. In 1946 through the Indian Claims Commission Act, Congress created the Indian Claims Commission (ICC) to expedite what had become an unwieldy process of restitution. The act authorized *groups*, as opposed to individual Indians, to file compensation claims with the ICC against the United States for loss of treaty land or other property taken on the basis of "fraud, duress, unconscionable consideration" or "mistake." The act also permitted tribes to seek damages for lost resources, such as timber and water.

By the end of the initial five-year period, 370 claims had been filed, so the ICC's life was extended into the late 1970s in order to conclude its business. Both sides had the right to appeal an ICC ruling to the Court of Claims and, in turn, to the Supreme Court. Congress finally dissolved the commission in 1978 and relegated all pending claims to the Court of Claims. Once all appeals are exhausted, Congress has the responsibility of allocating monetary awards to successful tribal plaintiffs. By 1992 more than $800 million had been distributed.

The Tucker Act of 1887 expressly waives the federal government's sovereign immunity and thus also authorizes tribes to seek monetary settlements against the United States. At the same time, the act permits tribes to recover for breach of contract or negligent conduct on the part of the government. Claims under the Tucker Act can be filed in either the Court of Claims or federal district court. The statute of limitations is six years, and the monetary limit is $10,000 in federal court. *Duncan v. United States* (1981), a case involving the mismanagement of Indian tribal land, is the type of suit allowed under the act.

Disputes that do not involve monetary damages may be subject to review by the federal courts. For example, if a federal agency proposed a building project on treaty land, a tribe could sue for injunctive or declaratory relief. Federal agencies are generally subject to federal court review under the Administrative Procedure Act. The act does not allow for court involvement if a statute prohibits judicial review or if the law permits agency discretion, as set forth in Title 28, section 1331. The act takes on particular significance because the majority of federal government actions are transacted through its agencies. For example, effective judicial review provides tribes the opportunity to protect themselves against abuses of authority on the part of the Bureau of Indian Affairs.

In *Chevron, U.S.A., Inc. v. Natural Resources Defense Council, Inc.* (1984), the Supreme Court set legal guidelines for judicial review of statutory interpretations by government agencies. The Court held that if Congress has spoken clearly on an issue, that issue is settled. In cases involving ambiguous language, the court must determine if the agency involved has provided a "permissible construction of the statute." The way in which the Environmental Protection Agency verbally interpreted a statutory provision of the Clean Water Act in light of the Supreme Court decision is an example of what is known as the Chevron Doctrine when applied to Indian law.

Judicial Review and Tribal Government

Absent a clear waiver by a tribe or congressional cancellation, a tribe cannot be sued. In *Oklahoma Tax Commission v. Citizen Band Potawatomi Indian Tribe* (1991), the Supreme Court reaffirmed the sovereign immunity of Indian tribes. Periodically, however, Congress has adopted laws to allow specific suits against a tribe. For example, in the 1980s it authorized the Navajo and Hopi to sue each other in an effort to resolve a long-standing property dispute. Environmental lawsuits, such as *Blue Legs v. BIA* (1989) involving hazardous waste, have also been permitted.

In 1978 the Court had held that the Indian Civil Rights Act of 1968 did not waive the sovereign immunity of tribal governments. Habeas corpus—the right to bail and a trial by jury—remained the only means for judicial review under the act, as held in *Santa Clara Pueblo v. Martinez* (1978). Additionally, the courts have ruled that neither Public Law 83-280, which gives some states control over law enforcement on Indian reservations (*Three Affiliated Tribes v. Wold Engineering* [1986]), nor the Indian Self-Determination and Education Assistance Act of 1975, which widens tribal government powers (*Evans v. McKay* [1989]), allows suits against tribal governments.

Land determined to be in trust status is not subject to judicial review according to the Federal Quiet Title Act of 1994. Among the types of cases *not* permitted due to sovereign immunity are those challenging tribal fishing and hunting laws (*People of California ex rel. Department of Fish and Game v. Quechan Tribe of Indians* 1979), tribal zoning regulations (*Trans-Canada Enterprises, Ltd. v. Muckleshoot Indian Tribe* [1980]), and tribal bingo ordinances (*Pan American Co. v. Syucan Band of Mission Indians* [1989]).

In *Bottomly v. Passamoquoddy Tribe* (1979), the Supreme Court reaffirmed tribes' sovereign immunity against suits brought by individuals. Tribal officers are also immune in cases where federal law allows suits against state officials, because according to *Wells v. Philbrick* (1980), officers acting within their authority cannot be sued. If, however, an officer acts outside of the scope of his or her authority, federal courts have generally held that he or she can be sued.

Tribal corporations also retain sovereign immunity unless a tribe waives this right. There are, however, significant disadvantages to corporations that cannot be sued. For example, they find it more difficult to borrow money and to sell their products because potential buyers and creditors may not want to do business with an organization immune to legal action.

Summary

Under the doctrine of sovereign immunity, a tribal, state, or federal government cannot be sued without its consent. In cases involving tribal suits against a state agency, Native Americans generally prefer to approach federal courts to uphold their claims. Four provisions of Title 28 of the United States Code are most relevant in these situations. Congress has waived sovereign immunity for the federal government for monetary damages under the Federal Tort Claims Act and through the Court of Claims. The Tucker Act specifically waives such protection from suits. Federal agencies may be sued by tribal governments through the Administrative Procedure Act. Tribal governments have retained sovereign immunity over a wide array of issues. Courts have held that the Indian Civil Rights Act, Public Law 83-280, and the Indian Self-Determination and Education Assistance Act do not allow suits against tribes.

Bibliography

Pevar, Stephen L. 1992. *The Rights of Indians and Tribes.* Carbondale: Southern Illinois University Press.

9 Native Americans and Equal Protection

Carole Goldberg

In the United States, federal law provides distinctive legal status for Indian tribes, their members, and sometimes Indians more broadly defined. Over the years the federal government has drawn upon its constitutional provisions to make treaties with Indian tribes and to issue statutes, executive orders, and other regulations concerning Indian affairs that reflect this status. Article I of the Constitution empowers Congress to regulate commerce with Indian tribes, acknowledging the legitimacy of the government to deal with Indian nations as discrete entities. Examples of the different treatment afforded Indians vis-à-vis other U.S. citizens include allowing Indians access to certain controlled substances and animal parts needed for ceremonial use, treaty rights to harvest fish, exemption from state taxes, employment preference within the Bureau of Indian Affairs (BIA), a special regime of federal criminal jurisdiction, and preferences in foster care and adoptive placement of Indian children.

States also have some laws that provide different rights to Indians than to other citizens. For example, some states exempt Native American ceremonial users of peyote from prosecution and give special consideration to Native Americans when issuing scholarships to state universities. In Hawaii, Native Hawaiians were granted exclusive rights to vote for an agency to oversee indigenous lands. Native Americans also have their own systems of classification within tribal law, sometimes privileging tribal members over others and at other times distinguishing Indians from all other peoples. An illustration of the former is a federal employment rights ordinance that institutes a tribally specific preference for all employment on tribal projects. An illustration of the latter is a law that restricts adoption of Indian children to individuals who are Indian, regardless of their tribe.

Since the 1970s, federal, state, and tribal laws affirming distinctive arrangements with tribes and their members have encountered legal challenges based on federal constitutional and statutory guarantees of equal protection under the law. The Fourteenth Amendment of the Constitution prohibits states from denying to any person equal protection within their jurisdiction. The Due Process Clause of the Fifth Amendment has been interpreted as imposing an equal protection requirement on the federal government as well. The Indian Civil Rights Act of 1968 imposes the same responsibility on Indian nations.

As a general matter, equal protection limitations require that persons similarly situated be treated alike under the law. Disparate legal treatment must be justified by a reasonable difference in circumstances. In many situations this requirement is satisfied by fairly minimal differences. The many classifications inherent in complex tax and social benefits laws are valid whenever the distinctions bear a rational relationship to the achievement of a valid governmental objective.

Legislative classifications tend to be subject to judicial inquiry under equal protection standards when the basis of thc classification is an innate group characteristic, such as race, ancestry, national origin, alienage, sex, or illegitimacy. According to decisions of the Supreme Court, classifications based on race, ancestry, or national origin, in particular, are inherently suspect and thus subject to "strict scrutiny" by the courts. To sustain a legislative classification based on one of these three categories, a government must show that the classification serves to further a compelling governmental interest. Few classifications have survived strict scrutiny.

Federal Classifications

During the last quarter of the twentieth century, as the emphasis of the civil rights movement shifted from desegregation to affirmative action, the equality-based rhetoric used to attack Indian treaty rights and legal status similarly shifted. Foes of tribal rights began to advance the view that federal Indian law constitutes racial discrimination against non-Indians.

The first Supreme Court case to deal with such an argument was *Morton v. Mancari* (1974), an equal protection challenge to a provision of the federal Indian Reorganization Act of 1934 giving Indians employment preference at the Bureau of Indian Affairs. In the statute, "Indians" were defined as individuals of one-quarter or more tribal ancestry; the Department of the Interior added the requirement of membership in a federally recognized tribe. In deciding the case, the Court refused to analyze federal laws singling out Indians according to "strict scrutiny" based on classifications of race and ethnicity. The Court instead acknowledged that resolution of the constitutional question "turns on the unique legal status of Indian tribes under federal law and upon the plenary power of Congress, based on a history of treaties and the assumption of a 'guardian-ward' status, to legislate on behalf of federally recognized Indian tribes." Given the long history of federal measures "derived from historical relationships and explicitly designed to help only Indians," characterizing such laws as invidious racial discrimination would "effectively erase" the entire federal code concerned with Indian affairs and would jeopardize "the solemn commitment of the Government toward the Indians."

Invoking Congress's constitutional power to regulate Indian affairs should have been sufficient to resolve the legal challenge in *Mancari*. The specific language of the Indian Commerce Clause envisioning group-specific legislation should be capable of overriding any general constitutional guarantees of equal protection or due process. In the second strand of the opinion, however, the Court asserted that the employment preference in the Indian Reorganization Act did not qualify as racial discrimination at all, but rather was "political," resting on membership in a tribal governmental entity. According to the Court, the classification was political in another sense: it was designed to advance tribal interests in self-government by enabling them to participate more fully in the activities of the BIA, which exercises governmental functions affecting tribes and their members. In conclusion, the Court emphasized the legitimate nonracial goal of the legislation in question and held that special treatment of Indians would be upheld "as long as [they] can be tied rationally to the fulfillment of Congress' unique obligation toward the Indians."

The Supreme Court has continued to stress the first strand of *Mancari* in subsequent rulings, sustaining federal Indian legislation against equal protection challenges: federal regulation of Indian affairs "is rooted in the unique status of Indians as 'a separate people' with their own political institutions. Federal regulation of tribes, therefore, is governance of once-sovereign political communities; it is not to be viewed as legislation of a 'racial group consisting of Indians.' " Nonetheless, the second strand of *Mancari*—that Indian classifications are not based on race, ancestry, or national origin—has often been misunderstood and has generated confusion. Some have taken the Court's statement to mean that only classifications turning on formal tribal enrollment or citizenship can escape the charge of invidious discrimination based on ancestry and thus pass muster under the Fifth Amendment's requirement of equal protection. According to this view, only classifications based on tribal citizenship are truly "political" rather than racial.

This reading of *Mancari* fails to capture the strongest rationale for the Court's conclusion: the charter for federal regulation of Indian affairs found in the Indian Commerce Clause and associated provisions of the Constitution. First, even when federal classifications turn on formal tribal citizenship, the fact that Indian ancestry is normally required for such citizenship as a matter of tribal law suggests that the federal classification may be incorporating a racelike component. Some tribes do allow adoption of individuals with no Indian ancestry, but they are a small minority. A tribal member adversely affected by a legal classification has the option of renouncing tribal membership and thereby avoiding the application of any law that turns on membership rather than ancestry. This option, however, does not alter the fact that non-Indians in general lack the ability to acquire tribal membership. Thus, there is no easy escape from charges of discrimination based on disfavored characteristics, except for the Indian Commerce Clause.

Second, if classifying who is an Indian were truly nonracial, there would be virtually no limitation on Congress's ability to make such distinctions, and state classifications would be permissible as well. Yet *Mancari* limited federal classifications to situations involving federal fulfillment of obligations to the Indians, and subsequent cases limited state classifications to those operating to further those federal obligations. Both of these limitations suggest that the driving energy behind *Mancari* was the Constitution's Indian Commerce Clause and the broader federal power over Indian affairs, not a view that the classifications are truly nonracial. Third, a number of federal legal provisions affecting Indians, including several upheld by the Court, expressly allude to ancestry rather than tribal citizenship. These laws were designed to account for actions of the United States that disrupted tribes as governments. Federal intervention in tribal sociopolitical organization has made it difficult to legitimate tribal citizenship. For this reason, the federal government has long resisted limiting its trust responsibility to enrolled tribal members. For example, the federal criminal laws applicable to Indian country that displace state criminal law apply to "Indians," who are defined not by enrolled tribal membership but by ancestry and involvement in an Indian tribal community.

Thus, the United States has historically recognized that its trust responsibility persists even when tribal communities have been dispersed, relocated, and combined, and when Indian individuals have been relocated to urban areas or forced to create new means of subsistence because their methods have been disrupted. A sound reading of *Mancari* would acknowledge that even though ancestry may figure in determining who is an Indian, ultimately the most important inquiry is whether the law can be justified as fulfilling "Congress' unique obligation toward the Indians."

The Supreme Court has never overturned a statute or treaty under the *Mancari* standard, but some of its opinions suggest that there are boundaries. In *Mancari*, the Court noted that an exemption for Indians from all civil service examinations would be an "obviously more difficult question" than the BIA preference cited in the case. Any racially motivated law, if proven to be such, would fall outside the permissible bounds set by *Mancari*.

Some courts have tried to circumscribe *Mancari* by, for example, restricting its application to federal laws addressing "uniquely Indian interests, such as tribal land, affairs, self-government, religion, and culture." This approach has the weakness of forcing the federal government and Indian nations to rationalize federal Indian law in light of historic tribal practices, an overly rigid and anachronistic approach. Some courts have even questioned whether *Mancari* adheres to the Supreme Court's decisions invalidating all affirmative action programs that are not closely tied to remedying specific acts of past discrimination. Some rejected affirmative action laws did include "Native Americans and Alaska Natives" among the targeted groups. A least some of these laws failed, however, to demonstrate even a minimal connection to the federal government's exercise of the Indian Commerce Clause and its fulfillment of unique obligations to the Indians. Rather, many were generic efforts to achieve racial or ethnic diversity. Thus, their possible invalidity does not necessarily undermine the holding of *Mancari*.

While *Mancari* remains the precedent for equal protection cases, its legal test does not extend to cases arising under the Fifteenth Amendment, which prohibits states and the federal government from denying or abridging the right to vote on the basis of race, color, or previous condition of servitude. In *Rice v. Cayetano* (2000), a person who was not of Native Hawaiian descent challenged a state law that permitted only individuals of such descent to vote for trustees of an agency administering programs benefiting Native Hawaiians. Notwithstanding that the classification was state rather than federal, *Mancari* was potentially implicated because the state agency had been created to implement a federal requirement imposed at the time of Hawaiian statehood. The Hawaiian law establishing this agency also extended an obligation that the United States had assumed upon annexing the Hawaiian Islands without Native Hawaiians' consent and seizing all former Crown, government, and public lands. In order to trigger *Mancari's* more relaxed standard of review, the state of Hawaii argued that Native Hawaiians have a status comparable to Indian tribes and that the voting restriction afforded Native Hawaiians a measure of self-government. The Supreme Court avoided resolution of these points by holding that even if *Mancari* were applicable for purposes of equal protection under the Fourteenth Amendment, such an approach did not extend to voting restrictions challenged under the Fifteenth Amendment.

Rice v. Cayetano reaffirms *Mancari*, even if some of the language may be read to restrict its applications. The two cases are easily reconciled when one considers the differences between the Equal Protection Clause and the Fifteenth Amendment in relation to the Indian Commerce Clause. The authorization for special federal Indian laws imparted in the Indian Commerce Clause should be sufficient to override the general promise of equal protection found in the Fourteenth Amendment and read into the Fifth. The specific language of the Indian Commerce Clause, however, confronts equally specific language in the Fifteenth Amendment regarding racial distinctions in the voting process. Under these circumstances, a greater burden of justification may be exacted for Indian-related laws introducing racial distinctions into state or federal elections, at least when those distinctions rest entirely on ancestry and make no reference to community affiliation.

In sum, the unique status of Indian tribes under the Constitution and treaties establishes a legitimate legislative purpose for singling out Indians as a class. Legislation rationally related to this purpose is not proscribed by the equal protection principle. Legislation dealing with Indians as a discrete class but not reasonably related to their federal status should be tested against the stricter equal protection standards prohibiting discrimination based on race, ancestry, or national origin.

State and Tribal Classifications

State action presents additional equal protection questions. The Supreme Court's opinions sustaining federal Indian laws against equal protection attacks have, as stated, emphasized "Congress' unique obligation toward the Indians," and tribes have been described as under federal guardianship arising out of treaties, federal laws, and the Constitution itself. The Court has pointed out that the "[s]tates do not enjoy [the] same unique relationship with Indians" as the federal government. Some courts have concluded that unless a state law embodying an Indian classification is specifically authorized by a federal statute or treaty, it should not benefit from the more relaxed standard of review in *Mancari*. Others have taken a broader view, asserting that state laws may be reviewed under the more relaxed standard so long as they operate to implement, reflect, or effectuate federal laws, thereby fulfilling Congress's evident intent to benefit Indians. This broader view makes sense in light of Congress's evident power to suppress state laws that stray too far from federal policy aims.

Indian nations regularly distinguish between tribal members and between Indians and non-Indians in their constitutions and laws. The Indian Civil Rights Act of 1968 contains an equal protection provision that binds individual tribes and protects all persons within the tribe's jurisdiction. In *Santa Clara Pueblo v. Martinez*

(1978), the Supreme Court ruled that tribal courts have exclusive jurisdiction to enforce the act in civil matters. Between 1968 and 1978, however, lower federal courts hearing civil actions on enforcing the act recognized that equal protection may mean something different under the Indian Civil Rights Act than under the Fourteenth and Fifth Amendments. For example, tribal social organization and the very nature of tribal communities may entail tribal membership requirements that take ancestry into account as well as tribal voting requirements that treat clans or kinship groups rather than individuals as the primary units for purposes of representation. More recently, in *Rice v. Cayetano*, the Supreme Court contrasted tribal with federal and state elections in setting forth the equality requirements of the Fifteenth Amendment, which prohibits denial or abridgement of the right to vote on the basis of race. The Court made it clear that its condemnation of racial distinctions in state elections did not extend to tribal elections, where ancestry-based distinctions may be necessary to sustain tribal existence and from a federal perspective are internal affairs of the tribe.

10 Red, Black, and Divided: Federal Recognition and the Imposition of Identity on the Seminole Nation

Natsu Taylor Saito

> Because it is a systematic negation of the other person and a furious determination to deny the other person all attributes of humanity, colonialism forces the people it dominates to ask themselves the question constantly: In reality, who am I?
>
> Frantz Fanon, *Wretched of the Earth*

Since 1996 Sylvia Davis, an enrolled member of the Dosar Barkus band of the Seminole Nation of Oklahoma (SNO), has been waiting to see if the federal courts will overturn a decision of the Bureau of Indian Affairs (BIA) denying her son Donnell a $125 school clothing allowance from funds allocated to compensate the Seminoles for land taken from them in Florida. The Dosar Barkus and Bruner bands are Seminoles of African descent, and although they are the only branches being denied access to these funds, the BIA—supported by the governing council of the SNO—claims that it is not discriminating on the basis of race but simply enforcing a requirement that the funds be distributed to the descendants of "the Seminole Nation as it existed in Florida on September 18, 1823" (*Davis v. United States* 1999). Despite uncontroverted evidence that the Seminole nation has included persons of African descent since its inception in the mid-1700s—and thus since before the formation of the United States—the Estelusti, or black Seminoles, are being told that they were not members of the nation until the U.S. government decided to recognize them as such in 1866.

In the meantime, the leadership of the SNO, apparently under the mistaken impression that *all* judgment funds would be frozen pending the outcome of the lawsuit, voted to expel the Dosar Barkus and Bruner bands from the

Seminole Nation of Oklahoma, and in July 2000 the governing council approved amendments to its constitution to that effect. In September 2001 the District Court for the District of Columbia ruled in *Seminole Nation of Oklahoma v. Norton* that the amendments were not effective because the Seminoles did not complete the amendment process by obtaining the approval of the secretary of the interior, as required by the Seminole constitution. The SNO has ignored this ruling and has proceeded with elections under the amended constitution, but the BIA is refusing to recognize the new government.

Sometimes the right thing happens for the wrong reasons, and sometimes otherwise righteous arguments are put forth in the interest of distinctly unjust ends. In this case, the Seminole Nation of Oklahoma—actually, the representatives of the tribal government recognized by the United States—claims to be exercising its sovereign right to amend its constitution without the approval of the secretary of the interior, and more fundamentally, its sovereign right to determine its own membership. Ironically, all of the reasons the SNO put forth to exclude the Estelusti derive from the U.S. government's two-hundred-year history of refusing to properly recognize the Seminole nation and its relentless imposition of identity upon the Seminoles. In the meantime, the Estelusti have no access to the judgment funds, and after trying for several centuries the U.S. government may have finally succeeded in dividing the Seminole nation along the lines of federally imposed definitions of race. *Davis v. United States* and *Seminole Nation of Oklahoma v. Norton* provide an unusual opportunity to unravel the tangled history of federal recognition of the Seminole nation and to examine the devastating impact of the imposition of identity by the U.S. government upon a people it colonized.

The Seminole Nation, September 18, 1823

After the introduction of African slavery in North America, some runaway slaves, or Maroons, fled south, where they established independent communities and alliances with indigenous peoples in what is now Florida. As early as 1687, Maroons from South Carolina had made their way to St. Augustine, where they were given asylum by the Spanish governor. According to Joshua Giddings, an Ohio congressman,

> Their numbers had become so great in 1736, that they were formed into companies, and relied on by the Floridians as allies to aid in the defense of the territory. They were also permitted to occupy lands upon the same terms that were granted to the citizens of Spain; indeed, they in all respect became free subjects of the Spanish crown. (Giddings 1858, 6)

Word of slaves escaping to freedom tended to spread rapidly through the British colonies, and apprehending fugitive slaves became a top domestic priority for the newly formed United States and an important issue in its relations with Indian nations and European colonies on its borders.

In the meantime, in the late seventeenth century a number of indigenous nations had joined to form the Creek Confederacy in what is now Georgia and Alabama. By 1750, some twenty-five years before the establishment of the United States, a sector of the confederacy had declared itself independent of Creek authority and moved south to Florida. These Creeks united with Miccosukee Indians and Maroons to form the Seminole nation. The

Tenth Circuit Court of Appeals summarized this history as follows:

> The Seminole Nation . . . formed after the European conquest of America and [is] composed of both Native American and African peoples. Some members of the Seminole Nation are descended from escaped African slaves who resided among several Native American groups living in what is now Florida. These Native American groups, together with the Africans living among them, became known as the Seminoles. The Africans were referred to in the Seminole tongue as Estelusti. (*Davis* at 954)

The newly emergent United States, militarily weak and anxious to appear legitimate in a community of nations that did not look kindly upon colonies fighting for independence, entered into a number of treaties with Indian nations. In this context, the United States wanted the benefits of these agreements and the recognition that they would convey upon the United States as a legitimate nation. The U.S. government did not, however, want to recognize a nation comprised of Indians and Africans, because the United States owed its creation and existence to maintaining the institution of slavery. Under U.S. law, persons of African descent were presumed to be slaves, and one of the benefits the United States sought in treaties with Indian nations was a promise to return fugitive slaves.

With the first treaty ratified under the Constitution, the United States imposed identity through federal recognition or, in this case, nonrecognition, of the Seminole nation. The 1790 Treaty of New York purported to be an agreement between all the citizens of the United States and "all the individuals, towns and tribes of the Upper, Middle and Lower Creeks and Semanolies [*sic*] composing the Creek nation of Indians." In addition to ceding land, the Creeks agreed to deliver all "prisoners and Negroes" in the nation. The Seminoles repudiated the treaty on the grounds that they were not Creeks, had not been represented in the negotiations, and lived in Spanish Florida. The United States would persist, however, in its refusal to acknowledge the independent existence of the Seminole nation until 1823. In the meantime, slaveholders in Georgia and South Carolina pressured the federal government to protect their property, so the United States attempted, though unsuccessfully, to force Spain to turn over persons of African descent in Florida. By the early nineteenth century, persons of African descent had been living freely in Florida for five or six generations, and had been Seminoles for three or four generations.

As pressure mounted for Florida's annexation, Congress secretly approved a series of invasions, all of which were driven back by Spanish and Seminole resistance. In May 1816 General Andrew Jackson authorized U.S. troops to attack a fort on the Apalachicola River, sixty miles inside Florida, solely because it was controlled by Seminoles. U.S. forces killed 270 Seminoles and wounded all but 3 of the 334 Seminoles, mostly women and children. They also captured, tortured, and then killed two warriors, one Indian and one black, whom they designated the chiefs. The Seminoles who survived were taken to Georgia and, in Giddings words, "delivered over to men who claimed to have descended from planters who, some three or four generations previously, owned the ancestors of the prisoners" (Giddings 1858, 42).

Shortly thereafter, the Seminoles launched a retaliatory attack on a U.S. vessel on the Apalachicola. The government used the incident—without mention of the burning of the fort—to get Congress to allocate money for the First Seminole War. After several bloody but unsuccessful campaigns, pressure mounted for the federal government to purchase Florida. In 1819 Spain, drained by the Napoleonic Wars and unable to effectively counter rising U.S. military power, agreed to the sale, setting the stage for thirty years of warfare over the removal of the Seminoles to lands in the west.

The Second Seminole War (1835–1842) has been described by military historians as the "longest and most expensive Indian war" waged by the U.S. government, although General Thomas Jesup, commander of the U.S. forces in Florida, insisted that it was "a negro and not an Indian war" (Porter 1996, 107). The reasons the Seminoles fought with such determination and never surrendered are rooted in their identity as a red-black nation and in the United States' long-standing refusal to acknowledge their status as a nation independent of the Creeks. The Seminoles, of course, had no desire to leave their homelands in Florida for any reason or at any price. The removal conflict, which would have existed in any case, was compounded by the terms of an 1821 treaty imposed on the Creeks.

Georgia planters claiming that the Creeks had not returned "property" as required by earlier treaties pressured the federal government into negotiating the 1821 Treaty of Indian Springs, under which the Creeks, despite their protests that the Seminoles were a separate nation, were held responsible "not only for the slaves and their increase, but also for the loss of labor which they would have performed had they remained in bondage" (Giddings 1858, 63). More than half of the money given to the Creeks in exchange for ceding five million acres of land was set aside to pay the claims of slaveholders for "property" purportedly lost to the Creeks between 1775 and 1802. In exchange for this indemnification, all right and title to this property—the persons claimed as fugitive slaves and their descendants; in other words, the black Seminoles—was assigned and transferred to the United States, to be held in trust for the benefit of the Creeks.

The U.S. government, having been unsuccessful in controlling the Seminoles through the Creeks, acknowledged the Seminole nation for the first time by entering into the Treaty of Moultrie Creek, signed on September 18, 1823. Its terms, which the U.S. negotiator candidly acknowledged "[t]he Indians would never have voluntarily assented to . . . had they not believed that we had both the power and disposition to compel obedience," required the Seminoles to cede their very fertile land in northern Florida for a large but barren tract further south and bound them to turn over any "absconding slaves, or fugitives from justice" to a U.S. agent (Prucha 1994, 152).

After Congress passed the 1830 Indian Removal Act and attempted to force all Indians into the territory north of Texas and west of Arkansas, the government planned to put the Seminoles on land already occupied by the Creeks. In other words, the U.S. military planned to deliver the Seminoles over to a people from whom it had just taken $250,000 in exchange for "title" to a large portion of the Seminole population. Thus, for the Seminoles, in addition to losing their land, their removal equated, literally, with being sold into slavery.

In 1950 and 1951 the Seminole Nation of Oklahoma and Seminoles still living in Florida filed claims for compensation for lands in Florida ceded to the United States in 1823. Hoping to quiet title to the lands taken from the Seminoles, in 1976 the Indian Claims Commission (ICC) finally awarded $16 million to the "Seminole Nation as it existed in Florida on September 18, 1823." Congress, however, did not pass an act providing for distribution of the money until 1990, by which time the judgment fund, with interest, had grown to $56 million. It is ironic that the same government that steadfastly refused to acknowledge the existence of the Seminole nation until 1823, and then did so only to strip it of its property, proceeded to define the rights of that nation's citizens as of that date. Putting aside the presumptuousness of the formulation for the moment, however, who comprised the Seminole nation as of September 18, 1823?

The Treaty of Moultrie Creek required that the Seminoles provide a list of Indian towns and a census of their inhabitants. The leader of the Seminole delegation, Neamathla, listed thirty-seven towns with 4,883 inhabitants, but, familiar with the predatory practices of slave catchers, he refused to specify the number of blacks in the nation. According to George Klos (1995, 131), by this time "Seminole society had blacks of every status born free, or the descendants of fugitives, or perhaps fugitives themselves. Some were interpreters and advisers of importance, others were warriors and hunters or field hands. Intermarriage with Indians further complicated black status."

Even the white planters recognized the distinction between fugitive slaves and black Seminoles, for they complained that the latter "aided such slaves to select new and more secure places of refuge" (Klos 1995, 131). One planter, after visiting several "Negro Villages" looking for runaways, reported that he could not determine the number of slaves living among the Seminoles because "of their being protected by the Indian Negroes . . . [who are] so artfull that it is impossible to gain any information relating to such property from them" (Klos 1995, 132–133). In 1837 General Jesup wrote, "I have some hopes of inducing both Indians and Indian negroes to unite in bringing in the negroes taken from the citizens during the war" (Giddings 1858, 147).

The Treaty of Moultrie Creek had been signed by Abraham, a Seminole of African descent identified as "the prime minister and privy counsellor of Micanopy." It is reported that to overcome opposition to the treaty's terms, "six of the most influential chiefs were bribed by the reservation of extensive tracts of land" one of the chiefs being Mulatto King (Foreman 1972, 319). Oceola, one of the nation's best known leaders, was married to an Estelusti and engaged in some of his most daring exploits to retaliate for his wife having been stolen and sold into slavery. All of the removal records identify large numbers of black Seminoles among the groups sent west. Grant Foreman notes that to induce the Seminoles to accept the terms of one of the removal agreements, the 1837 Camp Dade treaty, "General Jesup was obliged to agree to the one condition that the Indians had insisted on from the beginning; and that was that . . . the free negroes, should also be secure in their persons and property" (1972, 344–345). Thus it is clear from the history of the Seminole nation and from observations made in 1823 that while there may have been fugitive slaves in Seminole communities at this time, persons of African descent constituted a significant portion of the nation and had done so for several generations.

Federal Determinations of Seminole Identity

The United States never achieved a military victory over the Seminole nation but, community by community, most of the Seminoles were eventually forced to move west. Large groups refused to move onto Creek lands and instead lived for years off the generosity of the Cherokees until they were finally provided land of their own by the U.S. government. Some remained in the Everglades, living quietly until white settler pressure for their land resulted in the Third Seminole War (1855–1858), which destroyed most of their remaining villages. In the west, until the end of the Civil War, they faced constant slave-catching raids in which black Seminoles, including children, were kidnapped from their homes and sold, regardless of their legal status.

After the passage of the Thirteenth Amendment, the federal government imposed treaties upon the Seminoles and a number of other Indian nations, some of whom owned slaves, that provided for the emancipation of any slaves and the incorporation of the "freedmen" into the nation "on an equal footing with the original members" (14 Stat. 755, Treaty with the Seminoles, March 21, 1866). Such actions effectuated the imposition of identity on all the nations involved, but in the Seminoles' case the problem was not that the law forced the nation to recognize people as citizens in violation of its own standards of membership, but that the U.S. government (despite all evidence to the contrary) interpreted it to mean that all black Seminoles had been slaves prior to 1866 and thus could not have been members of the nation, not that any Seminoles who may have been enslaved as of 1866 were now free citizens.

Under the General Allotment Act of 1887, also known as the Dawes Act, Congress attempted to dissolve what remained of Indian sovereignty by implementing a policy of "extinguishing Indian tribal lands, allotting the same in severalty among those entitled to receive them, and distributing Indian tribal funds." Despite tremendous Indian resistance, the federal government took all collectively held lands, allotted the worst portions to individual Indians, and sold the "surplus" to white settlers, a process that resulted in the loss of about two-thirds of all Indian-held lands. In 1901 the members of the Five Civilized Tribes, which include the Seminoles, were unilaterally declared to be U.S. citizens by an act of Congress. Later, in 1906, Congress effectively abolished the Seminole government and provided for an accounting, or tribal enrollment, of members of the nation, a task assigned to the commission headed by Sen. Henry Dawes.

The Dawes Commission created a list of approximately three thousand Seminoles, about one-third of whom were of African descent. Although the commission was not required to create any distinctions among those enrolled, it divided Seminole membership into a "Seminole Blood Roll" and a "Freedmen Roll." Despite the fact that there had been far more intermarriage between indigenous and African peoples than between Indians and Europeans, the commission applied the "racial" classification rules used generally in the Jim Crow laws of the day to create the "freedmen" roll of persons of visible African ancestry, not identified by "blood quantum," and a "blood" roll of persons of indigenous or Euro-Indian heritage identified as "full-blood," "half-blood," and so on.

As the Tenth Circuit Court of Appeals noted in *Davis*, even these distinctions were muddied due to the fact that "[b]ecause the Seminole Nation is matrilineal, if an individual's mother was a Freedman and his father was Indian by blood, that individual was enrolled in the Freedmen Roll." Conversely, someone whose mother was Indian and father was black would be identified as Indian "by blood." Here again, the federal government was imposing its notion of identity on the Seminole nation. Not only were persons recognized as "Seminole" only if they met standards imposed upon them by a group of Euro-American men representing the colonizing power, but the criteria chosen also imposed a notion of "blood quantum," an entirely alien concept to Seminole culture and an arbitrary segregation of the nation along lines of "race" as invented by the settlers. Nonetheless, all who were identified, whether on the Blood Roll or the Freedmen Roll, were officially citizens of the Seminole nation, and it is these rolls that are still used to determine membership in that nation.

Exclusion of the Estelusti from the Judgment Funds

How is it that persons who are acknowledged to be members of the Seminole nation, a nation that by all historical accounts has been a "red *and* black" group since its inception, can be denied benefits accruing to that nation solely because of their African ancestry? How is it that the federal agency that colluded with the leadership of the Seminole Nation of Oklahoma to exclude the Estelusti from judgment fund programs now refuses to recognize the SNO government as "legal" because it has moved to exclude the Estelusti from membership in the nation? This story illustrates much about the insidious way in which federal "recognition" of Indian nations and the concomitant control exercised over them has been and continues to be used to destroy these nations.

Overlapping claims for approximately 24 million acres of land taken in Florida were brought to the Indian Claims Commission by Seminoles in Florida and in Oklahoma. The ICC merged these claims and issued the collective judgment in 1976 in the amount of $16 million, to be allocated among the various Seminole communities. As noted, distribution of the fund was not authorized by Congress until April 1990, and the authorizing statute required that the SNO develop a plan for the distribution and use of the funds. A dispute over how the funds would be divided between Seminoles in Florida and those in Oklahoma resulted in a 27:73 split derived from a recommendation by the Bureau of Indian Affairs applying a "blood quantum" formula. The BIA further recommended finding "all Seminole Negroes and their descendants [including members of] the modern Seminole Nation of Oklahoma, to be ineligible to participate in the subject award [because they] had no interest in the Florida lands in 1823, and . . . did not acquire an interest in Oklahoma lands until 1866" (Bureau of Indian Affairs memorandum, November 26, 1976, filed in *Davis*). In short, the BIA solution completely disregarded black Seminole membership, recognized the extensive European admixture of the remaining Oklahoma Seminoles, and divided the proceeds by something purporting to correspond to the proportion of "Indian blood." Thus, the settler society again imposed on the Seminoles a racial construction and concept entirely alien to their culture, most particularly Seminole culture as of 1823.

Despite their actions to the contrary, the BIA and the SNO leadership were clear that Congress probably intended for the Estelusti to benefit from the judgment fund. Its authorization did not limit distribution to "Seminole blood members" as recommended by the BIA. Also, the statute provides that at least 80 percent of the fund go to collective programs and that any per capita distributions be made on the basis of "a roll of members of the Seminole Nation of Oklahoma," a group conceded by all parties to include the Estelusti. A BIA memorandum even states, "We sincerely believe that should a plan be submitted to Congress that excludes the Seminole Freedmen, who are currently members of the tribe, a joint resolution will be enacted by Congress disapproving such a plan" (Bureau of Indian Affairs memorandum, Springwater to Muskogee area director, May 4, 1990, filed in *Davis*). A few months later, a BIA solicitor met with the SNO leadership to inform them of their options regarding the "Freedmen issue," including the possibility of the "plan slipping through if Congress is busy with the Middle East crises on their mind" (Bureau of Indian Affairs memorandum, Garbow, tribal operations officer, to Muskogee area director, September 10, 1990, filed in *Davis*).

Rather than risk being overridden by Congress, the SNO leadership decided on a distribution plan that only included collective programs, thus avoiding per capita distributions altogether. They made eligibility for the programs contingent on descent from "a member of the Seminole Nation as it existed in Florida on September 18, 1823," counting on their ability to exclude the Estelusti on the basis of the clearly counterfactual argument articulated by the BIA in 1976 that the "freedmen" were not really members of the nation until the United States said they must be under the treaty of 1866. This formulation was allowed by Congress, funds were allocated, and Estelusti members were excluded from the benefits, leading, as all parties had predicted, to a suit against the BIA. At some point, a BIA representative warned the SNO governing council incorrectly that the entire judgment fund was likely to be frozen pending the outcome of *Davis*, and the council responded by scheduling a referendum to remove the "freedmen" from membership in the nation.

The Seminole nation, like other Indian nations removed to eastern Oklahoma, was not subject to the Indian Reorganization Act of 1934 (IRA)—which reconstituted, under BIA-imposed conditions, some nations previously dissolved under the Dawes Act. Nonetheless, in 1969 the Seminole Nation of Oklahoma adopted a constitution and form of government modeled after those imposed on most Indian nations by the IRA. Under Article 13 of the Seminoles' 1969 constitution, amendments are effective only if approved by the secretary of the Department of the Interior (DOI). In 1991 the SNO attempted to remove this provision, but did not obtain the requisite governmental approval for the amendment, so the BIA's position is that Article 13 still stands. In July 2000 the SNO approved several more amendments to the constitution that would effectively oust the Estelusti by adding "Seminole Indian blood quantum" requirements for membership. The BIA refused to consider these amendments valid, because the SNO again failed to obtain DOI approval. In September 2001 the U.S. District Court for the District of Columbia upheld the federal government's rejection of these amendments.

The Seminole Nation of Oklahoma argues that the government is violating its right to self-determination by not allowing it to amend its constitution and determine its own membership and at the same time is engaging in further mismanagement of trust fund assets by refusing to recognize the newly elected council and, therefore, refusing to release funds to that council. On the question of self-determination, the government responds:

> While Defendants agree that the Seminole Nation possesses this power [to define its own government, the Plaintiff ignores the fact that] . . . the Seminole Nation did indeed define how its government was to be structured when it created its Constitution, which includes an article . . . expressly providing that the Commissioner of Indian Affairs must approve any ratified constitutional amendments. . . . Plaintiff also ignores the fact that the Seminole Nation, in December of 1991, attempted to amend its Constitution to remove the Commissioner of Indian Affairs' approval authority, but that attempt failed when Defendants refused to approve the amendment, and the Interior Board of Indian Appeals upheld Defendants' action. (Reply memorandum, March 21, 2001, p. 7, filed in *Seminole Nation of Oklahoma v. Norton*)

Although the BIA and the SNO leadership are willing to accept the entirely artificial (and counterfactual) assertion that the Estelusti only became members of the nation as of 1866 in order to exclude them from the benefits of the judgment fund, defining the current membership of the nation has become a contest of competing sovereignties. Having spent more than two hundred years attempting to effectively reduce the Seminole nation to an internal colony, the federal government appears unwilling to cede any ground now.

Can the Right Thing Happen for the Right Reasons?

As of January 2000 the Seminole Nation of Oklahoma had begun lobbying Congress in connection with a $95 million mineral rights claim related to federal mismanagement of oil and mineral resources on Seminole land. Due to the fracturing of the nation and lack of a functioning government recognized by the United States, the resources claim—potentially worth twice as much as all of the compensation for land—now appears dead in the water, in part because the passage of compensatory legislation would require the support of the Congressional Black Caucus.

Nations are colonized in large measure to facilitate the extraction of their resources. Although the Seminole nation fought valiantly to prevent the expropriation of its people and its land, it may be that the United States has found an easier way to take its mineral wealth. Such a colonial relationship requires control, and to the extent that the colonizers can determine the identity of the colonized, that control need not be imposed directly by force. The power of naming is key to the imposition of identity, and "federal recognition" is yet another of the misnomers so frequently found in the discourse concerning things Indian. Recognition implies the acknowledgment of what exists, but the term is used here to mean the opposite—certification that that which did exist has, in fact, been supplanted thoroughly enough to warrant the colonizer's stamp of approval.

Has the federal government finally succeeded in getting the Seminole nation to internalize the racism so integral to the settler state? Has the long and twisted history of the United States' refusal to recognize the Seminole nation left the Seminoles of eastern Oklahoma without any principled positive outcomes? Is the only way to avoid the very immediate harm being visited on the Seminoles of African descent an arbitrary limitation of sovereignty and the imposition of federal will on an indigenous nation? Even if the black Seminoles remain technically members of the nation due to this flexing of federal muscle, will they continue to be arbitrarily excluded from desperately needed judgment fund programs because the federal and SNO governments colluded to disregard history and pretend that the

Estelusti only became Seminoles upon decree of the United States in 1866?

If the BIA or the SNO leadership actually cared about determining the membership of the nation as of September 18, 1823, they would not participate in the charade that the Estelusti only became Seminoles as a result of the 1866 treaty, a position that necessarily incorporates the position taken in U.S. law (but certainly not Seminole law) that persons of African descent were presumed to be property, and therefore could not be property owners. Both the BIA and the SNO leadership supported this pretext; their ranks were split only when, apparently in response to the *Davis* litigation, the SNO tried to remove the Estelusti as citizens of the nation without getting BIA approval. This is the basis for the current stand-off reflected in *Seminole Nation of Oklahoma v. Norton*.

Does the BIA really care about the well-being of the Dosar Barkus and Bruner bands? Probably not, given its role in conspiring to deny them benefits. Does it really care about the unity of the nation? Probably not, given that the impetus to the current movement to expel these bands was the statement by a BIA official to the effect that the entire judgment fund could be frozen pending the outcome of *Davis*, a statement he almost certainly knew was not true and with equal certainty knew would be extremely divisive. Given these positions, why is BIA fighting the expulsion? Probably because, as the SNO tried to argue, it really is opposed to any measure that removes power from the federal government and places it in indigenous hands.

The proud red-black Seminole nation that held the United States at bay in one of its longest and costliest wars—and should have "title" to virtually the entire state of Florida—is self-destructing over compensatory crumbs in the form of burial assistance, school clothing, and roof repair funds desperately needed by all members of the nation because they have all been reduced to poverty by federal policies. The United States has continued to use its ability to impose identity on the Seminoles to divide and conquer the nation. This longstanding and consistent practice dates from the United States' initial refusal to acknowledge the Seminoles' separate existence, to its insistence on treating all Seminoles of African descent as if they were enslaved, and finally to its contemporary refusal to either allow the Estelusti to participate in judgment fund programs or the leadership to expel them. That the Seminole nation's $95 million mineral rights claim now has almost no chance of serious congressional consideration demonstrates the effectiveness of this strategy.

What would it take to untangle this seemingly intractable problem? Given the history of U.S.-Seminole relations, it is hardly appropriate for federal courts to determine who was a member of the nation as of the day the United States finally recognized its existence. Procedurally, submitting the dispute to arbitration by a neutral third party capable of an honest assessment of Seminole history, citizenship criteria, and treaty interpretation under applicable international law would seem to be appropriate. Substantively, the actual recognition by all parties, including the federal courts, that there have been Seminoles of African descent as long as the Seminole nation has existed would seem to be a good place to start, followed, perhaps, by acknowledgment of the illegitimacy of all U.S. attempts to impose its racial definitions upon the Seminole nation. This would include its insistence on assuming that black Seminoles were slaves from 1790 to

1866 and its continuing imposition of this misreading of reality onto the Estelusti.

Such acknowledgment would need to encompass the U.S. refusal to treat with the Seminole nation until 1823; its attempts to force them to "reunite" with the Creeks when removed to Oklahoma; the arbitrary imposition of citizenship in the 1866; treaty and all that was embodied in the creation of the Dawes Commission rolls—from the very notion that a U.S.-appointed commission could appropriately decide Seminole membership to the creation of Jim Crow lists to the identification of people by the eugenicist notion of blood quantum to the forced allotment of land. Also requiring recognition are the imposition of a U.S.-designed "constitution" on the nation, the control exercised over trust monies rightfully belonging to the nation (including the allocation of those funds according to the bizarre calculation that weighs "Indian blood" to determine the size of the pot and then allows it to be shared with those of European heritage but not those of African heritage), the stripping of mineral rights in Oklahoma, and the ongoing refusal to allow actual self-government.

After the above issues have been resolved, the conversation could then turn to the development, from the inside out, of an equitable form of government and allocation of the nation's resources among *all* of the descendants of the Seminole nation as it existed in Florida prior to 1823. If the energy currently being expended in the fight over who gets school clothing could be turned to obtaining some of the real resources owed the nation, beginning with its mineral rights claims, perhaps the processes of internal colonialism at work here could be reversed rather than further entrenched. Frantz Fanon's statement that "colonialism forces the people it dominates to ask themselves the question constantly: In reality, who am I?" is true of *peoples* as well as individuals. It is the question faced by the Seminole nation today.

Bibliography

Churchill, Ward. n.d. "The Nullification of Native America? An Analysis of the 1990 American Indian Arts and Crafts Act." In *Perversions of Justice: Indigenous Peoples and Angloamerican Law*. San Francisco: City Lights, forthcoming 2003.

Fanon, Frantz. 1963. *The Wretched of the Earth*. New York: Grove Press.

Forbes, Jack D. 1993. *Africans and Native Americans: The Language of Race and the Evolution of Red-Black Peoples*. Urbana: University of Illinois Press.

Foreman, Grant. 1972. *Indian Removal: The Emigration of the Five Civilized Tribes of Indians*. Norman: University of Oklahoma Press.

Gibson, Arrell Morgan. 1988. "To Kill a Nation: Liquidation of the Five Indian Republics." In *The American Indian Experience, A Profile: 1524 to the Present*, edited by Philip Weeks. Arlington Heights, Ill.: Forum Press.

Giddings, Joshua R. 1858. *The Exiles of Florida; Or, The Crimes Committed by Our Government against the Maroons, Who Fled from South Carolina and Other Slave States, Seeking Protection under Spanish Law*. Columbus, Ohio: Follett, Foster and Company.

Jaimes, M. Annette. 1992. "Federal Indian Identification Policy: A Usurpation of Indigenous Sovereignty in North America." In *The State of Native America: Genocide, Colonization, and Resistance*, edited by M. Annette Jaimes. Boston: South End Press.

Klos, George. 1995. "Blacks and the Seminole Removal Debate, 1821–1835." In *The African American Heritage of Florida*, edited by David R. Colburn. Gainesville: University of Florida Press.

Mahon, John K. 1962. "The Treaty of Moultrie Creek, 1823." *Florida Historical Quarterly*, no. 40 (April).

Mulroy, Kevin. 1993. *Freedom on the Border: The Seminole Maroons in Florida, the Indian Territory, Coahuila, and Texas*. Lubbock: Texas Tech University Press.

Porter, Kenneth W. 1996. *The Black Seminoles: History of a Freedom-Seeking People*. Gainesville: University Press of Florida.

Prucha, Francis Paul. 1994. *American Indian Treaties: The History of a Political Anomaly*. Berkeley: University of California Press

———. 2000. *Documents of United States Indian Policy*. 3d ed. Lincoln: University of Nebraska Press.

11

The Indian Child Welfare Act of 1978: Barriers to Implementation and Recommendations for the Future

Carol A. Markstrom

A fundamental prerogative of a people is to establish and direct practices for the well-being and best interests of its young. At its best, the Indian Child Welfare Act (ICWA) of 1978 represents an advance in tribal self-determination through the delineation of procedures to establish tribal control of child welfare. Presumably, tribal decision-making processes in matters of child welfare should firmly embrace children within the cultural context of kin, clan, and tribe. Culturally specific socialization of Indian children should, in turn, enhance the preservation of tribal culture. The ICWA implicitly supports two notions: that tribal communities have a collective responsibility to love and nurture their children, and that Indian children have fundamental rights to obtain such love and nurturing from their communities (Graham 1998/99). Since children cannot select those who will serve as their primary sources of socialization, this responsibility falls within the domain of adults. Tribal communities are best positioned to determine what is appropriate and desirable for the rearing and socialization of their children.

Background and Implementation

The ICWA stems from a broad historical and political U.S. government agenda of attempting to assimilate Indians. The long-standing and widespread Bureau of Indian Affairs (BIA) boarding school tradition was explicit in its effort to replace students' Indian culture with the values, beliefs, and practices of U.S. mainstream society. This pattern of assimilation escalated with the BIA's 1957 Indian Adoption Project, which facilitated adoption of Indian children into non-Indian homes. The Project linked the removal of Indian children from their homes to economic factors, with perceived neglect of children serving as justification (Philips 1997). Apparent in such removals was the lack of understanding about tribal communities, customs, and culture by the non-Indian agents of social welfare and state courts.

Significant to the development of the ICWA were reports by alarmed tribal communities of disproportionately high removal rates and the children's subsequent placement in non-Indian homes for foster case and adoption. The Devils Lake Sioux tribe—now the Spirit Lake Tribe of Dakota Indians—and, shortly thereafter, the Standing Rock Sioux and Three Affiliated Tribes were the first to draw attention to this issue (Jones et al. 2000). Prior to passage of the ICWA, the Association of American Indian Affairs reported that one-third of all Indian children were in foster care, adoptive homes, or residential educational institutions (Graham 1998/99). Eight-five percent of these placements were in non-Indian homes and institutions.

The Indian Self-Determination and Education Assistance Act of 1975 was a precursor to the ICWA of 1978 in that it allowed tribes to assume control over some of their social services. Only after passage of the ICWA, however, were tribes granted a say in the best interests of Indian children. The ICWA strengthened tribal jurisdiction over child welfare concerns regarding foster care placement, termination of parental rights, and pre-adoptive and adoptive placement of Indian children (Jones et al. 2000). The act was expected to circumvent the removal of Indian children from their homes by states. If child placement or adoption became necessary, the stated procedures and policies of the act, when followed, would ensure that most Indian children be placed in foster and adoptive situations within their tribal culture. The ICWA assigned tribal courts exclusive jurisdiction over child welfare cases of children living within reservations and those off the reservation who were wards of tribal courts. State courts would be allowed to retain jurisdiction "where there is good cause not to transfer the proceeding to a tribal court, when either parent objects to the transfer, or when the tribal court itself declines jurisdiction" (Stiffarm 1995, 1156). The cooperation of state courts with tribal courts is paramount for carrying out the intent of Congress.

The Indian Child Welfare Act, with all of its good intentions, is yet to be fully implemented though there have been some advancements since its passage. There are more tribal child and family support programs and service delivery programs for abused and neglected children (Goodluck 1999). There has been increased training on the ICWA at the state and tribal levels, and many states and tribes have signed cooperative agreements. ICWA case law has evolved to support the goals of the original act in respect to the best interests of Indian children.

In the 1980s, despite the passage of the ICWA, removal and placement of Indian children actually rose. For instance, public welfare agencies were responsible for 52 percent of Indian child welfare cases, and only 35 percent of these children were placed in Indian homes (Earle 2000). Data are limited, but relative to the general population, disproportionate placements of Indian children in substitute care continue to this day (Red Horse et al. 2000). That one-fifth of Indian children are still being placed outside of tribal and family environments indicates the failure of courts, social welfare agencies, and attorneys to abide by the act (Graham 1998/99). There have been at least forty controversial Indian adoption cases since implementation of the ICWA (Philips 1997). In these cases, either attorneys or the courts chose not to follow the protocol of the act, with disastrous results for all involved.

The problematic aspects of implementation can be linked to a continued lack of priority regarding Indian concerns and interests and an ongoing tacit underlying agenda for the assimilation of Indians (George 1997). The ICWA is federal legislation, but it requires federal, state, and tribal cooperation for full implementation. Varying laws, values, loyalties, and jurisdictional concerns must be negotiated (Goodluck 1999), and historically tribes and states have had antagonistic and uncooperative relationships (Monsivais 1997). The indifference of some states reflects not only a lack of information about the act, but perhaps also underlying beliefs that the best interests of Indian children are outside the tribal community. Unfortunately, jurisdictional problems translate into lengthy delays in child custody and welfare proceedings that leave children in limbo.

One problematic aspect of the ICWA is that it does not specify the criteria of "good cause" for state courts to retain custody of Indian child welfare cases. This clause has led to varying interpretations by states and great controversy. In respect to less clearcut custody cases, the BIA issued non-binding interpretative guidelines recommending full justification when a state court decides not to follow placement priorities. The Supreme Court, in determining the outcome of the *Mississippi Band of Choctaw Indians v. Holyfield* (1989), argued against varying state interpretations of "good cause" and stated that Congress did not design the act to permit state by state variability in its application (Stiffarm 1995).

A further challenge to the ICWA is the Existing Indian Family Doctrine, which has been argued by state courts in several custody cases. Essentially this doctrine has served as an exception to the act in cases in which families of children appeared unconnected to their tribes. In the case of Baby Boy L., the child's family was not regarded as sufficiently "Indian" and, therefore, the child was deemed exempt from the ICWA (Monsivais 1997). The judicial exemption under the doctrine was sustained because it was decided that the parents were not connected, or were only minimally connected, to their tribal communities and cultures. This legal doctrine, however, was not a component of the original ICWA and, in fact, violates the act and was a clear affront to tribal sovereignty.

A lack of trained personnel has also been an issue in implementation of the ICWA. Social workers are frequently the first points of contact in child welfare cases, and if they lack knowledge of the ICWA or regard for it, deleterious consequences result for children, families, and communities. In a related matter, the available service models for children and families tend to be based in the values of the broader U.S. society and are not culturally applicable in a different context.

A lack of funding for tribes to establish and maintain child and family services programs and to accept jurisdiction over some Indian child welfare cases is another barrier in the implementation of the ICWA. The original act authorized federal funding to tribes, but these grants have not been sufficient to fund even 25 percent of the need and have diminished over time (Cross, Earle, and Simmons 2000). Major sources of federal funding for child welfare purposes are found in Title IV-E, Foster Care and Adoption Assistance, and other programs of the U.S. Department of Health and Human Services. Indian tribes have not, however, received full benefits because these programs were not planned with tribal culture in mind or the unique relationships between tribes and states and tribes and the federal government. Also, programs such as Title IV-E require the establishment of cooperative agreements between tribes and states, and impediments to such arrangements sometimes arise because of historical and current tensions between the two parties.

Recommendations for Future Legislation

The Indian Child Welfare Act has been one of the most controversial congressional measures, in part because it gives Native American communities and parents rights relating to the appropriate cultural and racial placement of Native American children. Nonetheless, it represents a progressive effort in Indian child welfare and should be regarded as legislation in evolution (Monsivais 1997). Various bills in the 2000–2002 congressional session—including H.R. 2644 and, prior to that, H.R. 1082, S. 569, and S. 1213—were introduced to rectify the ambiguity and loopholes of the original act. In July 2001 Reps. Don Young (R-Ark.), J. D. Hayworth (R-Ariz.), David Camp (R-Mich.), and Christopher Cannon (R-Utah) introduced H.R. 2644 to correct, in part, weaknesses relative to voluntary adoptions brought to light in certain high-profile cases. None of these bills has been passed, however, and as of early 2002 H.R. 2644 remained pending before the 107th Congress.

Education of state and child welfare workers about the ICWA is another step needed for full implementation of the act. Training should include information on the history of federal Indian policy, the premise of the ICWA and guidelines for its implementation, the examination of cultural factors in risk assessment of Indian child welfare cases, culturally applicable information and skills on prevention and intervention involving child abuse and neglect, guidance for successful cooperation with tribal programs, and cross-cultural delivery of services (Bending 1997; Cross, Earle, and Simmons 2000). Content of such training should also encompass strategies for building cooperative arrangements between tribes and tribal welfare workers and the state court and welfare workers.

Support for family and tribal services is a necessity for future legislative and service efforts regarding the welfare of Indian children, as are efforts that bolster and promote Indian culture. Traditional tribal communities had mechanisms for the protection of children in respect to abuse and neglect (Cross, Earle, and Simmons 2000); these traditions still exist and should be regarded as resources in family preservation (Red Horse et al. 2000). Current thinking requires a shift from a deficit model to models that recognize and respect the implicit strengths of Indian families and that incorporate indigenous models of kinship and parenting. Indian children have been and continue to be highly valued and are regarded as gifts rather than property. One strength of tribal cultures is the network of shared parenting created by the extended family structure prevalent among American Indians. Not only do children have many adults involved and interested in their development, but parental stress is minimized through the support offered by kin. The strengths of an extended kin network serve as indigenous forms of child protection.

The pursuit of family preservation is an orientation that should include culturally based service models to address prevention and intervention efforts relative to child welfare. The first goal, prevention, would eliminate the need to remove children from their homes through a process of strengthening families. In cases where removal is necessary, intervention would require efforts to rehabilitate families and reunite children with them (Jones et al. 2000). The Adoption Assistance and Child Welfare Act of 1980 represented an advance in family preservation models, but it was directed toward mainstream families and, therefore, inadequate for addressing the situation of American Indians (Red Horse et al. 2000). In respect to tribes, family preservation models should be rooted in the notion of internal sovereignty; that is, tribal definitions of families, kinship, and child rearing should prevail.

A final recommendation is for the establishment of mechanisms that allow tribes direct access to funds for child and family support and welfare services and for managing Indian child welfare cases. The National Indian Child Welfare Association has provided several excellent recommendations related to needed tribal resources for child welfare services and child protection (Cross, Earle, and Simmons 2000):

- greater access to child welfare and child abuse prevention funds through the U.S. Department of Health and Human Services and the Bureau of Indian Affairs
- amendment of Title IV-B, subpart 1, of child welfare services regulations to create a funding base level of no less than $20,000 per fiscal year for all tribes
- increased funding for evaluation of services and dissemination of this knowledge
- funded at the levels originally authorized for Public Law 95-608 (which, among other purposes, establishes placement standards for Indian children), ICWA, and Title II tribal child welfare services and programs
- funding at authorized levels for Public Law 101-630, the Indian Child Protection and Family Violence Prevention Act, and Title IV grant programs for prevention and treatment of child abuse.
- promotion and support of culturally based service methods
- full funding for Indian-specific training, technical assistance, and resources
- tribal access to trust-fund-type financing for child abuse prevention
- greater dissemination of information about efforts that have proved effective among Indians, and
- creation of a needs-based budgeting process for HHS and BIA that is relevant to the real needs of Indians.

Summary

Numerous cases in the literature illustrate the destructive effects of the removal of Indian children from their homes and cultures. The Indian Child Welfare Act of 1978 represented a progressive step toward ensuring that Indian people would no longer experience the devastation to their children, families, and culture that they had experienced in the past by acts of states and the federal government. Clearly, effective efforts to remedy shortfalls in the implementation of the ICWA require sensitivity to the unique characteristics of Indian tribes in respect to family and kinship networks, values regarding socialization and education of children, dynamics of tribal government, courts, and social service programs, and government-to-government relations with the states and federal government.

Bibliography

Bending, R. L. 1997. "Training Child Welfare Workers to Meet the Requirements of the Indian Child Welfare Act." In *The Challenge of Permanency Planning in a Multicultural Society*, edited by G. R. Anderson, A. S. Ryan, and B. R. Leashore, 151–164. New York: The Haworth Press.

Cross, T. A., K. A. Earle, and D. Simmons. 2000. "Child Abuse and Neglect in Indian Country: Policy Issues."

Families in Society: The Journal of Contemporary Human Services 81 (no. 1): 49–58.

Earle, K. A. 2000. *Child Abuse and Neglect: An Examination of American Indian Data.* Seattle, Wash.: Casey Family Programs.

George, L. J. 1997. "Why the Need for the Indian Child Welfare Act?" In *The Challenge of Permanency Planning in a Multicultural Society*, edited by G. R. Anderson, A. S. Ryan, and B. R. Leashore, 165–175. New York: The Haworth Press.

Goodluck, C. T. 1999. "Necessary Social Work Roles and Knowledge with Native Americans: Indian Child Welfare Act." In *Family Ethnicity: Strength in Diversity*, edited by H. P. McAdoo, 293–300. 2d ed. Thousand Oaks, Calif.: Sage.

Graham, L. M. 1998/99. "The Past Never Vanishes: A Contextual Critique of the Existing Indian Family Doctrine." *American Indian Law Review* 23 (no. 1): 1–54.

Jones, B. J., et al. 2000. *Indian Child Welfare Act: A Pilot Study of Compliance in North Dakota.* Seattle, Wash.: Casey Family Programs.

Monsivais, J. 1997. "A Glimmer of Hope: A Proposal to Keep the Indian Child Welfare Act of 1978 Intact." *American Indian Law Review* 22: 1–36.

Philips, S. 1997. "Indian Child Welfare Act in the Face of Extinction." *American Indian Law Review* 21: 351–364.

Red Horse, J. G., et al. 2000. *Family Preservation Concepts in American Indian Communities.* Seattle, Wash.: Casey Family Programs.

Stiffarm, D. L. 1995. "The Indian Child Welfare Act: Guiding the Determination of Good Cause to Depart from the Statutory Placement Preferences." *Washington Law Review* 70 (October): 1151–1174.

12

The Native American Graves Protection and Repatriation Act and American Indian Religious Freedom

James Riding In

The National Museum of the American Indian Act of 1989 (NMAIA) and the Native American Graves Protection and Repatriation Act of 1990 (NAGPRA) represent major steps by Congress to extend various protections to indigenous peoples—the American Indians, Alaskan Natives, and Native Hawaiians. These statutes resulted from bipartisan support in response to calls by indigenous peoples and millions of their supporters for human rights legislation aimed at granting them burial rights and religious freedom. These acts also provide a legal means for Native Americans to repatriate lost cultural objects held by federal agencies and museums. Although many non-Indians now champion Indian rights in these matters, history has bestowed a privileged status on certain individuals who share a normative commitment to preserving a status quo rooted in racism, sacrilege, and oppression. Put another way, gaps in federal and state policies and statutes, construction activities, and illegal grave-looting operations continue to impede the burial rights of indigenous people. Moreover, U.S. museums and federal agencies still hold thousands of human remains of indigenous peoples' ancestors and sacred objects in violation of Indian spiritual beliefs and legal, moral, and ethical considerations that apply to the rest of U.S. society.

Indigenous Burials and Sacred Objects

Like many other peoples of the world, American Indians and Native Hawaiians believe in the sanctity of the grave and in an afterlife. Although mortuary traditions and religious convictions vary among them, many feel that the spirit of a deceased individual is associated with the physical remains. Relatives and friends often place pottery, pipes, and other items considered necessary in the afterlife alongside the body of their deceased loved ones. Interment also varies, but the dead usually possess a sacredness that encompasses values and beliefs and has led to established, acceptable ways of acting while in cemeteries and in the presence of the deceased. Indigenous peoples consider their burial places sacred sites. Unauthorized tampering with graves constitutes desecration and sacrilege. According to many indigenous peoples, what affects the dead also affects the living.

Indigenous peoples use various types of ceremonial objects in their religious life. Oftentimes, they consider these objects as cultural property and as being so sacred that the keepers of the objects have to follow carefully crafted rules of inheritance. Among the Pawnees and others, for example, sacred bundles come from the Creator and must be used in the seasonal round of religious ceremonies. The Hopis use masks in their rituals. Giving or selling these objects to outsiders violates their laws and customs.

American Indians and Native Hawaiians lost their power to protect their dead and to use their sacred objects without interference through a series of policies, practices, and laws perpetrated by the United States and its citizens. Since the arrival of Columbus, Euro-Americans have considered indigenous peoples as inferior, pagan, barbaric, and lacking moral worthiness. These stereotypes served as convenient rationales for the colonizers to justify acts of aggression against indigenous peoples, as well as against their lands, resources, burials, and religions. In an Indian and Native Hawaiian context, the magnitude of the resulting desecration can be termed a spiritual holocaust and genocide.

Grave robbing in the United States has a dual legacy of infringing on human rights and creating conflict. In New York City during the early 1790s, rioting that resulted from the theft of bodies from local cemeteries by medical students led to the enactment of the first burial protection law in this country. Although every state had enacted laws protecting cemeteries from looters and vandalism, these statutes excluded Indian and Native Hawaiian burial places. In this milieu, looting indigenous graves became a fashionable pastime for fun, profit, and study. During the early 1800s, Samuel G. Morton, the father of physical anthropology, paid U.S. soldiers, federal Indian agents, and settlers to steal skulls from Indian graves and ship them to him for craniometric studies. Morton's research, designed to validate popular beliefs concerning the alleged intellectual and cultural superiority of Anglo-Saxons over non-Anglo peoples, led to other developments. In 1867 the U.S. surgeon general issued the first in a series of memoranda instructing army field surgeons to collect the skulls of Indians killed in battle and skeletal remains belonging to the Mound Indians for study at the Army Medical Museum (AMM). During the next thirty or so years, AMM curators amassed the crania or bodies of approximately four thousand Indians.

Federal workers and individuals in the sciences, museums, academia, and other areas rather simply established a fictive claim of ownership over indigenous graves when, in actuality, indigenous peoples never ceded ownership of their dead. During the late 1800s, professional and amateur archaeologists, joined by museum curators, waved the banner of science to justify their digs, collection practices, and studies. University graduate programs in physical anthropology and archaeology established a body of scholars that specialized in the exhumation and study of indigenous bodies and grave contents. Museums abetted in the sacrilege by acquiring, displaying, and warehousing stolen skulls, bones, and grave goods for the enjoyment of their patrons. These illicit operations produced an archaeology and museum industry that thrived on Indian grave contents. Such professional organizations as the Society for American Archaeology (SAA) and the American Association of Physical Anthropology (AAPA) surfaced as benefactors and promoters of "scientific" grave looting. In the twentieth century, grave looters—whether archaeologists, amateur pot hunters, or developers—disrupted the final resting place of perhaps as many as two million people.

The pillaging of indigenous graves led to American Indians and Native Hawaiians losing many sacred objects. During the 1880s federal policymakers, supported by public opinion and missionaries, criminalized many religious ceremonies of indigenous peoples. In the United States, the implementation of these oppressive measures occurred when Indian life had reached a nadir. Federal policy, designed to facilitate and legalize nationalistic expansion through diplomatic, militaristic, and coercive means, had left Indians subjugated, depopulated, economically dependent, and confined on reservations. Their removal from their homelands exposed the graves of their ancestors and loved ones to thieves. Federal agents took children from their families and placed them in distant boarding schools, used rations to impose social and political control over reservations, and disrupted cultural activities considered antiquated and "uncivilized." The threat of incarceration for using cultural objects for ceremonial purposes, the specter of hunger, and acts of religious conversion encouraged people to sell the sacred objects in their custody to museums and private collectors. These "voluntary" transactions often occurred in violation of tribal laws and customs. The loss of these sacred items meant that elders could not pass on religious knowledge to future generations. Many U.S. universities and museums, such as Chicago's Field Museum of Natural History and New York's American Museum of Natural History, acquired vast amounts of Indian religious items. Museums in other parts of the world also collected Indian religious materials and human remains, until federal legislation imposed legal sanctions of the activities of foreigners.

U.S. expansionism and the accompanying exploitation of indigenous graves and cultures cemented a bond between the archaeology and museum industry and the federal government. The Antiquities Act of 1906 classified the contents of Indian graves on federal lands, including Indian reservations, as cultural resources belonging to the United States. The law required archaeologists and others who wanted to excavate Indian sites on public lands to first obtain a permit and place all unearthed items in a repository for study in perpetuity. During the twentieth century, federal work relief programs, archaeology programs, and salvage archaeology operations excavated thousands of burials. Many states followed the federal model, enacting laws asserting state ownership of Indian remains on state lands. Indigenous graves on private lands in most states, however, remained under the control and ownership of the property holders. Meanwhile, collectors and auction houses placed a high premium on Indian religious objects and grave items, especially pottery and other cultural items.

Repatriation and Burial Protections Laws

It took a social movement rooted in the concepts of indigenous spirituality, justice, and sovereignty to produce change. Many Indians and Native Hawaiian activists view the looting of their graves of their ancestors as religious, moral, and criminal transgressions. To them, the removal of bodies and funerary objects from graves interrupts the spiritual journey of the deceased, creating the potential for harming the living. Reburial enables the spirits to resume their journey and restores a sense of balance among the living. The retrieval of sacred objects in museums gives them an opportunity to preserve and renew elements of their spirituality.

Beginning in the late 1960s, indigenous protestors challenged the privilege bestowed on the archaeology and museum industry and the legal discrimination that classified their dead as cultural resources of the United States. They demanded burial protections and the right to repatriate confiscated human remains, funerary offerings, and sacred objects belonging to them and their ancestors but held in museums. Thus, their movement was one that sought to obtain property rights and burial rights taken for granted by the rest of U.S. society. The legislation emanating from the struggle is human rights law underpinned by issues of religious freedom.

The repatriation advocates persevered in the face of overwhelming odds. Determined to maintain their sanctioned status, many archaeologists emphatically opposed virtually all proposed measures aimed at protecting indigenous cemeteries from desecration committed in the name of science. They equated the reburial of confiscated indigenous human remains with book burning and as a threat to their careers, livelihood, and reputations. Simultaneously, museum curators jealously guarded the items in their collections. Compounding matters, U.S. society had been conditioned to accept as legitimate the functions of archaeologists and museums in the collection, display, and study of indigenous bodies and sacred objects. Seldom, if ever, did a member of dominant society challenge the notion that Indian burials were also sacred places, not archaeological sites. Few, if any, questioned the morality of displaying cultural items that had been taken under duress, coercion, and hunger. Basically, the archaeology and museum industry had convinced the public that indigenous burials and cultural objects were, indeed, resources of the United States.

Despite opposition from the archaeology and museum industry, indigenous advocates of repatriation presented a powerful message that resonated loud and clear with the public and among politicians. Growing numbers of archaeologists broke ranks and supported repatriation. Their renunciation of "imperial archaeology" was not, however, purely altruistic and uncalculated. Many of them—thinking that the repatriation movement endangered archaeology—viewed alignment with the cause of indigenous rights as a way to gain the confidence of indigenous peoples and governments so that they could continue their work. Some states responded during the 1970s and 1980s by extending their burial protection laws to include Indian graves. Since then, other states, including Arizona, California, Nebraska, and North Dakota, have enacted laws enabling Indian nations to repatriate and rebury human remains and associated funerary objects ancestral to them.

When the 1980s closed, the public mood had swung in favor of a federal Indian repatriation policy. In 1989 in Santa Fe, New Mexico, Smithsonian Institution officials adopted an accord with Indian leaders and repatriation advocates. Later that year, Congress enacted this historical agreement by passing the National Museum of the American Indian Act. The statute enables Indian nations to repatriate from Smithsonian collections those human remains and funerary objects linked to them by a preponderance of evidence. The act's provisions, however, leave other Indian remains classified as "culturally unidentifiable" and funerary items in the possession of the Smithsonian.

The NMAIA repatriation provision applied only to the Smithsonian, but Congress now stood poised to make repatriation a national policy. The Native American Graves Protection and Repatriation Act, signed into law by President George Bush in November 1990, protects burials on federal and tribal lands and establishes a legal framework for American Indians and Native Hawaiian organizations to repatriate those human remains and funerary and cultural objects that are linked to them by a preponderance of evidence and held in museums, universities, and agencies that receive federal funding (except the Smithsonian). NAGPRA covers four major categories of objects: culturally affiliated human remains; affiliated and unassociated funerary objects; culturally unidentifiable human remains; and objects of cultural patrimony and sacred objects. It also criminalizes trafficking in American Indian human remains. To create statutory uniformity in federal repatriation policy, Congress subsequently amended NMAIA in 1996 to enable Indian nations and Native Hawaiian organizations to repatriate objects of cultural patrimony and sacred objects from the Smithsonian.

Both of these acts and state law have allowed indigenous peoples to make significant recoveries. Collectively, they have repatriated and reburied thousands of human remains and funerary objects from the Smithsonian, other museums, and federal agencies. They have also recovered a growing list of sacred objects and objects of cultural patrimony. In some instances, museums have taken religious objects off public display until the people affiliated with them can make final determinations about their disposition. Thus, the repatriation policy opened new and important avenues of dialogue and cooperation between museums and American Indians and Native Hawaiians, although some contention and mistrust remain. Many anthropologists, scholarly organizations, and museum administrators continue to be philosophically opposed to repatriation. Consequently, some repatriation efforts have become mired in controversy.

Unfinished Business

Despite the progress these laws represent, some of their inadequacies and problems are beyond the realm of acceptance. First, museums have occasionally returned objects contaminated with arsenic, mercury, strychnine, and DDT, poisonous chemicals applied to ceremonial masks and other objects as insect and rodent repellants. Objects treated in this manner cannot be used, touched, or worn without raising health concerns, including death. Bearing the cost of detoxifying such objects lies with the Indian nations, not the institution responsible for applying the chemicals. Second, a lack of funding has hampered repatriation efforts. NAGRPA grants are available for Indian nations and Native Hawaiian organizations to identify, document, and repatriate human remains and cultural items, including funerary objects, sacred objects, and objects of cultural patrimony. Museums may also apply for this funding. The competitive nature of the NAGPRA grant selection process, however, means that Indian nations without the resources to employ skilled grant writers are at a severe disadvantage. Third, some institutions, including various federal agencies, are not in compliance with NAGPRA because they have not completed their inventories of human remains and cultural objects as required by law. NAGPRA provides for the issuance of civil penalties by the secretary of the interior for noncompliance, but as of mid-2002 no penalties had been assessed. Whether because of inadequate resources, stalling, or opposition, such situations have frustrated Indian repatriation efforts.

A fourth source of tension and conflict between indigenous reburial advocates and the archaeology and museum industry is the fate of tens of thousands of human remains classified as "culturally unidentifiable" in museum collections. NAGPRA leaves the NAGPRA Review Committee, a body established under NAGPRA to monitor and review the act's implementation, with the responsibility of drafting regulations to determine the disposition of these remains. Five drafts have been completed, but none has gone to the secretary of the interior for approval, as required by law. Simply, the complexities of the repatriation controversy are extremely divisive, and the stakes are too high for both sides to reach a consensus. For many indigenous peoples, compromise is no solution; they categorically reject the NAGPRA designation of their ancestors still in museums and in graves as culturally unidentifiable. Claiming a biological and cultural affiliation with those human remains, Indians insist that the archaeology and museum industry has no moral, legal, or ethical grounds to maintain possession of these remains for study, even if tribal affiliation cannot be determined. Many Indians and Native Hawaiians feel that if they abandon the struggle to rebury their ancestors, non-Indian scientists will have a free hand to conduct destructive studies and treat these remains in other sacrilegious ways. They see the members of the archaeology and museum industry opposed to repatriation as "parasites" who function within an archaic realm heavily influenced by tenets of scientific racism, imperial archaeology, and discriminatory laws.

Federal policy supports the indigenous peoples' position, defining Native American human remains as those of people in North American before 1492 and their descendants, but the question of cultural affiliation looms large. Many archaeologists and museum curators want to maintain large collections of these remains for study. Yet, they profess a willingness to help indigenous peoples establish cultural affiliation with "culturally unidentifiable" remains through study. The Society of American Archaeology is a group that professes support for the repatriation of human remains in museums that can be linked to present-day peoples. In 1986 it issued a statement concerning the reburying of remains that reflects the inherent contradiction of the organization's actual position: "Whatever their ultimate disposition," it reads, "all human remains should receive appropriate scientific study, should be responsibly and carefully conserved, and should be accessible only for legitimate scientific or educational purposes." This position unquestionably favors a policy that would result in the retention of thousands of human remains in museums, leaving the older ones especially vulnerable.

While the SAA has taken a subtle approach to the disposition of the human remains identified as culturally unaffiliated, other groups and individuals have articulated unbridled contempt for NAGPRA and Indian rights, charging supporters of repatriation with political correctness and allowing politics to take precedence over science. Opponents' trivialization of indigenous rights and religious beliefs threatens the humanitarian and spiritual goals of the repatriation movement and, on the other hand, echoes a time-honored strategy for sowing the seeds of oppression.

Non-Indians still have the final say in matters pertaining to the disposition of the contents of indigenous burials. Not surprisingly, repatriation opponents, often found in federal, state, and private organizations, have negatively affected some high-profile reburial initiatives. In Nevada, the Northern Paiutes claimed the remains of a ten-thousand-year-old mummified body called Spirit Cave Man, who was found in the 1940s. After hearing the Paiutes present historical, ethnographic, and archaeological testimony, as well as oral tradition and statements concerning geography, the NAGPRA Review Committee decided that Spirit Cave Man is culturally affiliated with the Paiutes. The Bureau of Reclamation, the federal agency under the Department of the Interior responsible for managing millions of acres of federal lands in twelve western states, rejects this determination, and therefore Spirit Cave Man remains in an Idaho repository.

The 1996 disruption of a burial near Kennewick, Washington, on lands controlled by the Army Corps of Engineers touched off another bitter and acrimonious controversy involving scientists, assorted institutions, and five Indian nations. The disinterring of an individual estimated to be some nine thousand years old, and a local physical anthropologist's determination that the individual had "Caucasoid" features, led to wild speculation, complete with media coverage, that the man was of European origin and that Indians were not the first Americans. Some scientists call this individual Kennewick Man, while Indians refer to him as the Ancient One.

The Colville, Nez Perce, Umatilla, Yakama, and Wanapum governments claimed the Ancient One as their own. Rejecting a Corps of Engineers decision endorsing the Indians' claim, a group of scientists challenged the decision in federal court. The judge referred the matter to the Department of the Interior for resolution. On September 21, 2000, after reviewing the evidence and congressional intent, Secretary of the Interior Bruce Babbitt declared in a letter to the secretary of the army, "Section 12 of NAGPRA recognizes the unique legal relationship between the United States and Indian tribes. Given its purpose and this recognition, DOI construes the statute as Indian legislation. Therefore, any ambiguities in the language of the statute must be resolved liberally in favor of Indian interests" (Babbitt 2000).

Although Babbitt upheld the corps' decision, the scientists filed another lawsuit, blocking the return of the Ancient One. Among other legal arguments, they claimed that the judgment to repatriate violates their First Amendment right because the Constitution allows them the right to study the remains. The fate of the Ancient One's remains continues to rest in the hands of a federal judge. Whatever that judge's decision, it is likely that an appeal will follow.

A fifth problem is the placement of the administration of NAGPRA under the Archaeology and Ethnology Division (AED) of the National Park Service (NPS), which led to allegations of a conflict of interest. They assert that the AED has a pro-science bias that undermines and impedes the implementation of NAGPRA. In December 2001 responsibility for NAGPRA was delegated as a separate program, but many repatriation advocates are concerned that the AED still influences NAGPRA decisions. Sixth, backlogs in publishing repatriation notices in the *Federal Register*, caused primarily by an inadequate allocation of funding and perhaps meddling by the opponents of reburial, have delayed progress in repatriation.

These controversies notwithstanding, models and precedent do exist for the reburial of human remains classified as culturally unidentifiable. During the late 1990s the Colorado Historical Society, the University of Nebraska, Lincoln, and the state of Minnesota recognized the shared group identity of Indian nations with a historical connection to their states as the basis for entering into reburial compacts with them. These unprecedented agreements have enabled American Indians to go through the sad, but necessary, task of returning their ancestors, along with accompanying funerary objects, to the womb of Mother Earth.

The seventh problem arises because indigenous graves on state and private lands are unprotected from desecration. Despite federal policies protecting indigenous burials, grave looting continues in the absence of similar state laws. Individual pieces of pottery and other objects from indigenous graves can garner thousands of dollars in Europe and Japan. These potentially enormous economic gains encourage looters. Texas has refused or neglected to extend its antiquities and burial laws to cover private lands, thus inviting grave-looting activities. Landowners there still have the legal right to dispose of human remains found on their property as they see fit. They can excavate the burials themselves, allow others to do so, or leave them intact. In Utah, a landowner recently offered to sell permits for $2,500 a day to individuals to excavate Anasazi town and burial sites on his property.

Eighth, enforcement of extant burial protection laws constitutes another problem. Because of inadequate resources for the police and for the protection of burial sites, state laws often do not deter grave robbers from plying their trade. In Arizona, regardless of whether state laws apply to private lands, pot hunters operate in isolated settings without fear of apprehension or punishment. Some criminals have been convicted in a few instances of violating the law, but the unwillingness of prosecutors to bring offenders to justice may encourage criminal activities. In Tennessee, county prosecutors have failed to act against a property owner who has refused to obey a court order to cover burials exposed by erosion.

Finally, breaching the law in some cases provides scientists access to very old Indian remains. During the 1990s the Nebraska State Historical Society and a Douglas County sheriff allowed a four-thousand-year-old human remain found along the banks of Papillion Creek to be shipped to a physical anthropologist at the Smithsonian Institution under the guise of a forensic case. Who did the parties involved plan to bring to justice? No one. Under Nebraska law, uncovered human remains classified as forensic do not fall under the purview of the state's burial protection law.

Courts have occasionally provided Indian nations with some relief. In 1999 in Washington, the Lummis discovered that the city of Blaine had desecrated an ancestral cemetery at Semiahmoo, one of their old town sites on Puget Sound. After the expansion of a city sewage treatment plant had unearthed nearly fifty skeletons, the construction archaeologist had the remains placed in cardboard boxes and sent to Colorado. Other human remains from the site were crushed with the soil and used in a landfill. Outraged by the callous disregard for their dead, the Lummis stopped the excavation by filing suit against Blaine. The city agreed to pay the Lummi nation $1.25 million to cover the cost of recovering and reburying the scattered remains. Significant harm had, however, been done.

In a 2002 case, U.S. District Judge Lawrence L. Piersol ruled that the state of South Dakota and the Army Corps of Engineers had violated the law by failing to adequately protect human remains and artifacts inadvertently uncovered by workers along the Missouri River. Rather than following NAGPRA and consulting with the Arikara, Omaha, Ponca, and Sioux peoples who had once lived in the area, a corps archaeologist shipped the bones and cultural objects to a Rapid City facility. The state then denied an Indian request for access to the site for ceremonial purposes. The judge granted the plaintiffs an injunction ordering the Corps of Engineers to comply with the law and the state to grant Indians access to the site for religious purposes.

Solutions

As noted, NAGPRA leaves unresolved the fate of tens of thousands of "culturally unidentifiable" human remains now in museums and federal repositories. These remains represent perhaps as many as 200,000 individuals. In June 2002 the National Park Service presented a set of proposed regulations to the Review Committee that triggered new tensions. If approved by the Department of the Interior following a period of public comment, these regulations would empower institutions to make final determinations regarding the disposition of all human remains in question in their collections. Indians and Native Hawaiians fear that such authority would undermine their ability to repatriate and rebury all of their ancestors and that it elevates the interest of science over those of indigenous peoples.

Compounding matters, this NPS draft ignores recommendations adopted by representatives of American Indian nations and Native Hawaiian organizations in a December 2002 meeting at Arizona State University's law school. The preamble to these recommendations contains an affirmative declaration of Indian and Native Hawaiian ownership of the contested human remains. The recommendations are as follows:

1. Culturally unidentifiable Native American human remains are culturally affiliated to contemporary Native peoples, including federally recognized tribes, non-federally recognized tribes, Native Alaskan peoples, and Native Hawaiian people.
2. All Native American human remains and associated funerary objects, including those deemed "culturally unidentifiable," shall be under the ownership and control of contemporary Native peoples.
3. All "culturally unidentifiable" Native American human remains shall be speedily repatriated to Native peoples in accordance with procedures to be determined by contemporary Native American groups.
4. All scientific study of "culturally unidentifiable" Native American human remains shall immediately cease.
5. The federal government shall be responsible for funding the costs of this repatriation (Recommendations for Disposition of "Culturally Unidentifiable" Native American Human Remains under NAGPRA).

Additionally, the country must take all measures necessary to protect the sacred soils where indigenous remains are buried. It must punish those who desecrate those graves and who violate the law.

Conclusion

The National Museum of the American Indian Act and the Native American Graves Protection and Repatriation Act have created legal avenues for American Indians and Native Hawaiians to reclaim their lost human rights and cultural objects. These peoples, however, are still battling for the rights taken for granted by other Americans. They want the right to repatriate their deceased ancestors unencumbered, the right to a lasting burial, and the right of religious freedom. Their burial grounds are sacred sites that nonnatives have routinely desecrated in the name of progress, science, and profit. Further, museums still hold tens of thousands of indigenous human remains, along with funerary objects, classified by them as culturally unidentifiable.

If the United States is to live up to its democratic ideals, a national strategy and course of action aimed at protecting indigenous spirituality and burial rights must be developed. Indigenous representatives, organizations, and scholars must take a leading role in all dialogues and decision-making processes affecting their rights. It is a simple matter of justice to remove the barriers that prevent them from exercising the inherent rights that they enjoy under U.S. law. Because of the federal government's collusion in the desecration of indigenous sites, the United States also has an obligation to cover the costs of reburial.

Bibliography

Babbit, Bruce. 2000. Letter to Louis Caldera, Secretary of the Army. September 21. Available at www.cr.nps.gov/aad/kennewick/babb_letter.htm.

Bieder, Robert E. 1986. *Science Encounters the Indian, 1820–1880: The Early Years of American Ethnology.* Norman: University of Oklahoma Press.

Echo-Hawk, C. Roger, and Walter R. Echo-Hawk. 1994. *Battlefields and Burial Grounds: The Indian Struggle To Protect Ancestral Graves in the United States.* Minneapolis: Lerner Publications.

Harper, Kenn. 2000. Reprint. *Give Me My Father's Body: The Life of Minik, the New York Eskimo.* South Royalton, Vt.: Steerforth Press. Original edition, 1986. Frobisher Bay, Canada: Blacklead Books.

Mihesuah, Devon, ed. 2000. *Repatriation Reader: Who Owns American Indian Remains?* Lincoln: University of Nebraska Press.

Riding In, James. 2002. "Our Dead Are Never Forgotten: American Indian Struggles for Burial Rights and Protections." In *"They Made Us Many Promises": The American Indian Experience, 1524 to the Present,* edited by Philip Weeks. Wheeling, Ill.: Harlan Davidson.

Society of American Archaeology. 1986. "Statement Concerning the Treatment of Human Remains." May. Available at www.saa.org/Repatriation/repat_policy.html.

Thomas, David Hurst. 2000. *Skull Wars: Kennewick Man, Archaeology, and the Battle for Native American Identity.* New York: Basic Books.

13 The American Indian Religious Freedom Act of 1978

Lawrence W. Gross

On August 12, 1978, President Jimmy Carter signed into law the American Indian Religious Freedom Act, also known as Public Law 95-341. The legislation is brief. An introduction comprises the first section, which states the need for the act, reaffirming the importance of the freedom of religion, recognizing the centrality of traditional religions to American Indian life, and acknowledging that federal policies have often abridged the religious rights of American Indians. The relevant language reads as follows:

> *Resolved by the Senate and House of Representatives of the United States of America in Congress assembled,*
>
> That henceforth it shall be the policy of the United States to protect and preserve for American Indians their inherent right of freedom to believe, express, and exercise the traditional religions of the American Indian, Eskimo, Aleut, and Native Hawaiians, including but not limited to access to sites, use and possession of sacred objects, and the freedom to worship through ceremonials and traditional rites.

The second section directs the president to instruct the various entities of the federal government to examine their policies and procedures in consultation with the leaders of traditional American Indian religions. It further requires that the president report back to Congress within one year with the results of the evaluation and suggestions for legislative action.

Efforts at regulating and suppressing Native American spirituality date from the initial contact between Europeans and American Indians. In the English, French, and Spanish spheres of influence, colonists took measures early on to supplant native religions with Christianity. The U.S. government later took this same approach. In 1883 the United States established a system of tribal courts on Indian reservations for the express purpose of eliminating native religions. These courts of Indian offenses had the power to imprison Native Americans for practicing their traditions, although initial violations generally resulted in the withholding of rations.

The suppression of Indian religions remained federal policy until 1934, when John Collier became commissioner of Indian affairs during the administration of Franklin D. Roosevelt. Collier was a longtime student and admirer of Indian culture, having spent a significant amount of time among the Hopi. On January 3, 1934, he issued Circular 2970, *Indian Religious Freedom and Indian Culture*, a policy directive marking a sea change in the government's approach toward Indian religions. In regard to the Bureau of Indian Affairs, the circular reads, "No interference with Indian religious life or ceremonial expression will hereafter be tolerated." Additionally, punishment for the practice of Indian religions was banned. It should be noted, however, that this policy directive applied only to the Bureau of Indian Affairs in its dealings with Native Americans and had no effect on other federal, state, or local government entities.

While overt government policies opposing the practice of Indian religions came to an end in the 1930s, other federal policies and laws continued to inhibit Native Americans from engaging in indigenous religious expression. The turning point came in the mid-1970s, with grassroot organizational and protest efforts by spiritual and political tribal leaders at the American Indian Law Center in New Mexico. By 1977 the state of Indian religions was being investigated by a congressional conference committee. A report that would accompany the American Indian Religious Freedom Act details how Indians continued to have a number of problems with the free exercise of religion (U.S. Senate 1978b, 2–5). Enumerating these concerns, the report notes the denial of access to sacred areas, including to Indian cemeteries in use at the time of "Federal subjugation." An additional issue involved restrictions on substances. There the term *substances* was used in a broad sense to include a wide range of plant materials, although peyote was singled out as the most important example. Legal substances, such as sweet grass, were sometimes confiscated under the suspicion of being illegal drugs. Also, federal officials opened sealed medicine bundles, thus rendering their sacred power ineffective. Possession of animal items was also problematic. Turkey feathers were confiscated, while possession of authentic eagle feathers for religious purposes was prosecuted. Finally, government officials interfered directly and indirectly with religious events. Such incidents made apparent the necessity of protecting Indian religions from government interference.

Legislative History

The American Indian Religious Freedom Act was introduced in the Senate by James Abourezk (D-S.D.) on December 15, 1977, as Senate Joint Resolution 102. Later, James Udall (D-N.M.) introduced the bill to the House of Representatives as House Joint Resolution 738. The Senate held hearings on the bill, but the House did not. Testimony came mainly from two groups: American Indians and government entities (U.S. Senate 1978a). The Indians testified overwhelmingly in favor of the legislation.

Most testimony from the executive branch supported the bill. Secretary of Agriculture Bob Bergland was particularly enthusiastic about the act. In his written statement, Bergland indicated that he had already implemented a task force to review his department's policies and expressed his hope the department's task force could serve as a model for other parts of the government (U.S. Senate 1978b, 7). Thaddeus Rojek, chief counsel of the Customs Service, also declared his support (U.S. Senate 1978a, 145–147; 1978b, 7–9).

In contrast, the Department of Justice expressed reservations about the legislation (U.S. Senate 1978b, 10–11). Larry Simms, representing the Office of Legal Counsel, stated that in the view of the department, there were two issues of concern: the Establishment Clause of the Constitution limits the degree to which the government can give preferential treatment to Indians, and the act might override existing legislation. Both concerns were eventually mitigated by the expressed intent of Congress and the language of the act.

The report Senator Abourezk prepared to accompany the act addressed the intent of Congress in the Section-by-Section Analysis: "The clear intent of [section one] is to insure for traditional native religions the same rights of free exercise enjoyed by more powerful religions. However, it is in no way intended to provide Indian religions with a more favorable status than other religions, only to insure that the U.S. Government treats them equally" (U.S. Senate 1978b, 6). The final language of the act contained no provisions for the legislation to supersede existing law. Instead, it merely required that the president in his report make suggestions about changes in the law that might be necessary to ensure the intent of the bill. The Department of Justice gave its support to the legislation once its concerns were allayed, and the act went on to pass the Senate by unanimous consent (*Congressional Record* 1978, 8365–8366).

The act met with more resistance in the House of Representatives (*Congressional Record* 1978, 21443–21446). During the floor debate, representatives raised a number of issues. One of the central concerns involved the right of ingress and egress to private property. Reservations were also expressed about the sites that would be affected. Questions even arose about the definition of *American Indians*, and, as in the Senate, whether existing law would be superseded and whether the act violated the Establishment Clause by creating a protected class of citizens.

Each of these matters was addressed in defense of the act. Supporters pointed out that the act did not involve private property, only federal lands, mainly in the West and in Alaska. It was argued that because the government did not keep a list of sacred sites for other religions, doing so for Indians would not be appropriate. *American Indians* was defined by statutes dealing with Indian rights, and it was stated in the act that the new legislative wording would not affect existing laws. Finally, bill supporters clarified that the act would not establish a protected class of people, but merely reaffirm the free exercise rights of American Indians.

Representative Udall added to the record a letter from the Department of Justice supporting the bill, stating that it was the understanding of the department that the act would not infringe upon the Establishment Clause and that the act would not affect existing law (Carter 1978, 2:1417–1418). The final language of the act would provide no right for substantive claims to be made. Also of significance were statements made on the floor by Udall in which he said of the act, "It has no teeth in it. It is the sense of the Congress" (*Congressional Record* 1978, 21445). These words would figure greatly in the subsequent court history of the act, as its weakness would become abundantly evident. With representatives' concerns allayed, the bill went on to pass the House by a vote of 396-2, with 34 abstentions.

As noted, the act mandates that a task force report back to Congress relating administrative changes made in light of the act and recommendations for changes to existing law. The task force, chaired by Secretary of the Interior Cecil D. Andrus, dutifully submitted the *American Indian Religious Freedom Act Report* to Congress in August 1979 (U.S. Federal Agencies Task Force 1979). The document includes hundreds of pages of records of consultations with various government entities, most of which claim no conflict with Indian religious freedom. Still, the task force presented thirty-seven pages of recommendations in such areas as cemeteries, sacred objects, and ceremonies and traditional rites (ibid., 51–87). Few administrative changes were suggested, and Congress did not change any laws. In the meantime, the act began to enter the arena of judicial action.

Court History

Throughout the 1980s a number of cases involving Indian religious freedom came before the courts at various levels (O'Brien 1991). Many of the cases concerned the issues raised in the 1978 report by the Senate Select Committee on Indian Affairs (U.S. Senate 1978b). Of particular interest were the issues of access to land and use of peyote, which were eventually brought before the Supreme Court in *Lyng v. Northwest Indian Cemetery Protective Association* (1988) and *Employment Division, Department of Human Resources of Oregon v. Smith* (1988), respectively.

Lyng involves land in the Sierra Nevada Mountains of California, where in the late 1960s the Forest Service had proposed building a road through the Six Rivers National Forest. The primary purpose of the road was to facilitate logging in the area, although easier access for recreational use and administrative oversight were also presented as justifications for construction. The forest, however, is sacred land to the Karok, Tolowa, and Yurok. These Indians continued to inhabit the lower reaches of a number of rivers in northern California and had long used the "high country," as they called the mountains, for religious purposes centering around access to sacred power through isolated visuals. A pristine environment and undisturbed silence are necessary conditions for these religious activities. Additionally, while certain locations are favored, the sacred quality of the land as a whole provides inspiration for the religions of these tribes.

After enactment of the American Indian Religious Freedom Act, the Forest Service, following the dictates of the law, commissioned a study to examine the impact of the proposed road on Indian religious practices. The investigators, in the Theodoratus Report, so-called after the lead author, Dorothea Theodoratus, concluded that the road would destroy the character of the wilderness necessary for the continuation of the practice of the Indians' religion and thus their worldview (Theodoratus, Chartkoff, and Chartkoff 1979). Further, they found the road of only marginal importance to the Forest Service in that alternative routes were already available. The report concludes, in no uncertain terms, that the road should not be built.

Ignoring the results of the report, the Forest Service proceeded with its plans to build the road. After construction began, the Karok, Tolowa, and Yurok, along with a number of other parties, including the state of California, sued to stop the project. The district court and the court of appeals both agreed with the Indians and the state. The evidence, as summarized by the Theodoratus Report, clearly showed that building the road would have a detrimental impact on the religious practice of the Indians, so the Forest Service was enjoined to stop construction.

In late 1987 *Lyng* reached the Supreme Court, which handed down a decision on April 19, 1988, overturning the lower court rulings. In short, as stated by Justice Sandra Day O'Conner, "Whatever rights the Indians may have to the use of the area those rights do not divest the Government of its right to use what is, after all, its land" (at 453). The Court held, in effect, that the government can do whatever it wants with its property, even if such use will most likely result in the destruction of a religion.

In regard to the American Indian Religious Freedom Act, the Court noted that the legislative intent of the bill did not "confer special religious rights on Indians," and as such, provided Indians with no judicial recourse. In reviewing the legislative history of the act, the Court noted that Representative Udall specifically stated that the act "has no teeth in it" (at 455). Additionally, the Court found that the Forest Service had fulfilled the mandate of the law in consulting with religious leaders, as included in the Theodoratus Report, even though the Forest Service ignored the results of that consultation. In essence, the Court ruled that merely consulting with religious leaders was sufficient; the government was under no obligation to act on the advice of Indians. In this case, neither the First Amendment of the Constitution nor the American Indian Religious Freedom Act was sufficient to secure Indian religious rights.

Employment Division v. Smith involves the use of peyote by two people participating in a ritual of the Native American Church. Alfred L. Smith and Galen W. Black were substance abuse counselors working with the Douglas County Council on Alcohol and Drug Abuse Prevention and Treatment in Oregon. While off duty, they ingested peyote at a ritual conducted by the Native American Church, for which they were subsequently dismissed from their jobs. The Oregon Employment Division ruled that they were fired for just cause and thus not eligible for unemployment benefits.

Smith took his case to court and won in state court, with the Oregon Supreme Court finding that the state of Oregon had violated his freedom of religion. The state appealed to the U.S. Supreme Court. For its part, the Court initially remanded the case back to the Oregon Supreme Court to determine whether Oregon state law prohibited the use of peyote without exception. The Oregon Supreme Court determined that while state law provides for no exceptions, First Amendment protections plus the intent of the American Indian Religious Freedom Act, among other considerations, grant constitutional protection for the use of peyote by members of the Native American Church.

The state of Oregon again appealed to the U.S. Supreme Court, which in 1990 dealt a severe blow to the Free Exercise Clause of the Constitution in general and Indian religious freedom in particular. Before *Employment Division v. Smith*, the compelling interest test, which had been the standard for judging freedom of religion cases, required that the government show a compelling state interest in order to override the exercise of religious freedom. In this case, the Supreme Court abandoned this approach. Instead, in a 6-3 opinion written by Justice Antonin Scalia, the Court focused on the nature of state law in Oregon, which was neutral in its applications, and banned the use of peyote without exception. The Court found that the state of Oregon was under no obligation to take considerations of religious practice into account, so denying Smith unemployment benefits was not unconstitutional. In effect, the Supreme Court found that legislatures, such as in Oregon, may pass laws that infringe on the free exercise of religion so long as the laws are otherwise neutral in their application to the general public.

The majority opinion made no mention of the American Indian Religious Freedom Act, but the minority opinion considered the act relevant to the case (at 921). Citing portions of section one, the minority noted that the act is the expressed resolve of Congress to protect and preserve American Indian religions. There was recognition by the court that the act does not create "rights enforceable against government action restricting religious freedom" (at 921), but the minority argued that unless the Court carefully attends to the religious claims of American Indians, "both the First Amendment and the stated policy of Congress will only offer to Native Americans merely an unfulfilled and hollow promise" (at 921).

Subsequent History

The *Lyng* and *Smith* decisions are important in that they generated congressional responses involving the American Indian Religious Freedom Act. As a result of *Lyng*, in 1988 Representative Udall proposed an amendment to the act directing managers of federal lands to allow American Indians access to them for religious purposes. Congress did not initially enact the amendment and continued to reject it when it was reintroduced with modifications throughout the 1991 session.

In addition to other legislative action, Congress passed the American Indian Religious Freedom Act Amendments of 1994 (Public Law 103-344). The amendments deal specifically with the results of *Smith* and make lawful the religious use of peyote. Additionally, it states that applicable benefits under public assistance programs will not be denied to Indians who use peyote for bona fide religious purposes—the very issue that gave rise to *Smith* in the first place. Indeed, as the House Committee on Natural Resources made clear in a 1994 report, part of the intent of the amendments is to undo *Smith* (U.S. House 1994, 5–8).

Various court decisions, but particularly *Lyng* and *Smith*, have demonstrated the inability of the original American Indian Religious Freedom Act to provide relief for the protection of the free exercise of religion. It is unclear, however, what effect the amendments of 1994 will have on future cases involving the religious use of peyote.

Bibliography

Carter, Jimmy. 1978. *Public Papers of the Presidents of the United States: Jimmy Carter.* 2 vols. Washington, D.C.: Government Printing Office.

Congressional Record. 1978. 95th Cong., 2d sess. Vol. 124. April 3: 8365–8366; July 18: 21443–21446.

Department of the Interior. 1934. Bureau of Indian Affairs. *Indian Religious Freedom and Indian Culture*, by John Collier. Circular 2970. January 3.

O'Brien, Sharon. 1991. "A Legal Analysis of the American Indian Religious Freedom Act." In *Handbook of American Indian Religious Freedom*, edited by Christopher Vecsey. New York: Crossroad.

Theodoratus, Dorothea J., Joseph L. Chartkoff, and Kerry K. Chartkoff. 1979. *Cultural Resources of the Chimney Rock Section, Gasquet-Orleans Road, Six Rivers National Forest.* Fair Oaks, Calif.: Theodoratus Cultural Research, for the U.S. Forest Service.

U.S. Federal Agencies Task Force. 1979. *American Indian Religious Freedom Act Report.* PL 95-341. Washington, D.C.: Department of the Interior.

U.S. House of Representatives. 1978. Committee on Interior and Insular Affairs. *American Indian Religious Freedom.* 95th Cong., 2d sess. House Rept. 95-1308.

———. 1994. Committee on Natural Resources. *American Indian Religious Freedom Act Report.* 103d Cong., 2d sess. House Rept. 103-675.

U.S. Public Law 95-341. *American Indian Religious Freedom Act.* 95th Cong., 2d sess., April 3, 1978.

U.S. Public Law 103-344. *American Indian Religious Freedom Act Amendments.* 103d Cong., 2d sess., October 6, 1994.

U.S. Senate. 1978a. Select Committee on Indian Affairs. *American Indian Religious Freedom.* 95th Cong., 2d sess. Senate Hearings 961-9 and 961-10. February 24 and 27.

———. 1978b. Select Committee on Indian Affairs. *Native Americans' Right to Believe and Exercise Their Traditional Native Religions Free of Federal Government Interference.* 95th Cong., 2d sess. S. Rept. 95-709.

State and Federal Power

14 The Scope of State Power in American Indian Affairs

David E. Wilkins

In *United States v. Kagama* (1886), the Supreme Court handed down one of its most powerful opinions on the political status of indigenous peoples and defined their relationship to the federal government and the states. The case dramatically transformed tribal-federal relations by sharply diminishing tribal sovereignty on the grounds that tribes and their citizens were "wards" under federal "guardianship." In the arena of tribal-state relations, the Court's comments were more in keeping with the U.S. Constitution and the political history of Indian-white relations than with the wishes of American Indian people. The Court maintained that "they [tribes] owe no allegiance to the States, and received from them no protection. Because of the local ill feeling, the people of the States where they are found are often their deadliest enemies." This description of tribal-state affairs is nearly as apropos at the beginning of the twenty-first century as it was at the end of the nineteenth century.

Conflicts and occasional agreements over such diverse subjects as education, taxation, law enforcement, burial sites and funerary objects, water, hunting and fishing practices, environmental regulations, and, the most recent and one of the most explosive topics, gaming on Indian lands, represent some of the issues that the tribes and states deal with in their intergovernmental relations. When the federal government joins the fray, the situation has the potential of being exacerbated or ameliorated.

Although tribal-state relations invoke a host of substantive political, constitutional, and cultural issues, there is a paucity of literature about this subject, and confusion predominates, largely because the literature and discourse remains heavily slanted toward describing and defining the tribal-federal relationship. It is certainly understandable why this relationship receives so much attention: the federal government remains the dominant politico-economic unit, although that reality has changed in recent years with the Supreme Court's redefinition of federalism and its resuscitation of state sovereignty on virtual par with federal sovereignty in many aspects of American Indian policy.

Nevertheless, since early in the Republic's existence, tribal-state affairs have developed concurrently, if sporadically, alongside those on the tribal-federal, state-state, tribe-tribe, and tribal-local levels. In fact, recent federal legislation and litigation suggests that the relationship between tribes and states has gained sufficient stature as to be of nearly equal political significance to the tribal-federal relationship. This development has potentially profound implications for tribal sovereignty and jurisdictional authority.

A Federalized Relationship

The political relationship between indigenous nations and the federal government is codified in Article 1, section 8, of the U.S. Constitution: "the Congress shall have Power . . . to regulate Commerce with foreign Nations, and among the several States, and with the Indian tribes." Furthermore, the government-to-government affairs between tribes and the U.S. government are evidenced in myriad treaties and agreements, executive orders, case law, statutes, regulations, and congressional appropriations.

The same does not hold true for the tribal-state relationship. There is no express guidance on this matter in the Constitution, it is not outlined in tribal or state constitutions, and it flails from ad hoc and inconsistent federal policy directives. Tribal nations, state governments, and the federal government acknowledge that the primary relationship for most federally recognized tribes—only a small number of tribes are recognized by states but not by the federal government—is with the federal government on a nation-to-nation, or government-to-government level, which is rooted in the doctrines of inherent tribal sovereignty, congressional plenary power (read, exclusive authority) to manage the federal government's affairs with tribes, and the treaty process.

Despite the federalized nature of this relationship, over the course of history tribes and states have arrived at a mutual, if uneven, coexistence. In the thirty-four states where federally recognized tribes reside, the two distinctive polities share contiguous lands, with every reservation, Indian allotment, and Indian community surrounded by the state border. States and tribes also share some common citizens in that Indians are citizens of their tribal nation as well as the state, while non-Indians only enjoy state.

Although states and tribes share some citizens and lands, in their relations as sovereign entities historically they have each jealously guarded their collective rights to political powers, economic and natural resources, and cultural historics. As a result, tension has been a hallmark of tribal-state relations. Tribes have resented state attempts to tax and regulate their lands, wages, and industries and are displeased that many states remain reluctant to concede the reality of tribal sovereignty. States resent the fact that while they have jurisdiction over all activities and persons within their borders, this does not generally apply to tribal affairs or to Indians residing on reservations or trust lands, which are not subject to state jurisdiction or taxation.

The reasons for this tension date back to the colonial period and the debates about whether the national government or the individual colonies, and later states, would manage the nation's Indian affairs. At the Constitutional

Convention in 1787, delegates determined that Congress would have exclusive control over trade relations with indigenous peoples and that the national government, not the states, would retain treaty-making power in the country's relations with indigenous. As the United States expanded westward, the enabling acts and constitutions of most western states, home to most Indian reservations, were required to contain disclaimer clauses in which the states agreed to recognize the federal government's exclusive jurisdiction over the nation's Indian affairs. The federal government also required states to promise never to tax Indians within reservations or Indian trust lands.

Thus, five factors—congressional plenary (exclusive) power in Indian affairs, treaty-making capacity, Supreme Court precedent acknowledging federal sovereignty in Indian affairs, and state constitutional clauses, along with the inherent sovereignty of tribal nations—generally served to effectively preclude state governments from any direct involvement in tribal affairs. Notwithstanding these constitutional and legal protections, over time states assumed a greater jurisdictional presence inside Indian country. A major factor was the immigration of white settlers onto Indian lands. For as whites moved in, so too did various elements of state law and authority. These state intrusions, which occurred without tribal consent, were precipitated by federal action either in the form of Supreme Court decisions—for example, *United States v. McBratney* (1881) and *Ward v. Race Horse* (1896)—or federal laws—for example, the General Allotment Act (1887), Public Law 83-280 (1953), various termination statutes (1953–1960s), and the Indian Gaming Regulatory Act (1988).

With the exception of these measures and the special political circumstances of New York and Oklahoma, which for historical reasons exercise considerable jurisdiction over the Indians within their borders, the general rule until the 1980s was that state laws had no force within Indian country unless Congress had expressly delegated authority to the state or unless a question involving Indians also involved non-Indians to a degree significant enough to call state jurisdiction into play.

Increasing State Presence in Indian Country

As the Supreme Court became more ideologically conservative in the 1980s, it shifted away from a reliance solely on tribal sovereignty as a check on state law and toward a two-part test to determine which state laws could be applied to Indians on trust land without congressional consent: a federal preemption test (a state law is void if it is inconsistent with federal law or interferes with overriding federal and tribal interests) and an infringement test (a state action is null if it infringes on the right of reservation Indians to be self-governing).

A number of more recent Supreme Court opinions have, however, seriously eroded even these tests: *Brendale v. Confederated Tribes and Bands of Yakima Indian Nation* (1989), *Cotton Petroleum v. New Mexico* (1989), *County of Yakima v. Yakima Nation* (1992), *Seminole Tribe of Florida v. Florida* (1996), *Strate v. A-1 Contractors* (1997), and *South Dakota v. Yankton Sioux Tribe* (1998). The current operating presumption of the Rehnquist Court is that state law is applicable in Indian country unless the affected tribe can show that the state's action will have a significantly adverse effect on the tribe or its resources or that Congress has expressly precluded the state's intrusion. This is a dramatic departure from the way the tribal-state relationship was understood until the last two decades of the twentieth century and runs afoul of tribal sovereignty, exclusive federal authority, the treaty relationship, and state constitutional disclaimer clauses.

Even as the Supreme Court challenges tribal sovereignty's force vis-à-vis states' rights, tribes and states in some cases have demonstrated a greater willingness to engage in constructive dialogue in an effort to avoid expensive litigation when their interests conflict. In recent years some tribes and states have entered into sovereignty accords—policy statements that formally recognize the sovereignty of each signer—participated in cooperative agreements, developed comprehensive policies on their relations, sought to eliminate negative Indian stereotypes and to educate citizens about Indian rights, and entered into negotiated settlements in an effort to establish friendlier relations.

Serious problems linger concerning the substance and meaning of tribal sovereignty, Indian gaming, hunting and fishing rights, religious freedom, and taxation. Litigation, therefore, remains the most common technique for settling differences, although there is little evidence that this process promotes a deeper understanding of each other's problems or needs.

Intergovernmental relations between tribes and states are dynamic and fluid. They are complicated by the overarching presence of the federal government, which on the one hand has treaty and trust obligations toward tribal nations but on the other hand is constitutionally wedded to the states. Relations will improve, from a tribal perspective, only if states recognize tribal sovereignty. States contend that tribes must in turn be willing to consider their interests if a tribal government embarks on economic development projects or makes environmental decisions with implications beyond reservation borders. While jurisdictional uncertainty and economic competition will most likely persist between tribes and states, there is growing hope that more positive relations will evolve between the governments of the two polities as the two sovereigns come to recognize the right of the other to protect the health, safety, and welfare of its citizens.

Bibliography

Cohen, Felix S. 1971. *Handbook of Federal Indian Law.* Albuquerque: University of New Mexico Press.

Deloria, Vine, Jr., and Clifford M. Lytle. 1983. *American Indians, American Justice.* Austin: University of Texas Press.

Deloria, Vine, Jr., and David E. Wilkins. 1999. *Tribes, Treaties, and Constitutional Tribulations.* Austin: University of Texas Press.

15 State and Federal Law and California Indians

Jack Norton

The constitutional treaty authority and legislative-judicial procedures that over the years guided U.S. relations with Native Americans also served to truncate and negate California Indian sovereignty. This contravention resulted from an admixture of the tenets of Manifest Destiny, the Mexican War (1846–1848), the Civil War (1861–1864), and Reconstruction and perceived Southern complicity in the effort. From the 1880s until well into the twentieth century, the U.S. government, preoccupied with economic and imperialistic surges abroad, abrogated its obligations to California Indian nations. As a consequence, these nations became scattered, isolated, and generally disorganized. By mid-century their governments and cultures had become targets for elimination based on a new government policy called "termination." During the last quarter of the century, California Indian nations reasserted their sovereignty through growing economic and political sophistication. The legal and political history of California Indians can best be presented by dividing it into six phases.

Phase I (1847–1849)

Official relations between California Indians and the federal government were established after the Californios, Mexican descendants of the Spanish settlers living in California, surrendered to U.S. forces at Cahuenga on January 13, 1847, during the Mexican American War. In March of that year, General Stephen W. Kearny, the first administrator of California, appointed John Sutter and Marino Vallejo as subagents of Indian affairs. During their tenures, they introduced patterns of exploitation and self-interest that would haunt California Indians for years. Sutter, for example, used Maidu and Nissen men, women, and children for economic and personal gain, and Vallejo captured and enslaved hundreds of Wappo and Pomo to work his estates north of San Francisco.

In May 1847 Col. Richard Mason, a Virginian that replaced Kearny as military governor, launched a series of restrictions on Indians similar to the Black Codes in the South after the Civil War. California Indians had to show upon demand certificates of employment and carry passes when moving from one area to another; they could not gather in groups or crowds without causing suspicion. In central California, Indians could not own horses or firearms. Further, Congress ratified the Treaty of Guadalupe Hidalgo in May 1849, ending the Mexican American War and ceding lands from New Mexico to California to the United States. As an international treaty, the civil rights of Mexican citizens, including Indians, superseded domestic laws in this realm (Art. VI, cl. 2). During this period, however, Congress was consumed with the debate over extending slavery into the newly acquired territories. Harsh military codes continued to be applied in California, and in November 1849, Peter Burnett and John McDougal, the first elected governor and lieutenant governor of California, respectively, called for the extermination of the Indians there. In April 1849 Adam Johnston was appointed the first U.S. Indian agent of California.

When gold was discovered in California in January 1848, more than a hundred thousand men inundated the territory. By the fall of 1849, the ratio of males to females was twelve to one. In the first years of the gold rush many men took Indian women as concubines and disrupted Indian lives with terror, disease, and murder. Reports of these conditions ultimately reached the Department of the Interior's newly formed Bureau of Indian Affairs.

Phase II (1850–1870s)

On April 22, 1850, the California legislature passed the Act for the Governance and Protection of Indians, bonding Indian persons of all ages to varying periods of servitude. The law stipulated that in "no case shall a white man be convicted of any offense upon the testimony of any Indian." In addition, California Indians could be arrested for loitering, drunkenness, or leading a profligate life. Indians had to labor from a week to several months to make bail. This law exceeded federal responsibilities and obligations and allowed for the rampant victimization of California native people. California Indians were generally paid small wages or compensated with discarded clothing and in many cases with hard liquor.

In 1860 this law was amended to liberalize the apprenticeship of Indian children, more than four thousand of whom were indentured in the northern counties. When the gold mines became less productive, some individuals turned to kidnapping and selling children, particularly young girls, to miners and farmers. Those who fought back were harried and in many cases murdered by federal troops and local volunteer units, who were paid by the state of California more than $1 million for their services. In addition, these volunteer groups were encouraged by government leaders to file for property within Indian homelands.

From 1851 to January 1852 the United States negotiated eighteen treaties against a backdrop of reports of genocidal activities from Johnston and others. The total acreage promised to California Indian nations was less than 3 percent of their aboriginal lands, yet the citizenry of California and the legislature pushed to reject ratification on the grounds that too much valuable land was being left to "savages."

On July 8, 1852, the U.S. Senate, under pressure from white leaders in California, rejected the treaties in closed session, ordered them filed, and denied public access to them. The California Indian signatories were not notified of the treaties' fate.

By September 1852 Congress superseded presidential treaty authority and appointed Edward Beale, a former naval officer in the Mexican American War, as superintendent of Indian affairs to California. Beale proposed establishing five military reservations—that is, reservations created by the War Department when dealing with hostile Indians—that would be supported by Indian labor. By fall 1853 Beale had established Fort Tejon and the Tejon reservation in southern California on the Sebastian reserve, a highly productive Indian community. The five military reservations (created between 1853 and 1864) and adjoining Indian farms were manipulated in size and number by the dictates of California citizens. In the meantime, Congress passed the California Land Claims Commission Act in March 1851, which primarily reviewed claims of ownership by former Californios. The act also charged the commission with protecting Indian ownership of land. All counties in the state were required to send Indian records to the three-member commission in San Francisco. Most counties refused to do so, and the commissioners failed to enforce compliance. Consequently, California Indian sovereignty was generally impaired.

In 1859 various county supervisors began rejecting Indian claims for goods and services within their jurisdictions. Further, the California legislature upheld these actions. In Mendocino County, for example, the Pomo Indians were directed to report to the Mendocino or Round Valley reservation. Many Indians refused because of the dismal and often life-threatening conditions on the reservations; several reservations lacked an adequate water supply. On the Mendocino reservation, irresponsible logging practices had destroyed the yearly salmon runs, a vital resource for many California Indians. Corruption and fraud were widespread within the California office of Indian affairs. In 1858 Superintendent Thomas Henly was charged and dismissed for fraud and malfeasance for diverting Indian assets to private accounts for personal gain. Congress responded by reducing the annual budget for California Indian services by two-thirds.

Phase III (1879–1920)

In 1869 President Ulysses S. Grant, embarrassed by the national scandal of corruption and incompetency within the Bureau of Indian Affairs, turned to religious denominations to find people to administer Indian policies. Congress, busy with Reconstruction programs, readily confirmed these religious nominees, thereby enacting Grant's so-called Quaker Policy. In California, the Catholic Church had converted, often by force, thousands of Indian people. The Episcopalians were assigned to many western reservations. In some areas of California, divisive and bitter debate over religious doctrine severed Indian groups and families. In addition, the religious administrators generally attempted to suppress Indian rituals and ceremonies, causing further isolation and disorientation. Maintaining their cultural identity was particularly difficult for California Indians. By 1900 only five thousand Indians were identified as living on reservations; the remaining eleven thousand were scattered throughout the general population or lived in small family groups in isolated areas. Furthermore, by 1883 the Bureau of Indian Affairs had codified a list of Indian offenses that included religious, medicinal, and marriage customs and using Indian languages.

Meanwhile, administrators implemented governmental assimilationist policies through Indian day schools in northern California on the Round Valley and Hoopa reservations. In 1887 Congress passed the General Allotment Act, or Dawes Act, which sought to divide reservations into family farms headed by adult males. The superiority of Christianity, values of Victorian domesticity, and Jeffersonian yeomanry of landownership formed the core of the act's program. In addition, Congress continued to encroach upon Indian sovereignty by passing the Major Crimes Act in 1885, which placed capital crimes committed on reservations under federal jurisdiction. Indian victims of white murderers, rapists, and robbers could not press charges in local or state courts. With the passage of the Indian Homestead Act of 1875, California Indians could choose to receive land, and in the process receive U.S. citizenship, or they could retain their tribal membership, and status as ward of the government, and continue to fend for themselves.

From 1900 to the 1920s the Bureau of Indian Affairs, through internal mandates, often denied medical and welfare services to Indian people. By 1906, for example, congressional investigations documented extraordinarily bad health conditions among California Indians due to near starvation, poverty, and tuberculosis and trachoma. Congress appropriated $100,000 for purchases of land and betterment of homeless California Indians. These reform efforts rectified some blatant governmental injustices. By 1910 the government had established an additional twenty-five reservations, or *rancherias*, across California. This federal policy of creating reservations continued and grew until 1950, resulting in the establishment of 117 new reservations in California that totaled less than 700,000 acres of the original 91 million acres of aboriginal territory. In the first half of the twentieth century, philanthropic organizations began to advocate for improvements to the Indians' situation. The Indian Board of Cooperation, a Methodist association founded in 1913, sought to improve Indian educational services in Mendocino County and supported *Anderson v. Mathews* (1917), which led to citizenship for California Indians. In the 1920s the association promoted a monetary per capita settlement for the lands set aside for the Indians, but never given to them, in the unratified treaties of 1851–1852. The Mission Indian Federation in southern California opposed such intrusive governmental policies as allotments by resisting them and advocating for upholding the rights of tribal sovereignty. The California Indian Brotherhood, the first all-Indian intertribal organization in California, was founded in the northern part of the state in 1926. Its primary goal was to provide public schooling for California Indian children, supporting them with lunches and clothing on their way to a college education.

Phase IV (1920–1950)

During the early 1920s many influential organizations, including the Commonwealth Club of San Francisco, the Federated Women's Club, the Native Sons of the Golden West, and others, agitated for compensating California Indians for confiscated lands. In 1927 the state authorized its attorney general to sue the federal government to grant remuneration for California Indian lands lost through the earlier unratified treaties. The following year, Congress passed the Jurisdictional Act, which enabled

California Indians to sue the federal government; the suit was filed before the U.S. Court of Claims as *Indians of California v. United States.* In a complex and protracted litigation, the U.S. government determined that all goods and services provided California Indians since 1852, including the cost of needles, shovels, harnesses, and old World War I uniforms, would be deducted from any award. In December 1944 the court awarded the Indians compensation of approximately $17 million, or $1.25 an acre. An offset of $12 million was deducted, and the remaining $5 million was distributed to 36,000 California Indians in the early 1950s.

The Indian Reorganization Act of 1934 (IRA) recognized that the Dawes Act had been disastrous and often used as a weapon to divest Indians of their homelands. Thus, the allotment policy was abandoned. The IRA encouraged self-government through tribal councils in California, and made available revolving loans for economic development. Most California Indian nations, however, refused to adopt the measures proposed under the act because of long-standing distrust of the U.S. government and its processes. Ironically, the Great Depression brought much-needed work to California Indian reservations through the Civilian Conservation Corps and the Forest Service as well as enlistment in the armed forces during World War II.

While *Indians of California v. United States* brought some government redress, many California Indians were outraged by the unjustness of the compensation they received. When Congress created the Indian Claims Commission in 1946 to sort through the growing number of land claims, California Indians sued for the remaining 91,764,600 acres of the state. By 1951 twenty-three separate claims had been filed before the commission. After a long and arduous fight, Congress finally authorized payment of an additional $29 million in 1964. The claims commission, however, reduced the litigated land to 64,425,000 acres and declared forty-seven cents per acre an equitable judgment. No adjudication, apology, or compensation for the genocide committed or for any moral wrongs or breach of fair or honest practices was forthcoming.

Phase V (1950–1970)

Meanwhile, in 1951 the commissioner of Indian affairs dispatched special agents to California to implement federal termination policies, which called for ending federal services to California Indians. The state passed a resolution supporting these procedures and in 1953 created the Senate Interim Committee on Indian Affairs to aid in the transfer of property and services to state control.

In 1953 the U.S. House of Representatives passed Concurrent Resolution 108, which instituted the termination policy, as well as H.R. 698, which created a program to relocate Indians from their reservations to urban areas, providing them with housing assistance and job training. By 1960 thousands of generally unskilled, poor, and culturally isolated Indians had moved to San Francisco and Los Angeles. (As a result of these acculturation efforts, Los Angeles County today is home to the largest Indian population in California.) The federal government arbitrarily limited services in health, education, and economic development programs. For instance, the Johnson-O'Malley Indian Education Fund was restricted severely. The Sherman Indian School was closed to California Indian students by the 1950s. Congress also passed Public Law 83-280, giving states, including California, criminal and civil jurisdiction over Indian nations. Although Public Law 83-280 intended to provide "law and order" on reservations, various counties began to use it to enforce local building codes and zoning ordinances.

In 1958 Congress implemented the Rancheria Act, which provided for the termination of federal trust responsibility and divided tribal assets among individual members. The Rancheria Act required that state standards be met in regard to health, water, and sanitation prior to the discontinuance of trust status. The Bureau of Indian Affairs often coerced California Indians into implementing the provisions of the act. Between the years 1958 and 1970, forty-one reservations, or *rancherias*, were officially terminated by the act, thus denying these communities federally recognized tribal status and governments.

Following the civil rights movement of the 1960s, federal and state investigative bodies and advisory commissions documented the oppressive conditions and high mortality rates among California Indians. The State of California created the Commission on Indian Affairs but overlooked Indian membership on the commission. By 1967 California Indians began to assert themselves through the American Indian Law Center and California Indian Legal Services, which litigated cases affecting the status of Indians throughout the state. Further, the California Indian Education Association challenged the exclusion of California Indians from the Sherman Indian School, as well as the reduction of Johnson-O'Malley funds for educational assistance. The Department of Public Health's Bureau of Maternal and Child Health established nine centers to assist young Indian mothers. In addition, the Indian Civil Rights Act of 1968, and later the Indian Self-Determination and Education Assistance Act of 1975, enhanced Indians' basic freedoms of speech, press, and assembly. The creation of the Intertribal Council of California in 1968 was a crucial step toward unifying and informing scattered tribes.

In 1969 several California universities began academic programs within Native American studies programs geared toward educating Indian scholars for participation in the broader academic community and fostering participation in the National Indian Education Association. The California Rural Indian Health Board began restoring health services throughout the state. Finally, the occupation of Alcatraz Island to dramatize the historical injustices and lack of treaty rights by a coalition of Californian Indian tribes marked the 1960s as a decade for reversing the historical legacy of 123 years of federal and state ineptitude and mistreatment.

Phase VI (1970–2001)

In California, the early 1970s brought Indian protests, demonstrations, and occupations of federal and state properties. The Pitt River nation occupied parts of Lassen National Forest, near present-day Redding, to protest the loss of aboriginal lands. A group of Hispanic and Indian students occupied an abandoned missile sight near Davis and established the Daganawida-Quetzacotl University, which dedicated itself to Indian and Chicano rights. Today, after years of governmental threats and meddling, the university is an accredited two-year community college.

In 1972 Title IV of the Elementary and Secondary Education Act recognized the additional educational needs of Indian youth in the public schools. The state of California passed Assembly Bill 872, which created an Indian

Education Department in the Department of Education, and Senate Bill 1258, which established ten centers for Indian early childhood learning. In 1974 Senate Bill 2264 was passed to support Indian education centers throughout the state.

The Indian Self-Determination and Education Assistance Act of 1975 encouraged direct contact between tribes and the federal government in meeting the unique needs of the Indian community. In 1976 the Indian Crimes Act guaranteed equal treatment for Indian people before the law. Furthermore, the American Indian Religious Freedom Act of 1978 declared the inherent right of Indians to believe, express, and exercise their religions under the protection of federal law. The Indian Child Welfare Act of 1978 recognized that a disproportionate number of Indian children were being adopted by non-Indian families, thereby threatening Indian identity and community continuance. The act encouraged adoption and guardianship of Indian children by Indian families.

Tillie Hardwicke v. United States (1983) reversed the termination efforts of the Rancheria Act and began the long process of retribalization and federal recognition of the forty-one California Indian nations terminated in the 1950s and 1960s. *Cabazon Band of Mission Indians v. California* (1987) brought about a critical change for California Indians, as the Supreme Court determined that California could not regulate bingo and gambling on Indian reservations. Within a few years, successful casino-style gambling operations opened, particularly in urban areas of southern California, and California Indians began the process of becoming economically independent and politically astute. The following year, however, Congress passed the Indian Gaming Regulatory Act, which required Indian nations to sign contractual agreements with state agencies before offering casino gambling. In 1998 and 2000 the California nations sponsored Proposition 5 and Initiative 1A to challenge these restrictive compacts. Voters supported both measures overwhelmingly. At the beginning of the twenty-first century, California Indian nations stand on the threshold of cultural regeneration. They continue, however, to face a legacy of state and local encroachment upon their land and resources, particularly as local populations are generally covetous of Indian nationhood and sovereignty.

Bibliography

Cook, Sherburne F. 1943. *The Conflict between White Civilization and California Indians.* Berkeley: University of California Press.

Forbes, Jack D. 1969. *Native Americans of California and Nevada.* Healdsburg, Calif.: Naturegraph Publishers.

Garner, Van. 1982. *The Broken Ring: The Destruction of California Indians.* Tucson, Ariz.: Westernlore Press.

Heizer, Robert F., and Alan F. Almquist. 1971. *The Other Californians: Prejudice and Discrimination under Spain, Mexico, and the United States to 1920.* Berkeley: University of California Press.

Phillips, George H. 1996. *The Enduring Struggle: Indians in California History.* Salinas: Boyd and Fraser Publishing.

Law and the Land

16 Native American Tribal Property

Stacy L. Leeds

The extent to which Native Americans hold rights to land and other valuable resources has been a source of political, theological, and legal debate since European contact. As the original inhabitants of North and South America, Native American tribes held original title, or absolute property rights, to most of the hemisphere. As Europeans arrived in the Americas, the question of what to do about the Native American's preexisting property rights had to be addressed. The first group of Europeans to offer political opinions on the issue were Christian theologians, led by Francisco de Vitoria in the mid-1500s. De Vitoria thought that the Native Americans had property rights that could not simply be taken away by European "discoverers." One way Native American property could, however, be taken was by consent.

Many European settlers simply disregarded Native American rights and took lands for their own use. The sovereign nations of Europe, however, recognized and reaffirmed Native American property rights through a series of treaties with tribal governments. Great Britain, Portugal, and Spain negotiated treaties with tribal governments long before the founding of the United States. Following the Revolutionary War, the new U.S. government continued the precedent of treaty making with tribal governments until Congress ended the practice in 1871. Many of these treaties were premised on the notion of tribal governments relinquishing claims to certain property in exchange for a pledge that their property rights to other lands were secure.

Native American property rights were not only acknowledged by treaty, but also through early actions of Congress and decisions of the Supreme Court. Congress began regulating the transfer of property rights from Native Americans in the Trade and Intercourse Act of 1790. Although this act was an infringement on tribal governments' ability to freely transfer their property, it also had the effect of protecting tribal property from being freely acquired by settlers.

The Supreme Court's first attempts at defining tribal property rights had an effect similar to the Trade and Intercourse Act: Native American rights to property were limited yet protected from the whim of settlers. The Court's decision in *Johnson v. McIntosh* (1823) is the foundation of tribal property law within the United States. The Court's decision, based on the doctrine of discovery, acknowledged that tribal governments kept "aboriginal title" to their property but also that they were only allowed to convey or sell their property to the "discovering" European nation, such as Great Britain, or its successor in interest, the United States. Native Americans could not convey or sell their property to individuals, each other, or foreign governments. The current state of Native American property rights evolved from this core concept.

During the mid-to-late 1800s the U.S. government relocated many tribes to their present-day reservations, which were generally established by treaty or by executive order as a final homeland for the tribes. In a practical sense, reservations were intended to restrict Indians to a specific area, where they would remain separate from white settlers, for the safety of both groups. From a property law standpoint, the tribe and its citizens had exclusive use and occupancy of these reservations. The federal government generally held the land in trust for the benefit of the tribe. The land was therefore treated as a trust corpus, by which the tribe was the beneficiary and the federal government the trustee. This fiduciary relationship gave rise to a federal trust responsibility for the management of tribal properties. The land could not be sold or otherwise used by anyone except the tribe and its citizens without first obtaining federal approval. A few tribes held their property in "fee" status, which meant that it could be freely conveyed without stipulation by the federal government. These tribes were the minority.

The tribes "owned" the land on the reservations subject to trust limitations. The entire tribe held the property in common, with no recognized individual ownership. Tribal citizens were afforded the right to use the land rather than given complete title in the form of individual ownership. Contemporary American Indian advocates and scholars challenge the theory that common ownership was the only property concept historically recognized by tribes and Indian peoples. They contend that the tribes had complex property law systems that recognized and protected individual as well as group property rights. Tribal law systems addressed property conveyances during life and in probate.

In the 1880s changes in federal Indian policy made an enormous impact on tribal property with the push for the allotment, or parceling, of Indian land to individual members of the tribes. Federal officials and so-called advocates for Indian rights widely believed that the only hope for the future of the Indians would be to transform their common property holdings into individually owned plots of land. Through allotment and the adaptation of the agrarian lifestyle that would follow, American Indians would abandon their old ways and ultimately become productive U.S. citizens.

The United States codified its allotment policy with the implementation of the General Allotment Act of 1887. This legislation required that commonly owned tribal property be divided and its ownership transferred to individual Indians. Heads of households generally received 160 acres. The tribes, as governmental entities, were never compensated for the loss of these lands. Rather, the federal government viewed this transfer as a simple change in the status of the land that was in the best interest of the tribe. It thus saw its allotment policy as consistent with its obligation as trustee.

Often, after tribal members had received their allotment, some land remained in common on the reservation. Rather than leaving the remainder under tribal ownership, the United States labeled it "surplus" land, for which non-Indian settlers could apply for homesteads. To the tribes, this aspect of the General Allotment Act proved even more troubling than the individual allotments because it created an abundance of non-Indian-owned land within reservation boundaries. Many of the tribal-federal treaties had promised federal removal of non-Indian intruders on the reservations. Instead, the General Allotment Act made reservation land available to non-Indians, inviting their settlement.

The individual Indian allotments on reservations were generally held in trust by the federal government in a capacity similar to that for trusts of tribally held lands. That is, the federal government held the land for the benefit and use of the individual Indian, the beneficiary of the trust. Federal officials believed that trust status would protect the land against alienation by taxation, forced sale for debts, or other conveyances for less than market value. The original trust periods elapsed after a certain number of years, and the allotment would then be held in fee ownership by the individual. Once Indian lands were freely alienable, a high percentage of the land was lost to non-Indian ownership. It is estimated that more than two-thirds of allotted lands eventually ended up in non-Indian hands. This estimate does not take into consideration the additional 60 million acres of Indian lands that were lost to non-Indians under the surplus land conveyances.

As a result of the overwhelming loss of the Indians' land base, the miserable economic conditions that resulted, and charges of inhumanity toward Native Americans, federal Indian policy shifted in the 1930s to an emphasis on protecting what land remained in Indian hands. In response, Congress passed the Indian Reorganization Act of 1934, which included two provisions of significance involving tribal property. First, it ended the allotment process and extended trust periods to protect lands against alienation, and, second, it provided a process for tribes to petition the secretary of the interior to return certain lands to trust status.

Although the Indian Reorganization Act and other legislation attempted to reverse the affects of allotment, its legacy would remain. Tribes could never regain the millions of acres lost to allotment and surplus land conveyances. Further, the present legal circumstances surrounding many allotments render the lands useless in terms of economic development because of the complicated pattern of ownership. Trust lands are generally passed down from generation to generation, increasing the number of owners on a particular tract of land.

For instance, if owner A received an allotment in 1887, her land would be passed to her two children at the time of her death, in equal undivided interest. Assume A's two children, B and C, each had two children of their own. When B and C died, A's original 160 acres would then pass in equal interest to her four grandchildren. If those four grandchildren each have two children, and the land passes accordingly, the original allotment would become even more fractioned. The federal government's conveyance of surplus lands ensured that there would never be additional land available for tribal descendants. Instead, they were destined to become fractional owners of minute interests in the allotted lands. The Supreme Court's description of this problem in *Hodel v. Irving* (1987) is poignant:

> Tract 1305 is 40 acres and produces $1080 in income annually. It is valued at $8,000. It has 439 owners, one-third of whom receive less than $.05 in annual rent and two-thirds of whom receive less than $1. . . . The common denominator used to compute fractional interests in the property is [3 trillion, 394 million, 923 million, 840 thousand]. The smallest heir receives $.01 every 177 years. . . . The administration costs of handling this tract are estimated by the Bureau of Indian Affairs at $17,560 annually.

The fractionated ownership of Indian lands is one of the most problematic contemporary legacies of federal Indian policy; attempts by Congress to remedy the situation have failed. Descendants of the original allottees are left lands that cannot be mortgaged or otherwise economically developed. Leasing and other property uses of Indian trust lands are subject to the approval of federal agencies. That is, should an individual Indian want to enter into a lease with an oil company for drilling on trust property, the contract or lease is subject to federal approval as part of the trust obligation. Individual Indians that hold land in fee status can lease or contract their lands without such approval.

Tribal governments are, like any other entity, free to purchase lands available on the market. If a tribe purchases land, that land will be held in fee, freely alienable, by the tribe. The tribe, if it wishes, may petition to have the federal government place the lands in trust. Trust status ensures that the land will not be subject to alienation by the state and will generally be viewed as within the tribe's jurisdiction for purposes of regulation. Trust status does, however, give the federal government superintendence over land uses and conveyances.

Bibliography

Bobroff, Kenneth H. 2001. "Retelling Allotment: Indian Property Rights and the Myth of Common Ownership." *Vanderbilt Law Review* 54: 1559.

Cohen, Felix S. 1982. *Felix S. Cohen's Handbook of Federal Indian Law*. Charlottesville, Va.: Mitchie/Bobbs-Merrill.

Deloria, Vine, Jr., and Clifford M. Lytle. 1983. *American Indians, American Justice*. Austin: University of Texas Press.

Guzman, Kathleen R. 2000. "Give or Take an Acre: Property Norms and the Indian Land Consolidation Act." *Iowa Law Review* 85: 595.

Prucha, Francis Paul, ed. 1990. *Documents of United States Indian Policy*. 2d ed. Lincoln: University of Nebraska Press.

Royster, Judith V. 1995. "The Legacy of Allotment." *Arizona State Law Review* 27: 1.

17 Native American Water Rights and the Winters Doctrine (1908)

M. A. Jaimes-Guerrero

Each law passed by Congress should be studied in the context of its practice and its theoretical construction, particularly in regard to Indian law and public policy. Such an approach is essential in comprehending the case of Native American water rights and the legislative act that came to be known as the Winters Doctrine (1908). Through this legislation the U.S. government ostensibly acknowledged the "first rights" of tribal peoples to their land-based waters, while at the same time diverting such water off Indian reservations to non-Indian urban centers and for industrial development. The diversion of water left most reservation lands barren, unfit for productive farming or useful toward a self-sufficient economy. How this came to be is a story of subterfuge and obfuscation by federal authorities overseeing Native American property under the U.S. "trust responsibility."

Origins of the Indian Water Rights Conflict

According to U.S. juridical doctrine, indigenous people retain rights to all their lands—including water as a natural resource—that they do not freely relinquish or that Congress does not expressly remove from them by statute. This concept was perhaps best articulated by the Eighth Circuit Court in *Wall v. Williamson* (1945): "It is only by positive enactments, even in the case of conquered and subdued nations, that their laws can be changed by the conqueror." On the one hand, such interpretations led to the passage of numerous statutes specifically diminishing Indian rights in regard to water and other natural resources on their lands, but on the other hand, such rulings also were interpreted to mean that any disputes over treaty language should be resolved in favor of the Indians' understanding of the text. In a previous opinion in *Worcester v. Georgia* (1832), Justice John McLean had put forth the idea that "the language used in treaties with the Indians should never be construed to their prejudice. . . . How the words of the treaty were understood by this unlettered people . . . should be for the rule of construction." The principle was further framed in *Carpenter v. Shaw* (1930): "Doubtful expressions are to be resolved in favor of the weak and defenseless people who are wards of the nation, dependent upon its protection and good faith." The justices, however, left it up to Congress, not the Indians, to decide what constitutes a "just resolution" in disputes on Indian matters and affairs. Over the years, especially in the arid and semiarid regions of the West, some forces have sought to separate tribal land rights and water rights. Among these forces have been the railroads, one of the first major development interests, which brought with them enterprising speculators and a wave of settlers motivated by the 1862 Homestead Act encouraging settlement of the West and other related congressional legislation (Gates 1968).

In 1887 Congress passed the General Allotment Act, also known as the Dawes Act, which forced Native American tribes to divide their landholdings among individual members and give the federal government authority over any "surplus" lands (which it then sold to non-Indians). Under the Carey Act of 1894, the federal government gave some 9.75 million acres of impounded, surplus Indian lands to various western states (see Glass 1964). The states, in turn, were expected to sell these lands to private parties, thereby raising needed capital to help solve the problem of water shortages.

In 1902 Theodore Roosevelt, the "conservationist president," went on record as stating, "It is right for the National Government to make the streams and rivers of the arid regions useful by engineering works for water storage" (Hays 1959, 104). Federal control over water resources was (and remains) crucial to any development scheme but fundamentally conflicts with the states' rights sentiments of the Carey Act and earlier statutes. Consequently, in the National Reclamation Act of 1902 Congress attempted to impose a federal coordinating mechanism for water development while simultaneously placating states' rights advocates. Meanwhile, the first *Annual Report* of the newly created Reclamation Service (later the Bureau of Reclamation) observed, "It appears probable that in some of the States radical changes in the laws must be made before important [national] projects can be undertaken" (Department of the Interior 1903, 33). The federal government's approach to water projects was stalled by the Supreme Court's decision in *Kansas v. Colorado* (1907), which decreed that under existing laws the central government had virtually no legal basis for exerting control over nonnavigable waters within its borders.

Although legalists and legislators concede that American Indians retain clear title to their reservation lands, it is also argued that water—particularly such waters as rivers, streams, and aquifers that are not completely bounded by reserved territory—is a different matter. The policies that devolved from this thinking were to leave these indigenous peoples in possession of their residual landholdings, thus upholding "the letter of the law," while diverting for non-Indian use and profit the water to support enterprise as well as larger populations outside tribal reservations.

The Fort Belknap Indian Water Rights Case

In 1905 Fort Belknap, an Indian reservation for the Gros Ventres and Assiniboines in Montana, experienced its first water shortage, which was the result of the diversion of the Milk River for white settlement in the area. This led to the Department of Justice filing suit in behalf of the Indians and their water rights. Assistant U.S. Attorney Carl Rasch argued to the federal court that water rights were implicitly reserved for the reservation under an 1855 treaty and reaffirmed by an 1888 agreement. He further argued that the Gros Ventres and Assiniboines possessed a riparian right to the Milk River that superseded the prior use doctrine in Montana law.

Riparian rights are not quantified, and the legal concept is interpreted to mean that title to land abutting a stream carries with it a right to withdraw from that stream any amount of water necessary for "reasonable use"; it applies to all neighboring users of the stream. Also, riparian rights are permanent, not subject to loss through non-use since title inheres in the land, and in times of shortage all users share equally (see Clark 1978). By contrast, the statutory codes of western states conform to the principle that water is allocated through a hierarchy of rights based on the chronological order in which users obtain permits to appropriate water from a given source. Hence, this right is limited to a specific "quantified" amount for an officially approved "beneficial use"; non-use can result in loss, while in times of shortage the users high on the list can retain their full quota.

In *United States v. Mose Anderson* (1905), the U.S. District Court in Montana found in favor of the Fort Belknap Indians and issued an injunction against non-Indian diversion, because the Milk River water was necessary to reservation life and its economy. In deciding the case, however, the court rejected Rasch's argument of riparian rights, instead basing its conclusion on treaty rights: "[The] Indians . . . reserved the right to the use of the waters of the Milk River, at least to the extent reasonably necessary to irrigate their lands." The decision therefore established a new legal doctrine concerning federal Indian water rights that was open-ended in quantifiable specifics about water—that is, in regard to Indian first water rights premised on treaty rights. The settlers immediately responded by filing an appeal in the Ninth Circuit Court, but were disappointed when their appeal worked in favor of the Indians. Thus an appeal of what was then called *Winters v. United States* was filed with the Supreme Court, and in 1908 the circuit court decision was affirmed:

> In upholding the circuit court decision, the Supreme Court agreed (1) that in keeping with the western states' water rights, the date a reservation was established was to be considered as the date the waters were reserved (thus making Indians the senior appropriators on many western streams since most reservations were founded from the 1850s through the 1880s); but (2) that unlike state appropriation doctrine, the reserved right was not liable to extinction through non-use; and (3) the right need not be quantified if the appropriated waters are used to fulfill the reservation's purpose. (Burton 1991, 21)

Although the Supreme Court's ruling appeared to support the Indians, its previous decision in *Lone Wolf v. Hitchcock* (1903) negated any real claim to tribal victory. In *Lone Wolf*, the Court asserted U.S. plenary power over Indian property. Carrying this argument forward in

Winters, the justices' ruling placed the waters at issue under federal, not Indian control, an approach that became known as the Winters Doctrine. In essence, the federal government could proceed with centralized development of water resources throughout the West. The Fort Belknap case is representative of the conflict between tribal Indians and federal and state authorities.

Ultimately, no laws bearing upon the substance of *Winters* were to be passed during the first half of the twentieth century. Congress appeared to be content to utilize the federal power attendant to the ambiguous situation created by the courts while allowing the western states to slide off the political hook. Meanwhile, on the judicial front the scope of federal power over western waters steadily increased. In 1908 the Ninth Circuit Court heard *Conrad Investment Co. v. United States*, in which it amplified *Winters* by holding that Indians on the Blackfeet reservation possessed a paramount right not simply to the water necessary to meet their present needs but to future needs as well. This was followed in 1921 by another Ninth Circuit decision, *Skeem v. United States*, that native water rights pertained to entire reservations rather than just the acreage abetting rivers and streams. In addition, Indians held the rights to lease these rights whenever they leased portions of their lands (Andrews and Sansone 1983). In other words, the undefined extent of "Indian" water could not be diminished under any circumstances.

It soon became apparent how the federal government would "protect" these Indian water rights, when in 1913 the secretary of the interior arbitrarily divided waters for use on the Yakima reservation between the Yakimas and a federal reclamation project, with the Indians getting the short end of the stick. Although the *Winters* precedent provided ample basis for litigation on behalf of the Yakimas, Congress provided a "legislative remedy" in 1915 by enacting a bill appropriating funds to buy water from its own Reclamation Service to give to the reservation to meet its needs (McCool 1987, 57–58).

Comparable situations were developing throughout the West at about the same time the Yakima situation was unfolding; for example, the Pima and Maricopa O'Odham peoples of the Gila River reservation, established in southern Arizona in 1869, were in a similar circumstance (McCool 1987, 58–59). The infamous story of the development of Arizona starts with the Reclamation Service's building of the Roosevelt Dam, with BIA endorsement, to divert tribal land waters to settlements for the benefit of non-Indian populations. The project devastated the arid Indian lands, making them useless for farming or economic subsistence (Bishop 1991). The Roosevelt Dam, along with a complementary smaller dam on the Gila River, was completed in 1929. Half of the water the system controlled was allocated for federally approved non-Indian users (Department of the Interior 1916, 43).

The Bureau of Reclamation, the Army Corps of Engineers, and Those "Dammed Indians"

Lloyd Burton explains federal manipulation of the Winters Doctrine as follows:

> An enduring, intractable, and—from the standpoint of legal ethics—morally indefensible conflict of interest pervaded [enforcement of native water rights] and continues to do so to this day. The Interior Department, which through the Bureau of Reclamation (BuRec) was encouraging the rapid appropriation and development of water resources by non-Indian

> users . . . was also responsible through [BIA] for protection of the Indians' reserved rights in the federal courts . . . but predictably, Interior was far more active and successful in disarming its former responsibility than its latter one. Without the political power necessary to get budgetary appropriations for Indian [projects], the tribes were incapable of converting the *Winters* rights guaranteed them by the Supreme Court into actual beneficial use of their waters. Meanwhile, the remaining water resources were rapidly being appropriated by non-Indians, with BuRec acquiescence and support [to federally approved users]. (Burton 1991, 23)

A large part of how this process has worked in the past involves interlocks, called an "iron triangle" by one researcher, among the Bureau of Reclamation, state officials, and major corporate interests (McCool 1987, 257–258). Once the courts established federal authority over western water issues, state governments adopted a more "cooperative" approach in their dealings with the bureau. In 1922 Arizona, California, Colorado, Nevada, New Mexico, Utah, and Wyoming negotiated a compact on water apportionment among themselves. The apportionment was that the upper Colorado basin states (north of the Grand Canyon) would claim 7.5 million acre-feet of Colorado River water each year (Warne 1973, 191–192). Representatives of the indigenous nations in the area were excluded from participation and apportionment (and ultimately Arizona declined to agree to the compact's terms). The Bureau of Reclamation strongly endorsed the effort, and the compact was ratified by Congress in 1928 (and would do the same for a 1944 compact). In 1932 the governors of the above seven states then joined the Bureau of Reclamation in forming the National Reclamation Association (later the National Waters Resource Association, NWRA). Working with other organizations, such as the American Public Power Association, NWRA became at that time "the most powerful water lobby in the nation" (Harrison 1981, S-11).

In the early 1960s water issues eventually led to interstate squabbling between Arizona and California over how to share the Colorado River, an issue in which reservation Indian interests were not seriously considered, if at all. At one point the conflict led the governor of Arizona to call out the National Guard in an attempt to physically block diversion of the Colorado's water to California. The matter was eventually settled in *Arizona v. California* (1963), which prohibited local control of any water in the West but affirmed Indian reservations being "quantified" for minimal use (for the Navajo Indian Irrigation Project), for the benefit of non-Indian metropolitan monopolies (Bishop 1991, 86). It is interesting to note that Arizona must mine for water to meet demand.

To appreciate the extent of water development, much of it for non-Indian commercial and corporate purposes at the expense of the American Indians, one must look beyond the Bureau of Reclamation to the Army Corps of Engineers, the quasi-autonomous governmental construction firm. In 1966 the corps reported that it had completed more than four thousand projects, valued at $88 billion, including the following: building some 19,000 miles of waterways, 500 harbors, 350 reservoirs, 9,000 miles of flood control structures, 7,500 miles of "improved" channels, and 50 hydropower facilities with a generating capacity of 12 million kilowatts (Department of Defense 1973, 25–26; 1976). Although much of this work did not affect water consumption or directly affect reservation lands, a sizable portion of it did. In 1964 the Kinzua Dam in

Pennsylvania, as a case in point, flooded most of the Seneca territory (Levine and Lurie 1965, 68). Moreover, when the Bureau of Reclamation and the Army Corps of Engineers were brought together in 1978 under the jurisdiction of the Senate Subcommittee for Water Resources (Committee on Environment and Public Works), the two formed a governmental "supergroup," which allowed them to approach their tasks in an even "more coordinated, efficient and industrious" manner (McCool 1987, 89).

The Pick-Sloan Plan is another case in point illustrating the deleterious effects of federal actions on American Indian tribes. The plan called for the Bureau of Reclamation and the Army Corps of Engineers to build a massive complex of 107 dams along the Missouri River during the 1950s and 1960s to generate hydroelectric power and facilitate water diversion. The Arikara, Mandan, and Hidatsa of the upper Missouri shared the lands of the Berthold reservation, "one-fourth of [which] was flooded, including the best and most valuable and productive land on the reservation—the bottom lands along the river where most of the people lived" (McCool 1987, 177; Berman 1989). Ultimately, the Pick-Sloan Plan cost the indigenous nations of the Missouri Valley an estimated 350,000 acres of their best lands, including a number of burial and other sacred sites. It also led to further impoverishment and severe cultural and emotional trauma. As researcher Bernard Shanks observes, "The Missouri River Basin Development Program (MRDP) replaced the subsistence economy of the Missouri River Indians with a welfare economy. As a result of the project, the Indians bore a disproportionate share of the social cost of development while having no share in the benefits" (Shanks 1982, 116; see also Shanks 1974, 576; Deloria 1982). Michael Lawson, in *Dammed Indians* (1982) relates numerous other development schemes that had a devastating effect on Indians and their lands.

By contrast to the vast emphasis on the water needs of non-Indians, the federal government did almost nothing to provide water to Indian users during the sixty years following the *Winters* decision. As of 1968, it was officially estimated that only about 4 to 5 percent of all potentially agricultural land on western reservations had been irrigated (Bishop 1991, 84). Today the lack of irrigation has become particularly acute in extremely arid locales, such as southern (Tucson) and central Arizona (Phoenix metropolis), where the non-Indian population is burgeoning. In fact, Arizona has the largest and fastest-growing population nationwide. As a Republican Party stronghold, the state has welcomed "snowbirds" and corporate interests, enticing them with notorious tax loopholes devised at the expense of its taxpaying residents, Indians and non-Indians alike. Arizona is also the state with the largest reservation-based Indian populations and landholdings. The Navajo / Dine reservation is the largest, even spreading into three other states—Colorado, New Mexico, and Utah (at Four Corners)—and overlapping the San Juan River. The Tohono O'Odham (Papago) is the second largest reservation, located between Phoenix and Tucson.

The State of Indian Water Affairs

Conflicts over Indian waters continue, with the federal government orchestrating the pitched battles of tribal reservation Indians with non-Indian users and state authorities. Tribal Indians have met with some success, especially in the Northwest. The Umatilla in Oregon filed suit in *Confederated Tribes of the Umatilla Reservation v. Alexander* (1977), arguing that the Army Corps of Engineers, through construction of the (ironically named) Chief Joesph Dam, illegally interfered with the water flow necessary for the spawning of salmon and steelhead trout, the basis of their traditional indigenous economy. At about the same time, in Washington State, another tribe filed a similar suit—*Colville Confederated Tribe v. Walton* (1978)—concerning the corps' Catherine Creek Lake Dam, that was upheld by the Ninth Circuit Court. In both cases, the courts ordered the creation of a plan "in the public interest" to correct the problem, thus leading to the evolution of an unlikely alliance between Indians, environmental activists, the non-Indian sport fishing industry, and the U.S. Forest Service to advocate that the dams be removed.

Other tribes have not, however, been so successful in their juridical complaints concerning water and land rights. Take, for example, the case of *United States v. Cappaert* (1974) involving the water rights of the Pyramid Lake Paiutes of Nevada and the Ak Chin O'Odham in Arizona. Some Florida Indians and the southern California Mission Indians have faired similarly (U.S. Senate 1987). Essentially, when Native Americans have attempted to assert rights deriving from their nationhood status, they have had to compete with larger and more powerful corporate interests and in situations in which they are perceived as "low man on the totem pole" in the name of the national and public good. The U.S. government, through its trust responsibility, has actually eroded Indians' "first rights" to their lands and natural resources, water being the most valuable resource for the Indians' subsistence and cultural survival.

Water as a development resource is big business; some observers predict that the next national crisis will be fought over water. Some Native Americans see their plight as an ecological as well as a politico-economic issue and therefore work in alliance with environmental activist organizations in maintaining a sense of bioregion for biodiversity (as cultural biology). Indeed, massive water projects that were inconceivable a few generations ago are still being taken seriously, in theory if not in practice. For example, some Native American activists are protesting the North American Water and Power Alliance (NAWAPA), portraying it as a plan to re-engineer the ecosystem of the entire continent. *Newsweek* called it "the greatest, the most colossal, stupendous, supersplendificent public-works project in history" (1965, 53). The scheme was devised by the Ralph M. Parsons Company of Los Angeles during the 1960s, with the stated intent "to divert 36 trillion, trillion gallons of water (per year) from the Yukon River in Alaska . . . [southward] to thirty-three states, seven Canadian provinces, and northern Mexico" (McCool 1987, 107–108). This massive project also included the Hudson and James Bays Projects. This project and ones like it are still possible if they receive adequate funding.

One of the reasons reservation-based Native Americans have turned to the gaming industry is to establish a cash economy to replace their codependency on the federal government, especially since they do not control the natural resources on their own lands. Native Americans have always viewed water as their lifeblood, and they will continue to assert their "first rights" to it in their ongoing struggle for self-determination, self-sufficiency, and history of living in reciprocity with Nature.

Bibliography

Andrews, Barbara T., and Sansone, Marie. 1983. *Who Runs the Rivers? Dams and Decisions in the New West.* Palo Alto, Calif.: Stanford Environmental Law Society.

Berman, Terry. 1989. "For the Taking: The Garrison Dam and the Tribal Taking Area." *Cultural Survival Quarterly* 12, no. 2.

Bishop, James Jr. 1991. "Wet Water Wars." *Phoenix Magazine*, June: 80–87.

Burton, Lloyd. 1991. *American Indian Water Rights and the Limits of the Law.* Lawrence: University Press of Kansas.

Clark, Ronald, ed. 1978. *Water and Water Rights.* Indianapolis: Smith and Co.

Deloria, Vine, Jr. 1982. "Sioux/ Lakota Burial and Sacred Sites." In *Dammed Indians: The Pick-Sloan Plan and the Missouri River Sioux, 1944–1980*, by Michael Lawson. Norman: University of Oklahoma Press.

Department of Defense. 1973. *Historical Highlights of the Army Corps of Engineers.* Washington, D.C.: Department of Defense.

———. 1976. *The Corps in Perspective since 1775.* Washington, D.C.: Government Printing Office.

Department of the Interior. 1903. Reclamation Service. *Annual Report, 1902–1903.* Washington, D.C.: Government Printing Office.

———. 1916. *Bureau of Indian Affairs Annual Report.* Washington, D.C.: Government Printing Office.

Gates, Paul. 1968. *The History of Public Land Law Development.* Washington, D.C.: Zanger Pub. Co., 1968.

Glass, Mary Ellen. 1964. *Water for Nevada: The Reclamation Controversy, 1885–1902.* Reno: University of Nevada Press.

Harrison, David C. 1981. *Do We Need a National Water Policy?* Washington, D.C.: National Academy of Public Administration, 1981.

Hays, Samuel P. 1959. *Conservation and the Gospel of Efficiency.* Cambridge, Mass.: Harvard University Press.

Lawson, Michael. 1982. *Dammed Indians: The Pick-Sloan Plan and the Missouri River Sioux, 1944–1980.* Norman: University of Oklahoma Press.

Levine, Stuart, and Nancy O. Lurie, eds. 1965. *The American Indian Today.* Deland, Fla.: Everett Edwards.

McCool, Daniel. 1987. *Command of the Waters: Iron Triangles, Federal Water Development, and Indian Water.* Berkeley: University of California Press.

Shanks, Bernard. 1974. "The American Indian and Missouri River Water Development." *Water Resources Bulletin* 10 (June): 576.

———. 1982. "Dams and Disasters: The Social Problems of Water Development Policies." In *Bureaucracy vs. Environment*, edited by J. Baden and R. L. Shoup. Ann Arbor: University of Michigan Press.

U.S. Senate. 1987. Select Committee on Indian Affairs. Senate Report 100-47, 100th Cong., 1st sess. Washington, D.C.: Government Printing Office.

Warne, William E. 1973. *The Bureau of Reclamation.* New York: Praeger.

18 Hunting, Fishing, and Gathering Rights

Philip L. Fetzer

Indians of the Northwest and the Great Lakes region depended upon fish in a way similar to the Plains Indians' dependence on the buffalo. As the Supreme Court said in *United States v. Winans* (1905), "[Rights to pursue wildlife] were not much less necessary to the existence of the Indians than the atmosphere they breathed." In treaties drafted between the United States and Indian nations, hunting and fishing were often discussed in the same section. In resolving federal-tribal disputes over the years, judges have tended to apply similar reasoning to cases involving either activity. The Supreme Court has interpreted treaties that apply to hunting and fishing to include trapping and gathering rights as well, as in *United States v. Aanerud* (1990).

In 1854 and 1855, Isaac Stevens, the first governor and superintendent of Indian affairs of the Washington Territory, negotiated five federal-Indian treaties in the Northwest, acquiring more than 100,000 square miles of land that includes most of present-day Idaho, Montana, and Washington. Among the five is the Treaty of Medicine Creek, which he negotiated in 1854. In it Stevens secured the Indians' right to take fish "at all usual and accustomed grounds and stations . . . in common with all citizens of the Territory." A central component of disagreements about Indian fishing and hunting rights is the meaning of the language found in tribal-federal treaties, including the foregoing, often used phrase.

In discussing treaty rights, it is important to recognize that certain canons of construction apply. What may appear to be straightforward language in congressional acts may not effectively terminate treaty rights. At the same time, imprecise terminology often protects these rights. In other words, two major rules apply to treaty interpretation: very broad construction to determine whether Indian rights exist, and very narrow construction to determine whether Indian rights have been abrogated.

An important principle of Indian law is that the contents of a treaty are *not rights granted to the Indians*, but a *grant of rights from them* with a reservation of all remaining rights, as the Supreme Court held in *Winans*. This rule is known as the reserved rights doctrine. Thus, in cases in which a treaty does not discuss hunting and fishing rights, the rule is that those rights remain with the tribe. It is also important to note that tribes on reservations created by federal executive order retain rights similar to those of Indians on reservations created by treaty. The Court has ruled that land which was once under Indian title but passed to non-Indian ownership does not impact upon prior rights, as per *Leech Lake Band of Chippewa Indians v. Herbst* (1971).

Most of the conflicts between Indians and non-Indians over fishing rights have been concentrated in the Great Lakes region and the Northwest, especially Washington. Most of the disagreements in Washington concern off-reservation fishing by treaty fishers. On the one side, thousands of commercial fishers and more than 200,000 sport fishers (supported by state agencies) have argued in favor of restricting Native American fishing rights on non-Indian lands. On the other side, a few thousand treaty Indian fishers advocate wide latitude in exercising their rights. The disagreements tend to focus on access to salmon and steelhead trout, which are born in fresh water, migrate to the ocean to live, and then return to fresh water to spawn.

Those opposed to full implementation of Native American treaty rights generally have made three arguments: the treaties are inconsistent with the exercise of a state's sovereign rights; are unequally applied to give unfair advantage to Indians; and are inconsistent with valid conservation goals. While monetary considerations are central to the position taken by commercial fishers, sport fishers tend to emphasize conservation as their fundamental concern. In *Cases and Materials on Federal Indian Law*, however, David Getches and his colleagues conclude, "[T]he argument that Indian treaty fishing or hunting practices have endangered fish or game is not supported by evidence" (Getches, Rosenfeld, and Wilkinson 1979, 617).

Opponents of treaty rights believe that the same rules for fishing should apply equally to Indians and to non-Indians. Many non-Indian fishers see as "unfair advantages" the fact that a state cannot require fishing licenses for treaty Indian fishers, as per *Tulee v. Washington* (1942). The courts have held that while a state may regulate treaty fishers to meet conservation goals, it "must [first] show that the conservation objective cannot be attained by restricting only citizens other than treaty Indians," as stated in *United States v. Washington* (1975). Off-reservation Indian fishers tend to fish for commercial purposes. Often they have the advantage of fishing on *and* off the reservation.

Off-Reservation Hunting and Fishing Rights

Many Indian tribes have federally protected rights to fish and hunt off the reservation. These rights exist by virtue of the reserved rights doctrine or because Congress has expressly granted a tribe off-reservation hunting and fishing rights. At the same time, over the years the courts have decided that hunting and fishing on these lands may be regulated in some instances, for example, by congressional action that expressly forbids taking certain wildlife. The dispute over off-reservation fishing has generated widespread controversy and, of course, judicial responses.

In 1942 the Supreme Court issued its ruling on *Tulee v. Washington*, in which it held that states have the power to regulate off-reservation fishing by treaty Indians. Speaking for a unanimous Court, Justice Hugo Black wrote that states could issue regulations "concerning the time and manner of fishing as necessary for the conservation of the fish."

In 1967 the Washington State Supreme Court ruled that states could regulate off-reservation fishing by Indians in the interest of conservation and that Native Americans therefore no longer held treaty rights to fish on former reservation lands. The following year the U.S. Supreme Court held in *Puyallup Tribe v. Department of Game* (1968) that because federal-tribal treaties did not mention the *manner* in which fishing was to be done, states could regulate off-reservation treaty fishing. Regulations could be adopted for conservation purposes as long as the standards were appropriate and non-discriminatory toward Indians. Legal scholars criticized the decision in *Federal Indian Law*, arguing that "there was no sound legal basis for the Puyallup ruling allowing limited state regulation of federally secured treaty rights" (Getches, Rosenfeld, and Wilkinson 1979, 633).

The current conservation standard for state regulation of off-reservation treaty fishing includes four components. The state must demonstrate that the regulation is rational and essential to maintaining the species; is minimally necessary to reach this objective; is non-discriminatory against Native Americans through avoiding application of extra restrictions on treaty fishers (compared with non-treaty fishers) or hindering them from taking their share as provided by treaty while following due process and allows tribes reasonable access to the resource in the affected area. After the Washington courts approved a ban on gill net fishing, arguing that it was "necessary for conservation," the U.S. Supreme Court in *Puyallup Tribe v. Department of Game* (1973) held that such a ban would effectively grant the total run of steelhead to sport fishers and was, therefore, discriminatory; nearly all Indian fishing is by net. The general rule is that although states have extensive authority to enforce regulations off the reservation, if Native Americans have off-reservation treaty rights, then those rights are superior to a state's laws. In another example, after Washington decided to ban off-reservation out-of-season deer hunting by Native Americans, the Supreme Court overturned the law in *Antoine v. Washington* (1975).

In one of the most important rulings on treaty rights, a federal district judge, George Boldt, concluded in *United States v. Washington* (1974) that the state could regulate off-reservation fishing only "insofar as necessary to achieve preservation of the resource" and that treaty Indians should have the opportunity to catch up to 50 percent of the harvestable fish in their traditional locations along rivers. Judge Boldt interpreted the phrase "in common with" from the Treaty of Medicine Creek to mean "sharing equally."

Courts in the Great Lakes area have generally upheld off-reservation treaty rights as well, as in *People v. LeBlanc* (1976) and *United States v. Michigan* (1979). Some courts, however, have allowed state regulation of off-reservation treaty fishing. For example, in *Wisconsin v.*

Gurnoe (1972) the Wisconsin Supreme Court allowed the state to control fishing in Lake Superior by treaty fishers. After reviewing the Chippewa Treaty of 1854, the court concluded that that the state was not prohibited from regulating the fishing so long as they were "reasonable and necessary'" to preserve fish in the state.

Finally, at the conclusion of a battle that lasted more than a decade, the Supreme Court held in *Washington v. Washington State Passenger Fishing Vessel Association* (1979) that the phrase "in common with" meant that Native American fishers had the right to take up to 50 percent of the available fish unless a smaller number would afford them a "moderate living."

On-Reservation Fishing, Hunting, and Gathering

Tribal power to regulate on-reservation fishing, hunting, and gathering is one aspect of Indian self-government and is, therefore, extensive. The U.S. Supreme Court affirmed the application of an 1854 treaty right to fish and hunt in Wisconsin in *Menominee Tribe v. United States* (1968). The Court ruled that the language "to be held as Indian lands are held" protected these rights even though no specific references were made to hunting or fishing.

Two later high court rulings have limited exercise of this power: *Puyallup Tribe v. Department of Game* (1977) and *United States v. Montana* (1981). The *Puyallup* Court held that a tribe did not have an exclusive right to take steelhead that passed through the reservation land. Instead, the treaty fishers had a limited right to take fish "in common with all citizens of the Territory." Additionally, the state could regulate on-reservation fishing in the interest of conservation. In *Montana*, the Court held that tribal power is limited when applied to non-Indian hunters and fishers on non-Indian-owned land within a reservation.

Unless granted explicit permission by Congress, states cannot exercise their authority to enforce their laws on a reservation. This rule includes treaty fishing and hunting rights. Public Law 83-280 (1953) specifically excludes state jurisdiction over these activities. *Confederated Tribes of the Colville Indian Reservation v. Washington* (1976) provides that states cannot enforce their laws on non-Indian fishers. The tribal right to control on-reservation fishing is protected under 18 United States Code Amended, section 1165. It is a violation of federal law to fish or hunt on reservation land unless in conformity with tribal law. Congress has also prohibited the sale, purchase, or transport of fish or game that violates tribal law. Such federal projects as dam building may not be undertaken on reservation land if they interfere with treaty hunting or fishing rights. Treaty fishers do not need to hunt or fish in the traditional manner. The taking of game by modern methods, such as with the use of speedboats and rifles, therefore, are acceptable. Taking shellfish from the beds of navigable rivers on reservation land is not viewed as fishing and is therefore not a treaty right.

Summary

Numerous tribes retained rights to fish, hunt, and gather through treaties they negotiated with the federal government. These rights were essential to the physical survival of Native Americans and frequently to their economic well-being. Two major principles have evolved in the area of fishing and hunting rights: treaties are grants of rights from Indians with a reservation of rights not granted and states can regulate treaty fishing to further conservation of the resource. State regulation of on-reservation hunting and fishing is generally permitted only for conservation purposes or cases involving non-Indians on non-Indian owned land within reservation boundaries.

Bibliography

Fetzer, Philip L. 1981. "Politics, Law and Indian Treaties." Ph.D. diss., University of Oregon.

Getches, David H., Daniel M. Rosenfeld, and Charles F. Wilkinson. 1979. *Federal Indian Law: Cases and Materials on Federal Indian Law.* St. Paul, Minn.: West Publishing.

Pevar, Stephen L. 1992. *The Rights of Indians and Tribes.* Carbondale: Southern Illinois University Press.

19 Tribal Governments and Environmental Protection

Dean B. Suagee

Modern tribal governments throughout the United States perform leading roles in protecting the environment and managing natural resources, often in ways similar to other governments and sometimes in ways that reflect their unique status as Indian tribes. Many tribes have established extensive natural resource management programs, through self-determination contracts and self-governance compacts with the Department of the Interior. Tribes are also creating environmental protection regulatory programs with assistance from the Environmental Protection Agency (EPA). Although tribes face formidable challenges in these endeavors, they continue to make real progress. These relatively recent advancements, however, should not obscure the fact that tribal Indian peoples have been fighting to protect the environment for many generations. Indeed, much of the history of relations between tribal peoples and the U.S. government can be seen as a history of conflicts over the ways people use the earth, and the other living things with which humans share the earth, to meet the needs of humanity.

The ways of life of American Indians and Alaska Natives are deeply rooted in the lands and waters of the territories in which their cultures developed. This connection between tribal peoples and their homelands manifests itself in many ways, including in methods of food production and providing for other basic human needs, knowledge of tribal history, and religious beliefs and burial practices. There is great diversity among the 558 federally recognized Indian tribes, so generalizations can be misleading. With that caveat, it remains true that most tribal peoples in the United States perceive their homelands as part of their cultural identity. Although many tribes in the contiguous forty-eight states were forcibly removed to reservations great distances from their homelands, most modern tribes' reservations include at least a small portion of their aboriginal territory. In Alaska, there are some 229 federally recognized tribes who generally live on a portion of their aboriginal territory, but as a result of the Alaska Native Claims Settlement Act of 1971, only one of these tribes has a formally recognized reservation. Despite their lack of reservations, Alaska Natives living in rural villages retain some federally protected rights that provide for their survival by allowing them to sustain their traditional reliance on fish and wildlife.

The members of modern tribes, especially the elders, often describe the relationship of the people with the land in religious terms. From the perspective of tribal cultural and religious traditions, people do not own the land but have responsibilities to it and the web of life, as well as to future generations who will also depend on the land and to ancestors whose remains are buried their. Tribes that were removed from their original territory may well have the same kind of relationship with their new homeland, even while they continue to regard places in their aboriginal territory as holding religious and cultural importance.

Trust Responsibilities and Treaty Rights

Many reservations were established by treaty, some by executive order, and others by an act of Congress. Until 1871 reservations tended to be established by treaties, or agreement between sovereign nations. These federal-tribal treaties were also land transactions. The United States wanted the Indians to relinquish much of their lands, so in return for land grants from the tribes, the federal government promised to protect the rights of tribes to continue to live as distinct peoples on the lands that they kept for themselves. In *Cherokee Nation v. Georgia* (1831) and *Worcester v. Georgia* (1832)—two decisions arising from the first tribal-related controversies to reach the Supreme Court—Chief Justice John Marshall explained that the United States promised in its treaties to protect tribal rights to the reserved lands and the tribes' right of self-government. In later cases, the Court held that a tribe reserved for itself everything that it did not specifically relinquish by treaty. In short, the tribe retains the right to make and be governed by its own laws and to carry on its way of life as its people choose.

These promises and rulings are key components of the modern legal doctrine of federal Indian law known as federal trust responsibility. This doctrine is also based on acts of Congress, such as laws that prohibit the sale or lease of Indian land without federal approval. Trust responsibility also has roots in the practice colonial-era practice of European sovereigns claiming legal title to Indian lands that they had "discovered," with the tribes retaining the right to use the lands that they did not relinquish by treaty. Upon achieving independence from Great Britain, the United States adopted this practice, now referred to as holding land in trust.

Having trust ownership means that the federal government has duties like those of any trustee, and the Indians have rights like those of any beneficiary of a trust. Historically, this has meant that the Bureau of Indian Affairs (BIA) was responsible for managing the natural resources of Indian trust lands (such as timber, minerals, fisheries, and grazing lands) and managing the income generated from such lands. Since the allotment era of federal Indian policy—1887 to 1934, when the federal government forced Indians to parcel reservation lands into individually owned plots—the BIA has also held duties for trust lands owned by individual Indians.

In some instances, federal courts have held the BIA liable for damages to Indian trust lands caused by its mismanagement. To avoid such situations, and in response to various laws passed by Congress, the BIA established programs to manage Indian trust resources. In the modern era of tribal self-determination, which began in the 1960s, the BIA has maintained some fiduciary responsibilities relating to Indian trust lands. Most tribes, however, have taken over many of the tasks associated with managing their natural resources through self-determination contracts and self-governance compacts granted since the 1970s. The trust doctrine is of ongoing importance to Indian natural resource management, however, since it is largely because of the federal trust responsibility that Congress appropriates money to tribal governments for relevant programs.

The federal government's trust duties also have implications for environmental protection in Indian country because certain kinds of activities that affect the environment may require the approval of the BIA as trustee. Typically, BIA approval is required for a transaction involving trust land that is encumbered for seven years or more or if an interest in the land, such as a lease or right-of-way, is granted. Any project that involves funding from the BIA or another federal agency renders the National Environmental Policy Act (NEPA) applicable, and, in most cases, an environmental assessment must be prepared. If the assessment does not support a finding of no significant impact (FONSI), then an environmental impact statement must be prepared, pursuant to regulations issued by the President's Council on Environmental Quality.

NEPA is a procedural statute that requires the preparation of documents to ensure that federal agencies have adequate information before making decisions that affect the environment; NEPA does not mandate that a federal agency choose the action with the least adverse effects. In the self-determination era, it should not be surprising that the BIA does not often reject projects that tribal governments support. There are numerous examples, however, of changes being made to projects as a result of preparing NEPA documents and some examples of projects that tribal governments have ceased to support as a result of the NEPA process. In any case, if federal action triggers the preparation of NEPA documents, the trust responsibility doctrine buttresses other legal requirements that such documents adequately discuss the environmental impacts of the proposed action and alternatives to the proposed action, and that federal agencies actually rely on NEPA documents in making decisions.

Cooperative Environmental Federalism

Treaty rights and the federal trust responsibility underscore the importance of the land and the web of life, or total ecosystem, for the survival of tribal cultures. In the modern United States, the web of life is under assault from environmentally damaging activities that did not exist when tribal peoples developed their ways of life. In the 1970s Congress enacted a number of laws that created a legal framework—cooperative environmental federalism—for protecting the environment. This new framework recognized that a national system for protection was needed but that the states must act to make the system work. From the 1970s onward, cooperative environmental federalism has been manifest in such federal environmental statutes as the Clean Water Act of 1972, Safe Drinking Water Act of 1974, Clean Air

Act of 1970, Resource Conservation and Recovery Act of 1976, and Comprehensive Environmental Response, Compensation and Liability Act of 1980.

The Clean Water Act provides a useful example here. The pressing need to control water pollution was identified, so Congress, aware that water pollution crosses state boundaries, decided on a national approach to the problem. With the Clean Water Act, Congress gave the Environmental Protection Agency the authority to set limits on pollution released from industrial facilities and to issue permits for "point sources" of water pollution. It directed the states to establish quality standards for all surface waters within their boundaries and gave them the authority to veto point source permits issued by EPA if the permit would result in a violation of state water quality standards. In addition, states could apply to EPA to take responsibility for certain EPA programs, such as issuing permits for point sources.

When Congress passed the first generation of major federal environmental statutes in the 1970s, it paid very little attention to how these statutes would be carried out within Indian reservations and other tribal areas. In historical context, this omission should not be surprising, since it occurred during the early years of the self-determination era. In 1970 President Richard M. Nixon rejected the federal policy of termination of all federal services to Indian nations, which the government had adopted in the 1950s. In 1975 Congress enacted the Indian Self-Determination and Education Assistance Act. When it came to laws that did not solely concern Indian policy, however, Congress seemed to overlook the fact that Indian tribes are sovereign governments with a range of powers comparable to the states. Under established principles of federal Indian law, states generally lack authority over tribes and tribal members within reservations. They may also lack authority over non-Indians within reservations if preempted by federal law or if state authority infringes on tribal self-government. Although the federal environmental statutes did not expressly provide for tribes to perform roles, they also did not give the states authority within Indian country. As a result, the omission of Indian tribes from environmental statutes left gaps in the national system that put Indian reservations at risk.

To protect the environmental quality on reservations while also respecting tribal sovereignty, EPA took the position that it, rather than the states, should perform the lead role in implementing environmental laws in Indian country. In keeping with principles of federal Indian law and the policy of tribal self-determination, EPA adopted policies that sought to vest tribes with as much authority as permissible under the federal statutes. EPA also supported legislation to amend statutes so that tribes would be treated more like the states; between 1986 and 1990 Congress did amend several statutes with this intent.

The federal courts resolved a number of conflicts that arose in the process of carrying out federal environmental laws in Indian country. Under the Clean Air Act of 1970, EPA established national ambient air quality standards, which were essentially targets for reducing air pollution in areas where the air quality is worse than the standards. After being sued by an environmental group, EPA issued rules to protect the air quality of regions that were cleaner than required by the standards. Under these rules for the "prevention of significant deterioration" of air quality, most regions were initially designated "class II," and the governors of states and the governing bodies of tribes could "redesignate" air regions within their jurisdiction to a more stringent "class I" or a less stringent "class III." The Northern Cheyenne in Montana redesignated their reservation to class I, and various parties challenged EPA's approval of this classification. In *Nance v. EPA* (1981), a federal appeals court upheld EPA's decision and the regulations on which the decision was based. While the case was pending, Congress had changed the law to explicitly allow tribes to redesignate their reservations, as the Northern Cheyenne had done.

The Resource Conservation and Recovery Act of 1976 applies to hazardous wastes and municipal solid waste landfills. Under the act, EPA regulates hazardous wastes, but the states can establish their own programs, and if EPA approves, the state's program supersedes EPA's. When the state of Washington sought EPA approval to apply its hazardous program to Indian reservations within the state, EPA denied the request because Congress had not granted the states authority to regulate hazardous waste in Indian country. A federal appeals court ruled in favor of EPA in *Washington Department of Ecology v. EPA* (1985).

In 1991 EPA issued a rule establishing a process for tribes to set water quality standards under the Clean Water Act, which had been amended in 1987 to allow EPA to treat tribes like states. One of the first reservations to adopt water quality standards was the Isleta Pueblo in New Mexico, where tribal leaders were concerned about pollution in the Rio Grande from the wastewater treatment plant in Albuquerque, a few miles upstream from the pueblo. Members of the pueblo carry out traditional religious ceremonies in the river that involve ingesting small amounts of water, so the pueblo set its water quality standards to protect this designated use of the river. The city of Albuquerque sued EPA, but a federal appeals court upheld EPA's approval of the pueblo's standards in *City of Albuquerque v. Browner* (1996).

Another case involving tribal water quality standards arose on the reservation of the Confederated Salish and Kootenai tribes in Montana. The tribes applied to EPA for authorization to set standards for all waters within their reservation, where nearly half the land had passed out of trust status as a result of allotments. EPA approved the application, based in part on its reading of Supreme Court decisions regarding tribal authority over non-Indians on non-trust reservation lands. The state of Montana sued EPA, arguing that the tribes did not have authority to regulate conduct on privately owned land within the reservation. The federal appeals court ruled in favor of EPA and the tribes in *Montana v. EPA* (1998).

In 1998 the EPA issued a final rule to carry out the provisions of the Clean Air Act Amendments of 1990 that authorized it to treat tribes like states. Among other things, EPA interpreted the amendments as a delegation of power from Congress to tribes to develop Tribal Implementation Plans to regulate all sources and persons within reservation boundaries, regardless of the ownership status of the land. This rule was challenged in court before any tribe had applied to EPA for a plan approval, and a federal appeals court upheld EPA's interpretation in *Arizona Public Service Company v. EPA* (2000).

The Resource Conversation and Recovery Act has not yet been amended to authorize EPA to treat tribes like states, but the agency nevertheless approved the application of the Campo band of Mission Indians to regulate a municipal solid waste landfill as a state would under the act. A federal court, however, held that EPA's interpretation of the statute was wrong in *Backcountry Against Dumps v. EPA* (1996). The court decided that although the issue is within the tribe's sovereignty to regulate, the recovery act does not authorize EPA to treat the tribe like a state.

Off-Reservation Rights

Many tribes are concerned about environmental and natural resource issues beyond reservation boundaries, because off-reservation activities sometimes affect reservations. These tribes have used the review process established by NEPA, as well as procedures established under other federal laws, to voice their concerns about such activities. Tribal concerns about off-reservation issues also derive from treaty rights to certain resources outside reservation boundaries. For example, many of the tribes in the Pacific Northwest and the Great Lakes region have off-reservation fishing rights. Over the last three decades, conflicts involving these rights have attracted quite a bit of media attention. For tribes with these rights, fishing was, and remains, central to their way of life. In the nineteenth century when the United States engaged the Indians in treaty negotiations, these tribes agreed to give up much of the land that they could have claimed as their territory in exchange for promises that they could continue to take fish at their customary places within the lands they agreed to cede.

About thirty years ago, conflicts involving off-reservation treaty rights began reaching the federal courts, with some cases decided by the Supreme Court. In essence, the courts have ruled that these rights still exist, that treaty tribes are entitled to substantial shares of the fish that can be harvested, and that states generally cannot regulate tribal members in the exercise of these rights. Another outcome of these cases has been the creation of intertribal organizations, such as the Columbia River Intertribal Fish Commission and the Great Lakes Intertribal Fish Commission, which have developed a great deal of capacity for resource management. Tribes are now involved directly and through such organizations in cooperative efforts with federal and state agencies to manage fish populations and habitat and to carry out restoration projects where fish habitat has been degraded. In the Pacific Northwest, tribes have been active in advocating for measures to restore habitats to promote the recovery of wild salmon, including the removal of some hydroelectric dams.

In addition to treaty rights, pursuant to the Native American Graves Protection and Repatriation Act of 1990, tribes have authority over the graves of their ancestors and rights to cultural items buried on federal lands and non-trust lands within reservation boundaries. Any affiliated tribes must be consulted if an excavation of such items is planned or if such items are inadvertently discovered. While they do not have authority to prevent excavation, culturally affiliated tribes do have rights to take possession of items that are excavated.

For many tribes, places outside their reservation still hold religious and cultural significance to them. In recognition of this, and the fact that tribal religions have been suppressed through much of U.S. history, Congress passed the American Indian Religious Freedom Act of 1978. In subsequent litigation, however, the Supreme Court—in *Lyng v. Northwest Indian Cemetery Protective Association* (1988)—not only held that the act does not create rights that are enforceable in court, but also that the First

Amendment's promise of freedom of religion does not prevent the federal government from destroying tribal sacred places on federal lands.

Places that hold religious and cultural importance for tribes may receive a measure of protection under federal law if they also possess enough historical significance to be eligible for listing on the National Register of Historic Places. As amended in 1992, the National Historic Preservation Act provides that when a federal agency is considering an action that may have an effect on a historic property with religious and cultural importance for a tribe, the agency must consult with that tribe. This right was implemented through regulations issued in December 2000 by the Advisory Council on Historic Preservation, and some tribes have successfully used it to persuade federal agencies to protect their sacred and cultural sites.

It is important to remember that what sets Indian tribes apart from other minority groups in this country is that they are sovereign governments, and they can deal with environmental problems by enacting and carrying out their own laws. Federal environmental laws provide a framework that supports tribal sovereignty in this area. In most of the cases cited here involving tribal authority within reservation boundaries, the federal courts have ruled in favor of EPA and the tribes; in other cases, the Supreme Court has denied petitions to review lower court decisions. Despite court rulings upholding tribal authority, tribes continue to face legal challenges in exercising it to protect the environment, particularly when they try to regulate the conduct of non-Indians. During the last few decades, the Supreme Court has issued a number of decisions resulting in major changes to federal Indian law, with some of these rulings providing opponents of tribal sovereignty with new arguments.

Over the course of U.S. history, Congress has held the constitutional authority to define the country's relations with the Indian tribes, but in recent years the Supreme Court has increasingly assumed this role for itself. As the status of the tribes in the federal system continues to evolve, it is increasingly unclear whether their rights will be determined by Congress or the Court. It may come to pass that this issue will be resolved in the context of environmental protection. If so, it is important for the American public to understand that tribes, as sovereign entities, are engaged in a wide range of programs to protect and restore the environments of their reservations and the regions in which their reservations are located. The political history of Indian tribes in the United States does not yet have a conclusion.

Bibliography

Coursen, David F. 1993. "Tribes as States: Indian Tribal Authority to Regulate and Enforce Federal Environmental Law and Regulations." *Environmental Law Report* 23 (October): 10,579.

Frickey, Philip P. 1999. "A Common Law for Our Age of Colonialism: The Judicial Divestiture of Indian Tribal Authority over Nonmembers." *Yale Law Journal* 109: 1.

Getches, David H. 1996. "Conquering the Cultural Frontier: The New Subjectivism of the Supreme Court in Indian Law." *California Law Review* 84: 1573.

Grijalva, James. 1995. "Tribal Government Regulation of Non-Indian Polluters of Reservation Waters." *Notre Dame Law Review* 71: 433.

Suagee, Dean B. 1996. "Tribal Voices in Historic Preservation: Sacred Landscapes, Cross-Cultural Bridges, and Common Ground." *Vermont Law Review* 21: 145.

Tsosie, Rebecca. 1996. "Tribal Environmental Policy in an Era of Self-Determination: The Role of Ethics, Economics, and Traditional Ecological Knowledge." *Vermont Law Review* 21: 225.

Recent Movements

20 Indian Gaming

Philip L. Fetzer

Gaming is a relatively recent development of tribal life. It began in the 1980s as a means of generating revenue for Native Americans, who had few opportunities to alleviate widespread poverty and unemployment. By the turn of the century, tribal gaming had grown into an $8 billion a year industry. The Seminoles were the first tribe to sponsor reservation gambling when they opened a bingo hall in Florida. Once tribes in Florida and California began offering prizes that were larger than those allowed by state law, the states appeared ready to shut down their gambling facilities. The tribes responded to the threat by bringing suits in federal court. In 1981 the Fifth Circuit Court of Appeals held that Florida law could not be enforced against reservation Indians as applied to bingo games. Six years later in *California v. Cabazon* (1987), the Supreme Court held that the states were not authorized to regulate Indian gaming on reservations if similar activities were already permitted by the state off reservation. In reaching its decision, an important ruling in support of tribal sovereignty, the Court concluded that states could not exercise civil authority over tribal activities absent express congressional consent.

Indian Gaming Regulatory Act

Responding to *Cabazon*, in 1988 Congress adopted the Indian Gaming Regulatory Act (IGRA), or Public Law 100-497, which recognized Indian gaming rights. While states wanted the authority to regulate tribal gaming, the casino industry in Las Vegas and Atlantic City sought to avoid competition from Native American interests altogether. The act divides gaming into three categories (Class I, II, and III) and parcels oversight of reservation gaming activities among four jurisdictions (tribal governments, state governments, the federal government, and the National Indian Gaming Commission). Class I gaming involves activities in which prizes are of minimal value or are part of tribal ceremonies or festivities. Class II gaming includes bingo, certain card games (such as blackjack and baccarat), lotto, pull tabs, tip jars, and punch boards. Class III gaming entails slot machines, pari-mutuel horse racing and dog racing, craps, and lotteries.

Tribal governments have the primary responsibility of enforcing gaming regulations. Through tribal courts and the use of tribal police, tribes hold responsibility for issuing gaming licenses, establishing gaming commissions, and providing security at gaming establishments. Class I gaming falls under the exclusive jurisdiction of tribal governments. Class II gaming is also under tribal supervision so long as the terms of the IGRA are followed. Regulation of Class III gaming is governed by compacts reached between tribes and the states, which are expected to negotiate in "good faith." These compacts normally include the types of games that will be offered, betting limits, and the size of the facilities. States have the responsibility of conducting background checks on employees and management personnel at Class III operations. By 1996, 124 of the 557 federally recognized tribes had compacts in twenty-four states. Under the compacts tribal governments must be recognized as the principal beneficiaries of gaming.

Federal authority over Indian gaming involves the Department of the Interior, which includes the Bureau of Indian Affairs (BIA), and the Department of Justice, which includes the Federal Bureau of Investigation (FBI). Interior recommends tribal-state compacts, audits gaming operations, and issues rules on the allocation of funding plans. Justice is charged with investigations of gaming laws as well as their enforcement. The BIA and FBI have oversight responsibilities for criminal activities on reservations. The National Indian Gaming Commission is authorized to enforce civil penalties for gaming violations.

While tribes are not required to pay state or federal taxes on their income from gaming, they are expected to make mandated deductions and to withhold state and federal income taxes from nonresident Indians and employees who are not tribal members. Additionally, tribes must report game winnings to the Internal Revenue Service and are required by the Bank Security Act of 1995 to divulge cash transactions of more than $10,000 within twenty-four hours of the exchange.

The IGRA mandates that profits from tribal gaming are for the exclusive use of the tribal government and for the benefit of tribal members. Some of the ways tribes have expended gaming receipts include building hospitals and clinics, schools and day-care facilities, and infrastructure such as roads and sewer and water systems. Because states may not necessarily agree to compacts with tribes, the IGRA set time limits on negotiations. In cases in which states delay good-faith negotiations for more than 180 days, tribes may request that a federal court appoint a mediator. If at the end of sixty days mediation has failed, the mediator may impose the "last best offer" of either party.

In 1994 the Eleventh Circuit Court of Appeals ruled in *Seminole Tribe v. Florida* that Congress lacked the power to force states to negotiate compacts in good faith at the time the IGRA was adopted in 1988. States were protected against such suits by sovereign immunity under the Eleventh Amendment. Nonetheless, if a compact cannot be reached within the time limits set by Congress, the IGRA places final authority with the secretary of the interior. The act entails a reduction in the exercise of tribal sovereignty in that it permits the federal government and the states to play a role in regulating a lawful reservation activity that, prior to its passage, was under the exclusive authority of the tribe.

Economic Effects of Indian Gaming

The effects of gaming on the economic life of reservation Indians vary considerably. Unemployment in the aggregate changed little in the decade after the adoption of the IGRA. Reservation unemployment rates averaged 45 percent in 1990 and nearly 50 percent at the turn of the century. At the same time, the poverty rate over this period has worsened, with approximately one-third of Native Americans living below the poverty line. In 1997 only 28 percent of employed Indians earned more than $7,000 annually.

The growth in revenue from Indian gaming during the 1990s has been spectacular. In 1988 revenue from tribal gaming was only about $120,000. The situation changed dramatically in the next few years, with gaming grossing $1.5 billion in 1992 and an estimated $4 billion in 1993. By the end of the decade, gaming generated more than $8 billion annually. Nationwide, tribal gaming accounts for 10 percent of the entire industry. Between 1988 and 2000 tribal gaming grew nearly forty-fold. The National Indian Gaming Association estimates that 50,000 Native Americans were employed in some aspect of the tribal gaming industry by the late 1990s.

Examples of economic success from tribal gaming can be found in Connecticut, Minnesota, and Washington State. By the mid-1990s, the Foxwoods Casino (Mashentucket-Pequots) in Connecticut employed more than 20,000 people and generated a gross profit of more than $800 million. One hundred fifty members of the Prior Lake Skakopee Mdewakanton Dakota tribe became millionaires from the profits of the Mystic Lake Casino in Minnesota. Unemployment on the Tuliaps reservation in Washington dropped from 65 percent to 10 percent after the tribe opened its gaming facilities in 1991.

That most tribes do not participate in gaming activities is one of the factors for continued widespread poverty and unemployment in the midst of the economic boom in the Indian gaming industry. In 1996 only 91 of the 557 federally recognized tribes operated high-stakes gaming facilities. By 2000 there were 184 tribes involved in the industry, but only 10 to 15 could be considered highly profitable, with just 8 accounting for 40 percent of all income from gaming.

Tribal gaming has not been an unalloyed blessing. In some cases it has widened the income gap between urban and rural tribes. Tribes that have decided not to open casinos, such as the Navajo and Hopi, continue to suffer economically. At the same time, most of the employment related to gaming pays relatively low wages. Top-end jobs generally require a college degree, a qualification that only a small percentage of Native Americans possess.

Summary

Overall, the development of tribal gaming has had mixed results for Native Americans. On the one hand, the economic benefits to a limited number of participating tribes have been substantial. On the other hand, tribes lost some of their traditional sovereignty as a consequence of congressional adoption of the Indian Gaming Regulatory Act. The success of tribal gaming on some reservations should not obscure the fact that the vast majority of federally recognized tribes have not realized significant revenue through the evolution of this industry.

Bibliography

Anders, Gary C. 1999. "Indian Gaming: Financial and Regulatory Issues." In *Contemporary Native American Issues*, edited by Troy R. Johnson. Walnut Creek, Calif.: Altamira Press.

Mason, W. Dale. 2000. *Indian Gaming*. Norman: University of Oklahoma Press.

21 Native American Gaming in California

Joely De La Torre

The history of California's first peoples is one that is not well known. In fact, although the state of California has the largest number of federally recognized tribes, most people remained unaware of the issues surrounding them until the 1998 political campaign for Proposition 5, the Indian Self-Reliance Initiative on gaming on reservation lands.

The Indians' political, social, and cultural contacts with the Spanish, Mexican, and then European American colonists severely affected their populations. The confrontation since the eighteenth century between Euro-Americans and California Indians was particularly ugly and brutal. Throughout the state, indigenous peoples fell victim to almost inconceivable tragedy brought on by disease and starvation as well as outright genocidal campaigns against them (Eargle 1992, 28–38). The colonists displaced Indians from their ancestral homes, denied them access to areas for procuring food and medicine by erecting fences, claimed rights to Indian lands, and spoiled economic resources with their mining and logging activities. As a result, native peoples starved to death by the hundreds (Jackson and Castillo 1995, 41–73). During the first two decades of the European American conquest, the native population of California plummeted by 90 percent (Cook 1976, xv–43). Today California Indians number approximately 64,000 and belong to 109 federally recognized tribes.

In addition to suffering physical acts of brutality and genocide, the Indians also lost millions of acres of land because Congress refused to ratify eighteen treaties. In 1852, the federal government sent three commissioners to negotiate these treaties at various ranches and army posts, mainly in southern and central California. The commissioners met with 402 Indian leaders, but these delegates represented less than one-third of the state's native peoples. Regardless, the United States decided that these few could sign away the rights of the many. In exchange for relinquishing their claims to California, the Indians were to receive some 7.5 million acres of land—roughly about 8 percent of the state—for their sole use, along with certain quantities of clothing, food, livestock, farming implements, and educational services; because the treaties were never ratified, however, the United States effectively seized these lands. In 1944, after lengthy litigation, California Indians were awarded $17.5 million for the 7.5 million acres promised through treaties. From this award, the federal government deducted some $12 million to recoup all monies spent on the Indians during the last half of the nineteenth century, leaving scarcely $150 apiece for the 36,000 remaining native Californians.

Under the Indian Claims Commission Act, which enabled American Indian nations to seek compensation from the federal government, California's native peoples brought a second claim for reimbursement in 1946 for another 65 million acres taken on pretenses other than treaties; the property involved included the various Mexican land grants and reservations excluded from the earlier settlement (Deloria 1988, 52). Eighteen years later, the Indians were awarded $46 million. When all was said and done, the United States had "purchased" California for 47 cents an acre.

Today California Indians continue to fare poorly in their relations with the federal government. The Bureau of Indian Affairs (BIA), an agency of the Department of the Interior designated to assist American Indians, has been criticized for its many shortcomings. California Indians suffer one of the lowest ratios of BIA employees to Indian service population, and the Sacramento area has the smallest administrative building space of all BIA areas. These two factors inhibit BIA officials and tribal leaders from effectively addressing the social and economic issues confronting all California Indian communities, which are among the least served, if they are not *the* least served, Indian groups in the nation.

The history of California Indian relations with the federal government is one of a people neglected and abused. Prior to the 1990s economic boom in tribal gaming, California Indians were the poorest of all native populations. The introduction of gaming has helped California tribes become more self-determining. It has also afforded California tribes the opportunity to exercise power at the local, state, and national levels.

Tribal Gaming

During the 1990s Indian gaming was the fastest growing "industry" among tribal communities and the fastest growing area of the gaming industry (Kelly 1993, 1672). Large-scale Indian gaming operations began booming in the late 1970s. Currently Indian gaming is a multibillion dollar enterprise and a major source of income on a number of reservations. In March 1999 the National Indian Gaming Commission documented 310 Indian gaming operations based on 198 tribal-state compacts in twenty-eight states. With estimated revenues of $7.4 billion a year, tribal gaming still only accounts for 10 percent of all gaming nationwide. About 40 percent of gambling revenues come from state lotteries, and commercial entities in Nevada and New Jersey dominate the remaining 50 percent (Kelly 1993, 1672). Less than one-third of the federally recognized tribes in the United States have gaming operations (National Congress of American Indians 1999, 2). Since the Seminoles first opened a bingo parlor in Florida in the 1970s, reservation casinos have been challenged in state courts, Congress, and the Supreme Court. This contest between the states and tribes has become a battle between sovereign entities, with each wanting to determine for itself what takes place within its borders (Bureau of Indian Affairs 1999, 1).

Indian gaming came to national attention in the early 1980s as a result of two court cases: *Seminole Tribe of Florida v. Butterworth* (1979) and *Cabazon Band of Mission Indians v. California* (1987). In *Cabazon* the Court upheld the right of tribes as sovereign nations to conduct gaming on their lands free of state control when similar gaming is permitted by the state outside the reservation.

The most significant reason for contemporary governmental interest in and recognition of American Indians, however, has its roots in the advantages of tribal gaming. Tribal gaming has also provided for a "political awakening" in the sense that it sparked a sense of self-interest among American Indians, leading them to demand services to meet the needs defined by this self-interest. As a result of this new outlook, the American Indian community is exercising its growing influence in the social, economic, and political structures of U.S. society; southern California tribes are no exception. The Bureau of Indian Affairs reported that as of 1990 forty-one of the then–one hundred four Indian reservations, or *rancherias*, in California had gaming facilities. Total casino revenue generated by Indian gaming in the state approached $1.4 billion in 1997. Local California non-casino businesses earned revenue estimated at $273 million that year as a result of tribal gaming. The total economic impact of tribal gaming in California is approximately $4.4 billion per year (Analysis Group/Economics 1998).

Proposition 5

Relations between California Indian tribal governments and federal and state governments over tribal casinos are strained. A central issue in this era of tension has been Proposition 5, otherwise known as the Tribal Government and Economic Self-Sufficiency Act of 1998, or the California Indian Self-Reliance Initiative. The proposition, which was on California's November 1998 ballot, called for California's Indian tribes to operate types of casinos that the state had previously deemed illegal and allow for additional casinos in a number of Native American communities. Supporters of the initiative argued that the act was necessary to allow California Indians to keep the jobs and benefits provided by what limited gaming they had already established. Opponents of the proposition argued that it would allow unregulated and untaxed (and unfair) gambling.

During the campaign, California tribes wanted to focus on their needs, values, history, and rights. Fortunately for them, they had the economic resources to get an early start, so they launched an unprecedented media campaign to educate voters about California Indians. The opposition, a coalition of entertainment firms, including Nevada casinos, also had plentiful resources. Each side wanted to frame the issue before other races began to clutter the airwaves. The campaign for Proposition 5 was hugely successful, with 62.6 percent of voters supporting the measure (see Table 21.1).

The battle over the initiative became the most expensive campaign in California's history. The proposition's supporters raised $68.6 million and after the race $2.2 million remained for use in future political battles. The largest contributor was the San Manuel tribe,

Table 21.1 Proposition 5: Percentage of Vote by Race, Party, Gender, and Region

Category	*Yes on 5*	*No on 5*
Black	78	22
Latino	73	27
Asian	64	36
Other	57	43
Democrats	75	25
Independents	71	29
Republicans	48	54
Men	61	39
Women	64	36
Southern California	62	38
Los Angeles County	71	29
Northern California	55	45
Bay Area	73	27
Central Valley	49	51

Source: Los Angeles Times Poll, Study 420/Exit Poll, California General Election, November 3, 1998, http://www.latimes.com/extras/timespoll/stats/pdfs/420ss.pdf.

at $25.5 million (California Common Cause 2002). Some observers would later argue that the amount of money spent by the tribes was excessive, because Californians were sympathetic to their up-from-poverty message and would have approved the measure without such an extensive campaign. The tribes, however, had worried that they would not even be able to collect enough signatures to qualify the measure as a constitutional initiative; thus, they settled for a statutory initiative, which allows for a change in state law but not an overruling of the state constitution. The tribes ultimately collected more than a million signatures, surpassing the 700,000 they needed for a constitutional amendment (Vellinga 1998).

Both sides advertised heavily on television. The tribes, for instance, spent more than $31 million on television and radio ads between July 1 and October 17, 1998, while Nevada casinos spent $15.6 million on broadcast ads during the same period (Secretary of State of California 2002).

To counter some of the opposition's negative publicity about Indian gaming, the California-Nevada Indian Gaming Association aired a series of commercials on the positive effects of gambling for tribes. The ads pointed out that gaming profits would go toward ending welfare dependency, creating jobs, and improving housing and health care on reservations. In general, rather than responding in-kind to the opposition's negative campaign approach, the tribes remained committed to conducting an educational campaign, informing voters about Indian values, beliefs, and history. It was the first time that a campaign in California had taken such an approach, and it was also the first time in the state of California that an initiative put forth by an ethnic group had won.

A number of ads featured members of non-gaming tribes describing their lives in poverty, surviving without electricity and running water, before tribal gaming. Because of gaming, however, they now had such basics as electricity, because the gaming tribes shared their revenues with them. In addition to such commercials, the coalition of tribes supporting the "Yes on 5" campaign aired a half-hour educational program in various time slots and on channels throughout the state. The documentary providing viewers with political, social, and historical background on California Indians. Members of gaming and non-gaming tribes were featured in the program along with historians and legal scholars, politicians, actors, and contemporary California Indian political leaders.

The opposition to Proposition 5 consisted of a few very well financed special interests: labor unions, casinos (California and Nevada), horse racing tracks, card clubs, and the Walt Disney Corporation. This lineup stands in sharp contrast to the image that the "No on 5" coalition tried to convey of active citizen organizations concerned about the effects of gambling on their communities. One opposition ad complained that the initiative would allow hundreds of casinos to open throughout the state; another featured actors pushing their baby in a stroller along a residential street when out of nowhere a casino pops up in the middle of the neighborhood.

In spite of its name, the California Alliance United Against Gaming did not represent a large coalition of varied interests. Only for "Stand up for California. No on 5," another opposition group, did any labor organization register $10,000 or more in direct contributions. Of further interest is where the majority of donors to the "No on 5" campaign resided—Nevada. Only a few California-based organizations contributed to the opposition campaign, and only 22.35 percent of itemized contributions were made by California businesses (Secretary of State of California 2002).

The Court Challenge

The Proposition 5 victory was short lived. On November 20, 1998, a hotel and restaurant employees union and a Nevada and California card club–backed neighborhood group in northern California filed *Hotel Employees and Restaurant Employees International Union v. Wilson* and *Cortez v. Wilson* before the California Supreme Court to overturn Proposition 5. The tribes knew that such a challenge was inevitable and were aware of the strong possibility of losing because of a 1984 amendment to the California constitution prohibiting "Las Vegas–style" gaming.

The cases before the California court concerned whether Proposition 5 exceeded the scope of initiative power by requiring the governor to enter into tribal gaming compacts; violated California Constitution, Article 4, section 19, subdivision (e) prohibiting "casinos of the type currently operating in Nevada and New Jersey"; and was preempted by the federal Indian Gaming Regulatory Act. The California Supreme Court overturned Proposition 5 on August 23, 1999, based on the hotel and restaurant employees' suit.

Within weeks of the court's ruling, however, sixty tribal governments reached agreement with Governor Gray Davis on compacts allowing gaming on reservations. On September 10, 1999, in a historic ceremony in the governor's office, tribal government leaders and Governor Davis signed fifty-nine gaming compacts, the basic terms of which are as follows:

- California Indian tribes may continue limited gaming at Indian casinos on federally designated reservation lands.
- Permitted games include slot machines, house-banked card games, lottery games, and pari-mutuel wagering.
- Revenues from gaming must be shared with non-gaming tribes to support education, health care, housing, and economic development programs on their reservations.
- All tribes must prepare environmental impact reports on potential effects to areas outside the reservation when planning for any new construction related to a casino and allow the public to comment on the report and make good-faith efforts to mitigate any negative impacts.
- Gaming must be strictly regulated by tribal governments, the state of California, and relevant federal agencies.
- Reservations may have a maximum of two gaming facilities and may not have more than two thousand slot machines.
- Gaming tribes must pay a percentage of their revenue to state and local governments,

which would go toward supporting local programs and services in nearby communities and reimbursing state and local agencies for costs related to regulating Indian casinos.

- Employees working in most non-management jobs at Indian casinos must be allowed to join labor unions.
- Compact terms are valid for twenty years with the option to extend them; changes may be renegotiated after three years, but must be agreed to by the tribe and the state and approved by the federal government.

In the March 7, 2000, California primary elections, nearly 65 percent of voters approved Proposition 1a to amend the California constitution to permit California Indian tribes exclusivity in offering casino-type gaming, such as slot machines, lotteries, and house-banked card games. The measure was approved by lawmakers on the final day of the spring legislative session.

The California tribes were successful in their gaming effort in part because they had the necessary resources with which to tell their stories and relay their issues to the public. That they used California Indians to relate their issues to the public enhanced the strength of their message. By taking an educational approach, rather than arguing a market-based agenda, the tribes framed the issues of sovereignty and self-determination on a personal level, involving real people. The paths of Propositions 5 and 1a offer a unique glimpse of the tribes developing and defining their own political reality and shaping it, at times, through the shared symbolism of language. Economic resources provided a platform for their political development, but it was the message that persuaded non-Indian voters to support them.

Tribal Political Development

American Indians have much to say about their own political status and condition. California tribes see themselves as rejecting contemporary Western models of political development and striving to restore and promote the traditional ideas and values of their own society. Native scholar Vine Deloria Jr. clearly articulates this view of indigenous self-determination in his argument for cultural integrity, which he defines as follows: "Commitment to a central and easily understood purpose that motivates a group of people, enables them to form efficient, albeit informal social institutions, and provides for them a clear identity which cannot be eroded by the passage of time. It involves most of all a strong sense of community, a degree of self-containment, a pride that transcends all objective codes, rules and regulations" (Deloria 1979, 27).

Thus, based on Deloria's impressions, tribal sovereignty is not just a political power or legal concept but a reality that encompasses a tribe's cultural identity and is represented in the daily activities and interactions of tribal peoples. It is through their culture and values that tribes communicate their political existence to others. Tribes are a distinct people held together by a culture that includes shared values, not by political institutions, as is the case in the dominant society. Ultimately, what makes a tribe is its members' ability to commit to a central purpose. Unlike the dominant society, tribes are not motivated by individuals but by a vision of the group. The opponents of tribal gaming have attempted to frame tribal sovereignty as a "special privilege," thereby imparting upon this right negative connotations. As Deloria so clearly articulates, however, "Indian sovereignty consists more of continued cultural integrity than of political powers and to that degree a nation loses its sense of cultural identity, to that degree it suffers a loss of sovereignty" (Deloria 1979, 27). Therefore, California tribes, in their quest to operate tribal gaming, had to clearly present their view of tribal sovereignty. Ultimately, they did so successfully.

Each tribe must determine its central purpose or, in other words, the vision that leads it to be self-determining and sovereign. Several tribes that encourage native culture and values may share the same vision, as was the case with Proposition 5. Here the vision shared was to support tribal economies, families, health care, education, and the maintenance of tribal culture through tribal gaming. California Indians defined this vision for California Indians, thus leading to an effective presentation of their values and views. Tribes who allow their culture to determine the boundaries of their relationships with others empower themselves to manage their own destiny. If tribes want to have their issues heard, they must clearly articulate their vision and goals, or it will be done for them. As Deloria contends, "If sovereignty is restricted to a legal-political context, then it becomes a limiting concept, which serves to prevent solutions. The legal-political context is structured in an adversary situation, which precludes both understanding and satisfactory resolution of difficulties and should be considered as a last resort . . . in which human problems and relationships are seen" (Deloria 1979, 28).

Political Power and Influence

The amount of money spent on the two gaming initiatives is the clearest indicator of Indians' potential power and economic influence. Only recently, however, have tribes become large donors to political campaigns (see Figure 21.1). Of the state's top ten contributors to legislative candidates in 1998, three were Indian tribes. That year California gaming tribes gave Governor Davis $664,920.

The state's top twenty-two gaming tribes or organizations collectively donated more than $7 million to legislative or statewide candidates in 1997 and 1998, dwarfing all other interest groups, according to statistics compiled by California Common Cause (2002). The second biggest spender during this period was the state prison guard union, the California Correctional Peace Officers Association, which gave $1.9 million to candidates.

In comparison, in 1995 and 1996 the same tribal interests spent only $950,000 on campaigns. A decade prior, in the late 1980s before reservation casino gambling became a cash fountain, Indians spent virtually nothing on

Figure 21.1 Tribal Donations to Legislative Candidates, 1995–1998

Donations to statewide and legislative candidates in California by Indian organizations, individuals, and tribes involved in casino operations

1995	$ 78,117
1996	871,665
1997	26,687
1998	7,371,867
Total	$8,348,336

Top three tribal contributors to California political campaigns

$1,705,331	Morongo Band of Mission Indians, near Banning, Southern California
$1,626,269	Agua Caliente Band of Cahuilla Indians, near Palm Springs, Southern California
$1,346,109	San Manuel Band of Mission Indians, near Patton, Southern California
$4,677,709	Total

Source: California Common Cause 2002.

political campaigns, mainly because they did not have many resources. That there is not a single self-identified Indian state legislator makes donating to campaigns all the more crucial. "Nobody took notice of us before, and our issues were never addressed in Sacramento because we were not able to lobby before," said Barbara Gonzales Lyons, tribal council vice chairwoman of the Agua Caliente band of Cahuilla Indians, which runs a successful casino near Palm Springs. "Ten years ago, we didn't even have the funds to take care of our own people, let alone donate to campaigns. But now that we have gaming, we can move forward and protect not just our gaming interests, but our people's interests." These interests include everything from tribal versus state rights in child custody cases to environmental and fire control issues on lands bordering reservations. "It would be nice if everyone could be heard in Sacramento, regardless of their funding chest, but that would be an idealistic world," said Lyons. "We have to deal with the way things are." From 1995 to 1998 Lyons' tribe gave $1.6 million to statewide and national congressional candidates, an amount among California gaming tribes second only to donations from the Morongo band of Mission Indians, which gave $1.7 million (Fagan 2000).

California tribes currently earn revenue totaling some $1.4 billion a year, but because of newly allowed slot machines, this figure is expected to grow to an estimated $4.4 billion by 2004, making California the biggest gambling state outside Nevada (*Gambling Magazine* 1999). Despite their growing clout, gaming tribes are not yet in the same league as such powerful political donors as the National Rifle Association, AARP, and the tobacco companies. Non-Indian society and its political arms are, however, closely scrutinizing and judging the success and political influence wielded by the tribes. Good, bad, or indifferent, tribes are keenly aware of this, which is why they are so concerned with symbolism, language, imagery, and the maintenance of tribal political power and development.

What impact has this infusion of money into California's political campaigns had for tribes? Has this cash translated into American Indian policies being championed by elected officials? The answers to these questions remain unclear at present. California Indians formed the California Democratic Party Native American Caucus immediately following their 1998 Proposition 5 victory, representing the first time in the history of the Democratic Party that American Indian party members had gathered as a formal caucus to plot their political future. "It's a very exciting time," said Frank LaMere, a Winnebago and vice chairman of the Nebraska Democratic Party. Nearly 100 American Indian delegates and alternates from twenty-nine states attended the caucus gathering at the 2000 Democratic National Convention. "We want to map a strategy as to where we will go politically," LaMere said. "It is a tremendous step forward in terms of Native Americans and politics" (Associated Press 2000).

There are about two million American Indians in the United States. Of the 3,711 delegates at the Democratic National Convention, slightly more than 1 percent were American Indian, Eskimo, or Aleuts (Associated Press 2000). High on their list of concerns were issue of sovereignty for indigenous nations and its relationship to the Constitution. Brian Wallace, chairman of the Washoe tribe of Nevada and California, said that he hoped American Indians could gain political muscle nationwide. "It's been a long road," he offered. "The fact that the tribes are able to constitute themselves around specific issues of common interest is tremendously important" (Associated Press 2000).

Although gaming has offered some American Indians the opportunity to participate in politics, many remain uninvolved. One key to understanding this nonparticipation is the politics of exclusion. American Indians have never been fully accepted into the larger, Anglo-dominated society, which poses problems for integration into mainstream politics. Thus, tribes use the resources available to them. Political donations represent more than money to them; they are an opportunity to discuss the issues facing Indians with policymakers, many of whom are woefully uneducated on such topics. Chairman Richard Milanovich of the Agua Caliente band refers to political donations as "assured access" (Associated Press 2000).

California Indians have over the years demonstrated their resiliency. Much misunderstood and hard working, tribes have achieved under the most unfavorable of circumstances. Although California Indians have made strides politically, socially, and economically, cautious optimism remains in order regarding their political influence. The tribes of California differ from one another in language, ceremonies, economies, and philosophy. In addition, although the federal government acts as a trustee for the sovereign nations and is presumably responsible for providing services to them, California Indians (as well as most other Indians) still face problems involving education, housing, employment, and health. Their unique political and legal status is often not afforded respect.

Another barrier to American Indian political influence is the inability to sustain intertribal cooperation. When working together, tribes must hold true to the principles and values that brought them together in the first place. If tribes step away from what they have interpreted and defined as in their interest and worldview, they render their issues illegitimate. Legitimacy, or validity, is an important resource that if not sustained can lead to political disempowerment. For example, if tribes supporting Proposition 5 maintain that tribal gaming in California offers self-reliance to *all* tribes, including gaming and non-gaming tribes, then this should hold true. This means that the economic affluence provided by gaming must be shared with non-gaming tribes. Such sharing of resources might lead to increased participation by American Indians in the political process.

Looking toward the Future

Economists agree that within the next ten years the revenue generated from tribal gaming will approach $10 billion dollars per year. At present, there is some indication of "countermobilization" efforts, such as newspaper articles portraying California Indians in a negative light because of gambling sites. In another example, a 2002 report depicts California tribes as a political elite able to manipulate the political process because of their economic resources from gaming (California Common Cause 2002). The key to future American Indian success in the gaming arena appears to rest upon their successful participation in the political process and the (re)education of non-Indian Americans about Native Americans. In addition, coalition building with other groups may provide American Indians with more opportunities in the political arena. They might also benefit from the positive impacts that tribal gaming has had in California because of its focus on employment, infrastructure, social services, and education. Highlighting these enormous contributions will assist tribes in forging a better relationship with non-Indian counterparts. Additionally, California tribes must continue to focus on intertribal social and culture well-being. A 1998 study prepared by the Analysis Group/Economics on the economic and fiscal benefits of Indian gaming in California reported the following:

- Indian gaming contributes approximately $120 million in state and local tax receipts annually, including $36.6 million in state personal income taxes, $23.6 million in gaming taxes, and $9.0 million in other taxes and payments in lieu of taxes.
- Indian gaming is estimated to have reduced Aid for Dependent Children (AFDC) payments to tribal members by $21 million and $28.9 million to other former recipients.
- Some 74 percent of Indian gaming customers surveyed indicated that if Indian gaming were not available in California, they would go to casinos in Nevada, thereby reducing income, jobs, and tax receipts in California.
- Total casino revenue generated directly by Indian gaming in California, in casino concessions, approached an estimated $1.4 billion in 1997.
- Gaming patrons' expenditures at local non-casino businesses totaled an estimated $273 million in 1997.
- Indian casinos employ an estimated 14,571 California residents, 90 percent of whom are non-Indians.
- In addition to jobs at casinos, Indian gaming supports an estimated 33,800 additional jobs in California through spending by employees, tribal governments, vendors, construction firms, and other businesses.
- The jobs created by Indian gaming are predominantly in counties with historically high rates of unemployment and low per capita income. (National Indian Gaming Association n.d.)

California tribes must continue to look inward to define and redefine the goals, values and needs of the whole in order to envision their future and move forward as a nation. Their values and cultural attributes define tribes as a separate sovereign entity with the ability and right to govern and lead their people

California Indian families must be at the heart of all decisions that respective tribes make, for without the next generation understanding their culture, language, and relationship to the land, attempts at economic success will be in vain. Families must continue to raise their children with the central values of the tribe. California Indians face a paradox of sorts in regard to the economic success of gaming and the constant influence of consumer-driven media and capitalism. American Indians are not exempt from greed or extraordinary consumerism and should not be held accountable based on mythic concepts of who they are or are able to withstand. Instead the emphasis must be on the importance of families and culture. Many tribes in California have provided incentives through programs in the areas of educational and cultural growth. Indians must continue in this endeavor by writing their own stories and histories, teaching their own people, and encouraging physical, social, and mental wellness.

Tribal governments should be applauded for their efforts to effectively serve their people and function in times of severe strife, economic depression, and social despair. Tribal governments must continue in their endeavors to treat their citizens in the most fair and equitable way. Gaming revenue will provide tribes with the economic foundation on which to build full governance, including ways to deal with disputes and issues, which is a necessary function for an effective and honorable government.

Tribal governments should request greater participation from their citizens. Citizenship must supersede the notion of membership. Therefore, tribes must clarify what is expected of their citizenry, which might include defining roles and responsibilities to the tribal community and society at large; character; cultural appreciation and promotion; service to community; participation in community and tribal events; betterment of oneself and tribal community; and promotion and development of tribal youth.

Despite the gains of California Indians, conflict with states, private enterprise, and other competing interests remain inevitable. The increasing revenues generated by tribal gaming operations will likely ensure California Indians greater political influence at the local, state, and federal levels. This development in turn will secure greater political sovereignty for them and the ability of tribal governments to provide services to their citizens, including educational opportunities and advancement, health care and wellness, infrastructure, employment opportunities, cultural maintenance and advancement, and development and strength within the American political system.

Bibliography

Analysis Group/Economics. 1998. "The Economic and Fiscal Benefits of Indian Gaming in California." Prepared for Californians for Indian Self-Reliance. June 26.

Associated Press. 2000. "American Indians Hold First Caucus at DNC." *Lawrence World Journal* (Kansas). August 15.

Bureau of Indian Affairs. 1999. Tribal State Compact List, http://www.bia.gov.

California Common Cause. 2002. "Big Donors Enjoy Legislative Success." March 18, http://www.commoncause.org/states/california/press-rel/mar18-02.html.

Cook, Sherburne F. 1976. *The Population of the California Indians, 1769–1970.* Berkeley: University of California Press.

Deloria, Vine, Jr. 1979. "Self-Determination and the Concept of Sovereignty." In *Economic Development in American Indian Reservations.* Native American Studies Development 1. Albuquerque: Native American Studies, University of New Mexico.

———. 1988. *Custer Died for Your Sins.* Norman: University of Oklahoma Press.

Eargle, Dolan H., Jr. 1992. *California Indian Country: The Land and the People.* San Francisco: Trees Company Press.

Fagan, Kevin. 2000. "Tribes Flex Money Muscles: Campaign Cash Catches Attention of Politicians." *San Francisco Chronicle*, May 25.

Gambling Magazine. 1999. "Nevada Gaming Industry To Be Hurt by California Indian Casinos," http://www.gamblingmagazine.com/articles/14/14-1563.htm.

Jackson, Robert H., and Edward Castillo. 1995. *Indians, Franciscans, and Spanish Colonization.* Albuquerque: University of New Mexico Press.

Kelly, Josephy. 1993. "American Indian Gaming Law." *New Law Journal.* November 26.

National Congress of American Indians. 1999. "Tribal Gaming." Washington, D.C.

National Indian Gaming Association. n.d. "Indian Gaming Facts," http://indiangaming.org/library/index.html.

Secretary of State of California. 2002. "Campaign Finance Activity," http://cal-access.ss.ca.gov/Campaign/Committees.

Vellinga, Mary Lynne. 1998. "Proposition 5 Still Too Close to Call." *Bee Capitol Bureau.* November 5.

22 Native American Rights and the American Indian Movement

Donald A. Grinde Jr.

During the late 1960s in Minneapolis, the Native American population numbered more than 10,000, and dire economic conditions there helped to create a new era of American Indian militancy. In addition to facing low incomes, poor housing, and high unemployment, native peoples in the Twin Cities also endured police brutality and harassment. Employing methods similar to those used by the Black Panther Party in Oakland, California, American Indian leaders in Minneapolis created an "Indian patrol" to shadow the activities of the police in the urban Indian community of the Twin Cities. In Oakland, Black Panthers had trailed police cars carrying guns and law books in an attempt to uphold the constitutional rights of African Americans. During thirty-nine weeks of Indian patrols in the Twin Cities Indian ghetto, the arrest rate of Native Americans fell significantly.

In the summer of 1968, as a result of the success of the Indian patrol, Ojibway leaders Dennis Banks and George Mitchell founded the American Indian Movement (AIM). Mitchell, an introspective leader, drafted AIM's charter, and Banks, a more colorful leader, became the group's media spokesman. Although the initial purpose of AIM was to protect the rights of Native Americans living in urban areas, the organization soon began supporting native political activities in cities and on reservations nationwide. AIM quickly evolved into a militant Native American rights group. Its leaders became convinced that tribal governments and the federal government were virtually identical, so real reform would have to come from the outside, not from within.

Soon American Indian protests were being held across the country, from Plymouth Rock, Massachusetts, to Mount Rushmore, South Dakota, to Pit River, California. While many of these protests focused on broken treaties and promises, some demonstrations targeted elected tribal governments and the Bureau of

Indian Affairs (BIA). Indian activists criticizing the role of government in the lives of Native Americans contended that "BIA" stood for "Bossing Indians Around." In 1970 several dozen demonstrators were arrested when they tried to occupy BIA offices in California, Colorado, Illinois, Minnesota, New Mexico, Ohio, and Pennsylvania.

This new activism upset many tribal leaders, who felt that their traditional role among Native American people was being undermined by a group of militants. Even more disconcerting to the older leadership was the growing alliance between American Indian militants and traditionalists on and off the reservations. In the summer of 1972 several AIM leaders met with traditional elders at the annual Sun Dance on the Rosebud reservation in South Dakota. At the meeting, the activists received direction from the spiritual leaders. Finding common cause in their distrust of elected tribal governments, the two groups joined forces to nurture a gathering of hundreds of Indians under the banner of the "Trail of Broken Treaties" and to march on Washington in a peaceful and spiritual way. Vernon Bellecourt, the national coordinator of AIM, volunteered to organize the demonstration.

In late September 1972 dozens of leaders met in Denver to outline the details of the protest. Based on the plan adopted there, in early October 1972 caravans left Los Angeles, San Francisco, and Seattle for the trip east to Washington. En route, the riders recruited demonstrators. By mid-October, the caravans converged in Minneapolis, where protestors drafted "Twenty Points," a list of grievances forming the manifesto for American Indian liberation. The document called for the repeal of the 1871 federal statute outlawing additional government treaties with Native American nations and demanded the reestablishment of treaty relations between the federal government and Indian tribes and nations. In instituting this new relationship, American Indian nations would regain the sovereignty and autonomy they lost in the nineteenth century. American Indian governments would be free to reinstate traditional forms of government, and the U.S. government's power over Native American nations would be greatly diminished.

After arriving in Washington on November 3, 1972, the eve of President Richard Nixon's reelection, some five hundred Native American demonstrators gathered in the BIA auditorium to speak with government leaders about their concerns. Those attending quickly learned that only a few low-level bureaucrats were willing to meet with them, and they also found out that promised housing arrangements for their stay in Washington would not be forthcoming. As the workday came to a close, guards prepared to eject the demonstrators, and violence broke out; several people were injured. Disappointed and angry, the demonstrators decided to occupy the BIA office building. They made barricades of filing cabinets, office furniture, and copy machines and crafted arms out of broken table legs, scissor blades, and electrical insulation cables.

Although the occupation lasted only five days, a groundswell of support rose across the United States. Leaders of the occupation were in constant fear that they would be stormed by the police, but the two sides reached an agreement on November 7 to end the takeover. In return for peaceably leaving on November 8, the leaders were assured that a federal task force would be created to address the Twenty Points and $66,500 provided to transport the demonstrators home. When the activists left, they took with them files that they later used for documenting BIA malfeasance in the administration of Indian affairs.

On January 9, 1973, the federal task force charged with evaluating the Twenty Points rejected all of them, asserting that the reestablishment of treaty relations was impractical because Native Americans were now citizens of the United States. Undaunted, AIM leaders the next month resolved to occupy a small village on the Pine Ridge reservation. On February 27, 1973, two hundred Native American activists took over Wounded Knee. Convinced that the occupation would lead to a fatal confrontation, AIM leader Russell Means said, "I hope by my death, and the deaths of these Indian men and women, there will be an investigation into corruption on the reservations and there's no better place to start than Pine Ridge." The activists held Wounded Knee for more than seventy days; during the confrontation two Native American were killed and one federal marshal was paralyzed. Nightly exchanges of hundreds of rounds of ammunition could be heard. Finally, an agreement ended the occupation in April 1973.

In early May, President Nixon agreed to send a federal delegation to discuss the Sioux Treaty of 1868 in exchange for the Native Americans putting down their arms. The Treaty of 1868 contained longstanding land claims and sovereignty issues that the federal government had not subsequently upheld. Additionally, the government promised an investigation of tribal government corruption on the Pine Ridge reservation and prosecutions for all criminal and civil violations uncovered. On May 17, 1973, Native American traditionalists and the federal authorities met to discuss the Sioux treaties. Pressing for acknowledgment of their pre-1871 status, the Native Americans urged a reinstatement of Sioux sovereignty. The federal government, however, once again stated that no fundamental change in the status of American Indian nations was possible and that returning to pre-1871 treaty relations was in violation of the provisions of the Indian Reorganization Act of 1934 that created the existing tribal governments.

Soon after AIM's confrontations with the federal government in the early 1970s, it was revealed that the FBI had an informant inside the movement. In order to deter future infiltrations, AIM leaders decided to decentralize the organization, essentially creating autonomous but confederated state and regional chapters. For twenty years, this decentralized structure allowed AIM to survive despite governmental repression, disinformation campaigns, and provocateurs. AIM continued to focus on supporting American Indian autonomy at the local level and the fight to reassert treaty rights and sovereignty at the national and state levels. It also organized demonstrations against Columbus Day celebrations and such sports mascots as the Washington Redskins and Atlanta Braves. In the mid-1990s, Vernon Bellecourt and his brother Clyde attempted to establish a national AIM office in Minneapolis, in part to discredit the confederated AIM chapters led by Russell Means, Bobby Castillo, Ward Churchill, and Glenn Morris. The resulting bitter fight divided an already fragmented organization and rendered it less useful in the pursuit of American Indian rights. To this date, there has been no American Indian organization to supplant AIM, but its divisions have made it less effective in the last decade.

Bibliography

Churchill, Ward, and Jim Van Der Wall. 1988. *Agents of Repression: The FBI's Secret Wars against the Black Panther Party and the American Indian Movement.* Boston: South End Press.

Deloria, Vine, Jr. 1974. *Behind the Trail of Broken Treaties: An Indian Declaration of Independence.* New York: Delta Books.

Stern, Kenneth S. 2002. *Loud Hawk: The United States versus the American Indian Movement.* Norman: University of Oklahoma Press.

Weyler, Rex. 1992. *Blood of the Land: The FBI and the Corporate War against the American Indian Movement.* Philadelphia: Society Publishers.

Documents

Introduction to the Documents

A multitude of documents underscores the political history of Native Americans since the founding of the United States, outlining the various policies formulated and pursued by the federal government. The documents that follow reflect the legislative and executive branch decisions and court cases integral to federal-tribal relations.

A close look at American Indian history might lead one to question the fundamental humanistic and ethical assertions about U.S. history and government espoused over the centuries. Certainly, it can be claimed without reservation that the United States has treated Native Americans with great malice for a long period of time. American policies, which encouraged genocide and ethnocide against Native Americans, cannot be excused when placed beside long-standing professed principles of democracy, equality, and "Christian" values. Anyone searching for an American history that incorporates the failure of American ideals and ethical duplicity in U.S. behavior can find it repeatedly in the history of federal-tribal relations. Thus, American Indian history is a measure of the United States' failure, despite its many successes in other areas, to live up to the fundamental conceptual principles formulated at its creation.

The documents here were selected to paint a representative picture of federal-tribal relations from the late eighteenth century to the end of the twentieth century. They elucidate salient points in federal Indian policy involving Christianization, education, and property ownership. These documents also highlight Native Americans' dubious singularity as one of the few groups of people that possess individual citizen rights and group, or treaty, rights under the U.S. Constitution. Despite the codification of these rights, the federal government and the American people have failed in far too many instances to sustain these rights.

One of the factors in this failure to protect Native Americans' rights is the great wealth that Indian peoples possessed at the time of Columbus. American Indians are unique in American history in that they are the only non-white peoples that had enormous wealth at the time of contact with emigrating Europeans. Hence, much of the history of federal-tribal relations deals with the illegal and legal transfer of that wealth in the form of land and natural resources to non-Indians. The history of this process is far less ambiguous than in the areas of Indian education, health, and human rights. In a very real sense, American Indian law as demonstrated in these documents is what each generation of political leaders has made of it, but the consistent thread is the taking of the land through a variety of legal and extralegal devices.

The spellings and use of capitalization are primarily as they appear in the original documents. In some cases, brackets or bracketed information appears in the source document, and in others information has been added to clarify or correct the text. The formatting in a number of documents has been adjusted for presentation.

1 Northwest Territory, July 13, 1787

In 1787 the Continental Congress created the Northwest Territory and in the process developed federal policy toward Native Americans west of the Appalachian Mountains. The policy included the stated need for justice and good faith in relations with American Indians.

Article the Third. Religion, Morality and knowledge being necessary to good government and the happiness of mankind, Schools and the means of education shall forever be encouraged. The utmost good faith shall always be observed towards the Indians, their lands and property shall never be taken from them without their consent; and in their property, rights and liberty, they never shall be invaded or disturbed, unless in just and lawful wars authorised by Congress; but laws founded in justice and humanity shall from time to time be made, for preventing wrongs being done to them, and for preserving peace and friendship with them. . . .

Source: *Journals of the Continental Congress, 1774–1789*, ed. Worthington C. Ford et al. (Washington, D.C., 1904–1937), 32:340–341.

2 Establishment of the War Department, August 7, 1789

The First Congress placed implementation of Indian affairs and policies under the jurisdiction of the War Department in 1789. It remained there until the creation of the Department of the Interior in 1849.

An Act to establish an Executive Department, to be denominated the Department of War. . . .

That every person who shall attempt to trade with the Indian tribes, or be found in the Indian country with such merchandise in his possession as are usually vended to the Indians, without a license first had and obtained, as in this act prescribed, and being thereof convicted in any court proper to try the same, shall forfeit all the merchandise so offered for sale to the Indian tribes, or so found in the Indian country, which forfeiture shall be one half to the benefit of the person prosecuting, and the other half to the benefit of the United States. . . .

SEC. 4. *And be it enacted and declared*, That no sale of lands made by any Indians, or any nation or tribe of Indians within SECTION 1. *Be it enacted . . .* , That there shall be an executive department to be denominated the Department of War, and that there shall be a principal officer therein, to be called the Secretary for the Department of War, who shall perform and execute such duties as shall from time to time be enjoined on, or entrusted to him by the President of the United States, agreeably to the Constitution, relative to military commissions, or to the land or naval forces, ships, or warlike stores of the United States, or to such other matters respecting military or naval affairs, as the President of the United States shall assign to the said department, or relative to the granting of lands to persons entitled thereto, for military services rendered to the United States, or relative to Indian affairs; and furthermore, that the said principal officer shall conduct the business of the said department in such manner, as the President of the United States shall from time to time order or instruct. . . .

Source: *U.S. Statutes at Large*, 1:49–50.

3 Trade and Intercourse Act, July 22, 1790

Frontier violence quickly became a hallmark of the early history of the United States. Secretary of War Henry Knox and President George Washington asked Congress to enact legislation to mitigate the problem. In 1790 Congress acted to "regulate trade and intercourse with the Indian tribes." This law and subsequent ones sought to facilitate and enforce various treaties in frontier areas against the objections of many white settlers. These laws are cornerstones of fundamental aspects of U.S. Indian policy.

An Act to regulate trade and intercourse with the Indian tribes.

SECTION 1. *Be it enacted* . . . , That no person shall be permitted to carry on any trade or intercourse with the Indian tribes, without a license for that purpose under the hand and seal of the superintendent of the department, or of such other person as the President of the United States shall appoint for that purpose; which superintendent, or other person so appointed, shall, on application, issue such license to any proper person, who shall enter into bond with one or more sureties, approved of by the superintendent, or person issuing such license, or by the President of the United States, in the penal sum of one thousand dollars, payable to the President of the United States for the time being, for the use of the United States, conditioned for the true and faithful observance of such rules, regulations and restrictions, as now are, or hereafter shall be made for the government of trade and intercourse with the Indian tribes. The said superintendents, and persons by them licensed as aforesaid, shall be governed in all things touching the said trade and intercourse, by such rules and regulations as the President shall prescribe. And no other person shall be permitted to carry on any trade or intercourse with the Indians without such license as aforesaid. No license shall be granted for a longer term than two years. *Provided nevertheless,* That the President may make such order respecting the tribes surrounded in their settlements by the citizens of the United States, as to secure an intercourse without license, if he may deem it proper.

SEC. 2. *And be it further enacted,* That the superintendent, or person issuing such license, shall have full power and authority to recall all such licenses as he may have issued, if the person so licensed shall transgress any of the regulations or restrictions provided for the government of trade and intercourse with the Indian tribes, and shall put in suit such bonds as he may have taken, immediately on the breach of any condition in said bond: *Provided always,* That if it shall appear on trial, that the person from whom such license shall have been recalled, has not offended against any of the provisions of this act, or the regulations prescribed for the trade and intercourse with the Indian tribes, he shall be entitled to receive a new license.

SEC. 3. *And be it further enacted,* That every person who shall attempt to trade with the Indian tribes, or be found in the Indian country with such merchandise in his possession as are usually vended to the Indians, without a license first had and obtained, as in this act prescribed, and being convicted in any court proper to try the same, shall forfeit all the merchandise in his possession so offered for sale to the Indian tribes, or so found in the Indian country, which forfeiture shall be one half to the benefit of the person prosecuting, and the other half to the benefit of the United States.

SEC. 4. *And be it further enacted,* That no sale of lands made by any Indians, or any nation or tribe of Indians within the United States, shall be valid to any person or persons, or to any state, whether having the right of pre-emption to such lands or not, unless the same shall be made and duly executed at some public treaty, held under the authority of the United States.

SEC. 5. *And be it further enacted,* That if any citizen or inhabitant of the United States, or of either of the territorial districts of the United States, shall go into any town, settlement or territory belonging to any nation or tribe of Indians, and shall there commit any crime upon, or trespass against, the person or property of any peaceable and friendly Indian or Indians, which, if committed within the jurisdiction of any state, or within the jurisdiction of either of the said districts, against a citizen or white inhabitant thereof, would be punishable by the laws of such state or district, such offender or offenders shall be subject to the same punishment, and shall be proceeded against in the same manner as if the offence had been committed within the jurisdiction of the state or district to which he or they may belong, against a citizen or white inhabitant thereof.

SEC. 6. *And be it further enacted,* That for any of the crimes or offences aforesaid, the like proceedings shall be had for apprehending, imprisoning or bailing the offender, as the case may be, and for recognizing the witnesses for their appearance to testify in the case, and where the offender shall be committed, or the witnesses shall be in a district other than that in which the offence is to be tried, for the removal of the offender and the witnesses or either of them, as the case may be, to the district in which the trial is to be had, as by the act to establish the judicial courts of the United States, are directed for any crimes or offences against the United States.

SEC. 7. *And be it further enacted*, That this act shall be in force for the term of two years, and from thence to the end of the next session of Congress, and no longer.

Source: *U.S. Statutes at Large*, 1:137–138.

Establishment of Government Trading Houses, April 18, 1796

In 1795 President George Washington proposed that the United States create Indian trading houses to foster "trade with the several Indian nations." In 1796 the federal government created a "factory system" of trading houses with Indian nations. Subsequently, the United States extended this arrangement through a series of laws until the abolition of the policy in 1822.

An Act for establishing Trading Houses with the Indian Tribes.

SECTION 1. *Be it enacted . . .*, That it shall be lawful for the President of the United States, to establish trading houses at such posts and places on the western and southern frontiers, or in the Indian country, as he shall judge most convenient for the purpose of carrying on a liberal trade with the several Indian nations, within the limits of the United States.

SEC. 2. *And be it further enacted*, That the President be authorized to appoint an agent for each trading house established, whose duty it shall be, to receive, and dispose of, in trade, with the Indian nations afore-mentioned, such goods as he shall be directed by the President of the United States to receive and dispose of, as aforesaid, according to the rules and orders which the President shall prescribe; and every such agent shall take an oath or affirmation, faithfully to execute the trust committed to him; and that he will not, directly or indirectly, be concerned or interested in any trade, commerce or barter, with any Indian or Indians whatever, but on the public account.

SEC. 3. *And be it further enacted*, That the agents, their clerks, or other persons employed by them, shall not be, directly or indirectly, concerned or interested in carrying on the business of trade or commerce, on their own, or any other than the public account, or take, or apply to his or their own use, any emolument or gain for negotiating or transacting any business or trade, during their agency or employment, other than is provided by this act.

SEC. 4. *And be it further enacted*, That the prices of the goods supplied to, and to be paid for by the Indians, shall be regulated in such manner, that the capital stock furnished by the United States may not be diminished.

SEC. 5. *Be it further enacted*, That during the continuance of this act, the President of the United States be, and he is hereby authorized to draw annually from the treasury of the United States, a sum not exceeding eight thousand dollars, to be applied, under his direction, for the purpose of paying the agents and clerks; which agents shall be allowed to draw out of the public supplies, two rations each, and each clerk one ration per day.

SEC. 6. *And be it further enacted*, That one hundred and fifty thousand dollars, exclusive of the allowances to agents and clerks, he and they are hereby appropriated for the purpose of carrying on trade and intercourse with the Indian nations, in the manner aforementioned, to be paid out of any monies unappropriated in the treasury of the United States.

SEC. 7. *And be it further enacted*, That if any agent or agents, their clerks, or other persons employed by them, shall purchase, or receive of any Indian, in the way of trade or barter, a gun or other article commonly used in hunting; any instrument of husbandry, or cooking utensil, of the kind usually obtained by Indians in their intercourse with white people; any article of clothing (excepting skins or furs) he or they shall, respectively, forfeit the sum of one hundred dollars for each offence.

Source: *U.S. Statutes at Large*, 1:452–453.

5 Trade and Intercourse Act, March 30, 1802

In 1802 Congress supplanted the Indian Temporary Trade and Intercourse Acts of 1790, 1796, and 1799 with a more comprehensive act restating these earlier laws. This act remained the fundamental legislation governing Indian affairs until 1834, when Congress replaced it with a set of new laws.

An Act to regulate trade and intercourse with the Indians tribes, and to preserve peace on the frontiers.

SECTION 1. *Be it enacted . . .* , That the following boundary line, established by treaty between the United States and various Indian tribes, shall be clearly ascertained, and distinctly marked in all such places as the President of the United States shall deem necessary, and in such manner as he shall direct, to wit: [The boundary is described in detail.] . . . *Provided always*, that if the boundary line between the said Indian tribes and the United States shall, at any time hereafter, be varied, by any treaty which shall be made between the said Indian tribes and the United States, then all the provisions contained in this act shall be construed to apply to the said line so to be varied, in the same manner as said provisions apply, by force of this act, to the boundary line herein before recited.

SEC. 2. *And be it further enacted,* That if any citizen of, or other person resident in, the United States, or either of the territorial districts of the United States, shall cross over, or go within the said boundary line, to hunt, or in any wise destroy the game; or shall drive, or otherwise convey any stock of horses or cattle to range on any lands allotted or secured by treaty with the United States, to any Indian tribes, he shall forfeit a sum not exceeding one hundred dollars, or be imprisoned not exceeding six months.

SEC. 3. *And be it further enacted,* That if any such citizen or other person, shall go into any country which is allotted, or secured by treaty as aforesaid, to any of the Indian tribes south of the river Ohio, without a passport first had and obtained from the governor of some one of the United States, or the officer of the troops of the United States, commanding at the nearest post on the frontiers, or such other person as the President of the United States may, from time to time, authorize to grant the same, shall forfeit a sum not exceeding fifty dollars, or be imprisoned not exceeding three months.

SEC. 4. *And be it further enacted,* That if any such citizen, or other person, shall go into any town, settlement or territory, belonging, or secured by treaty with the United States, to any nation or tribe of Indians, and shall there commit robbery, larceny, trespass or other crime, against the person or property of any friendly Indian or Indians, which would be punishable, if committed within the jurisdiction of any state, against a citizen of the United States: or, unauthorized by law, and with a hostile intention, shall be found on any Indian land, such offender shall forfeit a sum not exceeding one hundred dollars, and be imprisoned not exceeding twelve months; and shall also, when property is taken or destroyed, forfeit and pay to such Indian or Indians, to whom the property taken and destroyed belongs, a sum equal to twice the just value of the property so taken or destroyed: and if such offender shall be unable to pay a sum at least equal to the said just value, whatever such payment shall fall short of the said just value, shall be paid out of the treasury of the United States: *Provided nevertheless*, that no such Indian shall be entitled to any payment out of the treasury of the United States, for any such property taken or destroyed, if he, or any of the nation to which he belongs, shall have sought private revenge, or attempted to obtain satisfaction by any force or violence.

SEC. 5. *And be it further enacted,* That if any such citizen, or other person, shall make a settlement on any lands belonging, or secured, or granted by treaty with the United States, to any Indian tribe, or shall survey, or attempt to survey, such lands, or designate any of the boundaries, by marking trees, or otherwise, such offender shall forfeit a sum not exceeding one thousand dollars, and suffer imprisonment, not exceeding twelve months. And it shall, moreover, be lawful for the President of the United States to take such measures, and to employ such military force, as he may judge necessary, to remove from lands, belonging or secured by treaty, as aforesaid, to any Indian tribe, any such citizen, or other person, who has made, or shall hereafter make, or attempt to make a settlement thereon.

SEC. 6. *And be it further enacted,* That if any such citizen, or other person, shall go into any town, settlement or territory belonging to any nation or tribe of Indians, and shall there commit murder, by killing any Indian or Indians, belonging to any nation or tribe of Indians, in amity with the United States, such offender, on being thereof convicted, shall suffer death.

SEC. 7. *And be it further enacted,* That no such citizen, or other person, shall be permitted to reside at any of the towns, or hunting camps, of any of the Indian tribes as a trader, without a license under the hand and seal of the superintendent of the department, or of such other person as the President of the United States shall authorize to grant licenses for that purpose: which superintendent, or person authorized, shall, on application, issue such license, for a term not exceeding two years, to such trader, who shall enter into bond with one or more sureties, approved of by the superintendent, or person issuing such license, or by the President of the United States, in the penal sum of one thousand dollars, conditioned for the true and faithful observance of such regulations and restrictions, as are, or shall be made for the government of trade and intercourse with the Indian tribes: and the superintendent, or person issuing such license, shall have full power and authority to recall the same, if the person so licensed shall transgress any of the regulations, or restrictions, provided for the government of trade and intercourse with the Indian tribes; and shall put in suit such bonds as he may have taken, on the breach of any condition therein contained.

SEC. 8. *And be it further enacted,* That any such citizen or other person, who shall attempt to reside in any town or hunting camp, of any of the Indian tribes, as a trader, without such license, shall forfeit all the merchandise offered for sale to the Indians, or found in his possession, and shall, moreover, be liable to a fine not exceeding one hundred dollars, and to imprisonment not exceeding thirty days.

SEC. 9. *And be it further enacted,* That if any such citizen, or other person, shall purchase, or receive of any Indian, in the way of trade or barter, a gun, or other article commonly used in hunting, any instrument of husbandry, or cooking utensil, of the kind usually obtained by the Indians, in their intercourse with white people, or any article of clothing, excepting skins or furs, he shall forfeit a sum not exceeding fifty dollars, and be imprisoned not exceeding thirty days.

SEC. 10. *And be it further enacted,* That no such citizen or other person shall be permitted to purchase any horse of an Indian, or of any white man in the Indian territory, without special license for that purpose; which license, the superintendent, or such other person as the President shall appoint, is hereby authorized to grant, on the same terms, conditions and restrictions, as other licenses are to be granted under this act: and any such person, who shall purchase a horse or horses, under such license, before he exposes such horse or horses for sale, and within fifteen days after they have been brought out of the Indian country, shall make a particular return to the superintendent, or other person, from whom he obtained his license, of every horse purchased by him, as aforesaid; describing such horses, by their colour, height, and other natural or artificial marks, under the penalty contained in their respective bonds. And every such person, purchasing a horse or horses, as aforesaid, in the Indian country, without a special license, shall for every horse thus purchased and brought into any settlement of citizens of the United States, forfeit a sum not exceeding one hundred dollars, and be imprisoned not exceeding thirty days. And every person, who shall purchase a horse, knowing him to he brought out of the Indian territory, by any person or persons, not licensed, as above, to purchase the same, shall forfeit the value of such horse.

SEC. 11. *And be it further enacted,* That no agent, superintendent, or other person authorized to grant a license to trade, or purchase horses, shall have any interest or concern in any trade with the Indians, or in the purchase or sale of any horse to or from any Indian, excepting for and on account of the United States; and any person offending herein, shall forfeit a sum not exceeding one thousand dollars, and be imprisoned not exceeding twelve months.

SEC. 12. *And be it further enacted,* That no purchase, grant, lease, or other conveyance of lands, or of any title or claim thereto, from any Indian, or nation, or tribe of Indians, within the bounds of the United States, shall be of any validity, in law or equity, unless the same be made by treaty or convention, entered into pursuant to the constitution: and it shall be a misdemeanor in any person, not employed under the authority of the United States, to negotiate such treaty or convention, directly or indirectly, to treat with any such Indian nation, or tribe of Indians, for the title or purchase of any lands by them held or claimed, punishable by fine not exceeding one thousand dollars, and imprisonment not exceeding twelve months: *Provided nevertheless,* that it shall be lawful for the agent or agents of any state, who may be present at any treaty held with Indians under the authority of the United States, in the presence, and with the approbation of the commissioner or commissioners of the United States, appointed to hold the same, to propose to, and adjust with the Indians, the compensation to be made, for their claims to lands within such state, which shall be extinguished by the treaty.

SEC. 13. *And be it further enacted,* That in order to promote civilization among the friendly Indian tribes, and to secure the continuance of their friendship, it shall be lawful for the President of the United States, to cause them to be furnished with useful domestic animals, and implements of husbandry, and with goods or money, as he shall judge proper, and to appoint such persons, from time to time, as temporary agents, to reside among the Indians, as he shall think fit: *Provided,* that the whole amount of such presents, and allowance to such agents, shall not exceed fifteen thousand dollars per annum.

SEC. 14. *And be it further enacted,* That if any Indian or Indians, belonging to any tribe in amity with the United States, shall come over or cross the said boundary line, into any state or territory inhabited by citizens of the United States, and there take, steal or destroy any horse, horses, or other property, belonging to any citizen or inhabitant of the United States, or of either of the territorial districts of the United States, or shall commit any murder, violence or outrage, upon any such citizen or inhabitant, it shall be the duty of such citizen or inhabitant, his representative, attorney, or agent, to make application to the superintendent, or such other person as the President of the United States shall authorize for that purpose; who, upon being furnished with the necessary documents and proofs, shall, under the direction or instruction of the President of the United States, make application to the nation or tribe, to which such Indian or Indians shall belong, for satisfaction; and if such nation or tribe shall neglect or refuse to make satisfaction, in a reasonable time, not exceeding twelve months, then it shall be the duty of such superintendent or other person authorized as aforesaid, to make return of his doings to the President of the United States, and forward to him all the documents and proofs in the case, that such further steps may be taken, as shall be proper to obtain satisfaction for the injury: and in the mean time, in respect to the property so taken, stolen or destroyed, the United States guarantee to the party injured, an eventual indemnification: *Provided always*, that if such injured party, his representative, attorney or agent, shall, in any way, violate any of the provisions of this act, by seeking, or attempting to obtain private satisfaction or revenge, by crossing over the line, on any of the Indian lands, he shall forfeit all claim upon the United States, for such indemnification: *And provided also*, that nothing herein contained shall prevent the legal apprehension or arresting, within the limits of any state or district, of any Indian having so offended: *And provided further*, that it shall be lawful for the President of the United States, to deduct such sum or sums, as shall be paid for the property taken, stolen or destroyed by any such Indian, out of the annual stipend, which the United States are bound to pay to the tribe, to which such Indian shall belong.

SEC. 15. [Detailed listing of courts with jurisdiction under the act.]

SEC. 16. *And be it further enacted*, That it shall be lawful for the military force of the United States to apprehend every person who shall, or may be found in the Indian country over and beyond the said boundary line between the United States and the said Indian tribes, in violation of any of the provisions or regulations of this act, and him or them immediately to convey, in the nearest, convenient and safe route, to the civil authority of the United States, in some one of the three next adjoining states or districts, to be proceeded against in due course of law: *Provided*, that no person, apprehended by military force as aforesaid, shall be detained longer than five days after the arrest and before removal. And all officers and soldiers who may have any such person or persons in custody, shall treat them with all the humanity which the circumstances will possibly permit; and every officer and soldier who shall be guilty of maltreating any such person, while in custody, shall suffer such punishment as a court martial shall direct

SEC. 17. *And be it further enacted*, That if any person, who shall be charged with a violation of any of the provisions or regulations of this act, shall be found within any of the United States, or either of the territorial districts of the United States, such offender may be there apprehended and brought to trial in the same manner, as if such crime or offence had been committed within such state or district; and it shall be the duty of the military force of the United States when called upon by the civil magistrate or any proper officer, or other person duly authorized for that purpose and having a lawful warrant, to aid and assist such magistrate, officer, or other person authorized, as aforesaid, in arresting such offender, and him committing to safe custody, for trial according to law.

SEC. 18. *And be it further enacted,* That the amount of fines, and duration of imprisonment, directed by this act as a punishment for the violation of any of the provisions thereof, shall be ascertained and fixed not exceeding the limits prescribed, in the discretion of the court, before whom the trial shall be had; and that all fines and forfeitures, which shall accrue under this act, shall be one half to the use of the informant, and the other half to the use of the United States; except where the prosecution shall be first instituted on behalf of the United States; in which case the whole shall be to their use.

SEC. 19. *And be it further enacted,* That nothing in this act shall be construed to prevent any trade or intercourse with Indians living on lands surrounded by settlements of the citizens of the United States, and being within the ordinary jurisdiction of any of the individual states; or the unmolested use of a road from Washington district to Mero district, or to prevent the citizens of Tennessee from keeping in repair the said road, under the direction or orders of the governor of said state, and of the navigation of the Tennessee river, as reserved and secured by treaty; nor shall this act be construed to prevent any person or persons travelling from Knoxville to Price's settlement, or to the settlement on Obed's river, (so called,) provided they shall travel in the trace or path which is usually travelled, and provided the Indians make no objection; but if the Indians object, the President of the United States is hereby authorized to issue a proclamation, prohibiting all travelling on said traces, or either of them, as the case may be, after which, the penalties of this act shall be incurred by every person travelling or being found on said traces, or either of them, to which the prohibition may apply, within the Indian boundary, without a passport.

SEC. 20. *And be it further enacted,* That the President of the United States be, and he is hereby authorized to cause to be clearly ascertained and distinctly marked, in all such places as he shall deem necessary, and in such manner as he shall direct, any other boundary lines between the United States and any Indian tribe, which now are, or hereafter may be established by treaty.

SEC. 21. *And be it further enacted,* That the President of the United States be authorized to take such measures, from time to time, as to him may appear expedient to prevent or restrain the vending or distributing of spirituous liquors among all or any of the said Indian tribes, any thing herein contained to the contrary thereof notwithstanding.

SEC. 22. *And be it further enacted,* That this act shall be in force from the passage thereof. . . .

Source: *U.S. Statutes at Large,* 2:139–146.

6 President Thomas Jefferson to William Henry Harrison, February 27, 1803

President Thomas Jefferson, in this letter to William Henry Harrison, governor of the Indiana territory, wrote frankly about his administration's Indian policy. Note that Jefferson advised Harrison to encourage Indian leaders to run up huge debts so that they would ultimately have to cede large parcels of land. While Jefferson expressed a concern for Native Americans who might become part of American society, he also advocated harsh policies for Native American peoples that resisted U.S. domination.

[T]his letter being unofficial and private, I may with safety give you a more extensive view of our policy respecting the Indians, that you better comprehend the parts dealt out to you in detail through the official channel, and observing the system which they make a part, conduct yourself in unison with it in cases where you are obliged to act without instruction. Our system is to live in perpetual peace with the Indians, to cultivate an affectionate attachment from them, but everything just and liberal which we can do for them within the bounds of reason, and by giving them effectual protection against wrongs from our own people. The decrease of game rendering their subsistence by hunting insufficient, we wish to draw them to agriculture, to spinning and weaving. The latter branches they take up with great readiness, because they fall to women, who gain by quitting the labors of the field for those which are exercised within doors. When they withdraw themselves to the culture of a small piece of land, they will perceive how useless to them are their extensive forests, and will be willing to pare them off from time to time in exchange for necessaries for their farms and families. To promote this disposition to exchange lands, which they have to spare and they want, we shall push our trading uses, and be glad to see the good and influential individuals among them run in debt, because we observe that when debts get beyond what individuals can pay, they become willing to lop them off by a cession of lands. . . . In this way our settlements will gradually circumscribe and approach the Indians, and they will in time either incorporate with us as citizens of the United States, or remove beyond the Mississippi. The former is the termination of their history most happy for themselves; but, in the whole course of this, it is essential to cultivate their love. As to their fear, we presume that our strength and their weakness is now so visible that they must see we have only to shut our hand to crush them, and that all our liberalities to them proceed from motives of pure humanity only. Should any tribe be foolhardy enough to take up the hatchet at any time, the seizing the whole country of that tribe, and driving them across the Mississippi, as the only condition of peace, would be an example to others, and a furtherance of our final consolidation. . . .

Source: *Writings of Thomas Jefferson*, ed. Andrew A. Lipscomb and Albert Ellery Bergh (Washington, D.C.: Thomas Jefferson Memorial Association, 1903–1904), 10:369–371.

7 President Thomas Jefferson to Secretary of War Henry Dearborn, August 28, 1807

In this letter to Secretary of War Henry Dearborn, President Thomas Jefferson outlines his administration's military policies toward Native American societies. American Indian nations that resisted U.S. domination would be subjected to genocide.

[A]s we have learnt that some tribes are already expressing intentions hostile to the United States, we think it proper to apprise them of the ground on which they now stand; for which purpose we make them this solemn declaration of our unalterable determination, that we wish them to live in peace with all nations as well as with us, and we have no intention ever to strike them or to do them an injury of any sort, unless first attacked or threatened; but that learning that some of them meditate war on us, we too are preparing for war against those, and those only who shall seek it; and that if ever we are constrained to lift the hatchet against any tribe, we will never lay it down till that tribe is driven beyond the Mississippi. Adjuring them, therefore, if they wish to remain on the land which covers the bones of their fathers, to keep the peace with a people who ask their friendship without needing it, who wish to avoid war without fearing it. In war, they will kill some of us; we shall destroy all of them. . . .

Source: *Writings of Thomas Jefferson*, ed. Andrew A. Lipscomb and Albert Ellery Bergh (Washington, D.C.: Thomas Jefferson Memorial Association, 1903–1904), 11:344–345.

8 Authorization of Indian Agents, 1818

Although Indian agents would become key figures in federal-tribal relations, the appointment of agents was not initially a formal process. Often, their appointment depended on clauses in treaties or a specific reference in the Trade and Intercourse Acts. Two 1818 acts of Congress formalized their status in the administration of American Indian affairs. The first act established the process of appointing Indian agents and the second delineated their salaries.

A. Manner of Appointing Agents, April 16, 1818

An Act directing the manner of appointing Indian Agents.

Be it enacted . . . that the superintendent of Indian trade, the agents and assistant agents of Indian trading houses, and the several agents of Indian affairs, shall be nominated by the President of the United States, and appointed by and with the advice and consent of the Senate.

SEC. 2. *And be it further enacted*, that from and after the eighteenth instant, no person shall act in either of the characters aforesaid, who shall not have been thus first nominated and appointed. And every agent as aforesaid, before he shall enter upon the duties of his office, shall give bond to the United States, with two or more sufficient securities, in the penal sum of ten thousand dollars, conditioned faithfully to perform all the duties which are or may he enjoined on them as agents as aforesaid.

Source: *U.S. Statutes at Large*, 3:428.

B. Compensation for Indian Agents, April 20, 1818

An Act fixing the compensation of Indian agents and factors.

Be it enacted . . . That, from and after the passage of this act, Indian agents and factors shall receive the following salaries per annum, in lieu of their present compensation, to wit;

The agent to the Creek nation, one thousand eight hundred dollars.
The agent to the Choctaws, one thousand eight hundred dollars.
The agent to the Cherokees on Tennessee River, one thousand three hundred dollars.
The agent to the Cherokees on the Arkansas River, one thousand five hundred dollars.
The agent to the Chickasaws, one thousand three hundred dollars.
The agent in the Illinois territory, one thousand three hundred dollars.
The agent at Prairie du Chien, one thousand two hundred dollars.
The agent at Natchitoches, one thousand two hundred dollars.
The agent at Chicago, one thousand three hundred dollars.
The agent at Green Bay, one thousand five hundred dollars.
The agent at Mackinac, one thousand four hundred dollars.
The agent at Vincennes, one thousand two hundred dollars.
The agent at Fort Wayne and Piqua, one thousand two hundred dollars.
The agent to the Lakes, one thousand three hundred dollars.
The agent in the Missouri territory, one thousand two hundred dollars.
And all sub-agents, five hundred dollars per annum.

SEC. 2. *And be it further enacted*, That all factors shall receive one thousand three hundred dollars, and assistant factors seven hundred dollars, per annum.

SEC. 3. *And be it further enacted*, That the sums hereby allowed to Indian agents and factors shall be in full compensation for their services; and that all rations, or other allowances, made to them, shall be deducted from the sums hereby allowed.

Source: *U.S. Statutes at Large*, 3:461.

9 Secretary of War John C. Calhoun on Indian Trade, December 5, 1818

Since regulating Native American trade was problematic, the House of Representatives asked John C. Calhoun, President James Monroe's secretary of war, to propose a trading system with the tribes. In response, Calhoun not only stated his ideas on the conduct of the American Indian trade but also on methods that could be used for "civilizing" Native Americans.

After giving the subject that full consideration which its importance merits, it appears to me that the provisions of the Ordinance of 1786, with a few additions and modifications, particularly in the administrative part, so as to adjust it to our present form of government, are, for this division of our Indian trade, the best that can be devised. The provisions of the acts now in force in relation to licenses are not as well guarded or as efficient as those of the ordinance referred to. The introduction of the factories seems to have relaxed the attention of Government to the system of trade under license. I would then propose to assume the provisions of the ordinance referred to, as the basis of a system to open the trade with the contiguous tribes of Indians to individual enterprise. Instead, however, of appointing two superintendents, I would propose a superintendent of Indian affairs, to be attached to the War Department, with a salary of $3,000 per annum; the superintendent to be under the control of the Secretary of War, and to be charged, subject to such regulations as the President may prescribe, with the correspondence, superintendence, and general management of Indian affairs; and to be authorized, with the approbation of the Secretary of War, to grant licenses to trade with the Indians. Licenses to be granted to citizens of good moral character, and to continue in force till revoked. A sum not less than $100, nor more than $500, to be determined under regulations to be prescribed by the President, to be paid for the privilege of using it at the time of granting the license, and annually during its continuance; and bonds, with sufficient security, to be taken to conform to law and regulations. Licenses to be revoked by the President whenever he may judge proper. To trade without license, to subject to a fine not exceeding $1,000, and imprisonment not to exceed six months, with a forfeiture of the goods. Licenses to be granted to trade at specified places, to be selected by the applicants, and not to be changed without the consent of the superintendent. All peddling and sales of spirituous liquors to be strictly prohibited. Each trading-house, or establishment, to require a separate license; and books to be kept at the establishment, in which the prices of the goods sold and the articles purchased should he regularly and fairly entered; and to be subject at all times to the inspection of the Indian agent, or such persons as the superintendent may appoint. . . .

But it will probably be objected that it is our interest, and, as we propose to monopolize their trade, our duty, too, to furnish the Indians with goods on as moderate terms as possible; and that the sum to be paid for a license, by acting as a duty on the goods sold under it, will tend to enhance their price. In answer to which it may he justly observed, that it is not a matter of so much importance that they should obtain their supplies for a few cents more or less, as that the trade should, as far as practicable, be put effectually under the control of the Government, in order that they may be protected against the fraud and the violence to which their ignorance and weakness would, without such protection, expose them. It is this very ignorance and weakness which render it necessary for the Government to interfere; and, if such interference is proper at all, it ought to be rendered effectual. Such will be the tendency of this provision. Its first and obvious effects will be to diminish more certainly, and with less injurious effect than any other provision which can be devised, the number of traders, and to increase the amount of capital which each would employ. The profit of a small capital of a few hundred dollars would scarcely pay for the license; while that on a large one would not be much diminished by it. Both of these effects—the diminution of the number of traders, and the increase of the capital—would add greatly to the control of the Government over the trade. It would be almost impossible to inspect the conduct, and consequently control the actions, of the multitude of traders with small capitals, diffused over the Indian country, and settled at remote and obscure places. The greatest vigilance on the part of the superintendent and his agents would be unequal to the task. By diminishing the number, and bringing each more permanently before the view of the Government, a due inspection and superintendence becomes practicable. . . .

The reasons for fixing the trading establishments are no less strong. By rendering them stationary, and compelling the proprietor to keep books, containing regular entries of all their sales and purchases, important checks will be presented to prevent fraud and exorbitant charges. It will also strongly tend to prevent collision between the traders, and, consequently, the creation of parties among the Indians for or against particular traders—a state of things unfriendly to their interest, and dangerous to the peace of the frontier. Besides, the trading establishments, being fixed, as they will be, in the most advantageous positions, will, in time, become the nucleus of Indian settlements, which, by giving greater density and steadiness to their population, will tend to introduce a division of real property, and thus hasten their ultimate civilization.

The time seems to have arrived when our policy towards them should undergo an important change. They neither are, in fact, nor ought to be, considered as independent nations. Our views of their interest, and not their own, ought to govern them. By a proper combination of force and persuasion, of punishments and rewards, they ought to be brought within the pales of law and civilization. Left to themselves, they will never reach that desirable condition. Before the slow operation of reason and experience can convince them of its superior advantages, they must be overwhelmed by the mighty torrent of our population. Such small bodies, with savage customs and character, cannot, and ought not, to be permitted to exist in an independent condition in the midst of civilized society. Our laws and manners ought to supersede their present savage manners and customs. Beginning with those most advanced in civilization, and surrounded by our people, they ought to be made to contract their settlements within reasonable bounds, with a distinct understanding that the United States intend to make no further acquisition of land from them, and that the settlements reserved are intended for their permanent home. The land ought to be divided among families; and the idea of individual property in the soil carefully inculcated. Their annuities would constitute an ample school fund; and education, comprehending as well the common arts of life, as reading, writing, and arithmetic, ought not to be left discretionary with the parents. Those who might not choose to submit, ought to be permitted and aided in forming new settlements at a distance from ours. When sufficiently advanced in civilization, they would be permitted to participate in such civil and political rights as the respective States within whose limits they are situated might safely extend to them. It is only by causing our opinion of their interest to prevail, that they can be civilized and saved from extinction. Under the present policy, they are continually decreasing and degenerating, notwithstanding the Government has, under all of its administrations, been actuated by the most sincere desire to promote their happiness and civilization. The fault has been, not in the want of zeal, but in the mode by which it has been attempted to effect these desirable objects. The Indians are not so situated as to leave it to time and experience to effect their civilization. By selecting prudently the occasion for the change, by establishing a few essential regulations, and by appointing persons to administer them fairly and honestly, our efforts could scarcely fail of success. Nor ought it to be feared that the power would be abused on our part; for, in addition to the dictates of benevolence, we have a strong interest in their civilization. The enmity even of the frontier settlers towards them is caused principally by the imperfection of the present system; and under the one which I have suggested, it will greatly abate, if not entirely subside. The natural humanity and generosity of the American character would no longer be weakened by the disorders and savage cruelty to which our frontiers are now exposed. A deep conviction of the importance of the subject, and a strong desire to arrest the current of events, which, if permitted to flow in their present channel, must end in the annihilation of those who were once the proprietors of this prosperous country, must be my apology for this digression.

Source: *The New American State Papers: Indian Affairs* (Wilmington, Del.: Scholarly Resources, 1972), 2:182–184.

10 Civilization Fund Act, March 3, 1819

As Native American contacts with white settlers increased, the federal government sought ways to promote the education of American Indian children. Benevolent societies became interested in educating Native Americans, so in 1819 Congress established an annual "civilization fund" to promote such a policy.

An Act making provision for the civilization of the Indian tribes adjoining the frontier settlements.

Be it enacted . . . that for the purpose of providing against the further decline and final extinction of the Indian tribes, adjoining the frontier settlements of the United States, and for introducing among them the habits and arts of civilization, the President of the United States shall be, and he is hereby authorized, in every case where he shall judge improvement in the habits and condition of such Indians practicable, and that the means of instruction can be introduced with their own consent, to employ capable persons of good moral character, to instruct them in the mode of agriculture suited to their situation; and for teaching their children in reading, writing, and arithmetic, and performing such other duties as may be enjoined, according to such instructions and rules as the President may give and prescribe for the regulation of their conduct, in the discharge of their duties.

SEC. 2. *And be it further enacted,* That the annual sum of ten thousand dollars be, and the same is hereby appropriated, for the purpose of carrying into effect the provisions of this act; and an account of the expenditure of the money, and proceedings in execution of the foregoing provisions, shall be laid annually before Congress.

Source: *U.S. Statutes at Large,* 3:516–517.

11 *Johnson and Graham's Lessee v. William McIntosh* (1823)

Johnson and Graham asserted title to American Indian lands in Illinois by having purchased it from Native Americans. William McIntosh claimed title through a grant from the federal government. The Supreme Court found in favor of McIntosh and reiterated the power of the federal government in land dealings.

The United States, then, have unequivocally acceded to that great and broad rule by which its civilized inhabitants now hold this country. They hold, and assert in themselves, the title by which it was acquired. They maintain, as all others have maintained, that discovery gave an exclusive right to extinguish the Indian title of occupancy, either by purchase or by conquest; and gave also a right to such a degree of sovereignty, as the circumstances of the people would allow them to exercise.

The power now possessed by the government of the United States to grant lands, resided, while we were colonies, in the crown, or its grantees. The validity of the titles given by either has never been questioned in our Courts. It has been exercised uniformly over territory in possession of the Indians. The existence of this power must negative [negate?] the existence of any right which may conflict with, and control it. An absolute title to lands cannot exist, at the same time, in different persons, or in different governments. An absolute, must be an exclusive title, or at least a title which excludes all others not compatible with it. All our institutions recognise the absolute title of the crown, subject only to the Indian right of occupancy, and recognise the absolute title of the crown to extinguish that right. This is incompatible with an absolute and complete title in the Indians.

We will not enter into the controversy, whether agriculturists, merchants, and manufacturers, have a right, on abstract principles, to expel hunters from the territory they possess, or to contract their limits. Conquest gives a title which the Courts of the conqueror cannot deny, whatever the private and speculative opinions of individuals may be, respecting the original justice of the claim which has been successfully asserted. The British government, which was then our government, and whose rights have passed to the United States, asserted a title to all the lands occupied by Indians, within the chartered limits of the British colonies. It asserted also a limited sovereignty over them, and the exclusive right of extinguishing the title which occupancy gave to them. These claims have been maintained and established as far west as the river Mississippi, by the sword. The title to a vast portion of the lands we now hold, originates in them. It is not for the Courts of this country to question the validity of this title, or to sustain one which is incompatible with it.

Although we do not mean to engage in the defence of those principles which Europeans have applied to Indian title, they may, we think, find some excuse, if not justification, in the character and habits of the people whose rights have been wrested from them.

The title by conquest is acquired and maintained by force. The conqueror prescribes its limits. Humanity, however, acting on public opinion, has established, as a general rule, that the conquered shall not be wantonly oppressed, and that their condition shall remain as eligible as is compatible with the objects of the conquest. Most usually, they are incorporated with the victorious nation, and become subjects or citizens of the government with which they are connected. The new and old members of the society mingle with each other; the distinction between them is gradually lost, and they make one people. Where this incorporation is practicable, humanity demands, and a wise policy requires, that the rights of the conquered to property should remain unimpaired; that the new subjects should be governed as equitably as the old, and that confidence in their security should gradually banish the painful sense of being separated from their ancient connexions, and united by force to strangers.

When the conquest is complete, and the conquered inhabitants can be blended with the conquerors, or safely governed as a distinct people, public opinion, which not even the conqueror can disregard, imposes these restraints upon him; and he cannot neglect them without injury to his fame, and hazard to his power.

But the tribes of Indians inhabiting this country were fierce savages, whose occupation was war, and whose subsistence was drawn chiefly from the forest. To leave them in possession of their country, was to leave the country a wilderness; to govern them as a distinct people, was impossible, because they were as brave and as high spirited as they were fierce, and were ready to repel by arms every attempt on their independence.

What was the inevitable consequence of this state of things? The Europeans were under the necessity either of abandoning the country, and relinquishing their pompous claims to it, or of enforcing those claims by the sword, and by the adoption of principles adapted to the condition of a people with whom it was impossible to mix, and who could not be governed as a distinct society, or of remaining in their neighbourhood, and exposing themselves and their families to the perpetual hazard of being massacred.

Frequent and bloody wars, in which the whites were not always the aggressors, unavoidably ensued. European policy, numbers, and skill, prevailed. As the white population advanced, that of the Indians necessarily receded. The country in the immediate neighbourhood of agriculturists became unfit for them. The game fled into thicker and more unbroken forests, and the Indians followed. The soil, to which the crown originally claimed title, being no longer occupied by its ancient inhabitants, was parcelled out according to the will of the sovereign power, and taken possession of by persons who claimed immediately from the crown, or mediately, through its grantees or deputies.

That law which regulates, and ought to regulate in general, the relations between the conqueror and conquered, was incapable of application to a people under such circumstances. The resort to some new and different rule, better adapted to the actual state of things, was unavoidable. Every rule which can be suggested will be found to be attended with great difficulty.

However extravagant the pretension of converting the discovery of an inhabited country into conquest may appear; if the principle has been asserted in the first instance, and afterwards sustained; if a country has been acquired and held under it; if the property of the great mass of the community originates in it, it becomes the law of the land, and cannot be questioned. So, too, with respect to the concomitant principle, that the Indian inhabitants are to be considered merely as occupants, to be protected, indeed, while in peace, in the possession of their lands, but to be deemed incapable of transferring the absolute title to others. However this restriction may be opposed to natural right, and to the usages of civilized nations, yet, if it be indispensable to that system under which the country has been settled, and be adapted to the actual condition of the two people, it may, perhaps, be supported by reason, and certainly cannot be rejected by Courts of justice.

It has never been contended that the Indian title amounted to nothing. Their right of possession has never been questioned. The claim of government extends to the complete ultimate title, charged with this right of possession, and to the exclusive power of acquiring that right.

After bestowing on this subject a degree of attention which was more required by the magnitude of the interest in litigation, and the able and elaborate arguments of the bar, than by its intrinsic difficulty, the Court is decidedly of opinion, that the plaintiffs do not exhibit a title which can be sustained in the Courts of the United States; and that there is no error in the judgment which was rendered against them in the District Court of Illinois.

Source: 8 Wheaton 543, 587–592, 603–605.

12 Creation of a Bureau of Indian Affairs in the War Department, March 11, 1824

In 1824, without congressional sanction, Secretary of War John C. Calhoun established the Bureau of Indian Affairs in the War Department. Calhoun made Thomas L. McKenney head of the new office. McKenney served in that capacity until 1830, when President Andrew Jackson dismissed him. In 1832 Congress designated a permanent commissioner of Indian affairs.

Department of War, March 11th, 1824

SIR: To you are assigned the duties [of] the Bureau of Indian Affairs in this Department, for the faithful performance of which you will be responsible. Mr. Hamilton and Mr. Miller are assigned to you, the former as chief, and the latter as assistant clerk.

You will take charge of the appropriations for annuities, and of the current expenses, and all warrants on the same will be issued on your requisitions on the Secretary of War, taking special care that no requisition be issued, but in cases where the money previously remitted has been satisfactorily accounted for, and on estimates in detail, approved by you, for the sum required. You will receive and examine the accounts and vouchers for the expenditure thereof, and will pass them over to the proper Auditor's Office for settlement, after examination and approval by you; submitting such items for the sanction of this Department as may require its approval. The administration of the fund for the civilization of the Indians is also committed to your charge, under the regulations established by the Department. You are also charged with the examination of the claims arising out of the laws regulating the intercourse with Indian Tribes, and will, after examining and briefing the same, report them to this Department, endorsing a recommendation for their allowance or disallowance.

The ordinary correspondence with the superintendents, the agents, and subagents, will pass through your Bureau.

I have the honor to be,
Your obedient servant,
J. C. Calhoun

Thos. L. McKenney, Esq.

Source: House Document 146, 19th Cong., 1st sess., serial 138, p. 6.

13 Authorization of Treaties and Trade Regulations, May 25, 1824

Frontier violence on the Missouri River caused fur traders to demand government protection, so Congress empowered the president to negotiate treaties with Indian nations west of the Mississippi River. It also authorized military escorts for treaty commissioners and designated sites for the conduct of trade with American Indians.

An Act to enable the President to hold treaties with certain Indian tribes, and for other purposes.

Be it enacted . . . that the sum of ten thousand dollars be, and the same hereby is, appropriated, to defray the expenses of making treaties of trade and friendship with the Indian tribes beyond the Mississippi: and that the said sum shall be paid out of any money in the treasury not otherwise appropriated.

SEC. 2. *And be it further enacted,* That, for the purpose of negotiating said treaties, on the part of the United States, the President shall be, and he hereby is, authorized to appoint suitable persons for commissioners, and to fix their compensation, so as not to exceed what has been heretofore allowed for like services.

SEC. 3. *And be it further enacted,* That the President shall be, and hereby is, authorized to appoint two sub-agents to be employed among the Indian tribes, on the waters of the Upper Missouri, whose annual salary shall be eight hundred dollars each, to be paid out of any money in the treasury not otherwise appropriated.

SEC. 4. *And be it further enacted,* That it shall be the duty of Indian agents to designate, from time to time, certain convenient and suitable places for carrying on trade with the different Indian tribes, and to require all traders to trade at the places thus designated, and at no other place or places.

SEC. 5. *And be it further enacted,* That the superintendent of Indian affairs at St. Louis, and his successors in office, shall possess all the powers, and be subject to all the duties of governors of territories, when exercising the office of superintendents of Indian affairs, and shall exercise a general supervision of the official conduct and accounts of Indian agents within his superintendency.

SEC. 6. *And be it further enacted,* That the sum of ten thousand dollars be, and the same is hereby, appropriated, to be paid out of any money in the treasury not otherwise appropriated, to enable the President of the United States to furnish a competent military escort to the commissioners authorized to be appointed by this act, if, in his opinion, the same shall be necessary.

Source: *U.S. Statutes at Large,* 4:35–36.

14 Indian Removal Act, May 28, 1830

After considerable debate in the press and Congress during the 1820s, Congress passed the Indian Removal Act, empowering President Andrew Jackson to negotiate removal treaties with American Indian nations east of the Mississippi River. Native American nations were to exchange lands in the East for lands in the trans-Mississippi West. To fund this policy, Congress appropriated $500,000. Subsequently, American Indians in the East were removed with often disastrous and genocidal consequences.

An Act to provide for an exchange of lands with the Indians residing in any of the states or territories. And for their removal west of the river Mississippi.

Be it enacted . . . , That it shall and may be lawful for the President of the United States to cause so much of any territory belonging to the United States, west of the river Mississippi, not included in any state or organized territory, and to which the Indian title has been extinguished, as he may judge necessary, to be divided into a suitable number of districts, for the reception of such tribes or nations of Indians as may choose to exchange the lands where they now reside, and remove there; and to cause each of said districts to be so described by natural or artificial marks, as to be easily distinguished from every other.

SEC. 2. *And be it further enacted,* That it shall and may be lawful for the President to exchange any or all of such districts, so to be laid off and described, with any tribe or nation of Indians now residing within the limits of any of the states or territories, and with which the United States have existing treaties, for the whole or any part or portion of the territory claimed and occupied by such tribe or nation, within the bounds of any one or more of the states or territories, where the land claimed and occupied by the Indians, is owned by the United States, or the United States are bound to the state within which it lies to extinguish the Indian claim thereto.

SEC. 3. *And be it further enacted,* That in the making of any such exchange or exchanges, it shall and may be lawful for the President solemnly to assure the tribe or nation with which the exchange is made, that the United States will forever secure and guaranty to them, and their heirs or successors, the country so exchanged with them; and if they prefer it, that the United States will cause a patent or grant to be made and executed to them for the same: *Provided always,* That such lands shall revert to the United States, if the Indians become extinct, or abandon the same.

SEC. 4. *And be it further enacted,* That if, upon any of the lands now occupied by the Indians, and to be exchanged for, there should be such improvements as add value to the land claimed by any individual or individuals of such tribes or nations, it shall and may be lawful for the President to cause such value to be ascertained by appraisement or otherwise, and to cause such ascertained value to be paid to the person or persons rightfully claiming such improvements. And upon the payment of such valuation, the improvements so valued and paid for, shall pass to the United States, and possession shall not afterwards be permitted to any of the same tribe.

SEC. 5. *And be it further enacted*, That upon the making of any such exchange as is contemplated by this act, it shall and may be lawful for the President to cause such aid and assistance to be furnished to the emigrants as may be necessary and proper to enable them to remove to, and settle in, the country for which they may have exchanged; and also, to give them such aid and assistance as may be necessary for their support and subsistence for the first year after their removal.

SEC. 6. *And be it further enacted*, That it shall and may be lawful for the President to cause such tribe or nation to be protected, at their new residence, against all interruption or disturbance from any other tribe or nation of Indians, or from any other person or persons whatever.

SEC. 7. *And be it further enacted*, That it shall and may be lawful for the President to have the same superintendence and care over any tribe or nation in the country to which they may remove, as contemplated by this act, that he is now authorized to have over them at their present places of residence: *Provided*, That nothing in this act contained shall be construed as authorizing or directing the violation of any existing treaty between the United States and any of the Indian tribes.

SEC. 8. *And be it further enacted*, That for the purpose of giving effect to the provisions of this act, the sum of five hundred thousand dollars is hereby appropriated, to be paid out of any money in the treasury, not otherwise appropriated.

Source: *U.S. Statutes at Large*, 4:411–412.

15 *Cherokee Nation v. Georgia* (1831)

In anticipation of removing Native Americans east of the Mississippi River to lands in the West, the state of Georgia claimed jurisdiction over Cherokee lands in the northern part of the state. The Cherokees filed suit against Georgia in the U.S. Supreme Court, claiming that Georgia had no jurisdiction over them. Chief Justice John Marshall, finding against the Cherokees, stated that the Court had no jurisdiction over the matter because the Cherokee nation and other American Indian nations were not "foreign nations" but "domestic dependent nations."

Mr. Chief Justice MARSHALL delivered the opinion of the Court.

This bill is brought by the Cherokee nation, praying an injunction to restrain the state of Georgia from the execution of certain laws of that state, which, as is alleged, go directly to annihilate the Cherokees as a political society, and to seize, for the use of Georgia, the lands of the nation which have been assured to them by the United States in solemn treaties repeatedly made and still in force.

If Courts were permitted to indulge their sympathies, a case better calculated to excite them can scarcely be imagined. A people once numerous, powerful, and truly independent, found by our ancestors in the quiet and uncontrolled possession of an ample domain, gradually sinking beneath our superior policy, our arts and our arms, have yielded their lands by successive treaties, each of which contains a solemn guarantee of the residue, until they retain no more of their formerly extensive territory than is deemed necessary to their comfortable subsistence. To preserve this remnant, the present application is made.

Before we can look into the merits of the case, a preliminary inquiry presents itself. Has this Court jurisdiction of the cause?

The third article of the [C]onstitution describes the extent of the judicial power. The second section closes an enumeration of the cases to which it is extended, with "controversies" "between a state or the citizens thereof, and foreign states, citizens, or subjects." A subsequent clause of the same section gives the Supreme Court original jurisdiction in all cases in which a state shall be a party. The party defendant may then unquestionably be sued in this Court. May the plaintiff sue in it? Is the Cherokee nation a foreign state in the sense in which that term is used in the [C]onstitution?

The counsel for the plaintiffs have maintained the affirmative of this proposition with great earnestness and ability. So much of the argument as was intended to prove the character of the Cherokees as a state, as a distinct political society, separated from others, capable of managing its own affairs and governing itself, has, in the opinion of a majority of the judges, been completely successful. They have been uniformly treated as a state from the settlement of our country. The numerous treaties made with them by the United States recognise them as a people capable of maintaining the relations of peace and war, of being responsible in their political character for any violation of their engagements, or for any aggression committed on the citizens of the United States by any individual of their community. Laws have been enacted in the spirit of these treaties. The acts of our government plainly recognise the Cherokee nation as a state, and the Courts are bound by those acts.

A question of much more difficulty remains. Do the Cherokees constitute a foreign state in the sense of the [C]onstitution?

The counsel have shown conclusively that they are not a state of the union, and have insisted that individually they are aliens, not owing allegiance to the United States. An aggregate of aliens composing a state must, they say, be a foreign state. Each individual being foreign, the whole must be foreign.

This argument is imposing, but we must examine it more closely before we yield to it. The condition of the Indians in relation to the United States is perhaps unlike that of any other two people in existence. In the general, nations not owing a common allegiance are foreign to each other. The term foreign nation is, with strict propriety, applicable by either to the other. But the relation of the Indians to the United States is marked by peculiar and cardinal distinctions which exist nowhere else.

The Indian territory is admitted to compose a part of the United States. In all our maps, geographical treatises, histories, and laws, it is so considered. In all our intercourse with foreign nations, in our commercial regulations, in any attempt at intercourse between Indians and foreign nations, they are considered as within the jurisdictional limits of the United States, subject to many of those restraints which are imposed upon our own citizens. They acknowledge themselves in their treaties to be under the protection of the United States; they admit that the United States shall have the sole and exclusive right of regulating the trade with them, and managing all their affairs as they think proper; and the Cherokees in particular were allowed by the treaty of Hopewell, which preceded the [C]onstitution, "to send a deputy of their choice, whenever they think fit, to Congress." Treaties were made with some tribes by the state of New York, under a then unsettled construction of the confederation, by which they ceded all their lands to that state, taking back a limited grant to themselves, in which they admit their dependence.

Though the Indians are acknowledged to have an unquestionable, and, heretofore, unquestioned right to the lands they occupy, until that right shall be extinguished by a voluntary cession to our government; yet it may well be doubted whether those tribes which reside within the acknowledged boundaries of the United States can, with strict accuracy, be denominated foreign nations. They may, more correctly, perhaps, be denominated domestic dependent nations. They occupy a territory to which we assert a title independent of their will, which must take effect in point of possession when their right of possession ceases. Meanwhile they are in a state of pupilage. Their relation to the United States resembles that of a ward to his guardian.

They look to our government for protection; rely upon its kindness and its power; appeal to it for relief to their wants; and address the president as their great father. They and their country are considered by foreign nations, as well as by ourselves, as being so completely under the sovereignty and dominion of the United States, that any attempt to acquire their lands, or to form a political connexion with them, would be considered by all as an invasion of our territory, and an act of hostility.

These considerations go far to support the opinion, that the framers of our [C]onstitution had not the Indian tribes in view, when they opened the Courts of the union to controversies between a state or the citizens thereof, and foreign states.

In considering this subject, the habits and usages of the Indians, in their intercourse with their white neighbours, ought not to be entirely disregarded. At the time the [C]onstitution was framed, the idea of appealing to an American Court of justice for an assertion of right or a redress of wrong, had perhaps never entered the mind of an Indian or of his tribe. Their appeal was to the tomahawk, or to the government. This was well understood by the statesmen who framed the [C]onstitution of the United States, and might furnish some reason for omitting to enumerate them among the parties who might sue in the Courts of the union. Be this as it may, the peculiar relations between the United States and the Indians occupying our territory are such, that we should feel much difficulty in considering them as designated by the term foreign state, were there no other part of the [C]onstitution which might shed light on the meaning of these words. But we think that in construing them, considerable aid is furnished by that clause in the eighth section of the third article, which empowers Congress to "regulate commerce with foreign nations, and among the several states, and with the Indian tribes."

In this clause they are as clearly contradistinguished by a name appropriate to themselves, from foreign nations, as from the several states composing the union. They are designated by a distinct appellation; and as this appellation can be applied to neither of the others, neither can the appellation distinguishing either of the others be in fair construction applied to them. The objects, to which the power of regulating commerce might be directed, are divided into three distinct classes—foreign nations, the several states, and Indian tribes. When forming this article, the convention considered them as entirely distinct. We cannot assume that the distinction was lost in framing a subsequent article, unless there be something in its language to authorize the assumption.

The Court has bestowed its best attention on this question, and, after mature deliberation, the majority is of opinion that an Indian tribe or nation within the United States is not a foreign state in the sense of the [C]onstitution, and cannot maintain an action in the Courts of the United States.

If it be true that the Cherokee nation have rights, this is not the tribunal in which those rights are to be asserted. If it be true that wrongs have been inflicted, and that still greater are to be apprehended, this is not the tribunal which can redress the past or prevent the future.

The motion for an injunction is denied.

Source: 5 Peters 15–20.

16 *Worcester v. Georgia* (1832)

The state of Georgia jailed Samuel A. Worcester, a white missionary to the Cherokees, on charges that he had refused to take an oath of allegiance to Georgia while in Cherokee country and had not obtained a permit from the state for entry. The Supreme Court held in favor of Worcester, asserting that the Cherokee nation was not subject to the laws of Georgia, a reversal of the decision in Cherokee Nation v. Georgia *(1831).*

Mr. Chief Justice MARSHALL delivered the opinion of the Court.

This cause, in every point of view in which it can be placed, is of the deepest interest. The defendant is a state, a member of the Union, which has exercised the powers of government over a people who deny its jurisdiction, and are under the protection of the United States.

The plaintiff is a citizen of the state of Vermont, condemned to hard labour for four years in the penitentiary of Georgia; under colour of an act which he alleges to be repugnant to the Constitution, laws, and treaties of the United States.

The legislative power of a state, the controlling power of the Constitution and laws of the United States, the rights, if they have any, the political existence of a once numerous and powerful people, the personal liberty of a citizen, are all involved in the subject now to be considered. . . .

The Indian nations had always been considered as distinct, independent political communities, retaining their original natural rights, as the undisputed possessors of the soil, from time immemorial, with the single exception of that imposed by irresistible power, which excluded them from intercourse with any other European potentate than the first discoverer of the coast of the particular region claimed; and this was a restriction which those European potentates imposed on themselves, as well as on the Indians. The very term "nation," so generally applied to them, means "a people distinct from others." The Constitution, by declaring treaties already made, as well as those to be made, to be the supreme law of the land, has adopted and sanctioned the previous treaties with the Indian nations, and consequently admits their rank among those powers who are capable of making treaties. The words "treaty" and "nation" are words of our own language, selected in our diplomatic and legislative proceedings, by ourselves, having each a definite and well understood meaning. We have applied them to Indians, as we have applied them to the other nations of the earth. They are applied to all in the same sense.

Georgia, herself, has furnished conclusive evidence that her former opinions on this subject concurred with those entertained by her sister states, and by the government of the United States. Various acts of her legislature have been cited in the argument, including the contract of cession made in the year 1802, all tending to prove her acquiescence in the universal conviction that the Indian nations possessed full right to the lands they occupied, until that right should be extinguished by the United States, with their consent; that their territory was separated from that of any state within whose chartered limits they might reside, by a boundary line, established by treaties; that within their boundary, they possessed rights with which no state could interfere; and that the whole power of regulating the intercourse with them was vested in the United States. A review of these acts, on the part of Georgia, would occupy too much time, and is the less necessary, because they have been accurately detailed in the argument at bar. Her new series of laws, manifesting her abandonment of these opinions, appears to have commenced in December, 1828.

In opposition to this original right, possessed by the undisputed occupants of every country; to this recognition of that right, which is evidenced by our history, in every change through which we have passed; is placed the charters granted by the monarch of a distant and distinct region, parceling out a territory in possession of others whom he could not remove, and the cession made of his claims by the treaty of peace.

The actual state of things at the time, and all history since, explain these charters; and the King of Great Britain, at the treaty of peace, could only cede what belonged to his crown. These newly asserted titles can derive no aid from articles so often repeated in Indian treaties; extending to them, first, the protection of Great Britain, and afterwards that of the United States. These articles are associated with others, recognizing their title to self-government. The very fact of repeated treaties with them recognizes it; and the settled doctrine of the law of nations is, that a weaker power does not surrender its independence—its right to self-government—by associating with a stronger, and taking its protection. A weak state, in order to provide for its safety, may place itself under the protection of one more powerful, without stripping itself of the right of government, and ceasing to be a state. Examples of this kind are not wanting in Europe. "Tributary and feudatory states," says Vattel, "do not thereby cease to be sovereign and independent states, so long as self-government and sovereign and independent authority are left in the administration of the state." At the present day, more than one state may be considered as holding its right of self-government under the guarantee and protection of one or more allies.

The Cherokee nation, then, is a distinct community, occupying its own territory, with boundaries accurately described, in which the laws of Georgia can have no force, and which the citizens of Georgia can have no force, and which the citizens of Georgia have not right to enter, but with the assent of the Cherokees themselves, or in conformity with treaties, and with acts of Congress. The whole intercourse between the United States and this nation, is, by our Constitution and laws, vested in the United States.

The act of the state of Georgia, under which the plaintiff in error was prosecuted, is consequently void, and the judgment a nullity. Can this Court revise and reverse it?

If the objection to the system of legislation, lately adopted by the legislature of Georgia, in relation to the Cherokee nation, was confined to its extra-territorial operation, the objection, though complete, so far as respected mere right, would give this Court no power over the subject. But it goes much further. If the review which has been taken be correct, and we think it is the acts of Georgia are repugnant to the Constitution, laws and treaties of the United States.

They interfere forcibly with the relations established between the United States and the Cherokee nation, the regulation of which, according to settled principles of our Constitution, are committed exclusively to the government of the Union.

They are in direct hostility with treaties, repeated in a succession of years, which mark out the boundary that separates the Cherokee country from Georgia; guaranty to them all the land within their boundary; solemnly pledge the faith of the United States to restrain their citizens from trespassing on it; and recognize the pre-existing power of the nation to govern itself.

They are in equal hostility with the acts of Congress for regulating this intercourse, and giving effect to the treaties.

The forcible seizure and abduction of the plaintiff in error, who was residing in the nation with its permission, and by authority of the President of the United States, is also a violation of the acts which authorize the chief magistrate to exercise this authority.

Will these powerful considerations avail the plaintiff in error? We think they will. He was seized, and forcibly carried away, while under guardianship of treaties guarantying the country in which he resided, and taking it under the protection of the United States. He was seized while performing, under the sanction of the chief magistrate of the Union, those duties which the humane policy adopted by Congress had recommended. He was apprehended, tried, and condemned, under colour of a law which has been shown to be repugnant to the Constitution, laws, and treaties of the United States. Had a judgment, liable to the same objections, been rendered for property, none would question the jurisdiction of this Court. It cannot be less clear when the judgment affects personal liberty, and inflicts disgraceful punishment, if punishment could disgrace when inflicted on innocence. The plaintiff in error is not less interested in the operation of this unconstitutional law than if it affected his property. He is not less entitled to the protection of the Constitution, laws, and treaties of his country. . . .

It is the opinion of this Court that the judgment of the Superior Court for the county of Gwinnett, in the state of Georgia, condemning Samuel A. Worcester to hard labour in the penitentiary of the state of Georgia, for four years, was pronounced by that Court under colour of a law which is void, as being repugnant to the Constitution, treaties, and laws of the United States, and ought, therefore, to be reversed and annulled. . . .

Source: 6 Peters 534–536, 558–563.

17 Authorization of a Commissioner of Indian Affairs, July 9, 1832

Congress formally authorized the office of commissioner of Indian affairs in 1832 and delegated the management and direction of Indian affairs to it. The new commissioner replaced the head of the Indian office created in the War Department in 1824 (Doc. 12). Congress also prohibited the distribution of alcohol in Indian country.

An Act to provide for the appointment of a commissioner of Indian Affairs, and for other purposes.

Be it enacted . . . , That the President shall appoint, by and with the advice and consent of the Senate, a commissioner of Indian affairs, who shall, under the direction of the Secretary of War, and agreeably to such regulations as the President may, from time to time, prescribe, have the direction and management of all Indian affairs, and of all matters arising out of Indian relations, and shall receive a salary of three thousand dollars per annum.

SEC. 2. *And be it further enacted,* That the Secretary of War shall arrange or appoint to the said office the number of clerks necessary therefor, so as not to increase the number now employed; and such sum as is necessary to pay the salary of said commissioner for the year one thousand eight hundred and thirty-two, shall be, and the same hereby is, appropriated out of any money in the treasury.

SEC. 3. *And be it further enacted,* That all accounts and vouchers for claims and disbursements connected with Indian affairs, shall be transmitted to the said commissioner for administrative examination, and by him passed to the proper accounting officer of the Treasury Department for settlement; and all letters and packages to and from the said commissioner, touching the business of his office, shall be free of postage.

SEC. 4. *And be it further enacted,* That no ardent spirits shall be hereafter introduced, under any pretence, into the Indian country.

SEC. 5. *And be it further enacted,* That the Secretary of War shall, under the direction of the President, cause to be discontinued the services of such agents, subagents, interpreters, and mechanics, as may, from time to time, become unnecessary, in consequence of the emigration of the Indians, or other causes.

Source: *U.S. Statutes at Large,* 4:564.

18 Indian Commissioner William Medill on Indian Territories, November 30, 1848

With white settlers traveling through Native American lands on the Great Plains in order to settle on the Pacific Coast, the Indian office, under Commissioner William Medill, advocated the creation of two American Indian "colonies" west of the Mississippi River to remedy problems of frontier violence. Medill's analysis reflects the racial stereotypes of the era.

. . . While, to all, the fate of the red man has, thus far, been alike unsatisfactory and painful, it has, with many, been a source of much misrepresentation and unjust national reproach. Apathy, barbarism, and heathenism must give way to energy, civilization, and Christianity; and so the Indian of this continent has been displaced by the European; but this has been attended with much less of oppression and injustice than has generally been represented and believed. If, in the rapid spread of our population and sway, with all their advantages and blessings to ourselves and to others, injury has been inflicted upon the barbarous and heathen people we have displaced, are we as a nation alone to be held up to reproach for such a result? Where, in the contest of civilization with barbarism, since the commencement of time, has it been less the case than with us; and where have there been more general and persevering efforts, according to our means and opportunities, than those made by us, to extend to the conquered all the superior resources and advantages enjoyed by the conquerors? Of the magnitude and extent of those efforts but little comparatively is generally known.

Stolid and unyielding in his nature, and inveterately wedded to the savage habits, customs, and prejudices in which he has been reared and trained, it is seldom the case that the full blood Indian of our hemisphere can, in immediate juxtaposition with a white population, be brought farther within the pale of civilization than to adopt its vices; under the corrupting influences of which, too indolent to labor, and too weak to resist, he soon sinks into misery and despair. The inequality of his position in all that secures dignity and respect is too glaring, and the contest he has to make with the superior race with which he is brought into contact, in all the avenues to success and prosperity in life, is too unequal to hope for a better result. The collision is to him a positive evil. He is unprepared and in all respects unfitted for it; and he necessarily soon sinks under it and perishes. It must be recollected, too, that our white population has rapidly increased and extended, and, with a widening contact, constantly pressed upon the Indian occupants of territory necessary for the accommodation of our own people; thus engendering prejudices and creating difficulties which have occasionally led to strife and bloodshed—inevitable between different races under such circumstances—in which the weaker party must suffer. Hence, it is to natural and unavoidable causes, easily understood and appreciated, rather than to willful neglect, or to deliberate oppression and wrong, that we must in a great measure attribute the rapid decline and disappearance of our Indian population. Cannot this sad and depressing tendency of things be checked, and the past be at least measurably repaired by better results in the future? It is believed they can; and, indeed, it has to some extent been done already, by the wise and beneficent system of policy put in operation some years since, and which, if steadily carried out, will soon give to our whole Indian system a very different and much more favorable aspect.

The policy already begun and relied on to accomplish objects so momentous and so desirable to every Christian and philanthropist is, as rapidly as it can safely and judiciously be done, to colonize our Indian tribes beyond the reach, for some years, of our white population; confining each within a small district of country, so that, as the game decreases and becomes scarce, the adults will gradually be compelled to resort to agriculture and other kinds of labor to obtain a subsistence, in which aid may be afforded and facilities furnished them out of the means obtained by the sale of their former possessions. To establish, at the same time, a judicious and well devised system of manual labor schools for the education of the youth of both sexes in letters—the males in practical agriculture and the various necessary and useful mechanic arts, and the females in the different branches of housewifery, including spinning and weaving; and these schools, like those already in successful operation, to be in charge of the excellent and active missionary societies of the different Christian denominations of the country, and to be conducted and the children taught by efficient, exemplary, and devoted men and women, selected with the approbation of the Department by those societies; so that a physical, intellectual, moral, and religious education will all be imparted together.

The strongest propensities of an Indian's nature are his desire for war and his love of the chase. These lead him to display tact, judgment, and energy, and to endure great hardships, privation, and suffering; but in all other respects he is indolent and inert, physically and mentally, unless on occasions for display in council, when he not frequently exhibits great astuteness and a rude eloquence, evincing no ordinary degree of intellect. But anything like labor is distasteful and utterly repugnant to his feelings and natural prejudices. He considers it a degradation. His subsistence and dress are obtained principally by means of the chase; and if this resource is insufficient, and it be necessary to cultivate the earth or to manufacture materials for dress, it has to be done by the women, who are their "hewers of wood and drawers of water." Nothing can induce him to resort to labor, unless compelled to do so by a stern necessity; and it is only then that there is any ground to work upon for civilizing and Christianizing him. But little, if any, good impression can be made upon him in these respects, so long as he is able freely to roam at large and gratify his two predominant inclinations. Nor can these be subdued in any other way than by the mode of colonization, to which reference has been made. When compelled to face the stern necessities of life and to resort to labor for a maintenance, he in a very short time becomes a changed being; and is then willing, and frequently eager, to receive information and instruction in all that may aid him in improving his condition. It is at this stage that he begins to perceive and appreciate the advantages possessed by the white man, and to desire also to enjoy them; and, if too far advanced in life for mental instruction himself, he asks that it may be provided for his children. Such is the experience in the cases of several of the tribes not long since colonized, who a few years ago were mere nomads and hunters; and, when settled in their new countries, were opposed to labor and to anything like schools or missionaries; but who are now desirous of both the latter for the benefit of their children and themselves, and are becoming prosperous and happy from having learned how to provide a certain and comfortable support for themselves and their families by the cultivation of the soil and other modes of labor. The most marked change, however, when this transition takes place, is in the condition of the females. She who had been the drudge and the slave then begins to assume her true position as an equal; and her labor is transferred from the field to her household—to the care of her family and children. This great change in disposition and condition has taken place, to a greater or less extent, in all the tribes that have been removed and permanently settled west of the Mississippi. It is true, that portions of some of them enjoyed a considerable degree of civilization before they were transplanted; but prior to that event they were retrograding in all respects; while now, they and others who have been colonized and confined within reasonable and fixed limits, are rapidly advancing in intelligence and morality, and in all the means and elements of national and individual prosperity; so that before many years, if we sacredly observe all our obligations towards them, they will have reached a point at which they will be able to compete with a white population, and to sustain themselves under any probable circumstances of contact can afford them protection from the Sioux, they may properly be compelled at an early day to remove and to keep within their own country; and thus be out of the way of our emigrants. They are so obnoxious to the tribes south that they could not, for the present at least, be colonized with them. They must eventually be driven west or exterminated by the Sioux, who have a strong antipathy to them, unless a better understanding can be effected between them and the southern tribes, which will admit of their being moved down among or in the rear of them. No reasonable amount of military force could prevent their being killed off in detail by the Sioux, if they remain long in their present country. The other tribes mentioned can gradually be removed down to the southern colony, as the convenience of our emigrants and the pressure of our white population may require; which may be the case at no distant day, as the greater portion of the lands they occupy are eligibly located on and near the Missouri river, and from that circumstance, and their superior quality, said to be very desirable. Indeed, it would be a measure of great humanity to purchase out and remove the Omahas and the Ottoes and Missourias at an early period, particularly the former, who are a very interesting people, being mild and tractable in disposition, and much attached to the whites. Were they in a better position, they might, with proper measures, be easily civilized, and be made the instruments of imparting civilization to others. . . .

Source: House Executive Document 1, 30th Cong., 2d sess., serial 537, pp. 385–389.

19 Treaty of Fort Laramie, September 17, 1851

As the westward movement of American settlers increased, the federal government devised military and diplomatic policies to facilitate peaceful relations with Native Americans. One of the results of this policy was the Treaty of Fort Laramie, in which the United States sought to secure safety for settlers along the Oregon Trail and other passages. With this treaty, the federal government established formal relations with American Indian nations on the northern Plains, fixed boundaries for the various Indian nations, obtained the right to build forts and roads through the area, and secured damages for settlers if they were harmed by Indians. In 1853 a similar treaty for the southern Plains was negotiated at Fort Atkinson.

Articles of a treaty made and concluded at Fort Laramie, in the Indian Territory, between D. D. Mitchell, superintendent of Indian affairs, and Thomas Fitzpatrick, Indian agent, commissioners specially appointed and authorized by the President of the United States, of the first part, and the chiefs, headmen, and braves of the following Indian nations, residing south of the Missouri River, east of the Rocky Mountains, and north of the lines of Texas and New Mexico, viz, the Sioux or Dahcotahs, Cheyennes, Arrapahoes, Crows, Assinaboines, Gros-Ventre Mandans, and Arrickaras, parties of the second part, on the seventeenth day of September, A.D. one thousand eight hundred and fifty-one.

ARTICLE 1. The aforesaid nations, parties to this treaty, having assembled for the purpose of establishing and confirming peaceful relations amongst themselves, do hereby convenant and agree to abstain in future from all hostilities whatever against each other, to maintain good faith and friendship in all their mutual intercourse, and to make an effective and lasting peace.

ARTICLE 2. The aforesaid nations do hereby recognize the right of the United States Government to establish roads, military and other posts, within their respective territories.

ARTICLE 3. In consideration of the rights and privileges acknowledged in the preceding article, the United States bind themselves to protect the aforesaid Indian nations against the commission of all depredations by the people of the said United States, after the ratification of this treaty.

ARTICLE 4. The aforesaid Indian nations do hereby agree and bind themselves to make restitution or satisfaction for any wrongs committed, after the ratification of this treaty, by any band or individual of their people, on the people of the United States, whilst lawfully residing in or passing through their respective territories.

ARTICLE 5. The aforesaid Indian nations do hereby recognize and acknowledge the following tracts of country, included within the metes and boundaries hereinafter designated, as their respective territories [descriptions of the boundaries].

It is, however, understood that, in making this recognition and acknowledgement, the aforesaid Indian nations do not hereby abandon or prejudice any rights or claims they may have to other lands; and further, that they do not surrender the privilege of hunting, fishing, or passing over any of the tracts of country heretofore described.

ARTICLE 6. The parties to the second part of this treaty having selected principals or head-chiefs for their respective nations, through whom all national business will hereafter be conducted, do hereby bind themselves to sustain said chiefs and their successors during good behavior.

ARTICLE 7. In consideration of the treaty stipulations, and for the damages which have or may occur by reason thereof to the Indian nations, parties hereto, and for their maintenance and the improvement of their moral and social customs, the United States bind themselves to deliver to the said Indian nations the sum of fifty thousand dollars per annum for the term of ten years, with the right to continue the same at the discretion of the President of the United States for a period not exceeding five years thereafter, in provisions, merchandise, domestic animals, and agricultural implements, in such proportions as may be deemed best adapted to their condition by the President of the United States, to be distributed in proportion to the population of the aforesaid Indian nations.

ARTICLE 8. It is understood and agreed that should any of the Indian nations, parties to this treaty, violate any of the provisions thereof, the United States may withhold the whole or a portion of the annuities mentioned in the preceding article from the nation so offending, until, in the opinion of the President of the United States, proper satisfaction shall have been made. . . .

Source: *Indian Affairs: Laws and Treaties*, ed. Charles J. Kappler (Washington, D.C.: Government Printing Office, 1903), 2:594–595.

20 Creation of an Indian Peace Commission, July 20, 1867

With warfare on the Great Plains increasing during and after the Civil War, Congress decided to take a more peaceful approach in the conduct of Indian affairs. In 1867 it created the Indian Peace Commission to examine why there were so many conflicts. The commission was also empowered to negotiate treaties and create reservations.

An Act to establish Peace with certain Hostile Indian Tribes.

Be it enacted . . . , That the President of the United States be, and he is hereby, authorized to appoint a commission to consist of three officers of the army not below the rank of brigadier general, who, together with N. G. Taylor, Commissioner of Indian Affairs, John B. Henderson, Chairman of the Committee of Indian Affairs of the Senate, S. F. Tappan, and John B. Sanborn, shall have power and authority to call together the chiefs and headmen of such bands or tribes of Indians as are now waging war against the United States or committing depredations upon the people thereof, to ascertain the alleged reasons for their acts of hostility, and in their discretion, under the direction of the President, to make and conclude with said bands or tribes such treaty stipulations, subject to the action of the Senate, as may remove all just causes of complaint on their part, and at the same time establish security for person and property along the lines of railroad now being constructed to the Pacific and other thoroughfares of travel to the western Territories, and such as will most likely insure civilization for the Indians and peace and safety for the whites.

SEC. 2. *And be it further enacted*, That said commissioners are required to examine and select a district or districts of country having sufficient area to receive all the Indian tribes now occupying territory east of the Rocky mountains, not now peacefully residing on permanent reservations under treaty stipulations, to which the government has the right of occupation or to which said commissioners can obtain the right of occupation, and in which district or districts there shall be sufficient tillable or grazing land to enable the said tribes, respectively, to support themselves by agricultural and pastoral pursuits. Said district or districts, when so selected, and the selection approved by Congress, shall be and remain permanent homes for said Indians to be located thereon, and no person[s] not members of said tribes shall ever be permitted to enter thereon without the permission of the tribes interested, except officers and employees of the United States: *Provided*, That the district or districts shall be so located as not to interfere with travel on highways located by authority of the United States, nor with the route of the Northern Pacific Railroad, the Union Pacific Railroad, the Union Pacific Railroad Eastern Division, or the proposed route of the Atlantic and Pacific Railroad by the way of Albuquerque.

SEC. 3. *And be it further enacted*, That the following sums of money are hereby appropriated out of any moneys in the treasury, to wit: To carry out the provisions of the preceding sections of this act, one hundred and fifty thousand dollars; to enable the Secretary of the Interior to subsist such friendly Indians as may have separated or may hereafter separate themselves from the hostile bands or tribes and seek the protection of the United States, three hundred thousand dollars.

SEC. 4. *And be it further enacted*, That the Secretary of War be required to furnish transportation, subsistence, and protection to the commissioners herein named during the discharge of their duties.

SEC. 5. *And be it further enacted*, That if said commissioners fail to secure the consent of the Indians to remove to the reservations and fail to secure peace, then the Secretary of War, under the direction of the President, is hereby authorized to accept the services of mounted volunteers from the Governors of the several States and Territories, in organized companies and battalions, not exceeding four thousand men in number, and for such term of service as, in his judgment, may be necessary for the suppression of Indian hostilities.

SEC. 6. *And be it further enacted*, That all volunteers so accepted shall be placed upon the same footing, in respect to pay, clothing, subsistence, and equipment, as the troops of the regular army.

SEC. 7. *And be it further enacted*, That said commissioners report their doings under this act to the President of the United States, including any such treaties and all correspondence as well as evidence by them taken.

Source: *U.S. Statutes at Large*, 15:17–18.

21 Treaty of Fort Laramie, April 29, 1868

In 1868 the Indian Peace Commission negotiated a treaty with the Sioux and other American Indian nations in the Dakotas. The treaty closed the Bozeman Trail, as well as the forts along the trail, and recognized the hunting rights of various nations along the Powder River. It also created a Sioux reservation west of the Missouri River in what would become the state of South Dakota.

Articles of a treaty made and concluded by and between Lieutenant-General William T. Sherman, General William S. Harney, General Alfred H. Terry, General C. C. Augur, J. B. Henderson, Nathaniel G. Taylor, John B. Sanborn, and Samuel F. Tappan, duly appointed commissioners on the part of the United States, and the different bands of the Sioux Nation of Indians, by their chiefs and headmen, whose names are hereto subscribed, they being duly authorized to act in the premises.

ARTICLE 1. From this day forward all war between the parties to this agreement shall forever cease. The Government of the United States desires peace, and its honor is hereby pledged to keep it. The Indians desire peace, and they now pledge their honor to maintain it.

If bad men among the whites, or among other people subject to the authority of the United States, shall commit any wrong upon the person or property of the Indians, the United States will, upon proof made to the agent and forwarded to the Commissioner of Indian Affairs at Washington City, proceed at once to cause the offender to be arrested and punished according to the laws of the United States, and also re-imburse the injured person for the loss sustained.

If bad men among the Indians shall commit a wrong or depredation upon the person or property of any one, white, black, or Indian, subject to the authority of the United States, and at peace therewith, the Indians herein named solemnly agree that they will, upon proof made to their agent and notice by him, deliver up the wrong-doer to the United States, to be tried and punished according to its laws; and in case they willfully refuse so to do, the person injured shall be re-imbursed for his loss from the annuities or other moneys due or to become due to them under this or other treaties made with the United States. And the President, on advising with the Commissioner of Indian Affairs, shall prescribe such rules and regulations for ascertaining damages under the provisions of this article as in his judgment may be proper. But no one sustaining loss while violating the provisions of this treaty or the laws of the United States shall be re-imbursed therefor.

ARTICLE 2. The United States agrees that the following district of country, to wit, viz: commencing on the east bank of the Missouri River where the forty-sixth parallel of north latitude crosses the same, thence along low-water mark down said east bank to a point opposite where the northern line of the State of Nebraska strikes the river thence west across said river, and along the northern line of Nebraska to the one hundred and fourth degree of longitude west from Greenwich, thence north on said meridian to a point where the forty-sixth parallel of north latitude intercepts the same, thence due east along said parallel to the place of beginning; and in addition thereto, all existing reservations on the east bank of said river shall be, and the same is, set apart for the absolute and undisturbed use and occupation of the Indians herein named, and for such other friendly tribes or individual Indians as from time to time they may be willing, with the consent of the United States, to admit amongst them; and the United States now solemnly agrees that no persons except those herein designated and authorized so to do, and except such officers, agents, and employees of the Government as may be authorized to enter upon Indian reservations in discharge of duties enjoined by law, shall ever be permitted to pass over, settle upon, or reside in the territory described in this article, or in such territory as may be added to this reservation for the use of said Indians, and henceforth they will and do hereby relinquish all claims or right in and to any portion of the United States or Territories, except such as is embraced within the limits aforesaid, and except as hereinafter provided.

ARTICLE 3. If it should appear from actual survey or other satisfactory examination of said tract of land that it contains less than one hundred and sixty acres of tillable land for each person who, at the time, may be authorized to reside on it under the provisions of this treaty, and a very considerable number of such persons shall be disposed to commence cultivating the soil as farmers, the United States agrees to set apart, for the use of said Indians, as herein provided, such additional quantity of arable land, adjoining to said reservation, or as near to the same as it can be obtained, as may be required to provide the necessary amount.

ARTICLE 4. The United States agrees, at its own proper expense, to construct at some place on the Missouri River, near the center of said reservation, where timber and water may be convenient, the following buildings, to wit: a warehouse, a store-room for the use of the agent in storing goods belonging to the Indians, to cost not less than twenty-five hundred dollars; an agency-building for the residence of the agent, to cost not exceeding three thousand dollars; a residence for the physician, to cost not more than three thousand dollars; and five other buildings, for a carpenter, farmer, blacksmith, miller, and engineer, each to cost not exceeding two thousand dollars; also a school-house or mission-building, so soon as a sufficient number of children can be induced by the agent to attend school, which shall not cost exceeding five thousand dollars.

The United States agrees further to cause to be erected on said reservation, near the other buildings herein authorized, a good steam circular-saw mill, with a grist-mill and shingle-machine attached to the same, to cost not exceeding eight thousand dollars.

ARTICLE 5. The United States agrees that the agent for said Indians shall in the future make his home at the agency-building; that he shall reside among them, and keep an office open at all times for the purpose of prompt and diligent inquiry into such matters of complaint by and against the Indians as may be presented for investigation under the provisions of their treaty stipulations, as also for the faithful discharge of other duties enjoined on him by law. In all cases of depredation on person or property he shall cause the evidence to be taken in writing and forwarded, together with his findings, to the Commissioner of Indian Affairs, whose decision, subject to the revision of the Secretary of the Interior, shall be binding on the parties to this treaty.

ARTICLE 6. If any individual belonging to said tribes of Indians, or legally incorporated with them, being the head of a family, shall desire to commence farming, he shall have the privilege to select, in the presence and with the assistance of the agent then in charge, a tract of land within said reservation, not exceeding three hundred and twenty acres in extent, which tract, when so selected, certified, and recorded in the "land-book," as herein directed, shall cease to be held in common, but the same may be occupied and held in the exclusive possession of the person selecting it, and of his family, so long as he or they may continue to cultivate it.

Any person over eighteen years of age, not being the head of a family, may in like manner select and cause to be certified to him or her, for purposes of cultivation, a quantity of land not exceeding eighty acres in extent, and thereupon be entitled to the exclusive possession of the same as above directed.

For each tract of land so selected a certificate, containing a description thereof and the name of the person selecting it, with a certificate endorsed thereon that the same has been recorded, shall be delivered to the party entitled to it, by the agent, after the same shall have been recorded by him in a book to be kept in his office, subject to inspection, which said book shall be known as the "Sioux Land-Book."

The President may, at any time, order a survey of the reservation, and, when so surveyed, Congress shall provide for protecting the rights of said settlers in their improvements, and may fix the character of the title held by each. The United States may pass such laws on the subject of alienation and descent of property between the Indians and their descendants as may be thought proper. And it is further stipulated that any male Indians, over eighteen years of age, of any band or tribe that is or shall hereafter become a party to this treaty, who now is or who shall hereafter become a resident or occupant of any reservation or Territory not included in the tract of country designated and described in this treaty for the permanent home of the Indians, which is not mineral land, nor reserved by the United States for special purposes other than Indian occupation, and who shall have made improvements thereon of the value of two hundred dollars or more, and continuously occupied the same as a homestead for the term of three years, shall be entitled to receive from the United States a patent for one hundred and sixty acres of land including his said improvements, the same to be in the form of the legal subdivisions of the surveys of the public lands. Upon application in writing, sustained by the proof of two disinterested witnesses, made to the register of the local land-office when the land sought to be entered is within a land district, and when the tract sought to be entered is not in any land district, then upon said application and proof being made to the Commissioner of the General Land Office, and the right of such Indian or Indians to enter such tract or tracts of land shall accrue and be perfect from the date of his first improvements thereon, and shall continue as long as he continues his residence and improvements, and no longer. And any Indian or Indians receiving a patent for land under the foregoing provisions, shall thereby and from thenceforth become and be a citizen of the United States, and be entitled to all the privileges and immunities of such citizens, and shall, at the same time, retain all his rights to benefits accruing to Indians under this treaty.

ARTICLE 7. In order to insure the civilization of the Indians entering into this treaty, the necessity of education is admitted, especially of such of them as are or may be settled on said agricultural reservations, and they therefore pledge themselves to compel their children, male and female, between the ages of six and sixteen years, to attend school; and it is hereby made the duty of the agent for said Indians to see that this stipulation is strictly complied with; and the United States agrees that for every thirty children between said ages who can be induced or compelled to attend school, a house shall be provided and a teacher competent to teach the elementary branches of an English education shall be furnished, who will reside among said Indians, and faithfully discharge his or her duties as a teacher. The provisions of this article to continue for not less than twenty years.

ARTICLE 8. When the head of a family or lodge shall have selected lands and received his certificate as above directed, and the agent shall be satisfied that he intends in good faith to commence cultivating the soil for a living, he shall be entitled to receive seeds and agricultural implements for the first year, not exceeding in value one hundred dollars, and for each succeeding year he shall continue to farm, for a period of three years more, he shall be entitled to receive seeds and implements as aforesaid, not exceeding in value twenty-five dollars.

And it is further stipulated that such persons as commence farming shall receive instruction from the farmer herein provided for, and whenever more than one hundred persons shall enter upon the cultivation of the soil, a second blacksmith shall be provided, with such iron, steel, and other material as may be needed.

ARTICLE 9. At any time after ten years from the making of this treaty, the United States shall have the privilege of withdrawing the physician, farmer, blacksmith, carpenter, engineer, and miller herein provided for, but in case of such withdrawal, an additional sum thereafter of ten thousand dollars per annum shall be devoted to the education of said Indians, and the Commissioner of Indian Affairs shall, upon careful inquiry into their condition, make such rules and regulations for the expenditure of said sum as will best promote the educational and moral improvement of said tribes.

ARTICLE 10. In lieu of all sums of money or other annuities provided to be paid to the Indians herein named, under any treaty or treaties heretofore made, the United States agrees to deliver at the agency-house on the reservation herein named, on or before the first day of August of each year, for thirty years, the following articles, to wit:

For each male person over fourteen years of age, a suit of good substantial woolen clothing, consisting of coat, pantaloons, flannel shirt, hat, and a pair of home-made socks.

For each female over twelve years of age, a flannel skirt, or the goods necessary to make it, a pair of woolen hose, twelve yards of calico, and twelve yards of cotton domestics.

For the boys and girls under the ages named, such flannel and cotton goods as may be needed to make each a suit as aforesaid, together with a pair of woolen hose for each.

And in order that the Commissioner of Indian Affairs may be able to estimate properly for the articles herein named, it shall be the duty of the agent each year to forward to him a full and exact census of the Indians, on which the estimate from year to year can be based.

And in addition to the clothing herein named, the sum of ten dollars for each person entitled to the beneficial effects of this treaty shall be annually appropriated for a period of thirty years, while such persons roam and hunt, and twenty dollars for each person who engages in farming, to be used by the Secretary of the Interior in the purchase of such articles as from time to time the condition and necessities of the Indians may indicate to be proper. And if within the thirty years, at any time, it shall appear that the amount of money needed for clothing under this article can be appropriated to better uses for the Indians named herein, Congress may, by law, change the appropriation to other purposes; but in no event shall the amount of this appropriation be withdrawn or discontinued for the period named. And the President shall annually detail an officer of the Army to be present and attest the delivery of all the goods herein named to the Indians, and he shall inspect and report on the quantity and quality of the goods and the manner of their delivery. And it is hereby expressly stipulated that each Indian over the age of four years, who shall have removed to and settled permanently upon said reservation and complied with the stipulations of this treaty, shall be entitled to receive from the United States, for the period of four years after he shall have settled upon said reservation, one pound of meat and one pound of flour per day, provided the Indians cannot furnish their own subsistence at an earlier date. And it is further stipulated that the United States will furnish and deliver to each lodge of Indians or family of persons legally incorporated with them, who shall remove to the reservation herein described and commence farming, one good American cow, and one good well-broken pair of American oxen within sixty days after such lodge or family shall have so settled upon said reservation.

ARTICLE 11. In consideration of the advantages and benefits conferred by this treaty, and the many pledges of friendship by the United States, the tribes who are parties to this agreement hereby stipulate that they will relinquish all right to occupy permanently the territory outside their reservation as herein defined, but yet reserve the right to hunt on any lands north of North Platte, and on the Republican Fork of the Smoky Hill River, so long as the buffalo may range thereon in such numbers as to justify the chase. And they, the said Indians, further expressly agree:

1st. That they will withdraw all opposition to the construction of the railroads now being built on the plains.

2nd. That they will permit the peaceful construction of any railroad not passing over their reservation as herein defined.

3d. That they will not attack any persons at home, or travelling, nor molest or disturb any wagon-trains, coaches, mules, or cattle belonging to the people of the United States, or to persons friendly therewith.

4th. They will never capture, or carry off from the settlements, white women or children.

5th. They will never kill or scalp white men, nor attempt to do them harm.

6th. They withdraw all pretence of opposition to the construction of the railroad now being built along the Platte River and westward to the Pacific Ocean, and they will not in future object to the construction of railroads, wagon-roads, mail-stations, or other works of utility or necessity, which may be ordered or permitted by the laws of the United States. But should such roads or other works be constructed on the lands of their reservation, the Government will pay the tribe whatever amount of damage may be assessed by three disinterested commissioners to be appointed by the President for that purpose, one of said commissioners to be a chief or headman of the tribe.

7th. They agree to withdraw all opposition to the military posts or roads now established south of the North Platte River, or that may be established, not in violation of treaties heretofore made or hereafter to be made with any of the Indian tribes.

ARTICLE 12. No treaty for the cession of any portion or part of the reservation herein described which may be held in common shall be of any validity or force as against the said Indians, unless executed and signed by at least three-fourths of all the adult male Indians, occupying or interested in the same; and no cession by the tribe shall be understood or construed in such manner as to deprive, without his consent, any individual member of the tribe of his rights to any tract of land selected by him, as provided in [A]rticle 6 of this treaty.

ARTICLE 13. The United States hereby agrees to furnish annually to the Indians the physician, teachers, carpenter, miller, engineer, farmer, and blacksmiths as herein contemplated, and that such appropriations shall he made from time to time, on the estimates of the Secretary of the Interior, as will be sufficient to employ such persons.

ARTICLE 14. It is agreed that the sum of five hundred dollars annually, for three years from date, shall be expended in presents to the ten persons of said tribe who in the judgment of the agent may grow the most valuable crops for the respective year.

ARTICLE 15. The Indians herein named agree that when the agency-house or other buildings shall be constructed on the reservation named, they will regard said reservation their permanent home, and they will make no permanent settlement elsewhere; but they shall have the right, subject to the conditions and modifications of this treaty, to hunt, as stipulated in Article 11 hereof.

ARTICLE 16. The United States hereby agrees and stipulates that the country north of the North Platte River and east of the summits of the Big Horn Mountains shall be held and considered to be unceded Indian territory, and also stipulates and agrees that no white person or persons shall be permitted to settle upon or occupy any portion of the same; or without the consent of the Indians first had and obtained, to pass through the same; and it is further agreed by the United States that within ninety days after the conclusion of peace with all the bands of the Sioux Nation, the military posts now established in the territory in this article named shall be abandoned, and that the road leading to them and by them to the settlements in the Territory of Montana shall be closed.

ARTICLE 17. It is hereby expressly understood and agreed by and between the respective parties to this treaty that the execution of this treaty and its ratification by the United States Senate shall have the effect, and shall be construed as abrogating and annulling all treaties and agreements heretofore entered into between the respective parties hereto, so far as such treaties and agreements obligate the United States to furnish and provide money, clothing or other articles of property to such Indians and bands of Indians as become parties to this treaty, but no further. . . .

Source: *Indian Affairs: Laws and Treaties*, ed. Charles J. Kappler (Washington, D.C.: Government Printing Office, 1903), 2:998–1003.

22 Report of the Board of Indian Commissioners, November 23, 1869

When the Board of Indian Commissioners drafted its first report in 1869, it offered recommendations for changes in American Indian policy and severely criticized the government's past dealings with Native Americans. Its recommendations set the agenda for policy reforms in the late nineteenth century.

SIR: The commission of citizens appointed by the President under the act of Congress of April 10, 1869, to co-operate with the administration in the management of Indian affairs, respectfully report: . . .

It is not proposed to make this report either final or in any degree exhaustive. In its moral and political, as well as economic aspects, the Indian question is one of the gravest importance. The difficulties which surround it are of a practical nature, as are also the duties of the commission with reference to them. We cannot offer recommendations as the result of theorizing, but must reach our conclusions through personal observation and knowledge, as well as testimony. The comparatively short period of the existence of the commission, and the preventing causes already mentioned, compel the board to pass over, for the present, some of the important points which have occupied their attention. Should the commission be continued, it is hoped that visits of inspection to the reservations will, in each case, be productive of benefits, and the aggregate of the information acquired will enable the board to make important suggestions, for which it is not now prepared. Should the commission be discontinued, it is hoped some other permanent supervisory body will be created, which, in its material, office, and powers, shall be as far as possible beyond suspicion of selfish motives or personal profits in connection with its duties.

While it cannot be denied that the government of the United States, in the general terms and temper of its legislation, has evinced a desire to deal generously with the Indians, it must be admitted that the actual treatment they have received has been unjust and iniquitous beyond the power of words to express.

Taught by the government that they had rights entitled to respect; when those rights have been assailed by the rapacity of the white man, the arm which should have been raised to protect them has been ever ready to sustain the aggressor.

The history of the government connections with the Indians is a shameful record of broken treaties and unfulfilled promises.

The history of the border white man's connection with the Indians is a sickening record of murder, outrage, robbery, and wrongs committed by the former as the rule, and occasional savage outbreaks and unspeakably barbarous deeds of retaliation by the latter as the exception.

The class of hardy men on the frontier who represent the highest type of the energy and enterprise of the American people, and are just and honorable in their sense of moral obligation and their appreciations of the rights of others, have been powerless to prevent these wrongs, and have been too often the innocent sufferers from the Indians revenge. That there are many good men on the border is a subject of congratulation, and the files of the Indian Bureau attest that among them are found some of the most earnest remonstrants against the evils we are compelled so strongly to condemn.

The testimony of some of the highest military officers of the United States is on record to the effect that, in our Indian wars, almost without exception, the first aggressions have been made by the white man, and the assertion is supported by every civilian of reputation who has studied the subject. In addition to the class of robbers and outlaws who find impunity in their nefarious pursuits upon the frontiers, there is a large class of professedly reputable men who use every means in their power to bring on Indian wars, for the sake of the profit to be realized from the presence of troops and the expenditure of government funds in their midst. They proclaim death to the Indians at all times, in words and publications, making no distinction between the innocent and the guilty. They incite the lowest class of men to the perpetration of the darkest deeds against their victims, and, as judges and jurymen, shield them from the justice due to their crimes. Every crime committed by a white man against an Indian is concealed or palliated; every offense committed by an Indian against a white man is borne on the wings of the post or the telegraph to the remotest corner of the land, clothed with all the horrors which the reality or imagination can throw around it. Against such influences as these the people of the United States need to be warned. The murders, robberies, drunken riots and outrages perpetrated by Indians in time of peace—taking into consideration the relative population of the races on the frontier—do not amount to a tithe of the number of like crimes committed by white men in the border settlements and towns. Against the inhuman idea that the Indian is only fit to be exterminated, and the influence of the men who propagate it, the military arm of the government cannot be too strongly guarded. It is hardly to be wondered at that inexperienced officers, ambitious for distinction, when surrounded by such influences, have been incited to attack Indian bands without adequate cause, and involve the nation in an unjust war. It should, at least, be understood that in the future such blunders should cost the officer his commission, and that such distinction is infamy.

Paradoxical as it may seem, the white man has been the chief obstacle in the way of Indian civilization. The benevolent measures attempted by the government for their advancement have been almost uniformly thwarted by the agencies employed to carry them out. The soldiers, sent for their protection, too often carried demoralization and disease into their midst. The agent, appointed to be their friend and counsellor, business manager, and the almoner of the government bounties, frequently went among them only to enrich himself in the shortest possible time, at the cost of the Indians, and spend the largest available sum of the government money with the least ostensible beneficial result. The general interest of the trader was opposed to their enlightenment as tending to lessen his profits. Any increase of intelligence would render them less liable to his impositions; and, if occupied in agricultural pursuits, their product of furs would be proportionally decreased. The contractor's and transporter's interests were opposed to it, for the reason that the production of agricultural products on the spot would measurably cut off their profits in furnishing army supplies. The interpreter knew that if they were taught, his occupation would be gone. The more submissive and patient the tribe, the greater the number of outlaws infesting their vicinity; and all these were the missionaries teaching them the most degrading vices of which humanity is capable. If in spite of these obstacles a tribe made some progress in agriculture, or their lands became valuable from any cause, the process of civilization was summarily ended by driving them away from their homes with fire and sword to undergo similar experiences in some new locality.

Whatever may have been the original character of the aborigines, many of them are now precisely what the course of treatment received from the whites must necessarily have made them—suspicious, revengeful, and cruel in their retaliation. In war they know no distinction between the innocent and the guilty. In his most savage vices the worst Indian is but the imitator of bad white men on the border. To assume that all of them, or even a majority of them, may be so characterized with any degree of truthfulness, would be no more just than to assume the same of all the white people upon the frontier. Some of the tribes, as a whole, are peaceful and industrious to the extent of their knowledge, needing only protection, and a reasonable amount of aid and Christian instruction, to insure the rapid attainment of habits of industry, and a satisfactory advance toward civilization. Even among the wildest of the nomadic tribes there are large bands, and many individuals in other bands, who are anxious to remain quietly upon their reservation, and are patiently awaiting the fulfillment of the government promise that they and their children shall be taught to "live like the white man."

To assert that "the Indian will not work" is as true as it would be to say that the white man will not work. In all countries there are non-working classes. The chiefs and warriors are the Indian aristocracy. They need only to be given incentives to induce them to work. Why should the Indian be expected to plant corn, fence lands, build houses, or do anything but get food from day to day, when experience has taught him that the product of his labor will be seized by the white man tomorrow? The most industrious white man would become a drone under similar circumstances. Nevertheless, many of the Indians are already at work, and furnish ample refutation of the assertion that "the Indian will not work." There is no escape from the inexorable logic of facts. . . .

The policy of collecting the Indian tribes upon small reservations contiguous to each other, and within the limits of a large reservation, eventually to become a State of the Union, and of which the small reservations will probably be the counties, seems to be the best that can be devised. Many tribes may thus be collected in the present Indian territory. The larger the number that can be thus concentrated the better for the success of the plan; care being taken to separate hereditary enemies from each other. When upon the reservation they should be taught as soon as possible the advantage of individual ownership of property; and should be given land in severalty as soon as it is desired by any of them, and the tribal relations should be discouraged. To facilitate the future allotment of the land the agricultural portions of the reservations should be surveyed as soon as it can be done without too much exciting their apprehensions. The titles should be inalienable from the family of the holder for at least two or three generations. The civilized tribes now in the Indian territory should be taxed, and made citizens of the United States as soon as possible.

The treaty system should be abandoned, and as soon as any just method can be devised to accomplish it, existing treaties should be abrogated.

The legal status of the uncivilized Indians should be that of wards of the government; the duty of the latter being to protect them, to educate them in industry, the arts of civilization, and the principles of Christianity; elevate them to the rights of citizenship, and to sustain and clothe them until they can support themselves.

The payment of money annuities to the Indians should be abandoned, for the reason that such payments encourage idleness and vice, to the injury of those whom it is intended to benefit. Schools should be established, and teachers employed by the government to introduce the English language in every tribe. It is believed that many of the difficulties with Indians occur from misunderstanding as to the meaning and intention of either party. The teachers employed should be nominated by some religious body having a mission nearest to the location of the school. The establishment of Christian missions should be encouraged, and their schools fostered. The pupils should at least receive the rations and clothing they would get if remaining with their families. The religion of our blessed Saviour is believed to be the most effective agent for the civilization of any people.

A reversal of the policy which has heretofore prevailed, of taking the goods of the peaceable and industrious and giving them to the vicious and unruly, should be insisted on. Every means in the power of the government and its agents should be employed to render settlement and industrious habits on the reservation attractive and certain in its rewards. Experience has already shown that this is the best mode of inducing the Indians to settle upon their reservations.

The honest and prompt performance of all the treaty obligations to the reservation Indians is absolutely necessary to success in the benevolent designs of the administration. There should be no further delay in the erection of the promised dwellings, school-houses, mills, &c., and the opening of the farms and furnishing instructors. There can be no question or doubt as to the wisdom of the President in selecting Indian superintendents and agents with a view to their moral as well as business qualifications, and aside from any political considerations. There should be some judicial tribunal constituted within the Indian territory competent to the prompt punishment of crime, whether committed by white man, Indian, or negro. The agent upon the reservation in which the offense is committed, the agent of the next nearest reservation, and the nearest post commander might constitute a court, all the agents being clothed with the necessary powers. The Indian treaties we have examined provide, in effect, that proof of any offense committed by a white man against an Indian shall be made before the agent, who shall transmit the same to the Commissioner of Indian Affairs, who shall proceed to cause the offender to be arrested and tried by the laws of the United States. If the Indian commits an offense, he shall be given up to be tried by the laws of the United States. It is a long process to get a white man tried; a shorter one for the Indian, in proportion to the difference in distance between the agency and the nearest white settlement and that to Washington City; and in the trials the Indian never escapes punishment; the white man rarely fails to be acquitted. . . .

Source: *Annual Report of the Board of Indian Commissioners* (Washington, D.C.: Government Printing Office, 1869), 5–11.

23 Indian Commissioner Ely S. Parker on the Treaty System, December 23, 1869

Brigadier General Ely S. Parker was a Seneca Indian and Ulysses S. Grant's adjutant during the Civil War. When Grant became president, he appointed Parker as the first Native American commissioner of Indian affairs; there would not be another American Indian appointed to that position until the Kennedy administration. Parker decided to resign effective August 1, 1871, after being exonerated following a congressional investigation into his alleged misuse of government funds. In this report, Parker criticizes the treaty-making system and calls for an end to it.

Arrangements now, as heretofore, will doubtless be required with tribes desiring to be settled upon reservations for the relinquishment of their rights to the lands claimed by them and for assistance in sustaining themselves in a new position, but I am of the opinion that they should not be of a treaty nature. It has become a matter of serious import whether the treaty system in use ought longer to be continued. In my judgment it should not. A treaty involves the idea of a compact between two or more sovereign powers, each possessing sufficient authority and force to compel a compliance with the obligations incurred. The Indian tribes of the United States are not sovereign nations, capable of making treaties, as none of them have an organized government of such inherent strength as would secure a faithful obedience of its people in the observance of compacts of this character. They are held to be the wards of the government, and the only title the law concedes to them to the lands they occupy or claim is a mere possessory one. But, because treaties have been made with them, generally for the extinguishment of their supposed absolute title to land inhabited by them, or over which they roam, they have become falsely impressed with the notion of national independence. It is time that this idea should be dispelled, and the government cease the cruel farce of thus dealing with its helpless and ignorant wards. Many good men, looking at this matter only from a Christian point of view, will perhaps say that the poor Indian has been greatly wronged and ill treated; that this whole country was once his, of which he has been despoiled, and that he has been driven from place to place until he has hardly left to him a spot where to lay his head. This indeed may be philanthropic and humane, but the stern letter of the law admits of no such conclusion, and great injury has been done by the government in deluding this people into the belief of their being independent sovereignties, while they were at the same time recognized only as its dependents and wards. As civilization advances and their possessions of land are required for settlement, such legislation should be granted to them as a wise, liberal, and just government ought to extend to subjects holding their dependent relation. In regard to treaties now in force, justice and humanity require that they be promptly and faithfully executed, so that the Indians may not have cause of complaint, or reason to violate their obligations by acts of violence and robbery.

While it may not be expedient to negotiate treaties with any of the tribes hereafter, it is no doubt just that those made within the past year, and now pending before the United States Senate, should be definitely acted upon. Some of the parties are anxiously waiting for the fulfillment of the stipulations of these compacts and manifest dissatisfaction at the delay.

Source: House Executive Document 1, 41st Cong., 2d sess., serial 1414, p. 448.

24 President Ulysses S. Grant's Peace Policy, December 5, 1870

To stop corruption in Indian affairs by crooked Indian agents and the political patronage system, President Ulysses S. Grant ordered Indian agencies to work with religious groups. These sects appointed agents, teachers, and other personnel. In 1870 Grant explained his actions in his second annual message to Congress.

Reform in the management of Indian affairs has received the special attention of the Administration from its inauguration to the present day. The experiment of making it a missionary work was tried with a few agencies given to the denomination of Friends, and has been found to work most advantageously. All agencies and superintendencies not so disposed of were given to officers of the Army. The act of Congress reducing the Army renders army officers ineligible for civil positions. Indian agencies being civil offices, I determined to give all the agencies to such religious denominations as had heretofore established missionaries among the Indians, and perhaps to some other denominations who would undertake the work on the same terms—i.e., as a missionary work. The societies selected are allowed to name their own agents, subject to the approval of the Executive, and are expected to watch over them and aid them as missionaries, to Christianize and civilize the Indian, and to train him in the arts of peace. The Government watches over the official acts of these agents, and requires of them as strict an accountability as if they were appointed in any other manner. I entertain the confident hope that the policy now pursued will in a few years bring all the Indians upon reservations, where they will live in houses, and have schoolhouses and churches, and will be pursuing peaceful and self-sustaining avocations, and where they may be visited by the law-abiding white man with the same impunity that he now visits the civilized white settlements. I call your special attention to the report of the Commissioner of Indian Affairs for full information on this subject. . . .

Source: *Messages and Papers of the Presidents*, comp. James D. Richardson (New York: Bureau of National Literature, 1897), 7:109–110.

25 Cherokee Tobacco Case, December 1870

Stand Watie and Elias C. Boudinot, members of the Cherokee nation, refused to pay taxes on tobacco levied under the Internal Revenue Act of 1868 because they believed that the Cherokee treaty of 1868 exempted them from taxation. The Supreme Court found in favor of the federal government, stating that the laws of Congress can supersede rights delineated in American Indian treaties.

The second section of the fourth article of the Constitution of the United States declares that "this Constitution and the laws of the United States which shall be made in pursuance thereof, and all treaties which shall be made under the authority of the United States, shall be the supreme law of the land."

It need hardly be said that a treaty cannot change the Constitution or be held valid if it be in violation of that instrument. This results from the nature and fundamental principles of our government. The effect of treaties and acts of Congress, when in conflict, is not settled by the Constitution. But the question is not involved in any doubt as to its proper solution. A treaty may supersede a prior act of Congress, and an act of Congress may supersede a prior treaty. In the cases referred to these principles were applied to treaties with foreign nations. Treaties with Indian nations within the jurisdiction of the United States, whatever considerations of humanity and good faith may be involved and require their faithful observance, cannot be more obligatory. They have no higher sanctity; and no greater inviolability or immunity from legislative invasion can be claimed for them. The consequences in all such cases give rise to questions which must be met by the political department of the government. They are beyond the sphere of judicial cognizance. In the case under consideration the act of Congress must prevail as if the treaty were not an element to be considered. If a wrong has been done the power of redress is with Congress not with the judiciary, and that body, upon being applied to, it is to be presumed, will promptly give the proper relief. . . .

Source: 11 Wallace 616, 620–621.

26 Abolition of Treaty Making, March 3, 1871

The Senate originally held treaty-making powers with American Indians. In 1871 in a rider to an Indian appropriations bill, the House of Representatives forbade further treaty making with American Indians. This unilateral action, taken without consultation with American Indian nations, changed the process of treaty making in the Senate to the negotiation of "executive agreements" ratified by both houses of Congress.

An Act making Appropriations for the current and contingent Expenses of the Indian Department. . . .

Yankton Tribe of Sioux.— . . . For insurance and transportation of goods for the Yanktons, one thousand five hundred dollars: *Provided*, That hereafter no Indian nation or tribe within the territory of the United States shall be acknowledged or recognized as an independent nation, tribe, or power with whom the United States may contract by treaty: *Provided, further*, That nothing herein contained shall be construed to invalidate or impair the obligation of any treaty heretofore lawfully made and ratified with any such Indian nation or tribe. . . .

Source: *U.S. Statutes at Large*, 16:566.

27 Indian Commissioner Ezra A. Hayt on Indian Police, November 1, 1877

After Indian agent John Clum had proven the efficacy of deploying American Indian police on the San Carlos Apache reservation, in 1877 Commissioner of Indian Affairs Ezra A. Hayt recommended the creation of an American Indian police force. In 1878 Congress funded 480 officers and privates and in 1878 increased the number of personnel to 900.

The preservation of order is as necessary to the promotion of civilization as is the enactment of wise laws. Both are essential to the peace and happiness of any people. As a means of preserving order upon an Indian reservation, an Indian police has been found to be of prime importance. I have recommended an additional outlay of money to enable the government to extend the usefulness of a police system now in its infancy with us. In Canada, the entire body of Indians are kept in order by such force. In this country, as far as it has been tried, it works admirably. I would recommend that the force be composed of Indians, properly officered and drilled by white men, and where capable Indians can be found, that they be promoted to command, as reward for faithful service. The Army has used Indians for scouts with great success, and wherever employed the Indian has been found faithful to the trust confided to him. I would also recommend that the police force be supplied with a uniform similar to the style of clothing which I shall hereafter suggest to be furnished for all Indians, with the addition of a few brass buttons by way of distinction. The employment of such a force, properly officered and handled, would, in great measure, relieve the Army from doing police duty on Indian reservations. I am thoroughly satisfied that the saving in life and property by the employment of such a force would be very large, and that it would materially aid in placing the entire Indian population of the country on the road to civilization.

Source: House Executive Document 1, 45th Cong., 2d sess., serial 1800, pp. 398–399.

28 *United States ex rel. Standing Bear v. Crook* (1879)

After the federal government forcibly removed members of the Ponca tribe from their reservation in Dakota to lands farther west in 1877, Standing Bear and a group of Poncas fled back to Dakota. After General George Crook arrested him, Standing Bear sued in federal court to obtain his release through a writ of habeas corpus. Judge Elmer S. Dundy of the U.S. Circuit Court, District of Nebraska, found in Standing Bear's favor and ordered his release.

DUNDY, District Judge. During the fifteen years in which I have been engaged in administering the laws of my country, I have never been called upon to hear or decide a case that appealed so strongly to my sympathy as the one now under consideration. On the one side, we have a few of the remnants of a once numerous and powerful, but now weak, insignificant, unlettered, and generally despised race; on the other, we have the representative of one of the most powerful, most enlightened, and most Christianized nations of modern times. On the one side, we have the representatives of this wasted race coming into this national tribunal of ours, asking for justice and liberty to enable them to adopt our boasted civilization, and to pursue the arts of peace, which have made us great and happy as a nation; on the other side, we have this magnificent, if not magnanimous, government, resisting this application with the determination of sending these people back to the country which is to them less desirable than perpetual imprisonment in their own native land. But I think it is creditable to the heart and mind of the brave and distinguished officer who is made respondent herein to say that he has no sort of sympathy in the business in which he is forced by his position to bear a part so conspicuous; and, so far as I am individually concerned, I think it not improper to say that, if the strongest possible sympathy could give the relators title to freedom, they would have been restored to liberty the moment the arguments in their behalf were closed. No examination or further thought would then have been necessary or expedient. But in a country where liberty is regulated by law, something more satisfactory and enduring than mere sympathy must furnish and constitute the rule and basis of judicial action. It follows that this case must be examined and decided on principles of law, and that unless the relators are entitled to their discharge under the constitution or laws of the United States, or some treaty made pursuant thereto, they must be remanded to the custody of the officer who caused their arrest, to be returned to the Indian Territory, which they left without the consent of the government. . . .

Every "person" who comes within our jurisdiction, whether he be European, Asiatic, African, or "native to the manor born," must obey the laws of the United States. Every one who violates them incurs the penalty provided thereby. When a "person" is charged, in a proper way, with the commission of crime, we do not inquire upon the trial in what country the accused was born, nor to what sovereign or government allegiance is due, nor to what race he belongs. The questions of guilt and innocence only form the subjects of inquiry. An Indian, then, especially off from his reservation, is amenable to the criminal laws of the United States, the same as all other persons. They being subject to arrest for the violation of our criminal laws, and being "persons" such as the law contemplates and includes in the description of parties who may sue out the writ, it would indeed be a sad commentary on the justice and impartiality of our laws to hold that Indians, though natives of our own country, cannot test the validity of an alleged illegal imprisonment in this manner, as well as a subject of a foreign government who may happen to be sojourning in this country, but owing it no sort of allegiance. I cannot doubt that [C]ongress intended to give to every person who might be unlawfully restrained of liberty under color of authority of the United States, the right to the writ and a discharge thereon. I conclude, then, that, so far as the issuing of the writ is concerned, it was properly issued, and that the relators are within the jurisdiction conferred by the habeas corpus act. . . .

I have searched in vain for the semblance of any authority justifying the commissioner in attempting to remove by force any Indians, whether belonging to a tribe or not, to any place, or for any other purpose than what has been stated. Certainly, without some specific authority found in an act of [C]ongress, or in a treaty with the Ponca tribe of Indians, he could not lawfully force the relators back to the Indian Territory, to remain and die in that country, against their will. In the absence of all treaty stipulations or laws of the United States authorizing such removal, I must conclude that no such arbitrary authority exists. It is true, if the relators are to be regarded as a part of the great nation of Ponca Indians, the government might, in time of war, remove them to any place of safety so long as the war should last, but perhaps no longer, unless they were charged with the commission of some crime. This is a war power merely, and exists in time of war only. Every nation exercises the right to arrest and detain an alien enemy during the existence of a war, and all subjects or citizens of the hostile nations are subject to be dealt with under this rule.

But it is not claimed that the Ponca tribe of Indians are at war with the United States, so that this war power might be used against them; in fact, they are amongst the most peaceable and friendly of all the Indian tribes, and have at times received from the government unmistakable and substantial recognition of their long-continued friendship for the whites. In time of peace the war power remains in abeyance, and must be subservient to the civil authority of the government until something occurs to justify its exercise. No fact exists, and nothing has occurred, so far as the relators are concerned, to make it necessary or lawful to exercise such an authority over them. If they could be removed to the Indian Territory by force, and kept there in the same way, I can see no good reason why they might not be taken and kept by force in the penitentiary at Lincoln, or Leavenworth, or Jefferson City, or any other place which the commander of the forces might, in his judgment, see proper to designate. I cannot think that any such arbitrary authority exists in this country.

The reasoning advanced in support of my views, leads me to conclude:

1. That an Indian is a "person" within the meaning of the laws of the United States, and has, therefore, the right to sue out a writ of habeas corpus in a federal court, or before a federal judge, in all cases where he may be confined or in custody under color of authority of the United States, or where he is restrained of liberty in violation of the [C]onstitution or laws of the United States.

2. That General George Crook, the respondent, being commander of the military department of the Platte, has the custody of the relators, under color of authority of the United States, and in violation of the laws thereof.

3. That no rightful authority exists for removing by force any of the relators to the Indian Territory, as the respondent has been directed to do.

4. That the Indians possess the inherent right of expatriation, as well as the more fortunate white race, and have the inalienable right to "life, liberty, and the pursuit of happiness," so long as they obey the laws and do not trespass on forbidden ground. And,

5. Being restrained of liberty under color of authority of the United States, and in violation of the laws thereof, the relators must be discharged from custody, and it is so ordered.

Source: 25 Federal Cases 695, 697, 700–701.

29 Indian Commissioner Hiram Price on Civilizing the Indians, October 24, 1881

By the 1880s federal policymakers abandoned efforts to physically eliminate Native American peoples and instead sought to destroy their culture by assimilating Indians into white American society. Proposals were made to divide, or allot, reservation lands into family farms in order to replace Native American manners, customs, and ways of life with those of the mainstream society.

It is claimed and admitted by all that the great object of the government is to civilize the Indians and render them such assistance in kind and degree as will make them self-supporting, and yet I think no one will deny that one part of our policy is calculated to produce the very opposite result. It must be apparent to the most casual observer that the system of gathering the Indians in bands or tribes on reservations and carrying to them victuals and clothes, thus relieving them of the necessity of labor, never will and never can civilize them. Labor is an essential element in producing civilization. If white men were treated as we treat the Indians the result would certainly be a race of worthless vagabonds. The greatest kindness the government can bestow upon the Indian is to teach him to labor for his own support, thus developing his true manhood, and, as a consequence, making him self-relying and self-supporting.

We are expending annually over one million dollars in feeding and clothing Indians where no treaty obligation exists for so doing. This is simply a gratuity, and it is presumed no one will question the expediency or the right of the government, if it bestows gratuities upon Indians, to make labor of some useful sort a condition precedent to such gift, especially when all of the products of such labor go to the Indian. To domesticate and civilize wild Indians is a noble work, the accomplishment of which should be a crown of glory to any nation. But to allow them to drag along year after year, and generation after generation, in their old superstitions, laziness, and filth, when we have the power to elevate them in the scale of humanity, would be a lasting disgrace to our government. The past experience of this government with its Indians has clearly established some points which ought to be useful as guides in the future.

There is no one who has been a close observer of Indian history and the effect of contact of Indians with civilization, who is not well satisfied that one of two things must eventually take place, to wit, either civilization or extermination of the Indian. Savage and civilized life cannot live and prosper on the same ground. One of the two must die. If the Indians are to be civilized and become a happy and prosperous people, which is certainly the object and intention of our government, they must learn our language and adopt our modes of life. We are fifty millions of people, and they are only one-fourth of one million. The few must yield to the many. We cannot reasonably expect them to abandon their habits of life and modes of living, and adopt ours, with any hope of speedy success as long as we feed and clothe them without any effort on their part.

In this connection I wish to call attention to the fact that in almost every case it is only the non-laboring tribes that go upon the war-path, and the stubborn facts of history compel me to say that the government is largely to blame for this.

The peaceable and industrious Indian has had less consideration than the turbulent and vicious. One instance in proof of this can be found at this moment in the case of the White River Utes (the murderers of Meeker) and the Utes on the Uintah Reservation. The White River Utes have just been moved to the Uintah Reservation alongside of the peaceable Uintah Utes. We feed the White River murderers and compel the peaceable Uintahs to largely care for themselves. This course induces the Indians to believe that if they are to get favors from the government they must refuse to work, refuse to be orderly and peaceable, and must commit some depredations or murder, and then a commission will be appointed to treat with them, and pay them in goods, provisions, and money to behave themselves. This looks to an Indian very much like rewarding enemies and punishing friends, and gives him a singular idea of our Christian civilization and our manner of administering justice, which has so much the appearance of rewarding vice and punishing virtue.

Another cause of the unsatisfactory condition of our Indian affairs is the failure of the government to give the Indian land in severalty, and to give it to him in such a way that he will know that it is his. He has learned by painful experience that a small piece of paper called scrip is not good for much as a title to land. He has again and again earnestly solicited the government to give him a title to a piece of land, that he might make for himself a home. These requests have, in a great many instances, been neglected or refused, and this is true even in cases where, by treaty stipulations, the government agreed to give the Indian a patent for his land. Under this state of facts, it is not to be wondered at that the Indian is slow to cultivate the soil. He says, when urged to do so, that he has no heart to do it, when in a month or a year he may be moved, and some white man be allowed to enjoy the fruit of his labor. That is the way the Indian talks, and that is the way a white man would talk under similar circumstances.

Another just cause of complaint which the Indians have is that in our treaties with them, in some instances, we agree to give them so many pounds of beef, flour, coffee, sugar, &c., and then a certain sum of money is appropriated for the purpose of fulfilling the promise, which sum so appropriated (as is the case the present year, because of the increased price of beef, &c.) will not buy the pounds; consequently, the Indians do not get what was promised them. This they construe as bad faith on the part of the government, and use it as an excuse for doing something wrong themselves; and thus troubles of a serious and extensive nature frequently arise. This would all be avoided if appropriations were sufficiently large to cover all contingencies, and such appropriations would not interfere with or violate the rules of strict economy; for any surplus (if there should be any) would be turned into the Treasury, as is always done, at the end of the fiscal year, when an unexpended balance remains of any particular appropriation. This would be keeping our contracts to the letter and would inspire confidence and respect on the part of the Indian for our government, and give him no excuse for wrong-doing.

But I am very decidedly of opinion that ultimate and final success never can be reached without adding to all other means and appliances the location of each family, or adult Indian who has no family, on a certain number of acres of land which they may call their own and hold by a title as good and strong as a United States patent can make it. Let it be inalienable for, say, twenty years; give the Indian teams, implements, and tools amply sufficient for farming purposes; give him seed, food, and clothes for at least one year; in short, give him every facility for making a comfortable living, and then compel him to depend upon his own exertions for a livelihood. Let the laws that govern a white man govern the Indian. The Indian must be made to understand that if he expects to live and prosper in this country he must learn the English language, and learn to work. The language will enable him to transact his business understandingly with his white neighbors, and his labor will enable him to provide the necessaries and comforts of life for himself and family. The policy thus indicated will in a few years rid the government of this vexed "Indian question," making the Indian a blessing instead of a curse to himself and country, which, judging the future by the past, will never be done by the present policy. . . .

Source: House Executive Document 1, 47th Cong., 1st sess., serial 2018, pp. 1–3.

30 General William T. Sherman Asserts the End of the Indian Problem, October 27, 1883

In 1883 Gen. William T. Sherman claimed that American Indian wars were over and that the "Indian question" was finally settled.

I now regard the Indians as substantially eliminated from the problem of the Army. There may be spasmodic and temporary alarms, but such Indian wars as have hitherto disturbed the public peace and tranquillity are not probable. The Army has been a large factor in producing this result, but it is not the only one. Immigration and the occupation by industrious farmers and miners of land vacated by the aborigines have been largely instrumental to that end, but the railroad which used to follow in the rear now goes forward with the picket-line in the great battle of civilization with barbarism, and has become the greater cause. I have in former reports, for the past fifteen years, treated of this matter, and now, on the eve of withdrawing from active participation in public affairs, I beg to emphasize much which I have spoken and written heretofore. The recent completion of the last of the four great transcontinental lines of railway has settled forever the Indian question, the Army question, and many others which have hitherto troubled the country. . . .

Source: House Executive Document 1, 48th Cong., 1st sess., serial 2182, pp. 45–46.

31 Courts of Indian Offenses, November 1, 1883

To stop Native American "heathenish practices," Secretary of the Interior Henry M. Teller established courts of Indian offenses on reservations. Although the original purpose of the courts was ethnocidal—that is, to eliminate Native American religious and other practices—the courts almost immediately began hearing cases involving minor and petty offenses on the reservation.

Many of the agencies are without law of any kind, and the necessity for some rule of government on the reservations grows more and more apparent each day. If it is the purpose of the Government to civilize the Indians, they must be compelled to desist from the savage and barbarous practices that are calculated to continue them in savagery, no matter what exterior influences are brought to bear on them. Very many of the progressive Indians have become fully alive to the pernicious influences of these heathenish practices indulged in by their people, and have sought to abolish them; in such efforts they have been aided by their missionaries, teachers, and agents, but this has been found impossible even with the aid thus given.

The Government furnishes the teachers, and the charitable people contribute to the support of missionaries, and much time, labor, and money is yearly expended for their elevation, and yet a few non-progressive, degraded Indians are allowed to exhibit before the young and susceptible children all the debauchery, diabolism, and savagery of the worst state of the Indian race. Every man familiar with Indian life will bear witness to the pernicious influence of these savage rites and heathenish customs.

On the 2d of December last, with the view of as soon as possible putting an end to these heathenish practices, I addressed a letter to the Commissioner of Indian Affairs, which I here quote as expressive of my ideas on this subject:

> I desire to call your attention to what I regard as a great hindrance to the civilization of the Indians, viz, the continuance of the old heathenish dances, such as the sun-dance, scalp-dance, &c. These dances, or feasts, as they are sometimes called, ought, in my judgment, to be discontinued, and if the Indians now supported by the Government are not willing to discontinue them, the agents should be instructed to compel such discontinuance These feasts or dances are not social gatherings for the amusement of these people, but, on the contrary, are intended and calculated to stimulate the warlike passions of the young warriors of the tribe. At such feasts the warrior recounts his deeds of daring, boasts of his inhumanity in the destruction of his enemies, and his treatment of the female captives, in language that ought to shock even a savage ear. The audience assents approvingly to his boasts of falsehood, deceit, theft, murder, and rape, and the young listener is informed that this and this only is the road to fame and renown. The result is the demoralization of the young, who are incited to emulate the wicked conduct of their elders, without a thought that in so doing they violate any law, but, on the contrary, with the conviction that in so doing they are securing for themselves an enduring and deserved fame among their people. Active measures should be taken to discourage all feasts and dances of the character I have mentioned.
>
> The marriage relation is also one requiring the immediate attention of the agents. While the Indians were in a state of at least semi-independence, there did not seem to be any great necessity for interference, even if such interference was practicable (which it doubtless was not). While dependent on the chase the Indian did not take many wives, and the great mass found themselves too poor to support more than one; but since the Government supports them this objection no longer exists, and the more numerous the family the greater the number of the rations allowed. I would not advise any interference with plural marriages now existing; but I would by all possible methods discourage future marriages of that character. The marriage relation, if it may be said [to] coexist at all among the Indians, is exceedingly lax in its character, and it will be found impossible, for some time yet, to impress them with our idea of this important relation.
>
> The marriage state, existing only by the consent of both parties, is easily and readily dissolved, the man not recognizing any obligation on his part to care for his offspring. As far as practicable, the Indian having taken to himself a wife should be compelled to continue that relation with her, unless dissolved by some recognized tribunal on the reservation or by the courts. Some system of marriage should be adopted, and the Indian compelled to conform to it. The Indian should also be instructed that he is under

obligations to care for and support, not only his wife, but his children, and on his failure, without proper cause, to continue as the head of such family, he ought in some manner to be punished, which should be either by confinement in the guard-house or agency prison, or by a reduction of his rations.

Another great hindrance to the civilization of the Indians is the influence of the medicine men, who are always found with the anti-progressive party. The medicine men resort to various artifices and devices to keep the people under their influence, and are especially active in preventing the attendance of the children at the public schools, using their conjurers' arts to prevent the people from abandoning their heathenish rites and customs. While they profess to cure diseases by the administering of a few simple remedies, still they rely mainly on their art of conjuring. Their services are not required even for the administration of the few simple remedies they are competent to recommend, for the Government supplies the several agencies with skillful physicians, who practice among the Indians without charge to them. Steps should be taken to compel these impostors to abandon this deception and discontinue their practices, which are not only without benefit to the Indians but positively injurious to them.

The value of property as an agent of civilization ought not to be overlooked. When an Indian acquires property, with a disposition to retain the same free from tribal or individual interference, he has made a step forward in the road to civilization. One great obstacle to the acquirement of property by the Indian is the very general custom of destroying or distributing his property on the death of a member of his family. Frequently on the death of an important member of the family all the property accumulated by its head is destroyed or carried off by the "mourners," and his family left in desolation and want. While in their independent state but little inconvenience was felt in such a case, on account of the general community of interest and property, in their present condition not only real inconvenience is felt, but disastrous consequences follow. I am informed by reliable authority that frequently the head of a family, finding himself thus despoiled of his property, becomes discouraged, and makes no further attempt to become a property owner. Fear of being considered mean, and attachment to the dead, frequently prevents the owner from interfering to save his property while it is being destroyed in his presence and contrary to his wishes.

It will be extremely difficult to accomplish much towards the civilization of the Indians while these adverse influences are allowed to exist.

The Government having attempted to support the Indians until such time as they shall become self-supporting, the interest of the Government as well as that of the Indians demands that every possible effort should be made to induce them to become self-supporting at as early a day as possible. I therefore suggest whether it is not practicable to formulate certain rules for the government of the Indians on the reservations that shall restrict and ultimately abolish the practices I have mentioned. I am not ignorant of the difficulties that will be encountered in this effort; yet I believe in all the tribes there will be found many Indians who will aid the Government in its efforts to abolish rites and customs so injurious to the Indians and so contrary to the civilization that they earnestly desire.

In accordance with the suggestions of this letter, the Commissioner of Indian Affairs established a tribunal at all agencies, except among the civilized Indians, consisting of three Indians, to be known as the court of Indian offenses. The members of this tribunal consist of the first three officers in rank of the police force, if such selection is approved by the agent; otherwise, the agent may select from among the members of the tribe three suitable persons to constitute such tribunal.

The Commissioner of Indian Affairs, with the approval of the Secretary of the Interior, promulgated certain rules for the government of this tribunal, defining offenses of which it was to take cognizance. It is believed that such a tribunal, composed as it is of Indians, will not be objectionable to the Indians and will be a step in the direction of bringing the Indians under the civilizing influence of law. Since the creation of this tribunal the time has not been sufficient to give it a fair trial, but so far it promises to accomplish all that was hoped for at the time of its creation. The Commissioner recommends an appropriation for the support of this tribunal, and in such recommendation I concur. . . .

Source: House Executive Document 1, 48th Cong., 1st sess., serial 2190, pp. x–xiii.

32 *Ex Parte Crow Dog* (1883)

In 1883 the First Judicial District Court of Dakota sentenced Crow Dog, a chief of the Brule Sioux, to death for the murder of Spotted Tail, a fellow Brule Sioux. Subsequently, Crow Dog's attorneys filed suit for his release, arguing that federal courts had no jurisdiction over crimes committed by one Native American against another on Indian reservations. The Supreme Court found in favor of Crow Dog and ordered his release.

The petitioner is in the custody of the marshal of the United States for the Territory of Dakota, imprisoned in the jail of Lawrence County, in the First Judicial District of that Territory, under sentence of death, adjudged against him by the district court for that district, to be carried into execution January 14th, 1884. That judgment was rendered upon a conviction for the murder of an Indian of the Brule Sioux band of the Sioux Nation of Indians, by the name of Sin-ta-ge-le-Scka, or in English, Spotted Tail, the prisoner also being an Indian, of the same band and nation, and the homicide having occurred as alleged in the indictment, in the Indian country, within a place and district of country under the exclusive jurisdiction of the United States and within the said judicial district. The judgment was affirmed, on a writ of error, by the Supreme Court of the Territory. It is claimed on behalf of the prisoner that the crime charged against him, and of which he stands convicted, is not an offence under the laws of the United States; that the district court had no jurisdiction to try him, and that its judgment and sentence are void. He therefore prays for a writ of habeas corpus, that he may be delivered from an imprisonment which he asserts to be illegal.

It must be remembered that the question before us is whether the express letter of [section] 2146 of the Revised Statutes, which excludes from the jurisdiction of the United States the case of a crime committed in the Indian country by one Indian against the person or property of another Indian, has been repealed. If not, it is in force and applies to the present case. The treaty of 1868 and the agreement and act of Congress of 1877, it is admitted, do not repeal it by any express words. What we have said is sufficient at least to show that they do not work a repeal by necessary implication.

It is a case involving the judgment of a court of special and limited jurisdiction, not to be assumed without clear warrant of law. It is a case of life and death. It is a case where, against an express exception in the law itself, that law, by argument and inference only, is sought to be extended over aliens and strangers; over the members of a community separated by race, by tradition, by the instincts of a free though savage life, from the authority and power which seeks to impose upon them the restraints of an external and unknown code, and to subject them to the responsibilities of civil conduct, according to rules and penalties of which they could have no previous warning; which judges them by a standard made by others and not for them, which takes no account of the conditions which should except them from its exactions, and makes no allowance for their inability to understand it. It tries them, not by their peers, nor by the customs of their people, nor the law of their land, but by superiors of a different race, according to the law of a social state of which they have an imperfect conception, and which is opposed to the traditions of their history, to the habits of their lives, to the strongest prejudices of their savage nature; one which measures the red man's revenge by the maxims of the white man's morality. It is a case, too, of first impression, so far as we are advised, for, if the question has been mooted heretofore in any courts of the United States, the jurisdiction has never before been practically asserted as in the present instance.

To give to the clauses in the treaty of 1868 and the agreement of 1877 effect, so as to uphold the jurisdiction exercised in this case, would be to reverse in this instance the general policy of the government towards the Indians, as declared in many statutes and treaties, and recognized in many decisions of this court, from the beginning to the present time. To justify such a departure, in such a case, requires a clear expression of the intention of Congress, and that we have not been able to find.

It results that the First District Court of Dakota was without jurisdiction to find or try the indictment against the prisoner, that the conviction and sentence are void, and that his imprisonment is illegal.

The writs of habeas corpus and certiorari prayed for will accordingly be issued.

Source: 109 U.S. 557, 571–572.

33 *Elk v. Wilkins* (1884)

When John Elk took up residence in Omaha, Nebraska, and tried to register to vote, he was denied the right because it was alleged that he was not a U.S. citizen. Asserting that he was made a citizen with the passage of the Fourteenth Amendment, Elk took his case to the Supreme Court, which held that he was not a citizen of the United States.

The plaintiff, in support of his action, relies on the first clause of the first section of the Fourteenth Article of Amendment of the Constitution of the United States, by which "all persons born or naturalized in the United States, and subject to the jurisdiction thereof, are citizens of the United States and of the State wherein they reside;" and on the Fifteenth Article of Amendment, which provides that "the right of citizens of the United States to vote shall not be denied or abridged by the United States or by any State on account of race, color, or previous condition of servitude."

The petition, while it does not show of what Indian tribe the plaintiff was a member, yet, by the allegations that he "is an Indian, and was born within the United States," and that "he had severed his tribal relation to the Indian tribes," clearly implies that he was born a member of one of the Indian tribes within the limits of the United States, which still exists and is recognized as a tribe by the government of the United States. Though the plaintiff alleges that he "had fully and completely surrendered himself to the jurisdiction of the United States," he does not allege that the United States accepted his surrender, or that he has ever been naturalized, or taxed, or in any way recognized or treated as a citizen, by the State or by the United States. Nor is it contended by his counsel that there is any statute or treaty that makes him a citizen.

The question then is, whether an Indian, born a member of one of the Indian tribes within the United States, is, merely by reason of his birth within the United States, and of his afterwards voluntarily separating himself from his tribe and taking up his residence among white citizens, a citizen of the United States, within the meaning of the first section of the Fourteenth Amendment of the Constitution.

Indians born within the territorial limits of the United States, members of, and owing immediate allegiance to, one of the Indian tribes (an alien, though dependent, power), although in a geographical sense born in the United States, are no more "born in the United States and subject to the jurisdiction thereof," within the meaning of the first section of the Fourteenth Amendment, than the children of subjects of any foreign government born within the domain of that government, or the children born within the United States, of ambassadors or other public ministers of foreign nations.

This view is confirmed by the second section of the Fourteenth Amendment, which provides that "representatives shall be apportioned among the several States according to their respective numbers, counting the whole number of persons in each State, excluding Indians not taxed." Slavery having been abolished, and the persons formerly held as slaves made citizens, this clause fixing the apportionment of representatives has abrogated so much of the corresponding clause of the original Constitution as counted only three-fifths of such persons. But Indians not taxed are still excluded from the count, for the reason that they are not citizens. Their absolute exclusion from the basis of representation, in which all other persons are now included, is wholly inconsistent with their being considered citizens. . . .

The plaintiff, not being a citizen of the United States under the Fourteenth Amendment of the Constitution, has been deprived of no right secured by the Fifteenth Amendment, and cannot maintain this action.

Source: 112 U.S. 98–99, 102, 109.

34 Major Crimes Act, March 3, 1885

In order to stop the release by federal courts of Native Americans based on Ex Parte Crow Dog *(1883) (Doc. 32), Congress passed a law giving federal courts jurisdiction over seven major crimes committed by one Native American against another on reservations. This legislation represented an attack on the autonomy of traditional Native American governments.*

An Act making appropriations for the current and contingent expenses of the Indian Department.

SEC. 9. That immediately upon and after the date of the passage of this act all Indians, committing against the person or property of another Indian or other person any of the following crimes, namely, murder, manslaughter, rape, assault with intent to kill, arson, burglary, and larceny within any Territory of the United States, and either within or without an Indian reservation, shall be subject therefor to the laws of such Territory relating to said crimes, and shall be tried therefor in the same courts and in the same manner and shall be subject to the same penalties as are all other persons charged with the commission of said crimes, respectively; and the said courts are hereby given jurisdiction in all such cases; and all such Indians committing any of the above crimes against the person or property of another Indian or other person within the boundaries of any State of the United Stares, and within the limits of any Indian reservation, shall be subject to the same laws, tried in the same courts and in the same manner and subject to the same penalties as are all other persons committing any of the above crimes within the exclusive jurisdiction of the United States.

Source: *U.S. Statutes at Large*, 23:385.

35 *United States v. Kagama* (1886)

The constitutionality of the Major Crimes Act (Doc. 34) was challenged in 1886 in a case involving two Native Americans accused of murder on the Hoopa Valley reservation in California. The Supreme Court upheld the validity of the new law.

The case of *Crow Dog*, 109 U.S. 556, in which an agreement with the Sioux Indians, ratified by an act of Congress, was supposed to extend over them the laws of the United States and the jurisdiction of its courts, covering murder and other grave crimes, shows the purpose of Congress in this new departure. The decision in that case admits that if the intention of Congress had been to punish, by the United States courts, the murder of one Indian by another, the law would have been valid. But the court could not see, in the agreement with the Indians sanctioned by Congress, a purpose to repeal [section] 2146 of the Revised Statutes, which expressly excludes from that jurisdiction the case of a crime committed by one Indian against another in the Indian country. The passage of the act now under consideration was designed to remove that objection, and to go further by including such crimes on reservations lying within a State.

Is this latter act a fatal objection to the law? The statute itself contains no express limitation upon the powers of a State or the jurisdiction of its courts. If there be any limitation in either of these, it grows out of the implication arising from the fact that Congress has defined a crime committed within the State, and made it punishable in the courts of the United States. But Congress has done this, and can do it, with regard to all offences relating to matters to which the Federal authority extends. Does that authority extend to this case?

It will be seen at once that the nature of the offence (murder) is one which in almost all cases of its commission is punishable by the laws of the States, and within the jurisdiction of their courts. The distinction is claimed to be that the offence under the statute is committed by an Indian, that it is committed on a reservation set apart within the State for residence of the tribe of Indians by the United States, and the fair inference is that the offending Indian shall belong to that or some other tribe. It does not interfere with the process of the State courts within the reservation, nor with the operation of State laws upon white people found there. Its effect is confined to the acts of an Indian of some tribe, of a criminal character, committed within the limits of the reservation.

It seems to us that this is within the competency of Congress. These Indian tribes are the wards of the nation. They are communities dependent on the United States. Dependent largely for their daily food. Dependent for their political rights. They owe no allegiance to the States, and receive from them no protection. Because of the local ill feeling, the people of the States where they are found are often their deadliest enemies. From their very weakness and helplessness, so largely due to the course of dealing of the Federal Government with them and the treaties in which it has been promised, there arises the duty of protection, and with it the power. This has always been recognized by the Executive and by Congress, and by this court, whenever the question has arisen.

The power of the General Government over these remnants of a race once powerful, now weak and diminished in numbers, is necessary to their protection, as well as to the safety of those among whom they dwell. It must exist in that government, because it never has existed anywhere else, because the theatre of its exercise is within the geographical limits of the United States, because it has never been denied, and because it alone can enforce its laws on all the tribes.

We answer the questions propounded to us, that the 9th section of the act of March, 1885, is a valid law in both its branches, and that the Circuit Court of the United States for the District of California has jurisdiction of the offence charged in the indictment in this case.

Source: 118 U.S. 375, 382–385.

36 General Allotment Act (Dawes Act), February 8, 1887

By the late nineteenth century, reformers were demanding that reservations be divided into family farms, replacing Native Americans' communal holdings of land with an ethnocidal policy of Euro-American agriculture and capitalism. To implement this policy, Congress passed the General Allotment Act of 1887, also known as the Dawes Act. It empowered the president to begin allotting land on reservations and declare recipients of allotments to be U.S. citizens.

An act to provide for the allotment of lands in severalty to Indians on the various reservations, and to extend the protection of the laws of the United States and the Territories over the Indians, and for other purposes.

Be it enacted . . . , That in all cases where any tribe or band of Indians has been, or shall hereafter be, located upon any reservation created for their use, either by treaty stipulation or by virtue of an act of Congress or executive order setting apart the same for their use, the President of the United States be, and he hereby is, authorized, whenever in his opinion any reservation or any part thereof of such Indians is advantageous for agricultural and grazing purposes, to cause said reservation, or any part thereof, to be surveyed, or resurveyed if necessary, and to allot the lands in said reservation in severalty to any Indian located thereon in quantities as follows:

To each head of a family, one-quarter of a section;

To each single person over eighteen years of age, one-eighth of a section;

To each orphan child under eighteen years of age, one-eighth of a section; and

To each other single person under eighteen years now living, or who may be born prior to the date of the order of the President directing an allotment of the lands embraced in any reservation, one-sixteenth of a section: *Provided*, That in case there is not sufficient land in any of said reservations to allot lands to each individual of the classes above named in quantities as above provided, the lands embraced in such reservation or reservations shall be allotted to each individual of each of said classes pro rata in accordance with the provisions of this act: *And provided further*, That where the treaty or act of Congress setting apart such reservation provides for the allotment of lands in severalty in quantities in excess of those herein provided, the President, in making allotments upon such reservation, shall allot the lands to each individual Indian belonging thereon in quantity as specified in such treaty or act: *And provided further*, That when the lands allotted are only valuable for grazing purposes, an additional allotment of such grazing lands, in quantities as above provided, shall be made to each individual.

SEC. 2. That all allotments set apart under the provisions of this act shall be selected by the Indians, heads of families selecting for their minor children, and the agents shall select for each orphan child, and in such manner as to embrace the improvements of the Indians making the selection. Where the improvements of two or more Indians have been made on the same legal subdivision of land, unless they shall otherwise agree, a provisional line may be run dividing said lands between them, and the amount to which each is entitled shall be equalized in the assignment of the remainder of the land to which they are entitled under this act: *Provided*, That if any one entitled to an allotment shall fail to make a selection within four years after the President shall direct that allotments may be made on a particular reservation, the Secretary of the Interior may direct the agent of such tribe or band, if such there be, and if there be no agent, then a special agent appointed for that purpose, to make a selection for such Indian, which selection shall be allotted as in cases where selections are made by the Indians, and patents shall issue in like manner.

SEC. 3. That the allotments provided for in this act shall be made by special agents appointed by the President for such purpose, and the agents in charge of the respective reservations on which the allotments are directed to be made, under such rules and regulations as the Secretary of the Interior may from time to time prescribe, and shall be certified by such agents to the Commissioner of Indian Affairs, in duplicate, one copy to be retained in the Indian Office and the other to be transmitted to the Secretary of the Interior for his action, and to be deposited in the General Land Office.

SEC. 4. That where any Indian not residing upon a reservation, or for whose tribe no reservation has been provided by treaty, act of Congress, or executive order, shall make settlement upon any surveyed or unsurveyed lands of the United States not otherwise appropriated, he or she shall be entitled, upon application to the local land-office for the district in which the lands are located, to have the same allotted to him or her, and to his or her children, in quantities and manner as provided in this act for Indians residing upon reservations; and when such settlement is made upon unsurveyed lands, the grant to such Indians shall be adjusted upon the survey of the lands so as to conform thereto; and patents shall be issued to them for such lands in the manner and with the restrictions as herein provided. And the fees to which the officers of such local land-office would have been entitled had such lands been entered under the general laws for the disposition of the public lands shall be paid to them, from any moneys in the Treasury of the United States not otherwise appropriated, upon a statement of an account in their behalf for such fees by the Commissioner of the General Land Office, and a certification of such account to the Secretary of the Treasury by the Secretary of the Interior.

SEC. 5. That upon the approval of the allotments provided for in this act by the Secretary of the Interior, he shall cause patents to issue therefor in the name of the allottees, which patents shall be of the legal effect, and declare that the United States does and will hold the land thus allotted, for the period of twenty-five years, in trust for the sole use and benefit of the Indian to whom such allotment shall have been made, or, in case of his decease, of his heirs according to the laws of the State or Territory where such land is located, and that at the expiration of said period the United States will convey the same by patent to said Indian, or his heirs as aforesaid, in fee, discharged of said trust and free of all charge or incumbrance whatsoever: *Provided*, That the President of the United States may in any case in his discretion extend the period. And if any conveyance shall be made of the lands set apart and allotted as herein provided, or any contract made touching the same, before the expiration of the time above mentioned, such conveyance or contract shall be absolutely null and void: *Provided*, That the law of descent and partition in force in the State or Territory where such lands are situated shall apply thereto after patents therefor have been executed and delivered, except as herein otherwise provided; and the laws of the State of Kansas regulating the descent and partition of real estate shall, so far as practicable, apply to all lands in the Indian Territory which may be allotted in severalty under the provisions of this act: *And provided further*, That at any time after lands have been allotted to all the Indians of any tribe as herein provided, or sooner if in the opinion of the President it shall be for the best interests of said tribe, it shall be lawful for the Secretary of the Interior to negotiate with such Indian tribe for the purchase and release by said tribe, in conformity with the treaty or statute under which such reservation is held, of such portions of its reservation not allotted as such tribe shall, from time to time, consent to sell, on such terms and conditions as shall be considered just and equitable between the United States and said tribe of Indians, which purchase shall not be complete until ratified by Congress, and the form and manner of executing such release shall also be prescribed by Congress: *Provided however*, That all lands adapted to agriculture, with or without irrigation so sold or released to the United States by any Indian tribe shall be held by the United States for the sole purpose of securing homes to actual settlers and shall be disposed of by the United States to actual and bona fide settlers only in tracts not exceeding one hundred and sixty acres to any one person, on such terms as Congress shall prescribe, subject to grants which Congress may make in aid of education: *And provided further*, That no patents shall issue therefor except to the person so taking the same as and for a homestead, or his heirs, and after the expiration of five years occupancy thereof as such homestead; and any conveyance of said lands so taken as a homestead, or any contract touching the same, or lien thereon, created prior to the date of such patent, shall be null and void. And the sums agreed to be paid by the United States as purchase money for any portion of any such reservation shall be held in the Treasury of the United States for the sole use of the tribe or tribes of Indians; to whom such reservations belonged; and the same, with interest thereon at three per cent per annum, shall be at all times subject to appropriation by Congress for the education and civilization of such tribe or tribes of Indians or the members thereof. The patents aforesaid shall be recorded in the General Land Office, and afterward delivered, free of charge, to the allottee entitled thereto. And if any religious society or other organization is now occupying any of the public lands to which this act is applicable, for religious or educational work among the Indians, the Secretary of the Interior is hereby authorized to confirm such occupation to such society or organization, in quantity not exceeding one hundred and sixty acres in any one tract, so long as the same shall be so occupied, on such terms as he shall deem just; but nothing herein contained shall change or alter any claim of such society for religious or educational purposes heretofore granted by law. And hereafter in the employment of Indian police, or any other employees in the public service among any of the Indian tribes or bands affected by this act, and where Indians can perform the duties required, those Indians who have availed themselves of the provisions of this act and become citizens of the United States shall be preferred.

SEC. 6. That upon the completion of said allotments and the patenting of the lands to said allottees, each and every member of the respective bands or tribes of Indians to whom allotments have been made shall have the benefit of and be subject to the laws, both civil and criminal, of the State or Territory in which they may reside; and no Territory shall pass or enforce any law denying any such Indian within its jurisdiction the equal protection of the law. And every Indian born within the territorial limits of the United States to whom allotments shall have been made under the provisions of this act, or under any law or treaty, and every Indian born within the territorial limits of the United States who has voluntarily taken up, within said limits, his residence separate and apart from any tribe of Indians therein, and has adopted the habits of civilized life, is hereby declared to be a citizen of the United States, and is entitled to all the rights, privileges, and immunities of such citizens, whether said Indian has been or not, by birth or otherwise, a member of any tribe of Indians within the territorial limits of the United States without in any manner impairing or otherwise affecting the right of any such Indian to tribal or other property.

SEC. 7. That in cases where the use of water for irrigation is necessary to render the lands within any Indian reservation available for agricultural purposes, the Secretary of the Interior be, and he is hereby, authorized to prescribe such rules and regulations as he may deem necessary to secure a just and equal distribution thereof among the Indians residing upon any such reservations; and no other appropriation or grant of water by any riparian proprietor shall be authorized or permitted to the damage of any other riparian proprietor.

SEC. 8. That the provision of this act shall not extend to the territory occupied by the Cherokees, Creeks, Choctaws, Chickasaws, Seminoles, and Osage, Miamies and Peorias, and Sacs and Foxes, in the Indian Territory, nor to any of the reservations of the Seneca Nation of New York Indians in the State of New York, nor to that strip of territory in the State of Nebraska adjoining the Sioux Nation on the south added by executive order.

SEC. 9. That for the purpose of making the surveys and resurveys mentioned in section two of this act, there be, and hereby is, appropriated, out of any moneys in the Treasury not otherwise appropriated, the sum of one hundred thousand dollars, to be repaid proportionately out of the proceeds of the sales of such land as may be acquired from the Indians under the provisions of this act.

SEC. 10. That nothing in this act contained shall be so construed as to affect the right and power of Congress to grant the right of way through any lands granted to an Indian, or a tribe of Indians, for railroads or other highways, or telegraph lines, for the public use, or to condemn such lands to public uses, upon making just compensation.

SEC. 11. That nothing in this act shall be so construed as to prevent the removal of the Southern Ute Indians from their present reservation in Southwestern Colorado to a new reservation by and with the consent of a majority of the adult male members of said tribe.

Source: *U.S. Statutes at Large*, 24:388–391.

37 Amendment to the General Allotment Act (Dawes Act), February 28, 1891

In 1891 Congress amended the General Allotment Act of 1887, the Dawes Act (Doc. 36), to allow equal allotments to all Native Americans and the leasing of allotments in certain cases.

An act to amend and further extend the benefits of the act approved February eighth, eighteen hundred and eighty-seven, entitled "An act to provide for the allotment of land in severalty to Indians on the various reservations, and to extend the protection of the laws of the United States over the Indians, and for other purposes."

Be it enacted . . . , That section one of the act entitled "An act to provide for the allotment of lands in severalty to Indians on the various reservations, and to extend the protection of the laws of the United States and the Territories over the Indians, and for other purposes," approved February eighth, eighteen hundred and eighty-seven, be, and the same is hereby, amended so as to read as follows:

SEC. 1. That in all cases where any tribe or band of Indians has been, or shall hereafter be, located upon any reservation created for their use, either by treaty stipulation or by virtue of an Act of Congress or Executive order setting apart the same for their use, the President of the United States be, and he hereby is, authorized, whenever in his opinion any reservation, or any part thereof, of such Indians is advantageous for agricultural or grazing purposes, to cause said reservation, or any part thereof, to be surveyed, or resurveyed, if necessary, and to allot to each Indian located thereon one-eighth of a section of land: *Provided*, That in case there is not sufficient land in any of said reservations to allot lands to each individual in quantity as above provided the land in such reservation or reservations shall be allotted to each individual pro rata, as near as may be, according to legal subdivisions: *Provided further*, That where the treaty or act of Congress setting apart such reservation provides for the allotment of lands in severalty to certain classes in quantity in excess of that herein provided the President, in making allotments upon such reservation, shall allot the land to each individual Indian of said classes belonging thereon in quantity as specified in such treaty or act, and to other Indians belonging thereon in quantity as herein provided: *Provided further*, That where existing agreements or laws provide for allotments in accordance with the provisions of said act of February eighth, eighteen hundred and eighty-seven, or in quantities substantially as therein provided, allotments may be made in quantity as specified in this act, with the consent of the Indians, expressed in such manner as the President, in his discretion, may require: *And provided further*, That when the lands allotted, or any legal subdivision thereof, are only valuable for grazing purposes, such lands shall be allotted in double quantities.

SEC. 2. That where allotments have been made in whole or in part upon any reservation under the provisions of said act of February eighth, eighteen hundred and eighty-seven, and the quantity of land in such reservation is sufficient to give each member of the tribe eighty acres, such allotments shall be revised and equalized under the provisions of this act: *Provided,* That no allotment heretofore approved by the Secretary of the Interior shall be reduced in quantity.

SEC. 3. That whenever it shall be made to appear to the Secretary of the Interior that, by reason of age or other disability, any allottee under the provisions of said act, or any other act or treaty can not personally and with benefit to himself occupy or improve his allotment or any part thereof the same may be leased upon such terms, regulations and conditions as shall be prescribed by such Secretary, for a term not exceeding three years for farming or grazing, or ten years for mining purposes: *Provided,* That where lands are occupied by Indians who have bought and paid for the same, and which lands are not needed for farming or agricultural purposes, and are not desired for individual allotments, the same may be leased by authority of the Council speaking for such Indians, for a period not to exceed five years for grazing, or ten years for mining purposes in such quantities and upon such terms and conditions as the agent in charge of such reservation may recommend, subject to the approval of the Secretary of the Interior.

SEC. 4. That where any Indian entitled to allotment under existing laws shall make settlement upon any surveyed or unsurveyed lands of the United States not otherwise appropriated, he or she shall be entitled, upon application to the local land office for the district in which the lands are located, to have the same allotted to him or her and to his or her children, in quantities and manner as provided in the foregoing section of this amending act for Indians residing upon reservations; and when such settlement is made upon unsurveyed lands the grant to such Indians shall be adjusted upon the survey of the lands so as to conform thereto; and patents shall be issued to them for such lands in the manner and with the restrictions provided in the act to which this is an amendment. And the fees to which the officers of such local land office would have been entitled had such lands been entered upon the general laws for the disposition of the public lands shall be paid to them from any moneys in the Treasury of the United States not otherwise appropriated, upon a statement of an account in their behalf for such fees by the Commissioner of the General Land Office, and a certification of such account to the Secretary of the Treasury by the Secretary of the Interior.

SEC. 5. That for the purpose of determining the descent of land to the heirs of any deceased Indian under the provisions of the fifth section of said act, whenever any male and female Indian shall have co-habited together as husband and wife according to the custom and manner of Indian life the issue of such co-habitation shall be, for the purpose aforesaid, taken and deemed to be the legitimate issue of the Indians so living together, and every Indian child, otherwise illegitimate, shall for such purpose be taken and deemed to be the legitimate issue of the father of such child. . . .

Source: *U.S. Statutes at Large,* 26:794–796.

38 Commission to the Five Civilized Tribes (Dawes Commission), March 3, 1893

The federal government originally excluded the Five Civilized Tribes—the Cherokee, Chickasaw, Choctaw, Muscogee (or Creek), and Seminole nations—from the dictates of the Dawes Act (Docs. 36 and 37) because they opposed it. Their reservations comprised a large enclave of lands held in common in present-day Oklahoma. To force the tribes into allotting their lands in severalty, the government created a special commission to facilitate the division. The commission thus charged is called the Dawes Commission, after its first chairman, Henry L. Dawes.

An Act making appropriations for current and contingent expenses . . .

SEC. 16. The President shall nominate and, by and with the advice and consent of the Senate, shall appoint three commissioners to enter into negotiations with the Cherokee Nation, the Choctaw Nation, the Chickasaw Nation, the Muscogee (or Creek) Nation; the Seminole Nation, for the purpose of the extinguishment of the national or tribal title to any lands within that Territory now held by any and all of such nations or tribes, either by cession of the same or some part thereof to the United States, or by the allotment and division of the same in severalty among the Indians of such nations or tribes, respectively, as may be entitled to the same, or by such other method as may be agreed upon between the several nations and tribes aforesaid, or each of them, with the United States, with a view to such an adjustment, upon the basis of justice and equity, as may, with the consent of such nations or tribes of Indians, so far as may be necessary, be requisite and suitable to enable the ultimate creation of a State or States of the Union which shall embrace the lands within said Indian Territory.

The commissioners so appointed shall each receive a salary, to be paid during such time as they may be actually employed, under direction of the President, in the duties enjoined by this act, at the rate of five thousand dollars per annum, and shall also be paid their reasonable and proper expenses incurred in prosecution of the objects of this act, upon accounts therefor to be rendered to and allowed by the Secretary of the Interior from time to time. That such commissioners shall have power to employ a secretary, a stenographer, and such interpreter or interpreters as may be found necessary to the performance of their duties, and by order to fix their compensation, which shall be paid, upon the approval of the Secretary of the Interior, from time to time, with their reasonable and necessary expenses, upon accounts to be rendered as aforesaid; and may also employ, in like manner and with the like approval, a surveyor or other assistant or agent, which they shall certify in writing to be necessary to the performance of any part of their duties.

Such commissioners shall, under such regulations and directions as shall be prescribed by the President, through the Secretary of the Interior, enter upon negotiation with the several nations, of Indians as aforesaid in the Indian Territory, and shall endeavor to procure, first, such allotment of lands in severalty to the Indians belonging to each such nation, tribe, or band, respectively, as may be agreed upon as just and proper to provide for each such Indian a sufficient quantity of land for his or her needs, in such equal distribution and apportionment as may be found just and suited to the circumstances; for which purpose, after the terms of such an agreement shall have been arrived at, the said commissioners shall cause the lands of any such nation or tribe or band to be surveyed and the proper allotment to be designated; and, secondly, to procure the cession, for such price and upon such terms as shall be agreed upon, of any lands not found necessary to be so allotted or divided, to the United States; and to make proper agreements for the investment or holding by the United States of such moneys as may be paid or agreed to be paid to such nation or tribes or bands, or to any of the Indians thereof, for the extinguishment of their [titles] therein. But said commissioners shall, however, have power to negotiate any and all such agreements as, in view of all the circumstances affecting the subject, shall be found requisite and suitable to such an arrangement of the rights and interests and affairs of such nations, tribes, bands, or Indians, or any of them, to enable the ultimate creation of a Territory of the United States with a view to the admission of the same as a [S]tate in the Union.

The commissioners shall at any time, or from time to time, report to the Secretary of the Interior their transactions and the progress of their negotiations, and shall at any time, or from time to time, if separate agreements shall be made by them with any nation, tribe or band, in pursuance of the authority hereby conferred, report the same to the Secretary of the Interior for submission to Congress for its consideration and ratification.

For the purpose aforesaid there is hereby appropriated, out of any money in the Treasury of the United States, the sum of fifty thousand dollars, to be immediately available.

Neither the provisions of this section nor the negotiations or agreements which may be had or made thereunder shall be held in any way to waive or impair any right of sovereignty which the Government of the United States has over or respecting said Indian Territory or the people thereof, or any other right of the Government relating to said Territory, its lands, or the people thereof.

Source: *U.S. Statutes at Large*, 27:645–646.

39 Report of the Dawes Commission, November 20, 1894

The Five Civilized Tribes—the Cherokee, Chickasaw, Choctaw, Muscogee (or Creek), and Seminole nations—vigorously resisted the work of the Dawes Commission to allot their lands. A Dawes Commission report of 1894 criticized landholding in "Indian Territory," and in essence supported the ethnocidal policies of the reformers that sought to eliminate the governmental autonomy of these tribes.

The barrier opposed at all times by those in authority in the tribes, and assuming to speak for them as to any change in existing conditions, is what they claim to be "the treaty situation." They mean by this term that the United States is under treaty obligations not to interfere in their internal policy, but has guaranteed to them self-government and absolute exclusion of white citizens from any abode among them; that the United States is bound to isolate them absolutely. It can not be doubted that this was substantially the original governing idea in establishing the Five Tribes in the Indian Territory, more or less clearly expressed in the treaties, which are the basis of whatever title and authority they at present have in the possession of that Territory, over which they now claim this exclusive jurisdiction. To that end the United States, in different treaties and patents executed in pursuance of such treaties, conveyed to the several tribes the country originally known as the "Indian Territory," of which their present possessions are a part only, and agreed to the establishment by them therein of governments of their own. The United States also agreed to exclude all white persons from their borders.

These treaties, however, embraced stipulations equally clear, that these tribes were to hold this territory for the use and enjoyment of all Indians belonging to their respective tribes, so that every Indian, as is expressed in some of the treaties, "shall have an equal right with every other Indian in each and every portion of the territory," and the further stipulation that their laws should not conflict with the Constitution of the United States. These were executory provisions to be observed in the future by both sides. Without regard to any observance of them on their part, the Indians claim that these treaties are irrevocably binding on the United States. These stipulations naturally grew out of the situation of the country at the time they were made, and of the character of the Indians with whom they were made. The present growth of the country and its present relations to this territory were not thought of or even dreamed of by either party when they entered into these stipulations. These Indians were then at a considerably advanced stage of civilization, and were thought capable of self-government, in conformity with the spirit if not the forms of the National Government, within whose limits they were to remain. It was not altogether unreasonable, therefore, to conclude that it would be possible, as it was by them desirable, that these Indians could have set apart to them a tract of country so far remote from white civilization and so isolated that they could work out the problem of their own preservation under a government of their own, and that not only with safety to the Union but with altogether desirable results to themselves.

For quite a number of years after the institution of this project it seemed successful, and the Indians under it made favorable advance toward its realization. But within the last few years all the conditions under which it was inaugurated have undergone so complete a change that it has become no longer possible. It is hardly necessary to call attention to the contrast between the present conditions surrounding this Territory and those under which it was set apart. Large and populous States of the Union are now on all sides of it, and one-half of it has been constituted a Territory of the United States. These States and this Territory are teeming with population and increasing in numbers at a marvelous rate. The resources of the Territory itself have been developed to such a degree and are of such immense and tempting value that they are attracting to it an irresistible pressure from enterprising citizens. The executory conditions contained in the treaties have become impossible of execution. It is no longer possible for the United States to keep its citizens out of the Territory. Nor is it now possible for the Indians to secure to each individual Indian his full enjoyment in common with other Indians of the common property of the Territory.

The impossibility of enforcing these executory provisions has arisen from a neglect on both sides to enforce them. This neglect is largely the result of outside considerations for which neither is responsible and of the influence of forces which neither can control. These executory conditions are not only impossible of execution, but have ceased to be applicable or desirable. It has been demonstrated that isolation is an impossibility, and that if possible, it could never result in the elevation or civilization of the Indian. It has been made clear that under its operations, imperfectly as it has been carried out, its effect has been to retard rather than to promote civilization, to impair rather than strengthen the observance of law and order and regard for human life and human rights or the protection or promotion of a virtuous life. To such a degree has this sad deterioration become evident that to-day a most deplorable and dangerous condition of affairs exist[s] in the Territory, causing widespread alarm and demanding most serious consideration.

All the functions of the so-called governments of these five tribes have become powerless to protect the life or property rights of the citizen. The courts of justice have become helpless and paralyzed. Violence, robbery, and murder are almost of daily occurrence, and no effective measures of restraint or punishment are put forth to suppress crime. Railroad trains are stopped and their passengers robbed within a few miles of populous towns and the plunder carried off with impunity in the very presence of those in authority. A reign of terror exists, and barbarous outrages, almost impossible of belief, are enacted, and the perpetrators hardly find it necessary to shun daily intercourse with their victims. We are now informed that, within the territory of one of these tribes, there were 53 murders during the month of

September and the first twenty-four days of October last, and not a single person brought to trial.

In every respect the present condition of affairs demonstrates that the permission to govern themselves, under the Constitution of the United States, which was originally embraced in the treaty, has proved a failure. So, likewise, has the provision that requires the United States to exclude white citizens from the Territory. The course of procedure by the governments of the Five Tribes has largely contributed to this result, and they are quite as much responsible as the United States for the fact that there are 250,000 white people residing in the Territory. These citizens of the United States have been induced to go there in various ways and by various methods by the Indian governments themselves. These governments consented to the construction of a number of railways through the Territory, and thereby consented that they bring into the Territory all that is necessary in the building and operation of such railroads—the necessary depots, stations, and the inevitable towns which their traffic was sure to build up, and the large building which white men alone could develop and which these railroads were sure to stimulate and make profitable.

Besides these, they have, by their laws, invited men from the border States to become their employees in the Territory, receiving into their treasuries a monthly tax for the privilege of such employment. They have also provided by law for the intermarriage of white persons with their citizens and adopted them into their tribes. By operation of these laws large numbers of white people have become adopted citizens, participating in the benefits of citizenship. A single instance of such marriage has enabled one white man under the laws to appropriate to his exclusive use 50,000 acres of valuable land. They have, by their legislation, induced citizens of the United States to come in from all sides and under leases and other agreements with private citizens, sanctioned by their own laws, farmed out to them large ranges of their domain, as well as inexhaustible coal deposits within their respective borders, and other material interests which civilized white men alone could turn to profit. In some sections of the Territory the production of cotton has proved so feasible and profitable that white men have been permitted to come in by thousands and cultivate it and build trading marts and populous towns for the successful operation of this branch of trade alone.

In a single town of 5,000 white inhabitants, built there by their permission and also for the profit of the Indian, there were during last year marketed 40,000 bales of cotton. They have also sold off to the United States one-half of their original territory, to be opened up to white settlement on their western borders, in which, with their consent thus obtained, 300,000 white citizens have made their homes, and a Territorial government by this means has been erected in the midst of their own territory, which is forbidden by one of the executory provisions of the treaty. The day of isolation has passed. Not less regardless have they been of the stipulations in their title that they should hold their territory for the common and equal use of all their citizens. Corruption of the grossest kind, openly and unblushingly practiced, has found its way into every branch of the service of the tribal governments. . . .

Towns of considerable importance have been built by white persons under leases obtained from Indians claiming the right to appropriate the common property of these uses. . . . The original idea of a community of property has been entirely lost sight of and disregarded in every branch of the administration of their affairs by the governments which have been permitted to control this Territory under the treaty stipulations which are now being invoked, by those who are in this manner administering them, as a protection for their personal holdings and enterprises.

The large payments of moneys to the Indians of these tribes within the last few years have been attended by many and apparently well-authenticated complaints of fraud, and those making such payments, with others associated with them in the business, have, by unfair means and improper use of the advantages thus afforded them, acquired large fortunes, and in many instances private persons entitled to payments have received but little benefit therefrom. And worse still is the fact that the places of payments were thronged with evil characters of every possible caste, by whom the people were swindled, defrauded, robbed, and grossly debauched and demoralized. And in case of further payments of money to them the Government should make such disbursements to the people directly, through one of its own officers.

We feel it our duty to here suggest that any measures looking to any change of affairs in this Territory should embrace special, strict, and effective provisions for protection of the Indian and other citizens from the introduction, manufacture, or sale of intoxicants of any kind in the Territory, with penalties therefor and for failure by officers to enforce same, sufficiently severe to cause their perfect execution. A failure to thus protect these Indians will, in a measure, work their extinction at no distant day.

It is a deplorable fact, which should not be overlooked by the Government, that there are thousands of white children in this territory who are almost wholly without the means of education, and are consequently growing up with no fitting preparation for useful citizenship. A matter of so much concern to the country should not be disregarded.

When the treaties were reaffirmed in 1866, a provision was made for the adoption and equality of rights of the freedmen, who had theretofore been slaves in the tribes, upon terms provided in the treaties. The Cherokees and Choctaws have appeared to comply with the letter of the prescribed terms, although very inadequately and tardily, and the Chickasaws at one time took some steps toward complying with these terms, but now deny that they ever adopted the freedmen, and are endeavoring to retrace the steps originally taken. They now treat the whole class as aliens without any legal right to abide among them, or to claim any protection under their laws. They are shut out of the schools of the tribe, and from their courts, and are granted no privileges of occupancy of any part of the land for a home, and are helplessly exposed to the hostilities of the citizen Indian and the personal animosity of the former master. Peaceable, law-abiding, and hard-working, they have sought in vain to be regarded as a part of the people to whose wealth their industry is daily contributing a very essential portion. They number in that tribe about 4,000, while the Chickasaws number 3,500. The United States is bound by solemn treaty to place these freedmen securely in the enjoyment of their rights as Chickasaw Indians, and cannot with honor ignore the obligation. . . .

The condition of the freedmen in the Choctaw and Cherokee tribes is little better than that of those among the Chickasaws, although they have been adopted according to the requirements of the treaties. They are yet very far from the enjoyment of all the rights, privileges, and immunities to which they are entitled under the treaties. In the Choctaw tribe, the 40 acres to which they are entitled for a home has not been set apart to them and no one has any title to a single foot of land he may improve or occupy. Whenever his occupancy of land is in the way of any citizen Indian he is at once, by means sufficiently severe and threatening, compelled to leave his improvements. He consequently has no abiding place, and what he is enabled to get from the soil for his support, he is compelled to gather either furtively or by the most absolute subserviency to the will, caprices, or exactions of his former master. But meager provision is made for the schooling of his children, and but little participation in the management of the government of which he is a citizen is permitted him. He is nevertheless moral, industrious, and frugal, peaceable, orderly, and obedient to the laws, taking no part in the crimes which have of late filled the country with alarm and put in peril the lives and property of law-abiding citizens. A number of these sought an interview with us on one occasion, but were, as we were informed, warned by a prominent Indian citizen that if they called upon us they would be killed, which warning they heeded.

In the Cherokee tribe the schools provided for the freedmen are of very inferior and inefficient character, and practically their children are growing up in deplorable ignorance. They are excluded from participation in the per capita distribution of all funds, and are ignored in almost all respects as a factor in the government of a people of whose citizenship they are by the treaties in all respects made a part. Yet in this tribe the freedmen are conspicuous for their morality, industrial and frugal habits, and for peaceable and orderly lives.

Justice has been utterly perverted in the hands of those who have thus laid hold of the forms of its administration in this Territory and who have inflicted irreparable wrongs and outrages upon a helpless people for their own gain. The United States put the title to a domain of countless wealth and unmeasured resources in these several tribes or nationalities, but it was a conveyance in trust for specific uses, clearly indicated in the treaties themselves, and for no other purpose. It was for the use and enjoyment in common by each and every citizen of his tribe, of each and every part of the Territory, thus tersely expressed in one of the treaties: "To be held in common, so that each and every member of either tribe shall have an equal undivided interest in the whole." The tribes can make no other use of it. They have no power to grant it to anyone, or to grant to anyone an exclusive use of any portion of it. These tribal governments have wholly perverted their high trusts, and it is the plain duty of the United States to enforce the trust it has so created and recover for its original uses the domain and all the gains derived from the perversions of the trust or discharge the trustee.

The United States also granted to these tribes the power of self-government, not to conflict with the Constitution. They have demonstrated their incapacity to so govern themselves, and no higher duty can rest upon the Government that granted this authority than to revoke it when it has so lamentably failed.

In closing this report we may be permitted to add that we have observed with pain and deep regret that the praiseworthy efforts of the Christian church, and of benevolent associations from different parts of the country, so long continued among the tribes, are being counteracted and rendered in a large measure nugatory by the untoward influences and methods now in force among them tending directly to destroy and obliterate the beneficial effects of their good work.

Source: Senate Miscellaneous Document 24, 53d Cong., 3d sess., serial 3281, pp. 8–12.

40 Curtis Act, June 28, 1898

The Curtis Act destroyed Native American tribal governments in Indian Territory, present-day Oklahoma. Whereas the Dawes Commission had failed to achieve this goal through negotiation (see Docs. 38 and 39), the Curtis Act eliminated the power of tribal governments through its provisions to establish and regulate town sites, manage mineral rights leases, and circumscribe aspects of Indian life. The sections below authorize Congress to develop tribal membership rolls, allot lands, and abolish American Indian courts in Indian Territory.

An Act for the protection of the people of the Indian Territory, and/or other purposes. . . .

SEC. 11. That when the roll of citizenship of any one of said nations or tribes is fully completed as provided by law, and the survey of the lands of said nation or tribe is also completed, the commission heretofore appointed under Acts of Congress, and known as the "Dawes Commission," shall proceed to allot the exclusive use and occupancy of the surface of all the lands of said nation or tribe susceptible of allotment among the citizens thereof, as shown by said roll, giving to each, so far as possible, his fair and equal share thereof, considering the nature and fertility of the soil, location, and value of same; but all oil, coal, asphalt, and mineral deposits in the lands of any tribe are reserved to such tribe, and no allotment of such lands shall carry the title to such oil, coal, asphalt, or mineral deposits; and all town sites shall also be reserved to the several tribes, and shall be set apart by the commission heretofore mentioned as incapable of allotment. There shall also be reserved from allotment a sufficient amount of lands now occupied by churches, schools, parsonages, charitable institutions, and other public buildings for their present actual and necessary use, and no more, not to exceed five acres for each school and one acre for each church and each parsonage, and for such new schools as may be needed; also sufficient land for burial grounds where necessary. When such allotment of the lands of any tribe has been by them completed, said commission shall make full report thereof to the Secretary of the Interior for his approval. . . .

SEC. 17. That it shall be unlawful for any citizen of any one of said tribes to inclose or in any manner, by himself or through another, directly or indirectly, to hold possession of any greater amount of lands or other property belonging to any such nation or tribe than that which would be his approximate share of the lands belonging to such nation or tribe and that of his wife and his minor children as per allotment herein provided; and any person found in such possession of lands or other property in excess of his share and that of his family, as aforesaid, or having the same in any manner inclosed, at the expiration of nine months after the passage of this Act, shall be deemed guilty of a misdemeanor. . . .

SEC. 19. That no payment of any moneys on any account whatever shall hereafter be made by the United States to any of the tribal governments or to any officer thereof for disbursement, but payments of all sums to members of said tribes shall be made under direction of the Secretary of the Interior by an officer appointed by him; and per capita payments shall be made direct to each individual in lawful money of the United States, and the same shall not be liable to the payment of any previously contracted obligation. . . .

SEC. 26. That on and after the passage of this Act the laws of the various tribes or nations of Indians shall not be enforced at law or in equity by the courts of the United States in the Indian Territory. . . .

SEC. 28. That on the first day of July, eighteen hundred and ninety-eight, all tribal courts of Indian Territory shall be abolished, and no officer of said courts shall thereafter have any authority whatever to do or perform any act theretofore authorized by any law in connection with said courts, or to receive any pay for same; and all civil and criminal causes then pending in any such court shall be transferred to the United States court in said Territory by filing with the clerk of the court the original papers in the suit: *Provided,* That this section shall not be in force as to the Chickasaw, Choctaw, and Creek tribes or nations until the first day of October, eighteen hundred and ninety-eight. . . .

Source: *U.S Statutes at Large,* 30:497–498, 502, 504–505.

41 *Stephens v. Cherokee Nation* (1899)

Members of the Five Civilized Tribes—the Cherokee, Chickasaw, Choctaw, Muscogee (or Creek), and Seminole nations—challenged the constitutionality of the Curtis Act (Doc. 40) and the division of property rights as proposed by the Dawes Commission. The Supreme Court asserted that the Curtis Act was constitutional.

We repeat that in view of the paramount authority of Congress over the Indian tribes, and of the duties imposed on the Government by their condition of dependency, we cannot say that Congress could not empower the Dawes Commission to determine, in the manner provided, who were entitled to citizenship in each of the tribes and make out correct rolls of such citizens, an essential preliminary to effective action in promotion of the best interests of the tribes. It may be remarked that the legislation seems to recognize, especially the act of June 28, 1898, a distinction between admission to citizenship merely and the distribution of property to be subsequently made, as if there might be circumstances under which the right to a share in the latter would not necessarily follow from the concession of the former. But in any aspect, we are of opinion that the constitutionality of these acts in respect of the determination of citizenship cannot be successfully assailed on the ground of the impairment or destruction of vested rights. The lands and moneys of these tribes are public lands and public moneys, and are not held in individual ownership, and the assertion by any particular applicant that his right therein is so vested as to preclude inquiry into his status involves a contradiction in terms.

The judgments in these cases were rendered before the passage of the act of June 28, 1898, commonly known as the Curtis Act, and necessarily the effect of that act was not considered. As, however, the provision for an appeal to this court was made after the passage of the act, some observations upon it are required, and, indeed, the inference is not unreasonable that a principal object intended to be secured by an appeal was the testing of the constitutionality of this act, and that may have had controlling weight in inducing the granting of the right to such appeal.

The act is comprehensive and sweeping in its character, and notwithstanding the abstract of it in the statement prefixed to this opinion, we again call attention to its provisions. The act gave jurisdiction to the United States courts in the Indian Territory in their respective districts to try cases against those who claimed to hold lands and tenements as members of a tribe and whose membership was denied by the tribe, and authorized their removal from the same if the claim was disallowed; and provided for the allotment of lands by the Dawes Commission among the citizens of any one of the tribes as shown by the roll of citizenship when fully completed as provided by law, and according to a survey also fully completed; and "that if the person to whom an allotment shall have been made shall be declared, upon appeal as herein provided for, by any of the courts of the United States in or for the aforesaid Territory, to have been illegally accorded rights of citizenship, and for that or any other reason declared to be not entitled to any allotment, he shall be ousted and ejected from said lands." . . .

For reasons already given we regard this act in general as not obnoxious to constitutional objection, but in so holding we do not intend to intimate any opinion as to the effect that changes made thereby, or by the agreements referred to, may have, if any, on the status of the several applicants, who are parties to these appeals. . . .

As we hold the entire legislation constitutional, the result is that all the judgments must be affirmed.

Source: 174 U.S. 445, 488–489, 491–492.

42 *Lone Wolf v. Hitchcock* (1903)

The 1867 Treaty of Medicine Lodge stipulates that no parts of the Kiowa-Comanche reservation can be ceded unless three-fourths of the adult males of the tribe agreed to it. Congress, after allotting their reservation lands, allowed the sale of the remaining tribal lands without approval of the male members. A lawsuit was therefore filed contending that Congress did not have the power to override the treaty. The Supreme Court found that Congress had plenary powers over Native American affairs and thus was within its rights in passing legislation negating treaty provisions.

The contention in effect ignores the status of the contracting Indians and the relation of dependency they bore and continue to bear towards the government of the United States. To uphold the claim would be to adjudge that the indirect operation of the treaty was to materially limit and qualify the controlling authority of Congress in respect to the care and protection of the Indians, and to deprive Congress, in a possible emergency, when the necessity might be urgent for a partition and disposal of the tribal lands, of all power to act, if the assent of the Indians could not be obtained.

Now, it is true that in decisions of this court, the Indian right of occupancy of tribal lands, whether declared in a treaty or otherwise created, has been stated to be sacred, or, as sometimes expressed, as sacred as the fee of the United States in the same lands. . . . But in none of these cases was there involved a controversy between Indians and the government respecting the power of Congress to administer the property of the Indians. The questions considered in the cases referred to, which either directly or indirectly had relation to the nature of the property rights of the Indians, concerned the character and extent of such rights as respected States or individuals. In one of the cited cases it was clearly pointed out that Congress possessed a paramount power over the property of the Indians, by reason of its exercise of guardianship over their interests, and that such authority might be implied.

Plenary authority over the tribal relations of the Indians has been exercised by Congress from the beginning, and the power has always been deemed a political one, not subject to be controlled by the judicial department of the government. Until the year 1871 the policy was pursued of dealing with the Indian tribes by means of treaties, and, of course, a moral obligation rested upon Congress to act in good faith in performing the stipulations entered into on its behalf. But, as with treaties made with foreign nations, Chinese Exclusion Case, 130 U.S. 581, 600, the legislative power might pass laws in conflict with treaties made with the Indians. . . .

The power exists to abrogate the provisions of an Indian treaty, though presumably such power will be exercised only when circumstances arise which will not only justify the government in disregarding the stipulations of the treaty, but may demand, in the interest of the country and the Indians themselves, that it should do so. When, therefore, treaties were entered into between the United States and a tribe of Indians it was never doubted that the power to abrogate existed in Congress, and that in a contingency such power might be availed of from considerations of governmental policy, particularly if consistent with perfect good faith towards the Indians.

In view of the legislative power possessed by Congress over treaties with the Indians and Indian tribal property, we may not specially consider the contentions pressed upon our notice that the signing by the Indians of the agreement of October 6, 1892, was obtained by fraudulent misrepresentations and concealment, that the requisite three-fourths of adult male Indians had not signed, as required by the twelfth article of the treaty of 1867, and that the treaty as signed had been amended by Congress without submitting such amendments to the action of the Indians, since all these matters, in any event, were solely within the domain of the legislative authority and its action is conclusive upon the courts. . . .

Source: 187 U.S. 553, 564–568.

43 Burke Act, May 8, 1906

In 1906 Congress significantly altered the General Allotment Act, also known as the Dawes Act (Docs. 36 and 37). The Burke Act allowed the federal government to lengthen the trust period over Indian lands at its discretion and stipulated that citizenship for Native Americans agreeing to allotment come at the end of the trust period rather than at the beginning as provided in previous legislation.

An Act to amend section six of an Act approved February eighth, eighteen hundred and eighty-seven, entitled "An Act to provide for the allotment of lands in severalty to Indians on the various reservations, and to extend the protection of the laws of the United States and the Territories over the Indians, and for other purposes."

Be it enacted . . . , That section six of an Act approved February eighth, eighteen hundred and eighty-seven, entitled "An Act to provide for the allotment of lands in severalty to Indians on the various reservations, and to extend the protection of the laws of the United States and the Territories over the Indians, and for other purposes," be amended to read as follows:

"SEC. 6. That at the expiration of the trust period and when the lands have been conveyed to the Indians by patent in fee, as provided in section five of this Act, then each and every allottee shall have the benefit of and be subject to the laws, both civil and criminal, of the State or Territory in which they may reside; and no Territory shall pass or enforce any law denying any such Indian within its jurisdiction the equal protection of the law. And every Indian born within the territorial limits of the United States to whom allotments shall have been made and who has received a patent in fee simple under the provisions of this Act, or under any law or treaty, and every Indian born within the territorial limits of the United States who has voluntarily taken up within said limits his residence, separate and apart from any tribe of Indians therein, and has adopted the habits of civilized life, is hereby declared to be a citizen of the United States, and is entitled to all the rights, privileges, and immunities of such citizens, whether said Indian has been or not, by birth or otherwise, a member of any tribe of Indians within the territorial limits of the United States without in any manner impairing or otherwise affecting the right of any such Indian to tribal or other property: *Provided*, That the Secretary of the Interior may, in his discretion, and he is hereby authorized, whenever he shall be satisfied that any Indian allottee is competent and capable of managing his or her affairs at any time to cause to be issued to such allottee a patent in fee simple, and thereafter all restrictions as to sale, incumbrance, or taxation of said land shall be removed and said land shall not be liable to the satisfaction of any debt contracted prior to the issuing of such patent: *Provided further*, That until the issuance of fee-simple patents all allottees to whom trust patents shall hereafter be issued shall be subject to the exclusive jurisdiction of the United States: *And provided further*, That the provisions of this Act shall not extend to any Indians in the Indian Territory."

That hereafter when an allotment of land is made to any Indian, and any such Indian dies before the expiration of the trust period, said allotment shall be cancelled and the land shall revert to the United States, and the Secretary of the Interior shall ascertain the legal heirs of such Indian, and shall cause to be issued to said heirs and in their names, a patent in fee simple for said land, or he may cause the land to be sold as provided by law and issue a patent therefor to the purchaser or purchasers, and pay the net proceeds to the heirs, or their legal representatives, of such deceased Indian. The action of the Secretary of the Interior in determining the legal heirs of any deceased Indian, as provided herein, shall in all respects be conclusive and final.

Source: *U.S. Statutes at Large*, 34:182–183.

44 Lacey Act, March 2, 1907

The Burke Act (Doc. 43) and the Dawes Act (Docs. 36 and 37) authorized the allotment of reservation lands to individual Native Americans. Neither act, however, extended Congress's power over communal trust funds. In 1907 Congressman John F. Lacey of Iowa authored legislation providing for the allotment of tribal funds to certain classes of American Indians.

An Act Providing for the allotment and distribution of Indian tribal funds.

Be it enacted . . . , That the Secretary of the Interior is hereby authorized, in his discretion, from time to time, to designate any individual Indian belonging to any tribe or tribes whom he may deem to be capable of managing his or her affairs, and he may cause to be apportioned and allotted to any such Indian his or her pro rata share of any tribal or trust funds on deposit in the Treasury of the United States to the credit of the tribe or tribes of which said Indian is a member, and the amount so apportioned and allotted shall be placed to the credit of such Indian upon the books of the Treasury, and the same shall thereupon be subject to the order of such Indian: *Provided*, That no apportionment or allotment shall be made to any Indian until such Indian has first made an application therefor: *Provided further*, That the Secretaries of the Interior and of the Treasury are hereby directed to withhold from such apportionment and allotment a sufficient sum of the said Indian funds as may be necessary or required to pay any existing claims against said Indians that may be pending for settlement by judicial determination in the Court of Claims or in the Executive Departments of the Government, at time of such apportionment and allotment.

SEC. 2. That the Secretary of the Interior is hereby authorized to pay any Indian who is blind, crippled, decrepit, or helpless from old age, disease, or accident, his or her share, or any portion thereof, of the tribal trust funds in the United States Treasury belonging to the tribe of which such Indian is a member, and of any other money which may hereafter be placed in the Treasury for the credit of such tribe and susceptible of division among its members, under such rules, regulations, and conditions as he may prescribe.

Source: *U.S. Statutes at Large*, 34:1221–1222.

Indian Commissioner Cato Sells, A Declaration of Policy, October 15, 1917

To hasten the process of freeing Native Americans from federal guardianship, Commissioner of Indian Affairs Cato Sells instituted a policy in 1917 that shortened the time period for deciding on the competence of individual American Indians. If declared competent, an Indian would no longer be considered a ward of the U.S. government.

A DECLARATION OF POLICY

A careful study of the practical effects of governmental policies for determining the wardship of the Indians of this country is convincing that the solution is individual and not collective. Each individual must be considered in the light of his own environment and capacity for larger responsibilities and privileges.

While ethnologically a preponderance of white blood has not heretofore been a criterion of competency, nor even now is it always a safe standard, it is almost an axiom that an Indian who has a larger proportion of white blood than Indian partakes more of the characteristics of the former than of the latter. In thought and action, so far as the business world is concerned, he approximates more closely to the white blood ancestry.

On April 17, 1917, there was announced a declaration of policy for Indian affairs, as follows:

A DECLARATION OF POLICY IN THE ADMINISTRATION OF INDAIN AFFAIRS.

During the past four years the efforts of the administration of Indian affairs have been largely concentrated on the following fundamental activities—the betterment of health conditions of Indians, the suppression of the liquor traffic among them, the improvement of their industrial conditions, the further development of vocational training in their schools, and the protection of the Indians' property. Rapid progress has been made along all these lines, and the work thus reorganized and revitalized will go on with increased energy. With these activities and accomplishments well under way, we are now ready to take the next step in our administrative program.

The time has come for discontinuing guardianship of all competent Indians and giving even closer attention to the incompetent that they may more speedily achieve competency.

Broadly speaking, a policy of greater liberalism will henceforth prevail in Indian administration to the end that every Indian, as soon as he has been determined to be as competent to transact his own business as the average white man, shall be given full control of his property and have all his lands and moneys turned over to him, after which he will no longer be a ward of the Government.

Pursuant to this policy, the following rules shall be observed:

1. Patents in fee.—To all able-bodied adult Indians of less than one-half Indian blood, there will be given as far as may be under the law full and complete control of all their property. Patents in fee shall be issued to all adult Indians of one-half or more Indian blood who may, after careful investigation, be found competent, provided, that where deemed advisable patents in fee shall be withheld for not to exceed 40 acres as a home.

   Indian students, when they are 21 years of age, or over, who complete the full course of instruction in the Government schools, receive diplomas and have demonstrated competency will be so declared.
2. Sale of lands.—A liberal ruling will be adopted in the matter of passing upon applications for the sale of inherited Indian lands where the applicants retain other lands and the proceeds are to be used to improve the homesteads or for other equally good purposes. A more liberal ruling than has hitherto prevailed will hereafter be followed with regard to the applications of noncompetent Indians for the sale of their lands where they are old and feeble and need the proceeds for their support.
3. Certificates of competency.—The rules which are made to apply in the granting of patents in fee and the sale of lands be made equally applicable in the matter issuing certificates of competency.
4. Individual Indian moneys.—Indians will be given unrestricted control of all their individual Indian moneys upon issuance of patents in fee or certificates of competency. Strict limitations will not be placed upon the use of funds of the old, the indigent, and the invalid.
5. Pro-rata shares—trust funds.—As speedily as possible their pro rata shares in tribal trust or other funds shall be paid to all Indians who have been declared competent, unless the legal status of such funds prevents. Where practicable the

pro rata shares of incompetent Indians will be withdrawn from the Treasury and placed in banks to their individual credit.

6. Elimination of ineligible pupils from the Government Indian schools.—In many of our boarding schools Indian children are being educated at Government expense whose parents are amply able to pay for their education and have public school facilities at or near their homes. Such children shall not hereafter be enrolled in Government Indian schools supported by gratuity appropriations, except on payment of actual per capita cost and transportation.

These rules are hereby made effective, and all Indian Bureau administrative officers at Washington and in the field will be governed accordingly.

This is a new and far-reaching declaration of policy. It means the dawn of a new era in Indian administration. It means that the competent Indian will no longer be treated as half ward and half citizen. It means reduced appropriations by the Government and more self-respect and independence for the Indian. It means the ultimate absorption of the Indian race into the body politic of the Nation. It means, in short, the beginning of the end of the Indian problem.

In carrying out this policy, I cherish the hope that all real friends of the Indian race will lend their aid and hearty cooperation.

CATO SELLS,
Commissioner

Approved:
FRANKLIN K. LANE,
Secretary

The cardinal principle of this declaration revolves around this central thought—that an Indian who is as competent as an ordinary white man to transact the ordinary affairs of life should be given untrammeled control of his property and assured his personal rights in every particular so that he may have the opportunity of working out his own destiny. The practical application of this principle will relieve from the guardianship of the Government a very large number of Indians who are qualified to mingle on a plane of business equality with the white people. It will also begin the reduction of expenditures, and afford a better opportunity for closer attention to those who will need our protecting care for some years longer.

A vitally important result also will be obtained in placing a true ideal before those Indians remaining under guardianship. It will be a strong motive for endeavoring to reach the goal of competency, and prove a material incentive to a sincere effort for that end.

This new declaration of policy is calculated to release practically all Indians who have one-half or more white blood, although there will be exceptions in the case of those who are manifestly incompetent. It will also give like freedom from guardianship to those having more than one-half Indian blood when, after careful investigation, it is determined that they are capable of handling their own affairs. This latter class, however, will be much more limited since only about 40 per cent of the Indians of the country speak the English language and the large majority of this latter class still greatly need the protecting arm of the Government. . . .

Source: *Annual Report of the Commissioner of Indian Affairs* (Washington, D.C.: Government Printing Office, 1917), 3–5.

46 Indian Citizenship Act, June 2, 1924

In 1924 Congress unilaterally made citizens all Native Americans born in the United States who had not been granted citizenship under previous legislative provisions. Many Native American groups protested this act, which they thought would erode their treaty rights.

An Act To authorize the Secretary of the Interior to issue certificates of citizenship to Indians.

Be it enacted . . . , That all non-citizen Indians born within the territorial limits of the United States be, and they are hereby, declared to be citizens of the United States:

Provided, That the granting of such citizenship shall not in any manner impair or otherwise affect the right of any Indian to tribal or other property.

Source: *U.S. Statutes at Large*, 43:253.

47 Johnson-O'Malley Act, April 16, 1934

In 1934, during the "Indian New Deal," Congress provided for federal contracts with states to pay for educational, medical, and other services delivered by the states to Native American peoples.

An Act Authorizing the Secretary of the Interior to arrange with States or Territories for the education, medical attention, relief of distress, and social welfare of Indians, and for other purposes.

Be it enacted . . ., That the Secretary of the Interior is hereby authorized, in his discretion, to enter into a contract or contracts with any State or Territory having legal authority so to do, for the education, medical attention, agricultural assistance, and social welfare, including relief of distress, of Indians in such State or Territory, through the qualified agencies of such State or Territory, and to expend under such contract or contracts moneys appropriated by Congress for the education, medical attention, agricultural assistance, and social welfare, including relief of distress, of Indians in such State.

SEC. 2. That the Secretary of the Interior, in making any contract herein authorized with any State or Territory, may permit such State or Territory to utilize for the purpose of this Act, existing school buildings, hospitals, and other facilities, and all equipment therein or appertaining thereto, including livestock and other personal property owned by the Government, under such terms and conditions as may be agreed upon for their use and maintenance.

SEC. 3. That the Secretary of the Interior is hereby authorized to perform any and all acts and to make such rules and regulations, including minimum standards of service, as may be necessary and proper for the purpose of carrying the provisions of this Act into effect: *Provided*, That such minimum standards of service are not less than the highest maintained by the States or Territories with which said contract or con tracts, as herein provided, are executed.

SEC. 4. That the Secretary of the Interior shall report annually to the Congress any contract or contracts made under the provisions of this Act, and the moneys expended thereunder.

SEC. 5. That the provisions of this Act shall not apply to the State of Oklahoma.

Source: *U.S. Statutes at Large*, 48:596.

48 Wheeler-Howard Act (Indian Reorganization Act), June 18, 1934

The Wheeler-Howard Act of 1934, also known as the Indian Reorganization Act, brought a halt to the allotment of reservation lands and sought to sustain American Indian tribal organizations. It was the culmination of the American Indian reform movement begun in the 1920s by John Collier when he was executive director of the American Indian Defense Association. President Franklin Delano Roosevelt appointed Collier commissioner of Indian affairs in 1933. Collier championed Wheeler-Howard.

An Act to conserve and develop Indian lands and resources; to extend to Indians the right to form business and other organizations; to establish a credit system for Indians; to grant certain rights of home rule to Indians; to provide for vocational education for Indians; and for other purposes.

Be it enacted . . . , That hereafter no land of any Indian reservation, created or set apart by treaty or agreement with the Indians, Act of Congress, Executive order, purchase, or otherwise, shall be allotted in severalty to any Indian.

SEC. 2. The existing periods of trust placed upon any Indian lands and any restriction on alienation thereof are hereby extended and continued until otherwise directed by Congress.

SEC. 3. The Secretary of the Interior, if he shall find it to be in the public interest, is hereby authorized to restore to tribal ownership the remaining surplus lands of any Indian reservation heretofore opened, or authorized to be opened, to sale, or any other form of disposal by Presidential proclamation, or by any of the public land laws of the United States: *Provided*, however, That valid rights or claims of any persons to any lands so withdrawn existing on the date of the withdrawal shall not be affected by this Act: . . .

SEC. 4. Except as herein provided no sale, devise, gift, exchange or other transfer of restricted Indian lands or of shares in the assets of any Indian tribe or corporation organized hereunder, shall be made or approved: *Provided, however*, That such lands or interests may, with the approval of the Secretary of the Interior, be sold, devised or otherwise transferred to the Indian tribe in which the lands or shares are located or from which the shares were derived or to a successor corporation; and in all instances such lands or interests shall descend or be devised, in accordance with the then existing laws of the State, or Federal laws where applicable, in which said lands are located or in which the subject matter of the corporation is located, to any member of such tribe or of such corporation or any heirs of such member: *Provided further*, That the Secretary of the Interior may authorize voluntary exchanges of lands of equal value and the voluntary exchange of shares of equal value whenever such exchange, in his judgment, is expedient and beneficial for or compatible with the proper consolidation of Indian lands and for the benefit of cooperative organizations.

SEC. 5. The Secretary of the Interior is hereby authorized, in his discretion, to acquire through purchase, relinquishment, gift, exchange, or assignment, any interest in lands, water rights or surface rights to lands, within or without existing reservations, including trust or otherwise restricted allotments whether the allottee be living or deceased, for the purpose of providing land for Indians.

For the acquisition of such lands, interests in lands, water rights, and surface rights, and for expenses incident to such acquisition, there is hereby authorized to be appropriated, out of any funds in the Treasury not otherwise appropriated, a sum not to exceed $2,000,000 in any one fiscal year: . . .

The unexpended balances of any appropriations made pursuant to this section shall remain available until expended.

Title to any lands or rights acquired pursuant to this Act shall be taken in the name of the United States in trust for the Indian tribe or individual Indian for which the land is acquired, and such lands or rights shall be exempt from State and local taxation.

SEC. 6. The Secretary of the Interior is directed to make rules and regulations for the operation and management of Indian forestry units on the principle of sustained-yield management, to restrict the number of livestock grazed on Indian range units to the estimated carrying capacity of such ranges, and to promulgate such other rules and regulations as may be necessary to protect the range from deterioration, to prevent soil erosion, to assure full utilization of the range, and like purposes.

SEC. 7. The Secretary of the Interior is hereby authorized to proclaim new Indian reservations on lands acquired pursuant to any authority conferred by this Act, or to add such lands to existing reservations: *Provided,* That lands added to existing reservations shall be designated for the exclusive use of Indians entitled by enrollment or by tribal membership to residence at such reservations.

SEC. 8. Nothing contained in this Act shall be construed to relate to Indian holdings of allotments or homesteads upon the public domain outside of the geographic boundaries of any Indian reservation now existing or established hereafter.

SEC. 9. There is hereby authorized to be appropriated, out of any funds in the Treasury not otherwise appropriated, such sums as may be necessary, but not to exceed $250,000 in any fiscal year, to be expended at the order of the Secretary of the Interior, in defraying the expenses of organizing Indian chartered corporations or other organizations created under this Act. . . .

SEC. 10. There is hereby authorized to be appropriated, out of any funds in the Treasury not otherwise appropriated, the sum of $10,000,000 to be established as a revolving fund from which the Secretary of the Interior, under such rules and regulations as he may prescribe, may make loans to Indian chartered corporations for the purpose of promoting the economic development of such tribes and of their members, and may defray the expenses of administering such loans. Repayment of amounts loaned under this authorization shall be credited to the revolving fund and shall be available for the purposes for which the fund is established. A report shall be made annually to Congress of transactions under this authorization.

SEC. 11. There is hereby authorized to be appropriated, out of any funds in the United States Treasury not otherwise appropriated, a sum not to exceed $250,000 annually, together with any unexpended balances of previous appropriations made pursuant to this section, for loans to Indians for the payment of tuition and other expenses in recognized vocational and trade schools: *Provided*, That not more than $50,000 of such sum shall be available for loans to Indian students in high schools and colleges. Such loans shall be reimbursable under rules established by the Commissioner of Indian Affairs.

SEC. 12. The Secretary of the Interior is directed to establish standards of health, age, character, experience, knowledge, and ability for Indians who may be appointed, without regard to civil-service laws, to the various positions maintained, now or hereafter, by the Indian Office, in the administration of functions or services affecting any Indian tribe. Such qualified Indians shall hereafter have the preference to appointment to vacancies in any such positions.

SEC. 13. The provisions of this Act shall not apply to any of the Territories, colonies, or insular possessions of the United States, except that sections 9, 10, 11, 12, and 16, shall apply to the Territory of Alaska: *Provided*, That Sections 2, 4, 7, 16, 17, and 18 of this Act shall not apply to the following-named Indian tribes, the members of such Indian tribes, together with members of other tribes affiliated with such named tribes located in the State of Oklahoma, as follows: Cheyenne, Arapaho, Apache, Comanche, Kiowa, Caddo, Delaware, Wichita, Osage, Kaw, Otoe, Tonkawa, Pawnee, Ponca, Shawnee, Ottawa, Quapaw, Seneca, Wyandotte, Iowa, Sac and Fox, Kickapoo, Pottawatomi, Cherokee, Chickasaw, Choctaw, Creek, and Seminole. Section 4 of this Act shall not apply to the Indians of the Klamath Reservation in Oregon.

SEC. 14. [Listing of provisions pertaining to Sioux allotments]

SEC. 15. Nothing in this Act shall be construed to impair or prejudice any claim or suit of any Indian tribe against the United States. It is hereby declared to be the intent of Congress that no expenditures for the benefit of Indians made out of appropriations authorized by this Act shall be considered as offsets in any suit brought to recover upon any claim of such Indians against the United States.

SEC. 16. Any Indian tribe, or tribes, residing on the same reservation, shall have the right to organize for its common welfare, and may adopt an appropriate constitution and bylaws, which shall become effective when ratified by a majority vote of the adult members of the tribe, or of the adult Indians residing on such reservation, as the case may be, at a special election authorized and called by the Secretary of the Interior under such rules and regulations as he may prescribe. Such constitution and bylaws when ratified as aforesaid and approved by the Secretary of the Interior shall be revocable by an election open to the same voters and conducted in the same manner as herein above provided. Amendments to the constitution and bylaws may be ratified and approved by the Secretary in the same manner as the original constitution and bylaws.

In addition to all powers vested in any Indian tribe or tribal council by existing law, the constitution adopted by said tribe shall also vest in such tribe or its tribal council the following rights and powers: To employ legal counsel, the choice of counsel and fixing of fees to be subject to the approval of the Secretary of the Interior; to prevent the sale, disposition, lease, or encumbrance of tribal lands, interests in lands, or other tribal assets without the consent of the tribe; and to negotiate with the Federal, State, and local Governments. The Secretary of the Interior shall advise such tribe or its tribal council of all appropriation estimates or Federal projects for the benefit of the tribe prior to the submission of such estimates to the Bureau of the Budget and the Congress.

SEC. 17. The Secretary of the Interior may, upon petition by at least one-third of the adult Indians, issue a charter of incorporation to such tribe: *Provided*, That such charter shall not become operative until ratified at a special election by a majority vote of the adult Indians living on the reservation. Such charter may convey to the incorporated tribe the power to purchase, take by gift, or bequest, or otherwise, own, hold, manage, operate, and dispose of property of every description, real and personal, including the power to purchase restricted Indian lands and to issue in exchange therefor interests in corporate property, and such further powers as may be incidental to the conduct of corporate business, not inconsistent with law, but no authority shall be granted to sell, mortgage, or lease for a period exceeding ten years any of the land included in the limits of the reservation. Any charter so issued shall not be revoked or surrendered except by Act of Congress.

SEC. 18. This Act shall not apply to any reservation wherein a majority of the adult Indians, voting at a special election duly called by the Secretary of the Interior, shall vote against its application. It shall be the duty of the Secretary of the Interior, within one year after the passage and approval of this Act, to call such an election which election shall be held by secret ballot upon thirty days' notice.

SEC. 19. The term "Indian" as used in this Act shall include all persons of Indian descent who are members of any recognized Indian tribe now under Federal jurisdiction, and all persons who are descendants of such members who were, on June 1, 1934, residing within the present boundaries of any Indian reservation and shall further include all other persons of one-half or more Indian blood. For the purposes of this Act, Eskimos and other aboriginal peoples of Alaska shall be considered Indians. The term "tribe" wherever used in this Act shall be construed to refer to any Indian tribe, organized band, pueblo, or the Indians residing on one reservation. The words "adult Indians" wherever used in this Act shall be construed to refer to Indians who have attained the age of twenty-one years.

Source: *U.S. Statutes at Large*, 48:984–988.

49 Indian Commissioner John Collier on the Wheeler-Howard Act, 1934

Commissioner of Indian Affairs John Collier, the fundamental architect of the policies of the Wheeler-Howard Act (Doc. 48), or Indian Reorganization Act, praised the legislation in a 1934 report.

"If we can relieve the Indian of the unrealistic and fatal allotment system, if we can provide him with land and the means to work the land; if, through group organization and tribal incorporation, we can give him a real share in the management of his own affairs, he can develop normally in his own natural environment. The Indian problem as it exists today, including the heaviest and most unproductive administration costs of public service, has largely grown out of the allotment system which has destroyed the economic integrity of the Indian estate and deprived the Indians of normal economic and human activity."

The allotment system with its train of evil consequences was definitely abandoned as the backbone of the national Indian policy when Congress adopted and the President approved the Wheeler-Howard bill. The first section of this act in effect repeals the General Allotment Act of 1887. During numerous committee hearings, during several redrafts and modifications affecting every other part of the measure, this first section was never questioned or revised. It reached the President's desk in its original form without the change of a word or a comma, indicating that Congress was thoroughly convinced of the allotment system's complete failure and was eager to abandon it as the governing policy.

THE ACT'S TWOFOLD AIM

The Wheeler-Howard Act, the most important piece of Indian legislation since the eighties, not only ends the long, painful, futile effort to speed up the normal rate of Indian assimilation by individualizing tribal land and other capital assets, but it also endeavors to provide the means, statutory and financial, to repair as far as possible, the incalculable damage done by the allotment policy and its corollaries. Unfortunately, the beginning of the repair work had to be in large part postponed because the authorized appropriations could not be made by Congress after the passage of the act during the closing days of the session.

The repair work authorized by Congress under the terms of the act aims at both the economic and the spiritual rehabilitation of the Indian race. Congress and the President recognized that the cumulative loss of land brought about by the allotment system, a loss reaching 90,000,000 acres—two-thirds of the land heritage of the Indian race in 1887—had robbed the Indians in large part of the necessary basis for self-support. They clearly saw that this loss and the companion effort to break up all Indian tribal relations had condemned large numbers of Indians to become chronic recipients of charity; that the system of leasing individualized holdings had created many thousands of petty landlords unfitted to support themselves when their rental income vanished; that a major proportion of the red race was, therefore, ruined economically and pauperized spiritually.

ECONOMIC REHABILITATION-LAND PURCHASES

To meet this situation, the act authorized a maximum annual appropriation of $2,000,000 for the purchase of land for landless Indians. This maximum appropriation, even if continued over a term of years, will meet only the most pressing emergency land needs of the Indians. It must be remembered that since 1887 the Indian race has lost the use of 90,000,000 acres, the cream of its land holding. With an annual appropriation of $2,000,000 and an average base price of $20 per acre, it would require 20 years to restore 2,000,000 acres for Indian use.

While Congress did not specifically direct the consolidation of Indian lands broken up and checkerboarded with white holdings in the allotment process, it authorized such consolidation and set up the machinery for it. Congress also authorized the establishment of new reservations for now completely landless and homeless Indians and directed that title to all newly purchased land should be taken in the name of the United States in trust for the Indian tribe or individual Indian, who will have the use and occupancy of the land. Thus the policy of common ownership of land enunciated in section 1 of the Wheeler-Howard Act is reaffirmed and implemented throughout the body of the statute.

Part of the effort at economic rehabilitation is the indefinite extension of all restrictions on the alienation of Indian trust lands as prescribed by section 2. However, this section merely locks the door out of which passed the valuable team of work horses, leaving the decrepit plug behind.

THE REVOLVING CREDIT FUND

The sponsors of the General Allotment Act of 1887 believed that the division of the tribal land among the members of the tribe would create in the Indian the pride of individual ownership and induce him to make use of his own land for the support of his family. Overlooked entirely was the cold fact that capital in some form is needed to transform even a piece of the best raw land into a productive farm. Since the Indian's newly acquired private land could not legally be pledged as security for bank or private loans, it was the duty of the Federal Government to place at the disposal of its wards, credit in sufficient volume to meet their need for operating capital.

This imperative duty the Federal Government never recognized. Instead, it chose the easier road. It rapidly relaxed its restrictions on leasing. Lacking equipment for farming, the average Indian family proceeded to lease its land to white farmers or stock-men for cash. The leasing system, demoralizing to the Indians and contributing to the surplus of commercial farm products, spread like the Russian thistle. To this day the Indians who rely on the shrinking volume of lease money for their main support far outnumber those who farm their own allotted land.

What was true 50 years ago is true today. Without a reasonable amount of capital for permanent improvements, livestock, seed, implements, etc., the Indian owner of a piece of land cannot hope to make his living from the cultivation of the soil. To meet this pressing need, the Wheeler-Howard Act authorizes a revolving credit fund of $10,000,000.

This fund is to supply the long-term and short-term credit requirements of some 250,000 persons. Much of it must be tied up in long-term loans for sawmills, homes, and other improvements. Yet there is a huge demand for short-term loans to finance seasonal farm operations. The new lands to be bought for landless Indians must be improved and fenced, homes must be built, implements and seed acquired for the settlers, almost solely out of the revolving credit fund. In all probability the demands of the forthcoming year will demonstrate that it is inadequate.

THE HEIRSHIP-LAND PROBLEM

In the natural course of events, privately owned Indian lands must on the death of the owner be divided among his heirs and, in turn, among the heirs of the heirs. This result of the allotment system brings about the forced sale of Indian heirship lands, usually to white buyers. If there are no buyers, the heirship land must be leased and the proceeds distributed among the numerous heirs at an expense out of all proportion to the size of the gross revenue.

The Wheeler-Howard Act is taking the first hesitant step toward the solution of this problem. The new law, while allowing Indian owners to leave or devise their restricted land to any member of the tribe or to their heirs regardless of tribal affiliations in accordance with applicable State or Federal laws, bars the owners or heirs from selling restricted Indian lands to anyone except the tribe or the tribal corporation in the jurisdiction of which the land is located.

Obviously this negative provision, inapplicable in Oklahoma and on the Klamath Reservation, does not solve the problem. Some 7,000,000 acres are now in the heirship status; the acreage is increasing every month. The tribes have not the money with which to purchase this land. At only $5 per acre, it would require $35,000,000 to reacquire this land; the maximum authorized appropriation for 17 years would be needed to return the land now in the heirship status for tribal use.

If the problem is to be solved within a reasonable time, the cooperation of the allottees and heirs must be had. They must learn that for the sake of their race and of their children they should voluntarily transfer the title to their individual holdings to the tribe or to the tribal corporation, receiving in return the same rights as they enjoy now; namely, the right to use and occupy the land and its improvements, to receive the income from the land and to leave the same rights to their children, except that the children and other heirs could not cut up the land into small, unusable pieces.

Where the land in process of inheritance has already been so divided among numerous heirs, they will have the opportunity to return the small parcels to the tribe or tribal corporation, receiving interests in the corporate property in exchange. Thus the tribe would acquire title to now unusable land which, after consolidation, could be assigned for the use of interest-holders in tracts of usable size.

SPIRITUAL REHABILITATION

Through 50 years of "individualization," coupled with an ever-increasing amount of arbitrary supervision over the affairs of individuals and tribes so long as these individuals and tribes had any assets left, the Indians have been robbed of initiative, their spirit has been broken, their health undermined, and their native pride ground into the dust. The efforts at economic rehabilitation cannot and will not be more than partially successful unless they are accompanied by a determined simultaneous effort to rebuild the shattered morale of a subjugated people that has been taught to believe in its racial inferiority.

The Wheeler-Howard Act provides the means of destroying this inferiority complex, through those features which authorize and legalize tribal organization and incorporation, which give these tribal organizations and corporations limited but real power, and authority over their own affairs, which broaden the educational opportunities for Indians, and which give Indians a better chance to enter the Indian Service.

Even before the passage of the Wheeler-Howard bill a great spiritual stirring had become noticeable throughout the Indian country. That awakening of the racial spirit must be sustained, if the rehabilitation of the Indian people is to be successfully carried through. It is necessary to face the fact that pauperization, as the result of a century of spoliation, suppression, and paternalism, has made deep inroads. Of necessity it will take time, patience, and intelligent, sympathetic help to rebuild the Indian character where it has been broken down.

The first step in this rebuilding process must be the reorganization of the tribes, authorized by the Wheeler-Howard Act. In the past they managed their own affairs effectively whenever there was no white interference for selfish ends. They can learn to do it again under present conditions with the aid of modern organization methods, once they realize that these organizations will be permanent and will not be subject to the whims of changing administrations. These organizations, both tribal and corporate, will make many initial mistakes; there will be many complaints against shouldering the load of responsibility that accompanies authority. The task of organizing and incorporating the tribes will be difficult and laborious, calling for the maximum amount of skill, tact, firmness, and understanding on the part of the organizers. But the result should be the development of Indian leadership capable of making the Indian tribal organizations and corporations function effectively with a minimum of governmental interference.

OKLAHOMA TRIBES PENALIZED

It is to be regretted that the Oklahoma tribes, containing almost one-third of the Indians of the United States, should have been excluded by Congress from many of the important provisions of the Wheeler-Howard Act. Through this exclusion the Oklahoma Indians lose the benefit of section 2, which automatically extends the protective trust period on all restricted land; no new reservations can be established in Oklahoma; Oklahoma tribes cannot organize under the new act, nor can they form tribal corporations. Because they are denied the incorporation privilege, they cannot receive loans from the revolving credit fund, which loans can be made only to tribal corporations. It is hoped that Congress will amend the act so as to extend all of the benefits of the legislation to all Oklahoma Indians.

LAW AND ORDER

The entire title creating a special court of Indian affairs was omitted and consideration of this subject adjourned until the next Congress. In view of the chaotic state of Indian law enforcement, it is important that this subject be given adequate consideration and that early remedial action be had.

INDIAN CLAIMS

Section 15 of the Wheeler-Howard Act declares that nothing in the statute shall prejudice or impair any Indian claim or suit against the United States. But this declaration does not cure the situation created by the snail-like pace of the hundreds of suits and claims by Indians against the Government. While these suits and claims remain unsettled, they will be used by designing white persons to prejudice the Indian mind against the Government, to raise false hopes of recovering fabulous sums, and by these hopes to make more difficult the task of getting the Indians to face reality and to strive in earnest to help themselves. It is hoped that the next Congress will enact legislation designed finally to settle all Indian claims in the shortest possible time. . . .

Source: *Annual Report of the Secretary of the Interior* (Washington, D.C.: Government Printing Office, 1934), 78–83.

50 Indian Claims Commission Act, August 13, 1946

Because Native Americans had difficulties filing suit against the United States in the U.S. Court of Claims, in 1946 Congress created the Indian Claims Commission to hear American Indian grievances.

An Act To create an Indian Claims Commission, to provide for the powers, duties, and functions thereof, and for other purposes.

Be it enacted . . . , That there is hereby created and established an Indian Claims Commission, hereafter referred to as the Commission.

SEC. 2. The Commission shall hear and determine the following claims against the United States on behalf of any Indian tribe, band, or other identifiable group of American Indians residing within the territorial limits of the United States or Alaska: (1) claims in law or equity arising under the Constitution, laws, treaties of the United States, and Executive orders of the President; (2) all other claims in law or equity, including those sounding in tort, with respect to which the claimant would have been entitled to sue in a court of the United States if the United States was subject to suit; (3) claims which would result if the treaties, contracts, and agreements between the claimant and the United States were revised on the ground of fraud, duress, unconscionable consideration, mutual or unilateral mistake, whether of law or fact, or any other ground cognizable by a court of equity; (4) claims arising from the taking by the United States, whether as the result of a treaty of cession or otherwise, of lands owned or occupied by the claimant without the payment for such lands of compensation agreed to by the claimant; and (5) claims based upon fair and honorable dealings that are not recognized by any existing rule of law or equity. No claim accruing after the date of the approval of this Act shall be considered by the Commission.

All claims hereunder may be heard and determined by the Commission notwithstanding any statute of limitations or laches, but all other defenses shall be available to the United States.

In determining the quantum of relief the Commission shall make appropriate deductions for all payments made by the United States on the claim, and for all other offsets, counterclaims, and demands that would be allowable in a suit brought in the Court of Claims under section 145 of the Judicial Code (36 Stat. 1136; 28 U.S.C. sec. 250), as amended; the Commission may also inquire into and consider all money or property given to or funds expended gratuitously for the benefit of the claimant and if it finds that the nature of the claim and the entire course of dealings and accounts between the United States and the claimant in good conscience warrants such action, may set off all or part of such expenditures against any award made to the claimant, except that it is hereby declared to be the policy of Congress that monies spent for the removal of the claimant from one place to another at the request of the United States, or for agency or other administrative, educational, health or highway purposes, or for expenditures made prior to the date of the law, treaty or Executive Order under which the claim arose, or for expenditures made pursuant to the Act of June 18, 1934 (48 Stat. 984), save expenditures made under section 5 of that Act, or for expenditures under any emergency appropriation or allotment made subsequent to March 4, 1933, and generally applicable throughout the United States for relief in stricken agricultural areas, relief from distress caused by unemployment and conditions resulting therefrom, the prosecution of public work and public projects for the relief of unemployment or to increase employment, and for work relief (including the Civil Works Program) shall not be a proper offset against any award. . . .

SEC. 10. Any claim within the provisions of this Act may be presented to the Commission by any member of an Indian tribe, band, or other identifiable group of Indians as the representative of all its members; but wherever any tribal organization exists, recognized by the Secretary of the Interior as having authority to represent such tribe, band, or group, such organization shall be accorded the exclusive privilege of representing such Indians, unless fraud, collusion, or laches on the part of such organization be shown to the satisfaction of the Commission. . . .

SEC. 13. (a) As soon as practicable the Commission shall send a written explanation of the provisions of this Act to the recognized head of each Indian tribe and band, and to any other identifiable groups of American Indians existing as distinct entities, residing within the territorial limits of the United States and Alaska, and to the superintendents of all Indian agencies who shall promulgate the same, and shall request that a detailed statement of all claims be sent to the Commission, together with the names of aged or invalid Indians from whom depositions should be taken immediately and a summary of their proposed testimonies.

SEC. 14. The Commission shall have the power to call upon any of the departments of the Government for any information it may deem necessary, and shall have the use of all records, hearings, and reports made by the committees of each House of Congress, when deemed necessary in the prosecution of its business.

At any hearing held hereunder, any official letter, paper, document, map, or record in the possession of any officer or department, or court of the United States or committee of Congress (or a certified copy thereof), may be used in evidence insofar as relevant and material, including any deposition or other testimony of record in any suit or proceeding in any court of the United States to which an Indian or Indian tribe or group was a party, and the appropriate department of the Government of the United States shall give to the attorneys for all tribes or groups full and free access to such letters, papers, documents, maps, or records as may be useful to said attorneys in the preparation of any claim instituted hereunder, and shall afford facilities for the examination of the same and, upon written request by said attorneys, shall furnish certified copies thereof.

SEC. 15. Each such tribe, band, or other identifiable group of Indians may retain to represent its interests in the presentation of claims before the Commission an attorney or attorneys at law, of its own selection, whose practice before the Commission shall be regulated by its adopted procedure. The fees of such attorney or attorneys for all services rendered in prosecuting the claim in question, whether before the Commission or otherwise, shall, unless the amount of such fees is stipulated in the approved contract between the attorney or attorneys and the claimant, be fixed by the Commission at such amount as the Commission, in accordance with standards obtaining for prosecuting similar contingent claims in courts of law, finds to be adequate compensation for services rendered and results obtained, considering the contingent nature of the case, plus all reasonable expenses incurred in the prosecution of the claim; but the amount so fixed by the Commission, exclusive of reimbursements for actual expenses, shall not exceed 10 per centum of the amount recovered in any case.

The Attorney General or his assistants shall represent the United States in all claims presented to the Commission.

Source: *U.S. Statutes at Large*, 60:1049–1056.

51 House Concurrent Resolution 108, August 1, 1953

In 1953 Congress stated its intent to abolish federal supervision of Native Americans by abolishing treaties with certain Indian nations and subjecting American Indian individuals to the same privileges, responsibilities, and laws extended to other U.S. citizens. After passage of House Concurrent Resolution 108, the federal government began to "terminate" its relations with selected Native American nations with which it had treaties. American Indians voiced strong opposition to the implementation of this unilateral federal policy.

Whereas it is the policy of Congress, as rapidly as possible, to make the Indians within the territorial limits of the United States subject to the same laws and entitled to the same privileges and responsibilities as are applicable to other citizens of the United States, to end their status as wards of the United States, and to grant them all of the rights and prerogatives pertaining to American citizenship; and

Whereas the Indians within the territorial limits of the United States should assume their full responsibilities as American citizens: Now, therefore, be it

Resolved by the House of Representatives (the Senate concurring),

That it is declared to be the sense of Congress that, at the earliest possible time, all of the Indian tribes and the individual members thereof located within the States of California, Florida, New York, and Texas, and all of the following named Indian tribes and individual members thereof, should be freed from Federal supervision and control and from all disabilities and limitations specially applicable to Indians: The Flathead Tribe of Montana, the Klamath Tribe of Oregon, the Menominee Tribe of Wisconsin, the Potowatamie Tribe of Kansas and Nebraska, and those members of the Chippewa Tribe who are on the Turtle Mountain Reservation, North Dakota. It is further declared to be the sense of Congress that, upon the release of such tribes and individual members thereof from such disabilities and limitations, all offices of the Bureau of Indian Affairs in the States of California, Florida, New York, and Texas and all other offices of the Bureau of Indian Affairs whose primary purpose was to serve any Indian tribe or individual Indian freed from Federal supervision should be abolished. It is further declared to be the sense of Congress that the Secretary of the Interior should examine all existing legislation dealing with such Indians, and treaties between the Government of the United States and each such tribe, and report to Congress at the earliest practicable date, but not later than January 1, 1954, his recommendations for such legislation as, in his judgment, may be necessary to accomplish the purposes of this resolution.

Source: *U.S. Statutes at Large*, 67:132.

52 Public Law 83-280, August 15, 1953

Public Law 83-280 of 1953 authorized state jurisdiction over offenses committed against or by Native Americans on certain reservations, dramatically abridging the self-determination of Native American societies and their relations with the federal government.

An Act To confer jurisdiction on the States of California, Minnesota, Nebraska, Oregon, and Wisconsin, with respect to criminal offenses and civil causes of action committed or arising on Indian reservations within such States, and for other purposes. . . .

SEC. 2. Title 18, United States Code, is hereby amended by inserting in chapter 53 thereof immediately after section 1161 a new section, to be designated as section 1162, as follows:

§1162. State jurisdiction over offenses committed by or against Indians in the Indian country

"(a) Each of the States listed in the following table shall have jurisdiction over offenses committed by or against Indians in the areas of Indian country listed opposite the name of the State to the same extent that such State has jurisdiction over offenses committed elsewhere within the State, and the criminal laws of such State shall have the same force and effect within such Indian country as they have elsewhere within the State:

"State of	Indian country affected
California	All Indian country within the State
Minnesota	All Indian country within the State, except the Red Lake Reservation
Nebraska	All Indian country within the State
Oregon	All Indian country within the State, except the Warm Springs Reservation
Wisconsin	All Indian country within the State, except the Menominee Reservation

"(b) Nothing in this section shall authorize the alienation, encumbrance, or taxation of any real or personal property, including water rights, belonging to any Indian or any Indian tribe, band, or community that is held in trust by the United States or is subject to a restriction against alienation imposed by the United States; or shall authorize regulation of the use of such property in a manner inconsistent with any Federal treaty, agreement, or statute or with any regulation made pursuant thereto; or shall deprive any Indian or any Indian tribe, band, or community of any right, privilege, or immunity afforded under Federal treaty, agreement, or statute with respect to hunting, trapping, or fishing or the control, licensing, or regulation thereof.

Source: *U.S. Statutes at Large*, 67:588–590.

53 Termination of the Menominee Indians, June 17, 1954

The Menominees of Wisconsin were one of the first tribes to feel the full effects of termination. Congress stated its intent to withdraw federal jurisdiction over the tribe in 1954, and by 1961 the Menominees were terminated as a federally recognized Native American nation. In 1973, after fifteen years of protest, the Menominees won restoration of their tribal status.

An Act To provide for a per capita distribution of Menominee tribal funds and authorize the withdrawal of the Menominee Tribe from Federal jurisdiction.

Be it enacted . . . , That the purpose of this Act is to provide for orderly termination of Federal supervision over the property and members of the Menominee Indian Tribe of Wisconsin.

SEC. 2. For the purposes of the Act—

(a) "Tribe" means the Menominee Indian Tribe of Wisconsin;
(b) "Secretary" means the Secretary of the Interior.

SEC. 3. At midnight of the date of enactment of this Act the roll of the tribe maintained pursuant to the Act of June 15, 1934 (48 Stat. 965), as amended by the Act of July 14, 1939 (53 Stat. 1003), shall be closed and no child born thereafter shall be eligible for enrollment: *Provided*, That applicants for enrollment in the tribe shall have three months from the date the roll is closed in which to submit applications for enrollment: *Provided further*, That the tribe shall have three months thereafter in which to approve or disapprove any application for enrollment: *Provided further*, That any applicant whose application is not approved by the tribe within six months from the date of enactment of this Act may, within three months thereafter, file with the Secretary an appeal from the failure of the tribe to approve his application or from the disapproval of his application, as the case may be. The decision of the Secretary on such appeal shall be final and conclusive. When the Secretary has made decisions on all appeals, he shall issue and publish in the Federal Register a Proclamation of Final Closure of the roll of the tribe and the final roll of the members. Effective upon the date of such proclamation, the rights or beneficial interests of each person whose name appears on the roll shall constitute personal property and shall be evidenced by a certificate of beneficial interest which shall be issued by the tribe. Such interests shall be distributable in accordance with the laws of the State of Wisconsin. Such interests shall be alienable only in accordance with such regulations as may be adopted by the tribe.

SEC. 4. Section 6 of the Act of June 15, 1934 (48 Stat. 965, 966) is hereby repealed.

SEC. 5. The Secretary is authorized and directed, as soon as practicable after the passage of this Act, to pay from such funds as are deposited to the credit of the tribe in the Treasury of the United States $1,500 to each member of the tribe on the rolls of the tribe on the date of the Act. Any other person whose application for enrollment on the rolls of the tribe is subsequently approved, pursuant to the terms of section 3 hereof, shall, after enrollment, be paid a like sum of $1,500: *Provided*, That such payments shall be made first from any funds on deposit in the Treasury of the United States to the credit of the Menominee Indian Tribe drawing interest at the rate of 5 per centum, and thereafter from the Menominee judgment fund, symbol 14X7142.

SEC. 6. The tribe is authorized to select and retain the services of qualified management specialists, including tax consultants, for the purpose of studying industrial programs on the Menominee Reservation and making such reports or recommendations, including appraisals of Menominee tribal property, as may be desired by the tribe, and to make other studies and reports as may be deemed necessary and desirable by the tribe in connection with the termination of Federal supervision as provided for hereinafter. Such reports shall be completed not later than December 31, 1957. Such specialists are to be retained under contracts entered into between them and authorized representatives of the tribe, subject to approval by the Secretary. Such amounts of Menominee tribal funds as may be required for this purpose shall be made available by the Secretary.

SEC. 7. The tribe shall formulate and submit to the Secretary a plan or plans for the future control of the tribal property and service functions now conducted by or under the supervision of the United States, including, but not limited to, services in the fields of health, education, welfare, credit, roads, and law and order. The Secretary is authorized to provide such reasonable assistance as may be requested by officials of the tribe in the formulation of the plan or plans heretofore referred to, including necessary consultations with representatives of Federal departments and agencies, officials of the State of Wisconsin and political subdivisions thereof, and members of the tribe: *Provided*, That the responsibility of the United States to furnish all such supervision and services to the tribe and to the members thereof, because of their status as Indians, shall cease on December 31, 1958, or on such earlier date as may be agreed upon by the tribe and the Secretary.

SEC. 8. The Secretary is hereby authorized and directed to transfer to the tribe, on December 31, 1958, or on such earlier date as may be agreed upon by the tribe and the Secretary, the title to all property, real and personal, held in trust by the United States for the tribe: *Provided, however*, That if the tribe obtains a charter for a corporation or otherwise organizes under the laws of a State or of the District of Columbia for the purpose, among any others, of taking title to all tribal lands and assets and enterprises owned by the tribe or held in trust by the United States for the tribe, and requests such transfer to be made to such corporation or organization, the Secretary shall make such transfer to such corporation or organization.

SEC. 9. No distribution of the assets made under the provisions of this Act shall be subject to any Federal or State income tax: *Provided*, That so much of any cash distribution made hereunder as consists of a share of any interest earned on funds deposited in the Treasury of the United States pursuant to the Supplemental Appropriation Act, 1952 (65 Stat. 736, 754), shall not by virtue of this Act be exempt from individual income tax in the hands of the recipients for the year in which paid. Following any distribution of assets made under the provisions of this Act, such assets and any income derived therefrom in the hands of any individual, or any corporation or organization as provided in section 8 of this Act, shall be subject to the same taxes, State and Federal, as in the case of non-Indians, except that any valuation for purposes of Federal income tax on gains or losses shall take as the basis of the particular taxpayer the value of the property on the date title is transferred by the United States pursuant to section 8 of this Act.

SEC. 10. When title to the property of the tribe has been transferred, as provided in section 8 of this Act, the Secretary shall publish in the Federal Register an appropriate proclamation of that fact. Thereafter individual members of the tribe shall not be entitled to any of the services performed by the United States for Indians because of their status as Indians, all statutes of the United States which affect Indians because of their status as Indians shall no longer be applicable to the members of the tribe, and the laws of the several States shall apply to the tribe and its members in the same manner as they apply to other citizens or persons within their jurisdiction. Nothing in this Act shall affect the status of the members of the tribe as citizens of the United States.

SEC. 11. Prior to the transfer pursuant to section 8 of this Act, the Secretary shall protect the rights of members of the tribe who are less than eighteen years of age, non compos mentis, or in the opinion of the Secretary in need of assistance in conducting their affairs, by causing the appointment of guardians for such members in courts of competent jurisdiction, or by such other means as he may deem adequate.

SEC. 12. The Secretary is authorized and directed to promulgate such rules and regulations as are necessary to effectuate the purposes of this Act.

SEC. 13. If any provision of this Act, or the application thereof to any person or circumstance, is held invalid, the remainder of the Act and the application of such provision to other persons or circumstances shall not be affected thereby.

Source: *U.S. Statutes at Large*, 68:250–252.

54 Transfer of Indian Health Services, August 5, 1954

In 1954, as part of termination policies, health care for Native Americans was transferred from the Bureau of Indian Affairs to the Public Health Service of the U.S. Department of Health, Education, and Welfare.

An Act To transfer the maintenance and operation of hospital and health facilities for Indians to the Public Health Service, and for other purposes.

Be it enacted . . . , That all functions, responsibilities, authorities, and duties of the Department of the Interior, the Bureau of Indian Affairs, Secretary of the Interior, and the Commissioner of Indian Affairs relating to the maintenance and operation of hospital and health facilities for Indians, and the conservation of the health of Indians, are hereby transferred to, and shall be administered by, the Surgeon General of the United States Public Health Service, under the supervision and direction of the Secretary of Health, Education, and Welfare: *Provided*, That hospitals now in operation for a specific tribe or tribes of Indians shall not be closed prior to July 1, 1956, without the consent of the governing body of the tribe or its organized council.

SEC. 2. Whenever the health needs of the Indians can be better met thereby, the Secretary of Health, Education, and Welfare is authorized in his discretion to enter into contracts with any State, Territory, or political subdivision thereof, or any private nonprofit corporation, agency or institution providing for the transfer by the

United States Public Health Service of Indian hospitals or health facilities, including initial operating equipment and supplies.

It shall be a condition of such transfer that all facilities transferred shall be available to meet the health needs of the Indians and that such health needs shall be given priority over those of the non-Indian population. No hospital or health facility that has been constructed or maintained for a specific tribe of Indians, or for a specific group of tribes, shall be transferred by the Secretary of Health, Education, and Welfare to a non-Indian entity or organization under this Act unless such action has been approved by the governing body of the tribe, or by the governing bodies of a majority of the tribes, for which such hospital or health facility has been constructed or maintained: *Provided*, That if, following such transfer by the United States Public Health Service, the Secretary of Health, Education, and Welfare finds the hospital or health facility transferred under this section is not thereafter serving the need of the Indians, the Secretary of Health, Education, and Welfare shall notify those charged with management thereof, setting forth needed improvements, and in the event such improvements are not made within a time to be specified, shall immediately assume management and operation of such hospital or health facility.

SEC. 3. The Secretary of Health, Education, and Welfare is also authorized to make such other regulations as he deems desirable to carry out the provisions of this Act. . . .

Source: *U.S. Statutes at Large*, 68:6.

55 Relocation of American Indians to Urban Areas, 1954

In the 1950s, during the termination era, the federal government sought to relocate American Indians to urban areas. In this report, Commissioner of Indian Affairs Glenn L. Emmons seeks to paint a positive picture of this policy.

During the 1954 fiscal year, 2,163 Indians were directly assisted to relocate under the Bureau's relocation program. This included 1,649 persons in over 400 family groups, and 514 unattached men and women. In addition, over 300 Indians left reservations without assistance to join relatives and friends who had been assisted to relocate. At their destination, Bureau Relocation Offices assisted this group also to adjust to the new community. The total number of relocations represented a substantial increase over relocations during the previous fiscal year.

Of the 2,163 Indians assisted to relocate, financial assistance, to cover all or part of the costs of transportation to the place of relocation and short-term temporary subsistence, [was] provided to 1,637 Indians, in addition to relocation services. This number included 1,329 persons in over 300 family groups, and 308 unattached men and women. An additional 526 Indians, including 320 in approximately 100 family groups and 206 unattached men and women, were assisted to relocate without financial assistance, but were provided relocation services only. These services included counseling and guidance prior to relocation, and assistance in establishing residence and securing permanent employment in the new community.

In addition to the above-mentioned persons who were assisted to relocate, Bureau Relocation Offices assisted a number of Indian workers to secure employment which did not involve relocation, and cooperated with public employment offices and the Railroad Retirement Board in recruitment of Indians for temporary and seasonal work. However, in order to concentrate on providing relocation services, placement activities which do not involve relocation have been progressively decreased and responsibility for such placement activities has been largely left to established employment agencies.

In recognition of this emphasis, and following the recommendation of the survey team for the Bureau of Indian Affairs, the name of the former Branch of Placement and Relocation was changed during the year to the Branch of Relocation.

Approximately 54 percent of the Indians assisted to relocate came from 3 northern areas (Aberdeen, Billings, and Minneapolis), and 46 percent came from 4 southern areas (Anadarko, Gallup, Muskogee, and Phoenix). They went to 20 different States. The Los Angeles and Chicago metropolitan areas continued to be the chief centers of relocation.

On the reservations there was continued interest in relocation throughout the year. Relocation assistance funds were used up in almost every area, and at the end of the year there was a backlog of applications for relocation. Letters from relocated Indians to friends and relatives back on the reservation, describing their experiences and new standards of living, served to stimulate interest as did a decrease in employment opportunities in the vicinity of some of the reservations and a marked decrease in railroad employment.

There was a slight tightening of the labor market during part of the year. However, through intensive efforts on the part of field relocation offices, it was still possible to assure permanent types of employment to almost all qualified workers who requested assistance in settling away from reservations. Field relocation offices followed a policy of securing employment for Indians in diversified industries and with a large number of employers. This policy proved of great benefit when industrial disputes developed in certain industries on the west coast.

To adjust to changes in the labor market which reduced employment in military installations and certain Government projects, the field relocation office formerly located in Salt Lake City was transferred to Oakland, Calif., effective June 1.

The Chicago Field Relocation Office, in recognition of the needs of the growing number of relocatees in that city and in accordance with the Bureau policy of encouraging the development of non-Bureau facilities for Indians, assisted in the establishment of an All-Tribes American Indian Center in Chicago. This center raised its own funds, and under the directorship of a board composed almost entirely of Indians, began providing opportunities for Indian relocatees to meet, engage in social and recreational programs, exchange experiences, and assist each other. Its operations were completely independent of the Bureau.

Source: *Annual Report of the Secretary of the Interior* (Washington, D.C.: Government Printing Office, 1954), 242–243.

56 *Native American Church v. Navajo Tribal Council* (1959)

In 1959 the Native American Church sought to strike down an ordinance of the Navajo tribal council that made the use of peyote a criminal offense. The church contended that the ordinance violated the First Amendment's religious freedom clause. The U.S. Court of Appeals, Tenth Circuit, upheld the tribal council's decision even though it had an adverse impact on religious freedom.

No law is cited and none has been found which undertakes to subject the Navajo tribe to the laws of the United States with respect to their internal affairs, such as police powers and ordinances passed for the purposes of regulating the conduct of the members of the tribe on the reservation. It follows that the Federal courts are without jurisdiction over matters involving purely penal ordinances passed by the Navajo legislative body for the regulation of life on the reservation.

But it is contended that the First Amendment to the United States Constitution applies to Indian nations and tribes as it does to the United States and to the States. It is, accordingly, argued that the ordinance in question violates the Indians' rights of religious freedom and freedom of worship guaranteed by the First Amendment. No case is cited and none has been found where the impact of the First Amendment, with respect to religious freedom and freedom of worship by members of the Indian tribes, has been before the court. . . .

The First Amendment applies only to Congress. It limits the powers of Congress to interfere with religious freedom or religious worship. It is made applicable to the States only by the Fourteenth Amendment. Thus construed, the First Amendment places limitations upon the action of Congress and of the States. But as declared in the decisions herein before discussed, Indian tribes are not states. They have a status higher than that of states. They are subordinate and dependent nations possessed of all powers as such only to the extent that they have expressly been required to surrender them by the superior sovereign, the United States. The Constitution is, of course, the supreme law of the land, but it is nonetheless a part of the laws of the United States. Under the philosophy of the decisions, it, as any other law, is binding upon Indian nations only where it expressly binds them, or is made binding by treaty or some act of Congress. No provision in the Constitution makes the First Amendment applicable to Indian nations nor is there any law of Congress doing so. It follows that neither, under the Constitution or the laws of Congress, do the Federal courts have jurisdiction of tribal laws or regulations, even though they may have an impact to some extent on forms of religious worship.

Source: 272 Federal Reporter, 2d series, 131, 134–135.

57 Declaration of Indian Purpose, June 1961

In 1961 American Indian leaders met at the University of Chicago to discuss the state of Native Americans. At the conclusion of the meeting, they issued a declaration that included proposals and recommendations on economic development, education, law, housing, health, welfare, and other issues.

WE BELIEVE in the inherent right of all people to retain spiritual and cultural values, and that the free exercise of these values is necessary to the normal development of any people. Indians exercised this inherent right to live their own lives for thousands of years before the white man came and took their lands. It is a more complex world in which Indians live today, but the Indian people who first settled the New World and built the great civilizations which only now are being dug out of the past, long ago demonstrated that they could master complexity.

WE BELIEVE that the history and development of America show that the Indian has been subjected to duress, undue influence, unwarranted pressures, and policies which have produced uncertainty, frustration, and despair. Only when the public understands these conditions and is moved to take action toward the formulation and adoption of sound and consistent policies and programs will these destroying factors be removed and the Indian resume his normal growth and make his maximum contribution to modern society.

WE BELIEVE in the future of a greater America, an America which we were first to love, where life, liberty, and the pursuit of happiness will be a reality. In such a future, with Indians and all other Americans cooperating, a cultural climate will be created in which the Indian people will grow and develop as members of a free society.

LEGISLATIVE AND REGULATORY PROPOSALS

In order that basic objectives may be restated and that action to accomplish these objectives may be continuous and may be pursued in a spirit of public dedication, it is proposed that recommendations be adopted to strengthen the principles of the Indian Reorganization Act and to accomplish other purposes. These recommendations would be comparable in scope and purpose to the Indian Trade and Intercourse Act of June 30, 1834, the Act of the same date establishing the Bureau of Indian Affairs, and the Indian Reorganization Act of June 18, 1934, which recognized the inherent powers of Indian Tribes.

The recommendations we propose would redefine the responsibilities of the United States toward the Indian people in terms of a positive national obligation to modify or remove the conditions which produce the poverty and lack of social adjustment as these prevail as the outstanding attributes of Indian life today. Specifically, the recommendations would:

(1) Abandon the so-called termination policy of the last administration by revoking House Concurrent Resolution 108 of the 83rd Congress.
(2) Adopt as official policy the principle of broad educational process as the procedure best calculated to remove the disabilities which have prevented Indians from making full use of their resources.

It has been long recognized that one Commissioner cannot give the personal attention to all tribal matters which they deserve. He cannot meet all callers to his office, make necessary visits to the field, and give full attention to the review of tribal programs and supporting budget requests. In view of these conditions, we most urgently recommend that the present organization of the Bureau of Indian Affairs be reviewed and that certain principles be considered no matter what the organizational change might be.

The basic principle involves the desire on the part of Indians to participate in developing their own programs with help and guidance as needed and requested, from a local decentralized technical and administrative staff, preferably located conveniently to the people it serves. Also in recent years certain technical and professional people of Indian descent are becoming better qualified and available to work with and for their own people in determining their own programs and needs. The Indians as responsible individual citizens, as responsible tribal representatives, and as responsible Tribal Councils want to participate, want to contribute to their own personal and tribal improvements and want to cooperate with their Government on how best to solve the many problems in a business-like, efficient and economical manner as rapidly as possible.

It is, therefore, recommended that:

1. Area offices be abolished and their authority be given to the agency superintendents.

2. The position of reservation Superintendent be strengthened to permit broader exercise of responsibility and authority to act on significant and important matters of daily operations of Indian problems, preventing undue delays.
3. Position qualifications require the employment of Superintendents with courage and determination, among other qualities, to help with local problems and be willing to make without further referral to higher levels, decisions commensurate with the delegated authorities.
4. The Superintendent be charged with the responsibilities of cooperating with the local tribal governing bodies in developing the Federal Program and Budget for that particular tribe or reservation.

CONCLUDING STATEMENT

To complete our Declaration, we point out that in the beginning the people of the New World, called Indians by accident of geography, were possessed of a continent and a way of life. In the course of many lifetimes, our people had adjusted to every climate and condition from the Arctic to the torrid zones. In their livelihood and family relationships, their ceremonial observances, they reflected the diversity of the physical world they occupied.

The conditions in which Indians live today reflect a world in which every basic aspect of life has been transformed. Even the physical world is no longer the controlling factor in determining where and under what conditions men may live. In region after region, Indian groups found their means of existence either totally destroyed or materially modified. Newly introduced diseases swept away or reduced regional populations. These changes were followed by major shifts in the internal life of tribe and family.

The time came when the Indian people were no longer the masters of their situation. Their life ways survived subject to the will of a dominant sovereign power. This is said, not in a spirit of complaint; we understand that in the lives of all nations of people, there are times of plenty and times of famine. But we do speak out in a plea for understanding.

When we go before the American people, as we do in this Declaration, and ask for material assistance in developing our resources and developing our opportunities, we pose a moral problem which cannot be left unanswered. For the problem we raise affects the standing which our nation sustains before world opinion.

Our situation cannot be relieved by appropriated funds alone, though it is equally obvious that without capital investment and funded services, solutions will be delayed. Nor will the passage of time lessen the complexities which beset a people moving toward new meaning and purpose.

The answers we seek are not commodities to be purchased, neither are they evolved automatically through the passing of time.

The effort to place social adjustment on a money-time interval scale, which has characterized Indian administration, has resulted in unwanted pressure and frustration.

When Indians speak of the continent they yielded, they are not referring only to the loss of some millions of acres in real estate. They have in mind that the land supported a universe of things they knew, valued, and loved.

With that continent gone, except for the few poor parcels they still retain, the basis of life is precariously held, but they mean to hold the scraps and parcels as earnestly as any small nation or ethnic group was ever determined to hold to identity and survival.

What we ask of America is not charity, not paternalism, even when benevolent. We ask only that the nature of our situation be recognized and made the basis of policy and action.

In short, the Indians ask for assistance, technical and financial, for the time needed, however long that may be, to regain in the America of the space age some measure of the adjustment they enjoyed as the original possessors of their native land.

Source: American Indian Chicago Conference, *Declaration of Indian Purpose: The Voice of the American Indian* (Chicago: University of Chicago, 1961), 5–6, 19–20.

58 President Lyndon B. Johnson, Special Message to Congress, March 6, 1968

In 1968 President Lyndon B. Johnson declared that self-determination was to be a hallmark of American Indian policies of the future. His statement was designed to repudiate termination policies and reinforce those promoting tribal autonomy.

I propose a new goal for our Indian programs: A goal that ends the old debate about "termination" of Indian programs and stresses self-determination; a goal that erases old attitudes of paternalism and promotes partnership self-help.

Our goal must be:

—A standard of living for the Indians equal to that of the country as a whole.

—Freedom of Choice: An opportunity to remain in their homelands, if they choose, without surrendering their dignity; an opportunity to move to the towns and cities of America, if they choose, equipped with the skills to live in equality and dignity.

—Full participation in the life of modern America, with a full share of economic opportunity and social justice.

I propose, in short, a policy of maximum choice for the American Indian: a policy expressed in programs of self-help, self-development, self-determination.

To start toward our goal in Fiscal 1969, I recommend that the Congress appropriate one-half a billion dollars for programs targeted at the American Indian—about 10 percent more than Fiscal 1968.

STRENGTHENED FEDERAL LEADERSHIP

In the past four years, with the advent of major new programs, several agencies have undertaken independent efforts to help the American Indian. Too often, there has been too little coordination between agencies; and no clear, unified policy which applied to all.

To launch an undivided, Government-wide effort in this area, I am today issuing an Executive Order to establish a National Council on Indian Opportunity.

The Chairman of the Council will be the Vice President who will bring the problems of the Indians to the highest levels of Government. The Council will include a cross section of Indian leaders, and high government officials who have programs in this field:

—The Secretary of the Interior, who has primary responsibility for Indian Affairs.
—The Secretary of Agriculture, whose programs affect thousands of Indians.
—The Secretary of Commerce, who can help promote economic development of Indian lands.
—The Secretary of Labor, whose manpower programs can train more Indians for more useful employment.
—The Secretary of Health, Education, and Welfare, who can help Indian communities with two of their most pressing needs—health and education.
—The Secretary of Housing and Urban Development, who can bring better housing to Indian lands.
—The Director of the Office of Economic Opportunity, whose programs are already operating in several Indian communities.

The Council will review Federal programs for Indians, make broad policy recommendations, and ensure that programs reflect the needs and desires of the Indian people. Most important, I have asked the Vice President, as Chairman of the Council, to make certain that the American Indian shares fully in all our federal programs.

SELF-HELP AND SELF-DETERMINATION

The greatest hope for Indian progress lies in the emergence of Indian leadership and initiative in solving Indian problems. Indians must have a voice in making the plans and decisions in programs which are important to their daily life.

Within the last few months we have seen a new concept of community development—a concept based on self-help—work successfully among Indians. Many tribes have begun to administer activities which Federal agencies had long performed in their behalf.

Passive acceptance of Federal service is giving way to Indian involvement. More than ever before, Indian needs are being identified from the Indian viewpoint—as they should be.

This principle is the key to progress for Indians—just as it has been for other Americans. If we base our programs upon it, the day will come when the relationship between Indians and the Government will be one of full partnership—not dependency. . . .

THE FIRST AMERICANS

The program I propose seeks to promote Indian development by improving health and education, encouraging long-term economic growth, and strengthening community institutions.

Underlying this program is the assumption that the Federal government can best be a responsible partner in Indian progress by treating the Indian himself as a full citizen, responsible for the pace and direction of his development.

But there can be no question that the government and the people of the United States have a responsibility to the Indians.

In our efforts to meet that responsibility, we must pledge to respect fully the dignity and the uniqueness of the Indian citizen.

That means partnership—not paternalism.

We must affirm the right of the first Americans to remain Indians while exercising their rights as Americans.

We must affirm their right to freedom of choice and self-determination.

We must seek new ways to provide Federal assistance to Indians—with new emphasis on Indian self-help and with respect for Indian culture.

And we must assure the Indian people that it is our desire and intention that the special relationship between the Indian and his government grow and flourish.

For, the first among us must not be last.

I urge the Congress to affirm this policy and to enact this program.

Source: *Public Papers of the Presidents of the United States: Lyndon B. Johnson, 1968–69* (Washington, D.C.: Government Printing Office, 1977), 1:336–337, 343–344.

59 Civil Rights Act, April 11, 1968

Titles II–VII of the Civil Rights Act of 1968 focuses on Native American issues. Important points concerning them include the application of the Bill of Rights to Native Americans in federal-tribal relations, the creation of a code for courts of Indian offenses, and the requirement of obtaining Native American consent for states to assume jurisdiction over reservations.

An Act To prescribe penalties for certain acts of violence or intimidation, and for other purposes.

TITLE II—RIGHTS OF INDIANS

DEFINITIONS

SEC. 201. For purposes of this title, the term—

(1) "Indian tribe" means any tribe, band, or other group of Indians subject to the jurisdiction of the United States and recognized as possessing powers of self-government;
(2) "powers of self-government" means and includes all governmental powers possessed by an Indian tribe, executive, legislative, and judicial, and all offices, bodies, and tribunals by and through which they are executed, including courts of Indian offenses; and
(3) "Indian court" means any Indian tribal court or court of Indian offense.

INDIAN RIGHTS

SEC. 202. No Indian tribe in exercising powers of self-government shall—

(1) make or enforce any law prohibiting the free exercise of religion, or abridging the freedom of speech, or of the press, or the right of the people peaceably to assemble and to petition for a redress of grievances;
(2) violate the right of the people to be secure in their persons, houses, papers, and effects against unreasonable search and seizures, nor issue warrants, but upon probable cause, supported by oath or affirmation, and particularly describing the place to be searched and the person or thing to be seized;
(3) subject any person for the same offense to be twice put in jeopardy;
(4) compel any person in any criminal case to be a witness against himself;
(5) take any private property for a public use without just compensation;

(6) deny to any person in a criminal proceeding the right to a speedy and public trial, to be informed of the nature and cause of the accusation, to be confronted with the witnesses against him, to have compulsory process for obtaining witnesses in his favor, and at his own expense to have the assistance of counsel for his defense;
(7) require excessive bail, impose excessive fines, inflict cruel and unusual punishments, and in no event impose for conviction of any one offense any penalty or punishment greater than imprisonment for a term of six months or a fine of $500, or both;
(8) deny to any person within its jurisdiction the equal protection of its laws or deprive any person of liberty or property without due process of law;
(9) pass any bill of attainder or ex post facto law; or
(10) deny to any person accused of an offense punishable by imprisonment the right, upon request, to a trial by jury of not less than six persons.

HABEAS CORPUS

SEC. 203. The privilege of the writ of habeas corpus shall be available to any person, in a court of the United States, to test the legality of his detention by order of an Indian tribe. . . .

TITLE III—MODEL CODE GOVERNING COURTS OF INDIAN OFFENSES

SEC. 301. The Secretary of the Interior is authorized and directed to recommend to the Congress, on or before July 1, 1968, a model code to govern the administration of justice by courts of Indian offenses on Indian reservations. Such code shall include provisions which will (1) assure that any individual being tried for an offense by a court of Indian offenses shall have the same rights, privileges, and immunities under the United States Constitution as would be guaranteed any citizen of the United States being tried in a Federal court for any similar offense, (2) assure that any individual being tried for an offense by a court of Indian offenses will be advised and made aware of his rights under the United States Constitution, and under any tribal constitution applicable to such individual, (3) establish proper qualifications for the office of judge of the courts of Indian offenses, and (4) provide for the establishing of educational classes for the training of judges of courts of Indian offenses. In carrying out the provisions of this title, the Secretary of the Interior shall consult with the Indians, Indian tribes, and interested agencies of the United States.

SEC. 302. There is hereby authorized to be appropriated such sum as may be necessary to carry out the provisions of this title. . . .

TITLE IV—JURISDICTION OVER CRIMINAL AND CIVIL ACTIONS ASSUMPTION BY STATE

SEC. 401. (a) The consent of the United States is hereby given to any State not having jurisdiction over criminal offenses committed by or against Indians in the areas of Indian country situated within such State to assume, with the consent of the Indian tribe occupying the particular Indian country or part thereof which could be affected by such assumption, such measure of jurisdiction over any or all of such offenses committed within such Indian country or any part thereof as may be determined by such State to the same extent that such State has jurisdiction over any such offense committed elsewhere within the State, and the criminal laws of such State shall have the same force and effect within such Indian country or part thereof as they have elsewhere within that State.

(b) Nothing in this section shall authorize the alienation, encumbrance, or taxation of any real or personal property, including water rights, belonging to any Indian or any Indian tribe, band, or community that is held in trust by the United States or is subject to a restriction against alienation imposed by the United States; or shall authorize regulation of the use of such property in a manner inconsistent with any Federal treaty, agreement, or statute or with any regulation made pursuant thereto; or shall deprive any Indian or any Indian tribe, band, or community of any right, privilege, or immunity afforded under Federal treaty, agreement, or statute with respect to hunting, trapping, or fishing or the control, licensing, or regulation thereof.

ASSUMPTION BY STATE OF CIVIL JURISDICTION

SEC. 402. (a) The consent of the United States is hereby given to any State not having jurisdiction over civil causes of action between Indians or to which Indians are parties which arise in the areas of Indian country situated within such State to assume, with the consent of the tribe occupying the particular Indian country or part thereof which would be affected by such assumption, such measure of jurisdiction over any or all such civil causes of action arising within such Indian country or any part thereof as may be determined by such State to the same extent that such State has jurisdiction over other civil causes of action, and those civil laws of such State that are of general application to private persons or private property shall have the same force and effect within such Indian country or part thereof as they have elsewhere within that State.

(b) Nothing in this section shall authorize the alienation, encumbrance, or taxation of any real or personal property, including water rights, belonging to any Indian or any Indian tribe, band, or community that is held in trust by the United States or is subject to a restriction against alienation imposed by the United States; or shall authorize regulation of the use of such property in a manner inconsistent with any Federal treaty, agreement, or statute, or with any regulation made pursuant thereto; or shall confer jurisdiction upon the State to adjudicate, in probate proceedings or otherwise, the ownership or right to possession of such property or any interest therein.

(c) Any tribal ordinance or custom heretofore or hereafter adopted by an Indian tribe, band, or community in the exercise of any authority which it may possess shall, if not inconsistent with any applicable civil law of the State, be given full force and effect in the determination of civil causes of action pursuant to this section.

RETROCESSION OF JURISDICTION BY STATE

SEC. 403. (a) The United States is authorized to accept a retrocession by any State of allot any measure of the criminal or civil jurisdiction, or both, acquired by such State pursuant to the provisions of section 1162 of title 18 of the United States Code, section 1360 of title 28 of the United States Code, or section 7 of the Act of August 15, 1953 (67 Stat. 588), as it was in effect prior to its repeal by subsection (b) of this section.

(b) Section 7 of the Act of August 15, 1953 (67 Stat. 588), is hereby repealed, but such repeal shall not affect any cession of jurisdiction made pursuant to such section prior to its repeal. . . .

SPECIAL ELECTION

SEC. 406. State jurisdiction acquired pursuant to this title with respect to criminal offenses or civil causes of action, or with respect to both, shall be applicable in Indian country only where the enrolled Indians within the affected area of such Indian country accept such jurisdiction by a majority vote of the adult Indians voting at a special election held for that purpose. The Secretary of the Interior shall call such special election under such rules and regulations as he may prescribe, when requested to do so by the tribal council or other governing body, or by 20 per centum of such enrolled adults. . . .

TITLE V—OFFENSES WITHIN INDIAN COUNTRY AMENDMENT

SEC. 501. Section 1153 of title 18 of the United States Code is amended by inserting Immediately after "weapon,", the following: "assault resulting in serious bodily injury," . . .

TITLE VI—EMPLOYMENT OF LEGAL COUNSEL APPROVAL

SEC. 601. Notwithstanding any other provision of law, if any application made by an Indian, Indian tribe, Indian council, or any band or group of Indians under any law requiring the approval of the Secretary of the Interior or the Commissioner of Indian Affairs of contracts or agreements relating to the employment of legal counsel (including the choice of counsel and the fixing of fees) by any such Indians, tribe, council, band, or group is neither granted nor denied within ninety days following the making of such application, such approval shall be deemed to have been granted. . . .

TITLE VII—MATERIALS RELATING TO CONSTITUTIONAL RIGHTS OF INDIANS

SECRETARY OF INTERIOR TO PREPARE

SEC. 701. (a) In order that the constitutional rights of Indians might be fully protected, the Secretary of the Interior is authorized and directed to—

(1) have the document entitled "Indian Affairs, Laws and Treaties" (Senate Document Numbered 319, volumes 1 and 2, Fifty-eighth Congress) revised and extended to include all treaties, laws, Executive orders, and regulations relating to Indian affairs in force on September 1, 1967, and to have such revised document printed at the Government Printing Office;
(2) have revised and republished the treatise entitled "Federal Indian Law"; and
(3) have prepared, to the extent determined by the Secretary of the Interior to be feasible, an accurate compilation of the official opinions, published and unpublished, of the Solicitor of the Department of the Interior relating to Indian affairs rendered by the Solicitor prior to September 1, 1967, and to have such compilation printed as a Government publication at the Government Printing Office.

(b) With respect to the document entitled "Indian Affairs, Laws and Treaties" as revised and extended in accordance with paragraph (1) of subsection (a), and the compilation prepared in accordance with paragraph (3) of such subsection, the Secretary of the Interior shall take such action as may be necessary to keep such document and compilation current on an annual basis.

(c) There is authorized to be appropriated for carrying out the provisions of this title, with respect to the preparation but not including printing, such sum as may be necessary.

Source: *U.S. Statutes at Large*, 82:77–81.

60 Return of Blue Lake Lands to Taos Pueblo, 1970

When President Theodore Roosevelt declared in 1906 that the Blue Lake lands of the Taos Pueblo in New Mexico were part of what is now Carson National Forest, he restricted American Indians' exclusive use of these lands. From 1906 to 1970 the American Indians of Taos Pueblo sought to regain control over this area, which was considered sacred and was used for religious purposes. In 1970 Congress provided for the return of the Blue Lake lands to the pueblo. President Richard M. Nixon emphasized the significance of this act at the signing of the legislation.

Return of the Lands, December 15, 1970

An Act To amend section 4 of the Act of May 31, 1933 (48 Stat. 108).

Be it enacted . . . , That section 4 of the Act of May 31, 1933 (48 Stat. 108), providing for the protection of the watershed within the Carson National Forest for the Pueblo de Taos Indians in New Mexico, be and hereby is amended to read as follows: . . .

"SEC. 4. (a) That, for the purpose of safeguarding the interests and welfare of the tribe of Indians known as the Pueblo de Taos of New Mexico, the following described lands and improvements thereon, upon which said Indians depend and have depended since time immemorial for water supply, forage for their domestic livestock, wood and timber for their personal use, and as the scene of certain religious ceremonials are hereby declared to be held by the United States in trust for the Pueblo de Taos:

[Description of boundaries.]

"(b) The lands held in trust pursuant to this section shall be a part of the Pueblo de Taos Reservation, and shall be administered under the laws and regulations applicable to other trust Indian lands: *Provided,* That the Pueblo de Taos Indians shall use the lands for traditional purposes only, such as religious ceremonials, hunting and fishing, a source of water, forage for their domestic livestock, and wood, timber, and other natural resources for their personal use, all subject to such regulations for conservation purposes as the Secretary of the Interior may prescribe. Except for such uses, the lands shall remain forever wild and shall be maintained as a wilderness as defined in section 2(c) of the Act of September 3, 1964 (78 Stat. 890). With the consent of the tribe, but not otherwise, nonmembers of the tribe may be permitted to enter the lands for purposes compatible with their preservation as a wilderness. The Secretary of the Interior shall be responsible for the establishment and maintenance of conservation measures for these lands, including, without limitation, protection of forests from fire, disease, insects or trespass; prevention or elimination of erosion, damaging land use, or stream pollution; and maintenance of streamflow and sanitary conditions; and the Secretary is authorized to contract with the Secretary of Agriculture for any services or materials deemed necessary to institute or carry out any of such measures.

"(c) Lessees or permittees of lands described in subsection (a) which are not included in the lands described in the Act of May 31, 1933, shall be given the opportunity to renew their leases of permits under rules and regulations of the Secretary of the Interior to the same extent and in the same manner that such leases or permits could have been renewed if this Act had not been enacted; but the Pueblo de Taos may obtain the relinquishment of any or all of such leases or permits from the lessees or permittees under such terms and conditions as may be mutually agreeable. The Secretary of the Interior is authorized to disburse, from the tribal funds in the Treasury of the United States to the credit of said tribe, so much thereof as may be necessary to pay for such relinquishments and for the purchase of any rights or improvements on said lands owned by non-Indians. The authority to pay for the relinquishment of a permit pursuant to this subsection shall not be regarded as a recognition of any property right of the permittee in the land or its resources.

"(d) The Indian Claims Commission is directed to determine in accordance with the provisions of section 2 of the Act of August 13, 1946 (60 Stat. 1049, 1050), the extent to which the value of the interest in land conveyed by this Act should be credited to the United States or should be set off against any claim of the Taos Indians against the United States.

"(e) Nothing in this section shall impair any vested water right."

Source: *U.S. Statutes at Large*, 84:1437–1439.

Remarks of President Nixon December 15, 1970

Ladies and gentlemen:

I want to welcome all of you here on this very special occasion during the Christmas season, and particularly our guests from the western part of the United States who have come from a long way to be with us.

We are here for a bill signing ceremony that has very special significance—the Taos-Blue Lake bill. It is a bill that has bipartisan support. Both Democrats and Republicans joined together to get it through the Congress so that the President could have the honor of signing it today.

And it is a bill which could be interpreted particularly in the Christmas season as one where a gift was being made by the United States to the Indian population of the United States.

That is not the case.

This is a bill that represents justice, because in 1906 an injustice was done in which land involved in this bill, 48,000 acres, was taken from the Indians involved, the Taos Pueblo Indians. And now, after all those years, the Congress of the United States returns that land to whom it belongs.

This bill also involves respect for religion. Those of us who know something about the background of the first Americans realize that long before any organized religion came to the United States, for 700 years the Taos Pueblo Indians worshiped in this place.

We restore this place of worship to them for all the years to come.

And finally, this bill indicates a new direction in Indian affairs in this country, a new direction in which we will have the cooperation of both Democrats and Republicans, one in which there will be more of an attitude of cooperation rather than paternalism, one of self-determination rather than termination, one of mutual respect.

I can only say that in signing the bill trust that this will mark one of those periods in American history where, after a very, very long time, and at times a very sad history of injustice, that we started on a new road—a new road which leads us to justice in the treatment of those who were the first Americans, of our working together for the better nation that we want this great and good country of ours to become.

Source: *Public Papers of the Presidents of the United States: Richard Nixon, 1970* (Washington, D.C.: Government Printing Office, 1977), 1131–1132.

61 Alaska Native Claims Settlement Act, December 18, 1971

With the discovery of oil in Alaska, it became necessary for the federal government to settle Alaska Native land claims. The resulting legislation authorized the enrollment of Alaska Natives, created regional native corporations in the state, conveyed lands to the various native corporations, and deposited monies in the Alaska Native Fund.

An Act To provide for the settlement of certain land claims of Alaska Natives, and for other purposes.

Be it enacted . . . , That this Act may be cited as the "Alaska Native Claims Settlement Act." . . .

DECLARATION OF POLICY

SEC. 2. Congress finds and declares that

(a) there is an immediate need for a fair and just settlement of all claims by Natives and Native groups of Alaska, based on aboriginal land claims;
(b) the settlement should be accomplished rapidly, with certainty, in conformity with the real economic and social needs of Natives, without litigation, with maximum participation by Natives in decisions affecting their rights and property, without establishing any permanent racially defined Institutions, rights, privileges, or obligations, without creating a reservation system or lengthy wardship or trusteeship, and without adding to the categories of property and institutions enjoying special tax privileges or to the legislation establishing special relationships between the United States Government and the State of Alaska;
(c) no provision of this Act shall replace or diminish any right, privilege, or obligation of Natives as citizens of the United States or of Alaska, or relieve, replace, or diminish any obligation of the United States or of the State of Alaska to protect and promote the rights or welfare of Natives as citizens of the United States or of Alaska; the Secretary [of the Interior] is authorized and directed, together with other appropriate agencies of the United States Government, to make a study of all Federal programs primarily designed to benefit Native people and to report back to the Congress with his recommendations for the future management and operation of these programs within three years of the date of enactment of this Act;
(d) no provision of this Act shall constitute a precedent for reopening, renegotiating, or legislating upon any past settlement involving land claims or other matters with any Native organization, or any tribe, band, or identifiable group of American Indians;

(e) no provision of this Act shall effect a change or changes in the petroleum reserve policy reflected in sections 7421 through 7438 of title 10 of the United States Code except as specifically provided in this Act;
(f) no provision of this Act shall be construed to constitute a jurisdictional act, to confer jurisdiction to sue, nor to grant implied consent to Natives to sue the United States or any of its officers with respect to the claims extinguished by the operation of this Act; and
(g) no provision of this Act shall be construed to terminate or otherwise curtail the activities of the Economic Development Administration or other Federal agencies conducting loan or loan and grant programs in Alaska. For this purpose only, the terms "Indian reservation" and "trust or restricted Indian-owned land areas" in Public Law 89-136, the Public Works and Economic Development Act of 1965, as amended, shall be interpreted to include lands granted to Natives under this Act as long as such lands remain in the ownership of the Native villages or the Regional Corporations. . . . .

DECLARATION OF SETTLEMENT

SEC. 4. (a) All prior conveyances of public land and water areas in Alaska, or any interest therein, pursuant to Federal law, and all tentative approvals pursuant to section 6 (g) of the Alaska Statehood Act, shall be regarded as an extinguishment of the aboriginal title thereto, if any.

(b) All aboriginal titles, if any, and claims of aboriginal title in Alaska based on use and occupancy, including submerged land underneath all water areas, both inland and offshore, and including any aboriginal hunting or fishing rights that may exist, are hereby extinguished.

(c) All claims against the United States, the State, and all other persons that are based on claims of aboriginal right, title, use, or occupancy of land or water areas in Alaska, or that are based on any statute or treaty of the United States relating to Native use and occupancy, or that are based on the laws of any other nation, including any such claims that are pending before any Federal or state court or the Indian Claims Commission, are hereby extinguished.

ENROLLMENT

SEC. 5. (a) The Secretary shall prepare within two years from the date of enactment of this Act a roll of all Natives who were born on or before, and who are living on, the date of enactment of this Act. Any decision of the Secretary regarding eligibility for enrollment shall be final.

(b) The roll prepared by the Secretary shall show for each Native, among other things, the region and the village or other place in which he resided on the date of the 1970 census enumeration, and he shall be enrolled according to such residence.

Except as provided in subsection (c), a Native eligible for enrollment who is not, when the roll is prepared, a permanent resident of one of the twelve regions established pursuant to subsection 7(a) shall be enrolled by the Secretary in one of the twelve regions, giving priority in the following order to

(1) the region where the Native resided on the 1970 census date if he had resided there without substantial interruption for two or more years;
(2) the region where the Native previously resided for an aggregate of ten years or more;
(3) the region where the Native was born; and
(4) the region from which an ancestor of the Native came.

The Secretary may enroll a Native in a different region when necessary to avoid enrolling members of the same family in different regions or otherwise avoid hardship.

(c) A Native eligible for enrollment who is eighteen years of age or older and is not a permanent resident of one of the twelve regions may, on the date he files an application for enrollment, elect to be enrolled in a thirteenth region for Natives who are nonresidents of Alaska, if such region is established pursuant to subsection 7(c). If such region is not established, he shall be enrolled as provided in subsection (b). His election shall apply to all dependent members of his household who are less than eighteen years of age, but shall not affect the enrollment of anyone else.

ALASKA NATIVE FUND

SEC. 6. (a) There is hereby established in the United States Treasury an Alaska Native Fund into which the following moneys shall be deposited:

(1) $462,500,000 from the general fund of the Treasury, which are authorized to be appropriated according to the following schedule:
    (A) $12,500,000 during the fiscal year in which this Act becomes effective;
    (B) $50,000,000 during the second fiscal year;
    (C) $70,000,000 during each of the third, fourth, and fifth fiscal years;
    (D) $40,000,000 during the sixth fiscal year; and
    (E) $30,000,000 during each of the next five fiscal years.

(2) Four percent interest per annum, which is authorized to be appropriated, on any amount authorized to be appropriated by this paragraph that is not appropriated within six months after the fiscal year in which payable.

(3) $500,000,000 pursuant to the revenue sharing provisions of section 9. . . .

REGIONAL CORPORATIONS

SEC. 7. (a) For purposes of this Act, the State of Alaska shall be divided by the Secretary within one year after the date of enactment of this Act into twelve geographic regions, with each region composed as far as practicable of Natives having a common heritage and sharing common interests. In the absence of good cause shown to the contrary, such regions shall approximate the areas covered by the operations of the following existing Native associations:

(1) Arctic Slope Native Association (Barrow, Point Hope);
(2) Bering Straits Association (Seward Peninsula, Unalakleet, Saint Lawrence Island);
(3) Northwest Alaska Native Association (Kotzebue);
(4) Association of Village Council Presidents (southwest coast, all villages in the Bethel area, including all villages on the Lower Yukon River and the Lower Kuskokwim River);
(5) Tanana Chiefs' Conference (Koyukuk, Middle and Upper Yukon Rivers, Upper Kuskokwim, Tanana River);
(6) Cook Inlet Association (Kenai, Tyonek, Eklutna, Iliamna);
(7) Bristol Bay Native Association (Dillingham, Upper Alaska Peninsula);
(8) Aleut League (Aleutian Islands, Pribilof Islands and that part of the Alaska Peninsula which is in the Aleut League);
(9) Chugach Native Association (Cordova, Tatitlek, Port Graham, English Bay, Valdez, and Seward);
(10) Tlingit-Haida Central Council (southeastern Alaska, including Metlakatla);
(11) Kodiak Area Native Association (all villages on and around Kodiak Island); and
(12) Copper River Native Association (Copper Center, Glennallen, Chitina, Mentasta).

Any dispute over the boundaries of a region or regions shall be resolved by a board of arbitrators consisting of one person selected by each of the Native associations involved, and an additional one or two persons, whichever is needed to make an odd number of arbitrators, such additional person or persons to be selected by the arbitrators selected by the Native associations involved.

(b) The Secretary may, on request made within one year of the date of enactment of this Act, by representative and responsible leaders of the Native associations listed in subsection (a), merge two or more of the twelve regions: *Provided,* That the twelve regions may not be reduced to less than seven, and there may be no fewer than seven Regional Corporations. . . .

CONVEYANCE OF LANDS

SEC. 14. (a) Immediately after selection by a Village Corporation for a Native village listed in section 11 which the Secretary finds is qualified for land benefits under this Act, the Secretary shall issue to the Village Corporation a patent to the surface estate in the number of acres shown in the following table:

If the village had on the 1970 census enumeration date a Native population between	It shall be entitled to a patent to an area of public lands equal to
25 and 99	69,120 acres
100 and 199	92,160 acres
200 and 399	115,200 acres
400 and 599	138,240 acres
600 or more	161,280 acres

The lands patented shall be those selected by the Village Corporation pursuant to subsection 12(a). In addition, the Secretary shall issue to the Village Corporation a patent to the surface estate in the lands selected pursuant to subsection 12(b).

(b) Immediately after selection by any Village Corporation for a Native village listed in Section 16 which the Secretary finds is qualified for land benefits under this Act, the Secretary shall issue to the Village Corporation a patent to the surface estate to 23,040 acres. The lands patented shall be the lands within the township or townships that enclose the Native village, and any additional lands selected by the Village Corporation from the surrounding townships withdrawn for the Native village by subsection 16 (a). . . .

Source: *U.S. Statutes at Large*, 85:688–692, 701–703.

62

On December 22, 1973, following American Indian protests and evidence of the deplorable effects of termination on the Menominee Indians of Wisconsin, Congress repealed the termination act of June 17, 1954 (Doc. 53), thus restoring the Menominees to federal status.

An Act To repeal the Act terminating Federal supervision over the property and members of the Menominee Indian Tribe of Wisconsin; to reinstitute the Menominee Indian Tribe of Wisconsin as a federally recognized sovereign Indian tribe; and to restore to the Menominee Tribe of Wisconsin those Federal services furnished to American Indians because of their status as American Indians; and for other purposes.

Be it enacted . . . , That:

This Act may be cited as the "Menominee Restoration Act.". . .

SEC. 2. For the purposes of this Act—

(1) The term "tribe" means the Menominee Indian Tribe of Wisconsin.

(2) The term "Secretary" means the Secretary of the Interior.
(3) The term "Menominee Restoration Committee" means that committee of nine Menominee Indians who shall be elected pursuant to subsections 4(a) and 4(b) of this Act.

SEC. 3. (a) Notwithstanding the provisions of the Act of June 17, 1954 (68 Stat. 250; 25 U.S.C. 891-902), as amended, or any other law, Federal recognition is hereby extended to the Menominee Indian Tribe of Wisconsin and the provisions of the Act of June 18, 1934 (48 Stat. 984; 25 U.S.C. 461 et seq.), as amended, are made applicable to

(b) The Act of June 17, 1954 (68 Stat. 250; 25 U.S.C. 891-902), as amended, is hereby repealed and there are hereby reinstated all rights and privileges of the tribe or its members under Federal treaty, statute, or otherwise which may have been diminished or lost pursuant to such Act.

(c) Nothing contained in this Act shall diminish any rights or privileges enjoyed by the tribe or its members now or prior to June 17, 1954, under Federal treaty, statute, or otherwise, which are not inconsistent with the provisions of this Act.

(d) Except as specifically provided in this Act, nothing contained in this Act shall alter any property rights or obligations, any contractual rights or obligations, including existing fishing rights, or any obligations for taxes already levied.

(e) In providing to the tribe such services to which it may be entitled upon its recognition pursuant to subsection (a) of this section, the Secretary of the Interior and the Secretary of Health, Education, and Welfare, as appropriate, are authorized from funds appropriated pursuant to the Act of November 2, 1921 (42 Stat. 208; 25 U.S.C. 13), the Act of August 5, 1954 (68 Stat. 674), as amended, or any other Act authorizing appropriations for the administration of Indian affairs, upon the request of the tribe and subject to such terms and conditions as may be mutually agreed to, to make grants and contract to make grants which will accomplish the general purposes for which the funds were appropriated. The Menominee Restoration Committee shall have full authority and capacity to be a party to receive such grants, to make such contracts, and to bind the tribal governing body as the successor in interest to the Menominee Restoration Committee: Provided, however, That the Menominee Restoration Committee shall have no authority to bind the tribe for a period of more than six months after the date on which the tribal governing body takes office.

SEC. 4. (a) Within fifteen days after the enactment of this Act, the Secretary shall announce the date of a general council meeting of the tribe to nominate candidates for election to the Menominee Restoration Committee. Such general council meeting shall be held within thirty days of the date of enactment of this Act. Within forty-five days of the general council meeting provided for herein, the Secretary shall hold an election by secret ballot, absentee balloting to be permitted, to elect the membership of the Menominee Restoration Committee from among the nominees submitted to him from the general council meeting provided for herein. The ballots shall provide for write-in votes. The Secretary shall approve the Menominee Restoration Committee elected pursuant to this section if he is satisfied that the requirements of this section relating to the nominating and election process have been met. The Menominee Restoration Committee shall represent the Menominee people in the implementation of this Act and shall have no powers other than those given to it in accordance with this Act. The Menominee Restoration Committee shall have no power or authority under this Act after the time which the duly-elected tribal governing body takes office: Provided, however, That this provision shall in no way invalidate or affect grants or contracts made pursuant to the provisions of subsection 3 (e) of this Act.

(b) In the absence of a completed tribal roll prepared pursuant to subsection (c) hereof and solely for the purposes of the general council meeting and the election provided for in subsection (a) hereof, all living persons on the final roll of the tribe published under section 3 of the Act of June 17, 1954 (25 U.S.C. 893), and all descendants, who are at least eighteen years of age and who possess at least one-quarter degree of Menominee Indian blood, of persons on such roll shall be entitled to attend, participate, and vote at such general council meeting and such election. Verification of descendancy, age, and blood quantum shall be made upon oath before the Secretary or his authorized representative and his determination thereon shall be conclusive and final. The Secretary shall assure that adequate notice of such meeting and election shall be provided eligible voters.

SEC. 5. (a) Upon request from the Menominee Restoration Committee, the Secretary shall conduct an election by secret ballot, pursuant to the provisions of the Act of June 18, 1934, as amended, for the purpose of determining the tribe's constitution and bylaws. The election shall be held within sixty days after final certification of the tribal roll.

(b) The Menominee Restoration Committee shall distribute to all enrolled persons who are entitled to vote in the election, at least thirty days before the election, a copy of the constitution and bylaws as drafted by the Menominee Restoration Committee which will be presented at the election, along with a brief impartial description of the constitution and bylaws. The Menominee Restoration Committee shall freely consult with persons entitled to vote in the election concerning the text and description of the constitution and bylaws. Such consultation shall not be carried on within fifty feet of the polling places on the date of the election.

(c) Within one hundred and twenty days after the tribe adopts a constitution and bylaws, the Menominee Restoration Committee shall conduct an election by secret ballot for the purpose of determining the individuals who will serve as tribal officials as provided in the tribal constitution and bylaws. For the purpose of this initial election and notwithstanding any provision in the tribal constitution and bylaws to the contrary, absentee balloting shall be permitted and all tribal members who are eighteen years of age or over shall be entitled to vote in the election. All further elections of tribal officers shall be as provided in the tribal constitution and bylaws and ordinances adopted thereunder.

(d) In any election held pursuant to this section, the vote of a majority of those actually voting shall be necessary and sufficient to effectuate the adoption of a tribal constitution and bylaws and the initial election of the tribe's governing body, so long as, in each such election, the total vote cast is at least 30 per centum of those entitled to vote. . . .

Source: *U.S. Statutes at Large*, 87:700ff.

63 American Indian Religious Freedom Act, August 11, 1978

In 1978, Congress attempted to grant religious freedom to Native Americans through the American Indian Religious Freedom Act. In the 1980s and early 1990s the Supreme Court would strike down most of its provisions.

Whereas the freedom of religion for all people is an inherent right, fundamental to the democratic structure of the United States and is guaranteed by the First Amendment of the United States Constitution;

Whereas the United States has traditionally rejected the concept of a government denying individuals the right to practice their religion and, as a result, has benefited from a rich variety of religious heritages in this country;

Whereas the religious practices of the American Indian (as well as Native Alaskan and Hawaiian) are an integral part of their culture, tradition and heritage, such practices forming the basis of Indian identity and value systems;

Whereas the traditional American Indian religions, as an integral part of Indian life, are indispensable and irreplaceable;

Whereas the lack of a clear, comprehensive, and consistent Federal policy has often resulted in the abridgment of religious freedom for traditional American Indians;

Whereas such religious infringements result from the lack of knowledge or the insensitive and inflexible enforcement of Federal policies and regulations premised on a variety of laws;

Whereas such laws were designed for such worthwhile purposes as conservation and preservation of natural species and resources but were never intended to relate to Indian religious practices and, therefore, were passed without consideration of their effect on traditional American Indian religions;

Whereas such laws and policies often deny American Indians access to sacred sites required in their religions, including cemeteries;

Whereas such laws at times prohibit the use and possession of sacred objects necessary to the exercise of religious rites and ceremonies;

Whereas traditional American Indian ceremonies have been intruded upon, interfered with, and in a few instances banned: Now, therefore, be it

Resolved by the Senate and House of Representatives of the United States of America in Congress assembled, That henceforth it shall be the policy of the United States to protect and preserve for American Indians their inherent right of freedom to believe, express, and exercise the traditional religions of the American Indian, Eskimo, Aleut, and Native Hawaiians, including but not limited to access to sites, use and possession of sacred objects, and the freedom to worship through ceremonials and traditional rights.

Adopted August 11, 1978.

Source: *U.S. Statutes at Large*, 92:469.

64 Indian Child Welfare Act, November 8, 1978

In the following portion of the U.S. Code relating to the Indian Child Welfare Act, the federal government outlines its historical and contemporary concerns about the welfare of Native American children. The act sought to redress some of the problems created by federal policies involving Native American ethnocide.

Sec. 1901. Congressional findings
Recognizing the special relationship between the United States and the Indian tribes and their members and the Federal responsibility to Indian people, the Congress finds—

(1) that clause 3, section 8, article I of the United States Constitution provides that "The Congress shall have Power. . . . To regulate Commerce . . . with Indian tribes" and, through this and other constitutional authority, Congress has plenary power over Indian affairs;
(2) that Congress, through statutes, treaties, and the general course of dealing with Indian tribes, has assumed the responsibility for the protection and preservation of Indian tribes and their resources;
(3) that there is no resource that is more vital to the continued existence and integrity of Indian tribes than their children and that the United States has a direct interest, as trustee, in protecting Indian children who are members of or are eligible for membership in an Indian tribe;

(4) that an alarmingly high percentage of Indian families are broken up by the removal, often unwarranted, of their children from them by nontribal public and private agencies and that an alarmingly high percentage of such children are placed in non-Indian foster and adoptive homes and institutions; and

(5) that the States, exercising their recognized jurisdiction over Indian child custody proceedings through administrative and judicial bodies, have often failed to recognize the essential tribal relations of Indian people and the cultural and social standards prevailing in Indian communities and families.

Source: *U.S. Statutes at Large*, 92:3069.

65 *Lyng v. Northwest Indian Cemetery Protective Association* (1988)

In 1988 the Supreme Court, in a 5-3 vote, struck down most of the important provisions of the American Indian Religious Freedom Act. With this ruling, the Court departed from the two-centuries-old precedent of using the First Amendment's Free Exercise Clause as the measure for upholding religious freedom, instead supplanting it with a test akin to "community values" and states rights. The dissenting opinion in this case was highly critical of the majority opinion. The legal result was disastrous for American Indian religious freedom.

JUSTICE O'CONNOR delivered the opinion of the Court.

This case requires us to consider whether the First Amendment's Free Exercise Clause prohibits the Government from permitting timber harvesting in, or constructing a road through, a portion of a National Forest that has traditionally been used for religious purposes by members of three American Indian tribes in northwestern California. We conclude that it does not.

I

As part of a project to create a paved 75-mile road linking two California towns, Gasquet and Orleans, the United States Forest Service has upgraded 49 miles of previously unpaved roads on federal land. In order to complete this project (the G-O road), the Forest Service must build a 6-mile paved segment through the Chimney Rock section of the Six Rivers National Forest. That section of the forest is situated between two other portions of the road that are already complete.

In 1977, the Forest Service issued a draft environmental impact statement that discussed proposals for upgrading an existing unpaved road that runs through the Chimney Rock area. In response to comments on the draft statement, the Forest

Service commissioned a study of American Indian cultural and religious sites in the area. The Hoopa Valley Indian Reservation adjoins the Six Rivers National Forest, and the Chimney Rock area has historically been used for religious purposes by Yurok, Karok, and Tolowa Indians. The commissioned study, which was completed in 1979, found that the entire area "is significant as an integral and indispensable part of Indian religious conceptualization and practice." Specific sites are used for certain rituals, and "successful use of the [area] is dependent upon and facilitated by certain qualities of the physical environment, the most important of which are privacy, silence, and an undisturbed natural setting." The study concluded that constructing a road along any of the available routes "would cause serious and irreparable damage to the sacred areas which are an integral and necessary part of the belief systems and lifeway of Northwest California Indian peoples." Accordingly, the report recommended that the G-O road not be completed.

In 1982, the Forest Service decided not to adopt this recommendation, and it prepared a final environmental impact statement for construction of the road. The Regional Forester selected a route that avoided archeological sites and was removed as far as possible from the sites used by contemporary Indians for specific spiritual activities. Alternative routes that would have avoided the Chimney Rock area altogether were rejected because they would have required the acquisition of private land, had serious soil stability problems, and would in any event have traversed areas having ritualistic value to American Indians. At about the same time, the Forest Service adopted a management plan allowing for the harvesting of significant amounts of timber in this area of the forest. The management plan provided for one-half mile protective zones around all the religious sites identified in the report that had been commissioned in connection with the G-O road.

After exhausting their administrative remedies, respondents—an Indian organization, individual Indians, nature organizations and individual members of those organizations, and the State of California—challenged both the road-building and timber-harvesting decisions in the United States District Court for the Northern District of California. Respondents claimed that the Forest Service's decisions violated the Free Exercise Clause, the Federal Water Pollution Control Act (FWPCA), the National Environmental Policy Act of 1969 (NEPA), several other federal statutes, and governmental trust responsibilities to Indians living on the Hoopa Valley Reservation.

After a trial, the District Court issued a permanent injunction prohibiting the Government from constructing the Chimney Rock section of the G-O road or putting the timber-harvesting management plan into effect. The court found that both actions would violate the Free Exercise Clause because they "would seriously damage the salient visual, aural, and environmental qualities of the high country." The court also found that both proposed actions would violate the FWPCA, and that the environmental impact statements for construction of the road were deficient under the NEPA. Finally, the court concluded that both projects would breach the Government's trust responsibilities to protect water and fishing rights reserved to the Hoopa Valley Indians.

While an appeal was pending before the United States Court of Appeals for the Ninth Circuit, Congress enacted the California Wilderness Act of 1984. Under that statute, much of the property covered by the Forest Service's management plan is now designated a wilderness area, which means that commercial activities such as timber harvesting are forbidden. The statute exempts a narrow strip of land, coinciding with the Forest Service's proposed route for the remaining segment of the G-O road, from the wilderness designation. The legislative history indicates that this exemption was adopted "to enable the completion of the Gasquet-Orleans Road project if the responsible authorities so decide." The existing unpaved section of road, however, lies within the wilderness area and is therefore now closed to general traffic.

A panel of the Ninth Circuit affirmed in part. The panel unanimously rejected the District Court's conclusion that the Government's proposed actions would breach its trust responsibilities to Indians on the Hoopa Valley Reservation. The panel also vacated the injunction to the extent that it had been rendered moot by the California Wilderness Act, which now prevents timber harvesting in certain areas covered by the District Court's order. The District Court's decision, to the extent that it rested on statutory grounds, was otherwise unanimously affirmed.

By a divided decision, the District Court's constitutional ruling was also affirmed. Relying primarily on the Forest Service's own commissioned study, the majority found that construction of the Chimney Rock section of the G-O road would have significant, though largely indirect, adverse effects on Indian religious practices. The majority concluded that the Government had failed to demonstrate a compelling interest in the completion of the road, and that it could have abandoned the road without thereby creating "a religious preserve for a single group in violation of the establishment clause." The majority apparently applied the same analysis to logging operations that might be carried out in portions of the Chimney Rock area not covered by the California Wilderness Act.

The dissenting judge argued that certain of the adverse effects on the Indian respondents' religious practices could be eliminated by less drastic measures than a ban on building the road, and that other actual or suggested adverse effects did not pose a serious threat to the Indians' religious practices. He also concluded that the injunction against timber harvesting needed to be reconsidered in light of the California Wilderness Act: "It is not clear whether the district court would have issued an injunction based upon the development of the remaining small parcels. Accordingly, I would remand to allow the district court to reevaluate its injunction in light of the Act."

II

We begin by noting that the courts below did not articulate the bases of their decisions with perfect clarity. A fundamental and longstanding principle of judicial restraint requires that courts avoid reaching constitutional questions in advance of the necessity of deciding them. This principle required the courts below to determine, before addressing the constitutional issue, whether a decision on that question could have entitled respondents to relief beyond that to which they were entitled on their statutory claims. If no additional relief would have been warranted, a constitutional decision would have been unnecessary and therefore inappropriate.

Neither the District Court nor the Court of Appeals explained or expressly articulated the necessity for their constitutional holdings. Were we persuaded that those holdings were unnecessary, we could simply vacate the relevant portions of the judgment below without discussing the merits of the constitutional issue. The structure and wording of the District Court's injunctive order, however, suggest that the statutory holdings would not have supported all the relief granted. The order is divided into four sections. Two of those sections deal with a 31,100-acre tract referred to as the Blue Creek Roadless Area. The injunction prohibits the Forest Service from engaging in timber harvesting or road building anywhere on the tract "unless and until" compliance with the NEPA and the FWPCA have been demonstrated. The sections of the injunction dealing with the smaller Chimney Rock area (i.e., the area affected by the First Amendment challenge) are worded differently. The Forest Service is permanently enjoined, without any qualifying language, from constructing the proposed portion of the G-O road "and/or any alternative route" through that area; similarly, the injunction forbids timber harvesting or the construction of logging roads in the Chimney Rock area pursuant to the Forest Service's proposed management plan "or any other land management plan." These differences in wording suggest, without absolutely implying, that an injunction covering the Chimney Rock area would in some way have been conditional, or narrower in scope, if the District Court had not decided the First Amendment issue as it did. Similarly, the silence of the Court of Appeals as to the necessity of reaching the First Amendment issue may have reflected its understanding that the District Court's injunction necessarily rested in part on constitutional grounds.

Because it appears reasonably likely that the First Amendment issue was necessary to the decisions below, we believe that it would be inadvisable to vacate and remand without addressing that issue on the merits. This conclusion is strengthened by considerations of judicial economy. The Government, which petitioned for certiorari on the constitutional issue alone, has informed us that it believes it can cure the statutory defects identified below, intends to do so, and will not challenge the adverse statutory rulings. In this circumstance, it is difficult to see what principle would be vindicated by sending this case on what would almost certainly be a brief round trip to the courts below.

III

A

The Free Exercise Clause of the First Amendment provides that "Congress shall make no law . . . prohibiting the free exercise [of religion]." It is undisputed that the Indian respondents' beliefs are sincere and that the Government's proposed actions will have severe adverse effects on the practice of their religion. Those respondents contend that the burden on their religious practices is heavy enough to violate the Free Exercise Clause unless the Government can demonstrate a compelling need to complete the G-O road or to engage in timber harvesting in the Chimney Rock area. We disagree.

In *Bowen v. Roy* (1986), we considered a challenge to a federal statute that required the States to use Social Security numbers in administering certain welfare programs. Two applicants for benefits under these programs contended that their religious beliefs prevented them from acceding to the use of a Social Security number for their 2-year-old daughter because the use of a numerical identifier would " 'rob the spirit' of [their] daughter and prevent her from attaining greater spiritual power." Similarly, in this case, it is said that disruption of the natural environment caused by the G-O road will diminish the sacredness of the area in question and create distractions that will interfere with "training and ongoing religious experience of individuals using [sites within] the area for personal medicine and growth . . . and as integrated parts of a system of religious belief and practice which correlates ascending degrees of personal power with a geographic hierarchy of power." The Court rejected this kind of challenge in Roy:

> The Free Exercise Clause simply cannot be understood to require the Government to conduct its own internal affairs in ways that comport with the religious beliefs of particular citizens. Just as the Government may not insist that [the Roys] engage in any set form of religious observance, so [they] may not demand that the Government join in their chosen religious practices by refraining from using a number to identify their daughter. . . .
>
> The Free Exercise Clause affords an individual protection from certain forms of governmental compulsion; it does not afford an individual a right to dictate the conduct of the Government's internal procedures.

The building of a road or the harvesting of timber on publicly owned land cannot meaningfully be distinguished from the use of a Social Security number in Roy. In both cases, the challenged Government action would interfere significantly with private persons' ability to pursue spiritual fulfillment according to their own religious beliefs. In neither case, however, would the affected individuals be coerced by the Government's action into violating their religious beliefs; nor would either governmental action penalize religious activity by denying any person an equal share of the rights, benefits, and privileges enjoyed by other citizens.

We are asked to distinguish this case from Roy on the ground that the infringement on religious liberty here is "significantly greater," or on the ground that the Government practice in Roy was "purely mechanical" whereas this case involves "a case-by-case substantive determination as to how a particular unit of land will be managed." Similarly, we are told that this case can be distinguished from Roy because "the government action is not at some physically removed location where it places no restriction on what a practitioner may do." The State suggests that the

Social Security number in Roy "could be characterized as interfering with Roy's religious tenets from a subjective point of view, where the government's conduct of 'its own internal affairs' was known to him only secondhand and did not interfere with his ability to practice his religion." In this case, however, it is said that the proposed road will "physically destro[y] the environmental conditions and the privacy without which the [religious] practices cannot be conducted."

These efforts to distinguish Roy are unavailing. This Court cannot determine the truth of the underlying beliefs that led to the religious objections here or in Roy and accordingly cannot weigh the adverse effects on the appellees in Roy and compare them with the adverse effects on the Indian respondents. Without the ability to make such comparisons, we cannot say that the one form of incidental interference with an individual's spiritual activities should be subjected to a different constitutional analysis than the other.

Respondents insist, nonetheless, that the courts below properly relied on a factual inquiry into the degree to which the Indians' spiritual practices would become ineffectual if the G-O road were built. They rely on several cases in which this Court has sustained free exercise challenges to government programs that interfered with individuals' ability to practice their religion.

Even apart from the inconsistency between Roy and respondents' reading of these cases, their interpretation will not withstand analysis. It is true that this Court has repeatedly held that indirect coercion or penalties on the free exercise of religion, not just outright prohibitions, are subject to scrutiny under the First Amendment. Thus, for example, ineligibility for unemployment benefits, based solely on a refusal to violate the Sabbath, has been analogized to a fine imposed on Sabbath worship. This does not and cannot imply that incidental effects of government programs, which may make it more difficult to practice certain religions but which have no tendency to coerce individuals into acting contrary to their religious beliefs, require government to bring forward a compelling justification for its otherwise lawful actions. The crucial word in the constitutional text is "prohibit": "For the Free Exercise Clause is written in terms of what the government cannot do to the individual, not in terms of what the individual can exact from the government."

Whatever may be the exact line between unconstitutional prohibitions on the free exercise of religion and the legitimate conduct by government of its own affairs, the location of the line cannot depend on measuring the effects of a governmental action on a religious objector's spiritual development. The Government does not dispute, and we have no reason to doubt, that the logging and road-building projects at issue in this case could have devastating effects on traditional Indian religious practices. Those practices are intimately and inextricably bound up with the unique features of the Chimney Rock area, which is known to the Indians as the "high country." Individual practitioners use this area for personal spiritual development; some of their activities are believed to be critically important in advancing the welfare of the Tribe, and indeed, of mankind itself. The Indians use this area, as they have used it for a very long time, to conduct a wide variety of specific rituals that aim to accomplish their religious goals. According to their beliefs, the rituals would not be efficacious if conducted at other sites than the ones traditionally used, and too much disturbance of the area's natural state would clearly render any meaningful continuation of traditional practices impossible. To be sure, the Indians themselves were far from unanimous in opposing the G-O road, and it seems less than certain that construction of the road will be so disruptive that it will doom their religion. Nevertheless, we can assume that the threat to the efficacy of at least some religious practices is extremely grave.

Even if we assume that we should accept the Ninth Circuit's prediction, according to which the G-O road will "virtually destroy the . . . Indians' ability to practice their religion," the Constitution simply does not provide a principle that could justify upholding respondents' legal claims. However much we might wish that it were otherwise, government simply could not operate if it were required to satisfy every citizen's religious needs and desires. A broad range of government activities—from social welfare programs to foreign aid to conservation projects—will always be considered essential to the spiritual well-being of some citizens, often on the basis of sincerely held religious beliefs. Others will find the very same activities deeply offensive, and perhaps incompatible with their own search for spiritual fulfillment and with the tenets of their religion. The First Amendment must apply to all citizens alike, and it can give to none of them a veto over public programs that do not prohibit the free exercise of religion. The Constitution does not, and courts cannot, offer to reconcile the various competing demands on government, many of them rooted in sincere religious belief, that inevitably arise in so diverse a society as ours. That task, to the extent that it is feasible, is for the legislatures and other institutions.

One need not look far beyond the present case to see why the analysis in Roy, but not respondents' proposed extension of Sherbert and its progeny, offers a sound reading of the Constitution. Respondents attempt to stress the limits of the religious servitude that they are now seeking to impose on the Chimney Rock area of the Six Rivers National Forest. While defending an injunction against logging operations and the construction of a road, they apparently do not at present object to the area's being used by recreational visitors, other Indians, or forest rangers. Nothing in the principle for which they contend, however, would distinguish this case from another lawsuit in which they (or similarly situated religious objectors) might seek to exclude all human activity but their own from sacred areas of the public lands. The Indian respondents insist that "[p]rivacy during the power quests is required for the practitioners to maintain the purity needed for a successful journey." Similarly: "The practices conducted in the high country entail intense meditation and require the practitioner to achieve a profound awareness of the natural environment. Prayer seats are oriented so there is an unobstructed view, and the practitioner must be surrounded by undisturbed naturalness." No disrespect for these practices is implied when one notes that such beliefs could easily require de facto beneficial ownership of some rather spacious tracts of public property. Even without anticipating future cases, the diminution of the Government's property rights, and the concomitant subsidy of the Indian religion, would in this case be far from trivial: the District Court's order permanently forbade commercial timber harvesting, or the construction of a two-lane road, anywhere within an area covering a full 27 sections (i.e., more than 17,000 acres) of public land.

The Constitution does not permit government to discriminate against religions that treat particular physical sites as sacred, and a law prohibiting the Indian respondents from visiting the Chimney Rock area would raise a different set of constitutional questions. Whatever rights the Indians may have to the use of the area, however, those rights do not divest the Government of its right to use what is, after all, its land.

B

Nothing in our opinion should be read to encourage governmental insensitivity to the religious needs of any citizen. The Government's rights to the use of its own land, for example, need not and should not discourage it from accommodating religious practices like those engaged in by the Indian respondents. It is worth emphasizing, therefore, that the Government has taken numerous steps in this very case to minimize the impact that construction of the G-O road will have on the Indians' religious activities. First, the Forest Service commissioned a comprehensive study of the effects that the project would have on the cultural and religious value of the Chimney Rock area. The resulting 423-page report was so sympathetic to the Indians' interests that it has constituted the principal piece of evidence relied on by respondents throughout this litigation.

Although the Forest Service did not in the end adopt the report's recommendation that the project be abandoned, many other ameliorative measures were planned. No sites where specific rituals take place were to be disturbed. In fact, a major factor in choosing among alternative routes for the road was the relation of the various routes to religious sites: the route selected by the Regional Forester is, he noted, "the farthest removed from contemporary spiritual sites; thus, the adverse audible intrusions associated with the road would be less than all other alternatives." Nor were the Forest Service's concerns limited to "audible intrusions." As the dissenting judge below observed, 10 specific steps were planned to reduce the visual impact of the road on the surrounding country.

Except for abandoning its project entirely, and thereby leaving the two existing segments of road to dead-end in the middle of a National Forest, it is difficult to see how the Government could have been more solicitous. Such solicitude accords with "the policy of the United States to protect and preserve for American Indians their inherent right of freedom to believe, express, and exercise the traditional religions of the American Indian . . . including but not limited to access to sites, use and possession of sacred objects, and the freedom to worship through ceremonials and traditional rites."

Respondents, however, suggest that AIRFA goes further and in effect enacts their interpretation of the First Amendment into statutory law. Although this contention was rejected by the District Court, they seek to defend the judgment below by arguing that AIRFA authorizes the injunction against completion of the G-O road. This argument is without merit. After reciting several legislative findings, AIRFA "resolves" upon the policy quoted above. A second section of the statute required an evaluation of federal policies and procedures, in consultation with native religious leaders, of changes necessary to protect and preserve the rights and practices in question. The required report dealing with this evaluation was completed and released in 1979. Nowhere in the law is there so much as a hint of any intent to create a cause of action or any judicially enforceable individual rights.

What is obvious from the face of the statute is confirmed by numerous indications in the legislative history. The sponsor of the bill that became AIRFA, Representative Udall, called it "a sense of Congress joint resolution," aimed at ensuring that "the basic right of the Indian people to exercise their traditional religious practices is not infringed without a clear decision on the part of the Congress or the administrators that such religious practices must yield to some higher consideration." Representative Udall emphasized that the bill would not "confer special religious rights on Indians," would "not change any existing State or Federal law," and in fact "has no teeth in it."

C

The dissent proposes an approach to the First Amendment that is fundamentally inconsistent with the principles on which our decision rests. Notwithstanding the sympathy that we all must feel for the plight of the Indian respondents, it is plain that the approach taken by the dissent cannot withstand analysis. On the contrary, the path towards which it points us is incompatible with the text of the Constitution, with the precedents of this Court, and with a responsible sense of our own institutional role.

The dissent begins by asserting that the "constitutional guarantee we interpret today . . . is directed against any form of government action that frustrates or inhibits religious practice." The Constitution, however, says no such thing. Rather, it states: "Congress shall make no law . . . prohibiting the free exercise [of religion]."

As we explained above, *Bowen v. Roy* rejected a First Amendment challenge to Government activities that the religious objectors sincerely believed would " ' "rob the spirit" of [their] daughter and prevent her from attaining greater spiritual power.' " The dissent now offers to distinguish that case by saying that the Government was acting there "in a purely internal manner," whereas land-use decisions "are likely to have substantial external effects." Whatever the source or meaning of the dissent's distinction, it has no basis in Roy. Robbing the spirit of a child, and preventing her from attaining greater spiritual power, is both a "substantial external effect" and one that is remarkably similar to the injury claimed by respondents in the case before us today. The dissent's reading of Roy would effectively overrule that decision, without providing any compelling justification for doing so.

The dissent also misreads *Wisconsin v. Yoder* (1972). The statute at issue in that case prohibited the Amish parents, on pain of criminal prosecution, from providing their children with the kind of education required by the Amish religion. The statute directly compelled the Amish to send their children to public high schools "contrary to the Amish religion and way of life." The Court acknowledged that the statute might be constitutional, despite its coercive nature, if the State could show with sufficient "particularity how its admittedly strong interest in compulsory education would be adversely affected by granting an exemption to the Amish." The dissent's out-of-context quotations notwithstanding, there is nothing whatsoever in the Yoder opinion to support the proposition that the "impact" on the Amish religion would have been constitutionally problematic if the statute at issue had not been coercive in nature.

Perceiving a "stress point in the longstanding conflict between two disparate cultures," the dissent attacks us for declining to "balanc[e] these competing and potentially irreconcilable interests, choosing instead to turn this difficult task over to the Federal Legislature." Seeing the Court as the arbiter, the dissent proposes a legal test under which it would decide which public lands are "central" or "indispensable" to which religions, and by implication which are "dispensable" or "peripheral," and would then decide which government programs are "compelling" enough to justify "infringement of those practices." We would accordingly be required to weigh the value of every religious belief and practice that is said to be threatened by any government program. Unless a "showing of 'centrality,' " is nothing but an assertion of centrality, the dissent thus offers us the prospect of this Court's holding that some sincerely held religious beliefs and practices are not "central" to certain religions, despite protestations to the contrary from the religious objectors who brought the lawsuit. In other words, the dissent's approach would require us to rule that some religious adherents misunderstand their own religious beliefs. We think such an approach cannot be squared with the Constitution or with our precedents, and that it would cast the Judiciary in a role that we were never intended to play.

IV

The decision of the court below, according to which the First Amendment precludes the Government from completing the G-O road or from permitting timber harvesting in the Chimney Rock area, is reversed. In order that the District Court's injunction may be reconsidered in light of this holding, and in the light of any other relevant events that may have intervened since the injunction issued, the case is remanded for further proceedings consistent with this opinion.

It is so ordered.

JUSTICE KENNEDY took no part in the consideration or decision of this case.

JUSTICE BRENNAN, with whom JUSTICE MARSHALL and JUSTICE BLACKMUN join, dissenting.

" '[T]he Free Exercise Clause,' " the Court explains today, " 'is written in terms of what the government cannot do to the individual, not in terms of what the individual can exact from the government.' " Pledging fidelity to this unremarkable constitutional principle, the Court nevertheless concludes that even where the Government uses federal land in a manner that threatens the very existence of a Native American religion, the Government is simply not "doing" anything to the practitioners of that faith. Instead, the Court believes that Native Americans who request that the Government refrain from destroying their religion effectively seek to exact from the Government de facto beneficial ownership of federal property. These two astonishing conclusions follow naturally from the Court's determination that federal land-use decisions that render the practice of a given religion impossible do not burden that religion in a manner cognizable under the Free Exercise Clause, because such decisions neither coerce conduct inconsistent with religious belief nor penalize religious activity. The constitutional guarantee we interpret today, however, draws no such fine distinctions between types of restraints on religious exercise, but rather is directed against any form of governmental action that frustrates or inhibits religious practice. Because the Court today refuses even to acknowledge the constitutional injury respondents will suffer, and because this refusal essentially leaves Native Americans with absolutely no constitutional protection against perhaps the gravest threat to their religious practices, I dissent.

I

For at least 200 years and probably much longer, the Yurok, Karok, and Tolowa Indians have held sacred an approximately 25-square-mile area of land situated in what is today the Blue Creek Unit of Six Rivers National Forest in northwestern California. As the Government readily concedes, regular visits to this area, known to respondent Indians as the "high country," have played and continue to play a "critical" role in the religious practices and rituals of these Tribes. Those beliefs, only briefly described in the Court's opinion, are crucial to a proper understanding of respondents' claims.

As the Forest Service's commissioned study, the Theodoratus Report, explains, for Native Americans religion is not a discrete sphere of activity separate from all others, and any attempt to isolate the religious aspects of Indian life "is in reality an exercise which forces Indian concepts into non-Indian categories." Thus, for most Native Americans, "[t]he area of worship cannot be delineated from social, political, cultur[al], and other areas o[f] Indian lifestyle." A pervasive feature of this lifestyle is the individual's relationship with the natural world; this relationship, which can accurately though somewhat incompletely be characterized as one of stewardship, forms the core of what might be called, for want of a better nomenclature, the Indian religious experience. While traditional Western religions view creation as the work of a deity "who institutes natural laws which then govern the operation of physical nature," tribal religions regard creation as an ongoing process in which they are morally and religiously obligated to participate. Native Americans fulfill this duty through ceremonies and rituals designed to preserve and stabilize the earth and to protect humankind from disease and other catastrophes. Failure to conduct these ceremonies in the manner and place specified, adherents believe, will result in great harm to the earth and to the people whose welfare depends upon it.

In marked contrast to traditional Western religions, the belief systems of Native Americans do not rely on doctrines, creeds, or dogmas. Established or universal truths—the mainstay of Western religions—play no part in Indian faith. Ceremonies are communal efforts undertaken for specific purposes in accordance with instructions handed down from generation to generation. Commentaries on or interpretations of the rituals themselves are deemed absolute violations of the ceremonies, whose value lies not in their ability to explain the natural world or to enlighten individual believers but in their efficacy as protectors and enhancers of tribal existence. Where dogma lies at the heart of Western religions, Native American faith is inextricably bound to the use of land. The site-specific nature of Indian religious practice derives from the Native American perception that land is itself a sacred, living being. Rituals are performed in prescribed locations not merely as a matter of traditional orthodoxy, but because land, like all other living things, is unique, and specific sites possess different spiritual properties and significance. Within this belief system, therefore, land is not fungible; indeed, at the time of the Spanish colonization of the American Southwest, "all . . . Indians held in some form a belief in a sacred and indissoluble bond between themselves and the land in which their settlements were located."

For respondent Indians, the most sacred of lands is the high country where, they believe, prehuman spirits moved with the coming of humans to the Earth. Because these spirits are seen as the source of religious power, or "medicine," many of the tribes' rituals and practices require frequent journeys to the area. Thus, for example, religious leaders preparing for the complex of ceremonies that underlie the Tribes' World Renewal efforts must travel to specific sites in the high country in order to attain the medicine necessary for successful renewal. Similarly, individual tribe members may seek curative powers for the healing of the sick, or personal medicine for particular purposes such as good luck in singing, hunting, or love. A period of preparation generally precedes such visits, and individuals must select trails in the sacred area according to the medicine they seek and their abilities, gradually moving to increasingly more powerful sites, which are typically located at higher altitudes. Among the most powerful of sites are Chimney Rock, Doctor Rock, and Peak 8, all of which are elevated rock outcroppings.

According to the Theodoratus Report, the qualities "of silence, the aesthetic perspective, and the physical attributes, are an extension of the sacredness of [each] particular site." The act of medicine making is akin to meditation: the individual must integrate physical, mental, and vocal actions in order to communicate with the prehuman spirits. As a result, "successful use of the high country is dependent upon and facilitated by certain qualities of the physical environment, the most important of which are privacy, silence, and an undisturbed natural setting." Although few Tribe members actually make medicine at the most powerful sites, the entire Tribe's welfare hinges on the success of the individual practitioners.

Beginning in 1972, the Forest Service began preparing a multiple-use management plan for the Blue Creek Unit. The plan's principal features included the harvesting of 733 million board feet of Douglas fir over an 80-year period and the completion of a 6-mile segment of paved road running between two northern California towns, Gasquet and Orleans (the G-O road). The road's primary purpose was to provide a route for hauling the timber harvested under the management plan; in addition, it would enhance public access to the Six Rivers and other national forests, and allow for more efficient maintenance and fire control by the Forest Service itself. In the mid-1970's, the Forest Service circulated draft environmental impact statements evaluating the effects of several proposed routes for the final segment of the G-O road, including at least two that circumnavigated the high country altogether. Ultimately, however, the Service settled on a route running along the Chimney Rock Corridor, which traverses the Indians' sacred lands.

Respondent Indians brought suit to enjoin implementation of the plan, alleging that the road construction and timber harvesting would impermissibly interfere with their religious practices in violation of the Free Exercise Clause of the First Amendment. Following a trial, the District Court granted the requested injunctive relief. The court found that "use of the high country is essential to [respondents'] 'World Renewal' ceremonies . . . which constitute the heart of the Northwest Indian religious belief system," and that "' [i]ntrusions on the sanctity of the Blue Creek high country are . . . potentially destructive of the very core of Northwest [Indian] religious beliefs and practices.'" Concluding that these burdens on respondents' religious practices were sufficient to trigger the protections of the Free Exercise Clause, the court found that the interests served by the G-O road and the management plan were insufficient to justify those burdens. In particular, the court found that the road would not improve access to timber resources in the Blue Creek Unit and indeed was unnecessary to the harvesting of that timber; that it would not significantly improve the administration of the Six Rivers National Forest; and that it would increase recreational access only marginally, and at the expense of the very pristine environment that makes the area suitable for primitive recreational use in the first place. The court further found that the unconnected segments of the road had independent utility, and that although completion of the Chimney Rock segment would reduce timber-hauling costs, it would not generate new jobs but would instead merely shift work from one area of the region to another. Finally, in enjoining the proposed harvesting activities, the court found that the Blue Creek Unit's timber resources were but a small fraction of those located in the entire National Forest and that the local timber industry would not suffer seriously if access to this fraction were foreclosed. Ibid.

While the case was pending on appeal before the Court of Appeals for the Ninth Circuit, Congress passed the California Wilderness Act of 1984, which designates most of the Blue Creek Unit a wilderness area, and thus precludes logging and all other commercial activities in most of the area covered by the Forest Service's management plan. Thereafter, the Court of Appeals affirmed the District Court's determination that the proposed harvesting and construction activities violated respondents' constitutional rights. Recognizing that the high country is "indispensable" to the religious lives of the approximately 5,000 Tribe members who reside in the area, the court concluded "that the proposed government operations would virtually destroy the . . . Indians' ability to practice their religion." Like the lower court, the Court of Appeals found the Government's interests in building the road and permitting limited timber harvesting—interests which of course were considerably undermined by passage of the California Wilderness Act—did not justify the destruction of respondents' religion.

II

The Court does not for a moment suggest that the interests served by the G-O road are in any way compelling, or that they outweigh the destructive effect construction of the road will have on respondents' religious practices. Instead, the Court embraces the Government's contention that its prerogative as landowner should always take precedence over a claim that a particular use of federal property infringes religious practices. Attempting to justify this rule, the Court argues that the First Amendment bars only outright prohibitions, indirect coercion, and penalties on the free exercise of religion. All other "incidental effects of government programs," it concludes, even those "which may make it more difficult to practice certain religions but which have no tendency to coerce individuals into acting contrary to their religious beliefs," simply do not give rise to constitutional concerns. Since our recognition nearly half a century ago that restraints on religious conduct implicate the concerns of the Free Exercise Clause, we have never suggested that the protections of the guarantee are limited to so narrow a range of governmental burdens. The land-use decision challenged here will restrain respondents from practicing their religion as surely and as completely as any of the governmental actions we have struck down in the past, and the Court's efforts simply to define away respondents' injury as nonconstitutional are both unjustified and ultimately unpersuasive.

A

The Court ostensibly finds support for its narrow formulation of religious burdens in our decisions in *Hobbie v. Unemployment Appeals Comm'n of Fla.* (1987), *Thomas v. Review Bd., Indiana Employment Security Division* (1981), and *Sherbert v.*

Verner (1963). In those cases, the laws at issue forced individuals to choose between adhering to specific religious tenets and forfeiting unemployment benefits on the one hand, and accepting work repugnant to their religious beliefs on the other. The religions involved, therefore, lent themselves to the coercion analysis the Court espouses today, for they proscribed certain conduct such as munitions work (Thomas) or working on Saturdays (Sherbert, Hobbie) that the unemployment benefits laws effectively compelled. In sustaining the challenges to these laws, however, we nowhere suggested that such coercive compulsion exhausted the range of religious burdens recognized under the Free Exercise Clause.

Indeed, in *Wisconsin v. Yoder* (1972), we struck down a state compulsory school attendance law on free exercise grounds not so much because of the affirmative coercion the law exerted on individual religious practitioners, but because of "the impact that compulsory high school attendance could have on the continued survival of Amish communities." Like respondents here, the Amish view life as pervasively religious and their faith accordingly dictates their entire lifestyle. Detailed as their religious rules are, however, the parents in Yoder did not argue that their religion expressly proscribed public education beyond the eighth grade; rather, they objected to the law because "the values . . . of the modern secondary school are in sharp conflict with the fundamental mode of life mandated by the Amish religion." By exposing Amish children "to a 'worldly' influence in conflict with their beliefs," and by removing those children "from their community, physically and emotionally, during the crucial and formative adolescent period of life" when Amish beliefs are inculcated, the compulsory school law posed "a very real threat of undermining the Amish community and religious practice." Admittedly, this threat arose from the compulsory nature of the law at issue, but it was the "impact" on religious practice itself, not the source of that impact, that led us to invalidate the law.

I thus cannot accept the Court's premise that the form of the government's restraint on religious practice, rather than its effect, controls our constitutional analysis. Respondents here have demonstrated that construction of the G-O road will completely frustrate the practice of their religion, for as the lower courts found, the proposed logging and construction activities will virtually destroy respondents' religion, and will therefore necessarily force them into abandoning those practices altogether. Indeed, the Government's proposed activities will restrain religious practice to a far greater degree here than in any of the cases cited by the Court today. None of the religious adherents in *Hobbie*, *Thomas*, and *Sherbert*, for example, claimed or could have claimed that the denial of unemployment benefits rendered the practice of their religions impossible; at most, the challenged laws made those practices more expensive. Here, in stark contrast, respondents have claimed—and proved—that the desecration of the high country will prevent religious leaders from attaining the religious power or medicine indispensable to the success of virtually all their rituals and ceremonies. Similarly, in *Yoder* the compulsory school law threatened to "undermin[e] the Amish community and religious practice," and thus to force adherents to "abandon belief . . . or . . . to migrate to some other and more tolerant region." Here the threat posed by the desecration of sacred lands that are indisputably essential to respondents' religious practices is both more direct and more substantial than that raised by a compulsory school law that simply exposed Amish children to an alien value system. And of course respondents here do not even have the option, however unattractive it might be, of migrating to more hospitable locales; the site-specific nature of their belief system renders it nontransportable.

Ultimately, the Court's coercion test turns on a distinction between governmental actions that compel affirmative conduct inconsistent with religious belief, and those governmental actions that prevent conduct consistent with religious belief. In my view, such a distinction is without constitutional significance. The crucial word in the constitutional text, as the Court itself acknowledges, is "prohibit" a comprehensive term that in no way suggests that the intended protection is aimed only at governmental actions that coerce affirmative conduct. Nor does the Court's distinction comport with the principles animating the constitutional guarantee: religious freedom is threatened no less by governmental action that makes the practice of one's chosen faith impossible than by governmental programs that pressure one to engage in conduct inconsistent with religious beliefs. The Court attempts to explain the line it draws by arguing that the protections of the Free Exercise Clause "cannot depend on measuring the effects of a governmental action on a religious objector's spiritual development," for in a society as diverse as ours, the Government cannot help but offend the "religious needs and desires" of some citizens. While I agree that governmental action that simply offends religious sensibilities may not be challenged under the Clause, we have recognized that laws that affect spiritual development by impeding the integration of children into the religious community or by increasing the expense of adherence to religious principles—in short, laws that frustrate or inhibit religious practice—trigger the protections of the constitutional guarantee. Both common sense and our prior cases teach us, therefore, that governmental action that makes the practice of a given faith more difficult necessarily penalizes that practice and thereby tends to prevent adherence to religious belief. The harm to the practitioners is the same regardless of the manner in which the government restrains their religious expression, and the Court's fear that an "effects" test will permit religious adherents to challenge governmental actions they merely find "offensive" in no way justifies its refusal to recognize the constitutional injury citizens suffer when governmental action not only offends but actually restrains their religious practices. Here, respondents have demonstrated that the Government's proposed activities will completely prevent them from practicing their religion, and such a showing, no less than those made out in *Hobbie*, *Thomas*, *Sherbert*, and *Yoder*, entitles them to the protections of the Free Exercise Clause.

B

Nor can I agree with the Court's assertion that respondents' constitutional claim is foreclosed by our decision in *Bowen v. Roy* (1986). There, applicants for certain welfare benefits objected to the use of a Social Security number in connection with the administration of their 2-year-old daughter's application for benefits, contending that such use would "rob the [child's] spirit" and thus interfere with her spiritual development. In rejecting that challenge, we stated that "[t]he Free Exercise Clause simply cannot be understood to require the Government to conduct its own internal affairs in ways that comport with the religious beliefs of particular citizens." Accordingly, we explained that Roy could

> no more prevail on his religious objection to the Government's use of a Social Security number for his daughter than he could on a sincere religious objection to the size or color of the Government's filing cabinets. The Free Exercise Clause affords an individual protection from certain forms of governmental compulsion; it does not afford an individual a right to dictate the conduct of the Government's internal procedures.

Today the Court professes an inability to differentiate *Roy* from the present case, suggesting that "[t]he building of a road or the harvesting of timber on publicly owned land cannot meaningfully be distinguished from the use of a Social Security number." I find this inability altogether remarkable. In Roy, we repeatedly stressed the "internal" nature of the Government practice at issue: noting that *Roy* objected to "the widespread use of the social security number by the federal or state governments in their computer systems," we likened the use of such recordkeeping numbers to decisions concerning the purchase of office equipment. When the Government processes information, of course, it acts in a purely internal manner, and any free exercise challenge to such internal recordkeeping in effect seeks to dictate how the Government conducts its own affairs.

Federal land-use decisions, by contrast, are likely to have substantial external effects that government decisions concerning office furniture and information storage obviously will not, and they are correspondingly subject to public scrutiny and public challenge in a host of ways that office equipment purchases are not. Indeed, in the American Indian Religious Freedom Act (AIRFA), Congress expressly recognized the adverse impact land-use decisions and other governmental actions frequently have on the site-specific religious practices of Native Americans, and the Act accordingly directs agencies to consult with Native American religious leaders before taking actions that might impair those practices. Although I agree that the Act does not create any judicially enforceable rights, the absence of any private right of action in no way undermines the statute's significance as an express congressional determination that federal land management decisions are not "internal" Government "procedures," but are instead governmental actions that can and indeed are likely to burden Native American religious practices. That such decisions should be subject to constitutional challenge, and potential constitutional limitations, should hardly come as a surprise.

The Court today, however, ignores *Roy*'s emphasis on the internal nature of the Government practice at issue there, and instead construes that case as further support for the proposition that governmental action that does not coerce conduct inconsistent with religious faith simply does not implicate the concerns of the Free Exercise Clause. That such a reading is wholly untenable, however, is demonstrated by the cruelly surreal result it produces here: governmental action that will virtually destroy a religion is nevertheless deemed not to "burden" that religion. Moreover, in AIRFA Congress explicitly acknowledged that federal "policies and regulations" could and often did "intrud[e] upon [and] interfer[e] with" site-specific Native American religious ceremonies, and in *Roy* we recognized that this Act—"with its emphasis on protecting the freedom to believe, express, and exercise a religion—accurately identifies the mission of the Free Exercise Clause itself." Ultimately, in Roy we concluded that, however much the Government's recordkeeping system may have offended Roy's sincere religious sensibilities, he could not challenge that system under the Free Exercise Clause because the Government's practice did not "in any degree impair Roy's 'freedom to believe, express, and exercise' his religion." That determination distinguishes the injury at issue here, which the Court finds so "remarkably similar" to *Roy*'s, for respondents have made an uncontroverted showing that the proposed construction and logging activities will impair their freedom to exercise their religion in the greatest degree imaginable, and Congress has "accurately identifie[d]" such injuries as falling within the scope of the Free Exercise Clause. The Court's reading of *Roy*, therefore, simply cannot be squared with our endorsement—in that very same case—of this congressional determination. More important, it lends no support to the Court's efforts to narrow both the reach and promise of the Free Exercise Clause itself.

C

In the final analysis, the Court's refusal to recognize the constitutional dimension of respondents' injuries stems from its concern that acceptance of respondents' claim could potentially strip the Government of its ability to manage and use vast tracts of federal property. In addition, the nature of respondents' site-specific religious practices raises the specter of future suits in which Native Americans seek to exclude all human activity from such areas. These concededly legitimate concerns lie at the very heart of this case, which represents yet another stress point in the longstanding conflict between two disparate cultures—the dominant Western culture, which views land in terms of ownership and use, and that of Native Americans, in which concepts of private property are not only alien, but contrary to a belief system that holds land sacred. Rather than address this conflict in any meaningful fashion, however, the Court disclaims all responsibility for balancing these competing and potentially irreconcilable interests, choosing instead to turn this difficult task over to the Federal Legislature. Such an abdication is more than merely indefensible as an institutional matter: by defining respondents' injury as "nonconstitutional," the Court has effectively bestowed on one party to this conflict the unilateral authority to resolve all future disputes in its favor, subject only to the Court's toothless exhortation to be "sensitive" to affected religions. In my view, however, Native Americans deserve—and the Constitution demands—more than this.

Prior to today's decision, several Courts of Appeals had attempted to fashion a test that accommodates the competing "demands" placed on federal property by the two cultures. Recognizing that the Government normally enjoys plenary authority over federal lands, the Courts of Appeals required Native Americans to demonstrate that any land-use decisions they challenged involved lands that were "central" or "indispensable" to their religious practices. Although this requirement limits the potential number of free exercise claims that might be brought to federal land management decisions, and thus forestalls the possibility that the Government will find itself ensnared in a host of Lilliputian lawsuits, it has been criticized as inherently ethnocentric, for it incorrectly assumes that Native American belief systems ascribe religious significance to land in a traditionally Western hierarchical manner. It is frequently the case in constitutional litigation, however, that courts are called upon to balance interests that are not readily translated into rough equivalents. At their most absolute, the competing claims that both the Government and Native Americans assert in federal land are fundamentally incompatible, and unless they are tempered by compromise, mutual accommodation will remain impossible.

I believe it appropriate, therefore, to require some showing of "centrality" before the Government can be required either to come forward with a compelling justification for its proposed use of federal land or to forgo that use altogether. "Centrality," however, should not be equated with the survival or extinction of the religion itself. In Yoder, for example, we treated the objection to the compulsory school attendance of adolescents as "central" to the Amish faith even though such attendance did not prevent or otherwise render the practice of that religion impossible, and instead simply threatened to "undermine" that faith. Because of their perceptions of and relationship with the natural world, Native Americans consider all land sacred. Nevertheless, the Theodoratus Report reveals that respondents here deemed certain lands more powerful and more directly related to their religious practices than others. Thus, in my view, while Native Americans need not demonstrate, as respondents did here, that the Government's land-use decision will assuredly eradicate their faith, I do not think it is enough to allege simply that the land in question is held sacred. Rather, adherents challenging a proposed use of federal land should be required to show that the decision poses a substantial and realistic threat of frustrating their religious practices. Once such a showing is made, the burden should shift to the Government to come forward with a compelling state interest sufficient to justify the infringement of those practices.

The Court today suggests that such an approach would place courts in the untenable position of deciding which practices and beliefs are "central" to a given faith and which are not, and invites the prospect of judges advising some religious adherents that they "misunderstand their own religious beliefs." In fact, however, courts need not undertake any such inquiries: like all other religious adherents, Native Americans would be the arbiters of which practices are central to their faith, subject only to the normal requirement that their claims be genuine and sincere. The question for the courts, then, is not whether the Native American claimants understand their own religion, but rather whether they have discharged their burden of demonstrating, as the Amish did with respect to the compulsory school law in Yoder, that the land-use decision poses a substantial and realistic threat of undermining or frustrating their religious practices. Ironically, the Court's apparent solicitude for the integrity of religious belief and its desire to forestall the possibility that courts might second-guess the claims of religious adherents leads to far greater inequities than those the Court postulates: today's ruling sacrifices a religion at least as old as the Nation itself, along with the spiritual well-being of its approximately 5,000 adherents, so that the Forest Service can build a 6-mile segment of road that two lower courts found had only the most marginal and speculative utility, both to the Government itself and to the private lumber interests that might conceivably use it.

Similarly, the Court's concern that the claims of Native Americans will place "religious servitudes" upon vast tracts of federal property cannot justify its refusal to recognize the constitutional injury respondents will suffer here. It is true, as the Court notes, that respondents' religious use of the high country requires privacy and solitude. The fact remains, however, that respondents have never asked the Forest Service to exclude others from the area. Should respondents or any other group seek to force the Government to protect their religious practices from the interference of private parties, such a demand would implicate not only the concerns of the Free Exercise Clause, but also those of the Establishment Clause as well. That case, however, is most assuredly not before us today, and in any event cannot justify the Court's refusal to acknowledge that the injuries respondents will suffer as a result of the Government's proposed activities are sufficient to state a constitutional cause of action.

III

Today, the Court holds that a federal land-use decision that promises to destroy an entire religion does not burden the practice of that faith in a manner recognized by the Free Exercise Clause. Having thus stripped respondents and all other Native Americans of any constitutional protection against perhaps the most serious threat to their age-old religious practices, and indeed to their entire way of life, the Court assures us that nothing in its decision "should be read to encourage governmental insensitivity to the religious needs of any citizen." I find it difficult, however, to imagine conduct more insensitive to religious needs than the Government's determination to build a marginally useful road in the face of uncontradicted evidence that the road will render the practice of respondents' religion impossible. Nor do I believe that respondents will derive any solace from the knowledge that although the practice of their religion will become "more difficult" as a result of the Government's actions, they remain free to maintain their religious beliefs. Given today's ruling, that freedom amounts to nothing more than the right to believe that their religion will be destroyed. The safeguarding of such a hollow freedom not only makes a mockery of the " 'policy of the United States to protect and preserve for American Indians their inherent right of freedom to believe, express, and exercise the[ir] traditional religions,' " it fails utterly to accord with the dictates of the First Amendment.

I dissent.

Source: 485 U.S. 439.

66 Native American Graves Protection and Repatriation Act, November 16, 1990

In the 1980s it came to light that federal agencies had possession of hundreds of thousands of Native American human remains. After a concerted effort by American Indian organizations and leaders, Congress enacted the Native American Graves Protection and Repatriation Act in 1990 (NAGPRA). The act had four basic provisions: federal agencies and private museums receiving federal monies must inventory their collections of American Indian funerary objects and human remains, and then the Indian nation of origin, if known, must be notified and, if it requests, the objects returned; native communities are the rightful owners of these objects; trafficking in these objects is illegal; and federal agencies and private museums must develop an itemized list of their Native American funerary and sacred objects so that any Native American nation proving possession can request and demand their return.

An Act to provide for the protection of Native American graves, and for other purposes.

SECTION 1. SHORT TITLE.

This Act may be cited as the "Native American Graves Protection and Repatriation Act".

SEC. 2. DEFINITIONS.

For purposes of this Act, the term—

(1) "burial site" means any natural or prepared physical location, whether originally below, on, or above the surface of the earth, into which as a part of the death rite or ceremony of a culture, individual human remains are deposited.

(2) "cultural affiliation" means that there is a relationship of shared group identity which can be reasonably traced historically or prehistorically between a pres-

ent day Indian tribe or Native Hawaiian organization and an identifiable earlier group.

(3) "cultural items" means human remains and—

(A) "associated funerary objects" which shall mean objects that, as a part of the death rite or ceremony of a culture, are reasonably believed to have been placed with individual human remains either at the time of death or later, and both the human remains and associated funerary objects are presently in the possession or control of a Federal agency or museum, except that other items exclusively made for burial purposes or to contain human remains shall be considered as associated funerary objects.

(B) "unassociated funerary objects" which shall mean objects that, as a part of the death rite or ceremony of a culture, are reasonably believed to have been placed with individual human remains either at the time of death or later, where the remains are not in the possession or control of the Federal agency or museum and the objects can be identified by a preponderance of the evidence as related to specific individuals or families or to known human remains or, by a preponderance of the evidence, as having been removed from a specific burial site of an individual culturally affiliated with a particular Indian tribe,

(C) "sacred objects" which shall mean specific ceremonial objects which are needed by traditional Native American religious leaders for the practice of traditional Native American religions by their present day adherents, and

(D) "cultural patrimony" which shall mean an object having ongoing historical, traditional, or cultural importance central to the Native American group or culture itself, rather than property owned by an individual Native American, and which, therefore, cannot be alienated, appropriated, or conveyed by any individual regardless of whether or not the individual is a member of the Indian tribe or Native Hawaiian organization and such object shall have been considered inalienable by such Native American group at the time the object was separated from such group.

(4) "Federal agency" means any department, agency, or instrumentality of the United States. Such term does not include the Smithsonian Institution.

(5) "Federal lands" means any land other than tribal lands which are controlled or owned by the United States, including lands selected by but not yet conveyed to Alaska Native Corporations and groups organized pursuant to the Alaska Native Claims Settlement Act of 1971.

(6) "Hui Malama I Na Kupuna O Hawai'i Nei" means the nonprofit, Native Hawaiian organization incorporated under the laws of the State of Hawaii by that name on April 17, 1989, for the purpose of providing guidance and expertise in decisions dealing with Native Hawaiian cultural issues, particularly burial issues.

(7) "Indian tribe" means any tribe, band, nation, or other organized group or community of Indians, including any Alaska Native village (as defined in, or established pursuant to, the Alaska Native Claims Settlement Act), which is recognized as eligible for the special programs and services provided by the United States to Indians because of their status as Indians.

(8) "museum" means any institution or State or local government agency (including any institution of higher learning) that receives Federal funds and has possession of, or control over, Native American cultural items. Such term does not include the Smithsonian Institution or any other Federal agency.

(9) "Native American" means of, or relating to, a tribe, people, or culture that is indigenous to the United States.

(10) "Native Hawaiian" means any individual who is a descendant of the aboriginal people who, prior to 1778, occupied and exercised sovereignty in the area that now constitutes the State of Hawaii.

(11) "Native Hawaiian organization" means any organization which—

(A) serves and represents the interests of Native Hawaiians,

(B) has as a primary and stated purpose the provision of services to Native Hawaiians, and

(C) has expertise in Native Hawaiian Affairs, and shall include the Office of Hawaiian Affairs and Hui Malama I Na Kupuna O Hawai'i Nei.

(12) "Office of Hawaiian Affairs" means the Office of Hawaiian Affairs established by the constitution of the State of Hawaii.

(13) "right of possession" means possession obtained with the voluntary consent of an individual or group that had authority of alienation. The original acquisition of a Native American unassociated funerary object, sacred object or object of cultural patrimony from an Indian tribe or Native Hawaiian organization with the voluntary consent of an individual or group with authority to alienate such object is deemed to give right of possession of that object, unless the phrase so defined would, as applied in section 7(c), result in a Fifth Amendment taking by the United States as determined by the United States Claims Court pursuant to 28 U.S.C. 1491 in which event the "right of possession" shall be as provided under otherwise applicable property law. The original acquisition of Native American human remains and associated funerary objects which were excavated, exhumed, or otherwise obtained with full knowledge and consent of the next of kin or the official governing body of the appropriate culturally affiliated Indian tribe or Native Hawaiian organization is deemed to give right of possession to those remains.

(14) "Secretary" means the Secretary of the Interior.

(15) "tribal land" means—

(A) all lands within the exterior boundaries of any Indian reservation;

(B) all dependent Indian communities;

(C) any lands administered for the benefit of Native Hawaiians pursuant to the Hawaiian Homes Commission Act, 1920, and section 4 of Public Law 86-3.

SEC 3. OWNERSHIP.

(a) NATIVE AMERICAN HUMAN REMAINS AND OBJECTS.—The ownership or control of Native American cultural items which are excavated or discovered on Federal or tribal lands after the date of enactment of this Act shall be (with priority given in the order listed)—

(1) in the case of Native American human remains and associated funerary objects, in the lineal descendants of the Native American; or

(2) in any case in which such lineal descendants cannot be ascertained, and in the case of unassociated funerary objects, sacred objects, and objects of cultural patrimony—

(A) in the Indian tribe or Native Hawaiian organization on whose tribal land such objects or remains were discovered;

Claims.

(B) in the Indian tribe or Native Hawaiian organization which has the closest cultural affiliation with such remains or objects and which, upon notice, states a claim for such remains or objects; or

(C) if the cultural affiliation of the objects cannot be reasonably ascertained and if the objects were discovered on Federal land that is recognized by a final judgment of the Indian Claims Commission or the United States Court of Claims as the aboriginal land of some Indian tribe—

(1) in the Indian tribe that is recognized as aboriginally occupying the area in which the objects were discovered, if upon notice, such tribe states a claim for such remains or objects, or

(2) if it can be shown by a preponderance of the evidence that a different tribe has a stronger cultural relationship with the remains or objects than the tribe or organization specified in paragraph (1), in the Indian tribe that has the strongest demonstrated relationship, if upon notice, such tribe states a claim for such remains or objects.

Regulations.

(b) UNCLAIMED NATIVE AMERICAN HUMAN REMAINS AND OBJECTS. Native American cultural items not claimed under subsection (a) shall be disposed of in accordance with regulations promulgated by the Secretary—in consultation with the review committee established under section 8—Native American groups, representatives of museums and the scientific community.

(c) INTENTIONAL EXCAVATION AND REMOVAL OF NATIVE AMERICAN HUMAN REMAINS AND OBJECTS.—The intentional removal from or excavation of Native American cultural items from Federal or tribal lands for purposes of discovery, study, or removal of such items is permitted only if—

(1) such items are excavated or removed pursuant to a permit issued under section 4 of the Archaeological Resources Protection Act of 1979 (93 Stat. 721; 16 U.S.C. 470aa et seq.) which shall be consistent with this Act;

(2) such items are excavated or removed after consultation with or, in the case of tribal lands, consent of the appropriate (if any) Indian tribe or Native Hawaiian organization;

(3) the ownership and right of control of the disposition of such items shall be as provided in subsections (a) and (b); and

(4) proof of consultation or consent under paragraph (2) is shown.

(d) INADVERTENT DISCOVERY OF NATIVE AMERICAN REMAINS AND OBJECTS.—(1) Any person who knows, or has reason to know, that such person has discovered Native American cultural items on Federal or tribal lands after the date of enactment of this Act shall notify, in writing, the Secretary of the department, or head of any other agency or instrumentality of the United States, having primary management authority with respect to Federal lands and the appropriate Indian tribe or Native Hawaiian organization with respect to tribal lands, if known or readily ascertainable, and, in the case of lands that have been selected by an Alaska Native Corporation or group organized pursuant to the Alaska Native Claims Settlement Act of 1971, the appropriate corporation or group. If the discovery occurred in connection with an activity, including (but not limited to) construction, mining, logging, and agriculture, the person shall cease the activity in the area of the discovery, make a reasonable effort to protect the items discovered before resuming such activity, and provide notice under this subsection. Following the notification under this subsection, and upon certification by the Secretary of the department or the head of any agency or instrumentality of the United States or the appropriate Indian tribe or Native Hawaiian organization that notification has been received, the activity may resume after 30 days of such certification. (2) The disposition of and control over any cultural items excavated or removed under this subsection shall be determined as provided for in this section. (3) If the Secretary of the Interior consents, the responsibilities (in whole or in part) under paragraphs (1) and (2) of the Secretary of any department (other than the Department of the Interior) or the head of any other agency or instrumentality may be delegated to the Secretary with respect to any land managed by such other Secretary or agency head.

(e) RELINQUISHMENT.—Nothing in this section shall prevent the governing body of an Indian tribe or Native Hawaiian organization from expressly relinquishing control over any Native American human remains, or title to or control over any funerary object, or sacred object.

SEC. 4. ILLEGAL TRAFFICKING.

(a) ILLEGAL TRAFFICKING.—Chapter 53 of title 18, United States Code, is amended by adding at the end thereof the following new section:

"1170. Illegal Trafficking in Native American Human Remains and Cultural Items

"(a) Whoever knowingly sells, purchases, uses for profit, or transports for sale or profit, the human remains of a Native American without the right of possession to those remains as provided in the Native American Graves Protection and Repatriation Act shall be fined in accordance with this title, or imprisoned not more than 12 months, or both, and in the case of a second or subsequent violation, be fined in accordance with this title, or imprisoned not more than 5 years, or both.

"(b) Whoever knowingly sells, purchases, uses for profit, or transports for sale or profit any Native American cultural items obtained in violation of the Native American Grave Protection and Repatriation Act shall be fined in accordance with this title, imprisoned not more than one year, or both, and in the case of a second or subsequent violation, be fined in accordance with this title, imprisoned not more than 5 years, or both.".

(b) TABLE OF CONTENTS.—The table of contents for chapter 53 of title 18, United States Code, is amended by adding at the end thereof the following new item:

"1170. Illegal Trafficking in Native American Human Remains and Cultural Items.".

SEC. 5. INVENTORY FOR HUMAN REMAINS AND ASSOCIATED FUNERARY OBJECTS.

(a) IN GENERAL.—Each Federal agency and each museum which has possession or control over holdings or collections of Native American human remains and associated funerary objects shall compile an inventory of such items and, to the extent possible based on information possessed by such museum or Federal agency, identify the geographical and cultural affiliation of such item.

(b) REQUIREMENTS.—(1) The inventories and identifications required under subsection (a) shall be—

(A) completed in consultation with tribal government and Native Hawaiian organization officials and traditional religious leaders;

(B) completed by not later than the date that is 5 years after the date of enactment of this Act, and

(C) made available both during the time they are being conducted and afterward to a review committee established under section 8.

(2) Upon request by an Indian tribe or Native Hawaiian organization which receives or should have received notice, a museum or Federal agency shall supply additional available documentation to supplement the information required by subsection (a) of this section. The term "documentation" means a summary of existing museum or Federal agency records, including inventories or catalogues, relevant studies, or other pertinent data for the limited purpose of determining the geographical origin, cultural affiliation, and basic facts surrounding acquisition and accession of Native American human remains and associated funerary objects subject to this section. Such term does not mean, and this Act shall not be construed to be an authorization for, the initiation of new scientific studies of such remains and associated funerary objects or other means of acquiring or preserving additional scientific information from such remains and objects.

(c) EXTENSION OF TIME FOR INVENTORY.—Any museum which has made a good faith effort to carry out an inventory and identification under this section, but which has been unable to complete the process, may appeal to the Secretary for an extension of the time requirements set forth in subsection (b)(1)(B). The Secretary may extend such time requirements for any such museum upon a finding of good faith effort. An indication of good faith shall include the development of a plan to carry out the inventory and identification process.

(d) NOTIFICATION—(1) If the cultural affiliation of any particular Native American human remains or associated funerary objects is determined pursuant to this section, the Federal agency or museum concerned shall, not later than 6 months after the completion of the inventory, notify the affected Indian tribes or Native Hawaiian organizations.

(2) The notice required by paragraph (1) shall include information—

(A) which identifies each Native American human remains or associated funerary objects and the circumstances surrounding its acquisition; (B) which lists the human remains or associated funerary objects that are clearly identifiable as to tribal origin; and

(C) which lists the Native American human remains and associated funerary objects that are not clearly identifiable as being culturally affiliated with that Indian tribe or Native Hawaiian organization, but which, given the totality of circumstances surrounding acquisition of the remains or objects, are determined by a reasonable belief to be remains or objects culturally affiliated with the Indian tribe or Native Hawaiian organization.

(3) A copy of each notice provided under paragraph (1) shall be sent to the Secretary who shall publish each notice in the Federal Register.

(e) INVENTORY.—For the purposes of this section, the term "inventory" means a simple itemized list that summarizes the information called for by this section.

SEC. 6. SUMMARY FOR UNASSOCIATED FUNERARY OBJECTS, SACRED OBJECTS, AND CULTURAL PATRIMONY.

(a) IN GENERAL.—Each Federal agency or museum which has museums in possession or control over holdings or collections of Native American unassociated funerary objects, sacred objects, or objects of cultural patrimony shall provide a written summary of such objects based upon available information held by such agency or museum. The summary shall describe the scope of the collection, kinds of objects included, reference to geographical location, means and period of acquisition and cultural affiliation, where readily ascertainable.

(b) REQUIREMENTS.— (1) The summary required under subsection (a) shall be—

(A) in lieu of an object-by-object inventory;

(B) followed by consultation with tribal government and Native Hawaiian organization officials and traditional religious leaders; and

(C) completed by not later than the date that is 3 years after the date of enactment of this Act.

(2) Upon request, Indian Tribes and Native Hawaiian organizations shall have access to records, catalogues, relevant studies or other pertinent data for the limited purposes of determining the geographic origin, cultural affiliation, and basic facts surrounding acquisition and accession of Native American objects subject to this section. Such information shall be provided in a reasonable manner to be agreed upon by all parties.

SEC. 7. REPATRIATION.

(a) REPATRIATION OF NATIVE AMERICAN HUMAN REMAINS AND OBJECTS POSSESSED OR CONTROLLED BY FEDERAL AGENCIES AND MUSEUMS.—(1) If, pursuant to section 5, the cultural affiliation of Native American human remains and associated funerary objects with a particular Indian tribe or Native Hawaiian organization is established, then the Federal agency or museum, upon the request of a known lineal descendant of the Native American or of the tribe or organization and pursuant to subsections (b) and (e) of this section, shall expeditiously return such remains and associated funerary objects.

(2) If, pursuant to section 6, the cultural affiliation with a particular Indian tribe or Native Hawaiian organization is shown with respect to unassociated funerary objects, sacred objects or objects of cultural patrimony, then the Federal agency or museum, upon the request of the Indian tribe or Native Hawaiian organization and pursuant to subsections (b), (c) and (e) of this section, shall expeditiously return such objects.

(3) The return of cultural items covered by this Act shall be in consultation with the requesting lineal descendant or tribe or organization to determine the place and manner of delivery of such items.

(4) Where cultural affiliation of Native American human remains and funerary objects has not been established in an inventory prepared pursuant to section 5, or the summary pursuant to section 6, or where Native American human remains and funerary objects are not included upon any such inventory, then, upon request and pursuant to subsections (b) and (e) and, in the case of unassociated funerary objects, subsection (c), such Native American human remains and funerary objects shall be expeditiously returned where the requesting Indian tribe or Native Hawaiian organization can show cultural affiliation by a preponderance of the evidence based upon geographical, kinship, biological, archaeological, anthropological, linguistic, folkloric, oral traditional, historical, or other relevant information or expert opinion.

(5) Upon request and pursuant to subsections (b), (c) and (e), sacred objects and objects of cultural patrimony shall be expeditiously returned where—

(A) the requesting party is the direct lineal descendant of an individual who owned the sacred object;

(B) the requesting Indian tribe or Native Hawaiian organization can show that the object was owned or controlled by the tribe or organization; or

(C) the requesting Indian tribe or Native Hawaiian organization can show that the sacred object was owned or controlled by a member thereof, provided that in the case where a sacred object was owned by a member thereof, there are no identifiable lineal descendants of said member or the lineal descendant, upon notice, have failed to make a claim for the object under this Act.

(b) SCIENTIFIC STUDY.—If the lineal descendant, Indian tribe, or Native Hawaiian organization requests the return of culturally affiliated Native American cultural items, the Federal agency or museum shall expeditiously return such items unless such items are indispensable for completion of a specific scientific study, the outcome of which would be of major benefit to the United States. Such items shall be returned by no later than 90 days after the date on which the scientific study is completed.

(c) STANDARD OF REPATRIATION.—If a known lineal descendant or an Indian tribe or Native Hawaiian organization requests the return of Native American unassociated funerary objects, sacred objects or objects of cultural patrimony pursuant to this Act and presents evidence which, if standing alone before the introduction of evidence to the contrary, would support a finding that the Federal agency or museum did not have the right of possession, then such agency or museum shall return such objects unless it can overcome such inference and prove that it has a right of possession to the objects.

(d) SHARING OF INFORMATION BY FEDERAL AGENCIES AND MUSEUMS.—Any Federal agency or museum shall share what information it does possess regarding the object in question with the known lineal descendant, Indian tribe, or Native Hawaiian organization to assist in making a claim under this section.

(e) COMPETING CLAIMS.—Where there are multiple requests for repatriation of any cultural item and, after complying with the requirements of this Act, the Federal agency or museum cannot clearly determine which requesting party is the most appropriate claimant, the agency or museum may retain such item until the requesting parties agree upon its disposition or the dispute is otherwise resolved pursuant to the provisions of this Act or by a court of competent jurisdiction.

(f) MUSEUM OBLIGATION.—Any museum which repatriates any item in good faith pursuant to this Act shall not be liable for claims by an aggrieved party or for claims of breach of fiduciary duty, public trust, or violations of state law that are inconsistent with the provisions of this Act.

SEC. 8. REVIEW COMMITTEE.

(a) ESTABLISHMENT.—Within 120 days after the date of enactment of this Act, the Secretary shall establish a committee to monitor and review the implementation of the inventory and identification process and repatriation activities required under sections 5, 6 and 7.

(b) MEMBERSHIP—(1) The Committee established under subsection (a) shall be composed of 7 members,

(A) 3 of whom shall be appointed by the Secretary from nominations submitted by Indian tribes, Native Hawaiian organizations, and traditional Native American religious leaders with at least 2 of such persons being traditional Indian religious leaders;

(B) 3 of whom shall be appointed by the Secretary from nominations submitted by national museum organizations and scientific organizations; and

(C) 1 who shall be appointed by the Secretary from a list of persons developed and consented to by all of the members appointed pursuant to subparagraphs (A) and (B).

(2) The Secretary may not appoint Federal officers or employees to the committee.

(3) In the event vacancies shall occur, such vacancies shall be filled by the Secretary in the same manner as the original appointment within 90 days of the occurrence of such vacancy.

(4) Members of the committee established under subsection (a) shall serve without pay, but shall be reimbursed at a rate equal to the daily rate for GS-18 of the General Schedule for each day (including travel time) for which the member is actually engaged in committee business. Each member shall receive travel expenses, including per diem in lieu of subsistence, in accordance with sections 5702 and 5703 of title 5, United States Code.

(c) RESPONSIBILITIES.—The committee established under subsection (a) shall be responsible for—

(1) designating one of the members of the committee as chairman;

(2) monitoring the inventory and identification process conducted under sections 5 and 6 to ensure a fair, objective consideration and assessment of all available relevant information and evidence;

(3) upon the request of any affected party, reviewing and making findings related to—

(A) the identity or cultural affiliation of cultural items, or

(B) the return of such items;

(4) facilitating the resolution of any disputes among Indian tribes, Native Hawaiian organizations, or lineal descendants and Federal agencies or museums relating to the return of such items including convening the parties to the dispute if deemed desirable;

(5) compiling an inventory of culturally unidentifiable human remains that are in the possession or control of each Federal agency and museum and recommending specific actions for developing a process for disposition of such remains;

(6) consulting with Indian tribes and Native Hawaiian organizations and museums on matters within the scope of the work of the committee affecting such tribes or organizations;

(7) consulting with the Secretary in the development of regulations to carry out this Act;

(8) performing such other related functions as the Secretary may assign to the committee; and

(9) making recommendations, if appropriate, regarding future care of cultural items which are to be repatriated.

(d) Any records and findings made by the review committee pursuant to this Act relating to the identity or cultural affiliation of any cultural items and the return of such items may be admissible in any action brought under section 15 of this Act.

(e) RECOMMENDATIONS AND REPORT.—The committee shall make the recommendations under paragraph (c)(5) in consultation with Indian tribes and Native Hawaiian organizations and appropriate scientific and museum groups.

(f) ACCESS.—The Secretary shall ensure that the committee established under subsection (a) and the members of the committee have reasonable access to Native American cultural items under review and to associated scientific and historical documents.

Regulations.

(g) DUTIES OF THE SECRETARY.—The Secretary shall—

(1) establish such rules and regulations for the committee as may be necessary, and

(2) provide reasonable administrative and staff support necessary for the deliberations of the committee.

(h) ANNUAL REPORT.—The committee established under subsection (a) shall submit an annual report to the Congress on the progress made, and any barriers encountered, in implementing this section during the previous year.

(i) TERMINATION.—The committee established under subsection (a) shall terminate at the end of the 120-day period beginning on the day the Secretary certifies, in a report submitted to Congress, that the work of the committee has been completed.

SEC. 9. PENALTY. Museums.

(a) PENALTY.—Any museum that fails to comply with the 25 U.S.C. 3007 requirements of this Act may be assessed a civil penalty by the Secretary of the Interior pursuant to procedures established by the Secretary through regulation. A penalty assessed under this subsection shall be determined on the record after opportunity for an agency hearing. Each violation under this subsection shall be a separate offense.

(b) AMOUNT OF PENALTY.—The amount of a penalty assessed under subsection (a) shall be determined under regulations promulgated pursuant to this Act, taking into account, in addition to other factors—

(1) the archaeological, historical, or commercial value of the item involved;

(2) the damages suffered, both economic and noneconomic, by an aggrieved party, and

(3) the number of violations that have occurred.

(c) ACTIONS TO RECOVER PENALTIES.—If any museum fails to pay costs, an assessment of a civil penalty pursuant to a final order of the Secretary that has been issued under subsection (a) and not appealed or after a final judgment has been rendered on appeal of such order, the Attorney General may institute a civil action in an appropriate district court of the United States to collect the penalty. In such action, the validity and amount of such penalty shall not be subject to review.

(d) SUBPOENAS.—In hearings held pursuant to subsection (a), subpoenas may be issued for the attendance and testimony of witnesses and the production of relevant papers, books, and documents. Witnesses so summoned shall be paid the same fees and mileage that are paid to witnesses in the courts of the United States.

SEC. 10. GRANTS.

(a) INDIAN TRIBES AND NATIVE HAWAIIAN ORGANIZATIONS.—The Secretary is authorized to make grants to Indian tribes and Native Hawaiian organizations for the purpose of assisting such tribes and organizations in the repatriation of Native American cultural items.

(b) MUSEUMS.—The Secretary is authorized to make grants to museums for the purpose of assisting the museums in conducting the inventories and identification required under sections 5 and 6.

SEC. 11. SAVINGS PROVISIONS.

Nothing in this Act shall be construed to—

(1) limit the authority of any Federal agency or museum to—

(A) return or repatriate Native American cultural items to Indian tribes, Native Hawaiian organizations, or individuals, and

(B) enter into any other agreement with the consent of the culturally affiliated tribe or organization as to the disposition of, or control over, items covered by this Act;

(2) delay actions on repatriation requests that are pending on the date of enactment of this Act;

(3) deny or otherwise affect access to any court;

(4) limit any procedural or substantive right which may otherwise be secured to individuals or Indian tribes or Native Hawaiian organizations; or

(5) limit the application of any State or Federal law pertaining to theft or stolen property.

SEC. 12. SPECIAL RELATIONSHIP BETWEEN FEDERAL GOVERNMENT AND INDIAN TRIBES.

This Act reflects the unique relationship between the Federal Government and Indian tribes and Native Hawaiian organizations and should not be construed to establish a precedent with respect to any other individual, organization or foreign government.

SEC. 13. REGULATIONS.

The Secretary shall promulgate regulations to carry out this Act within 12 months of enactment.

SEC. 14. AUTHORIZATION OF APPROPRIATIONS.

There is authorized to be appropriated such sums as may be necessary to carry out this Act.

SEC. 15. ENFORCEMENT.

The United States district courts shall have jurisdiction over any action brought by any person alleging a violation of this Act and shall have the authority to issue such orders as may be necessary to enforce the provisions of this Act.

Approved November 16, 1990.

Source: *U.S. Statutes at Large*, 104:3048.

67 American Indian Religious Freedom Act Amendments, January 25, 1994

After the Supreme Court struck down many of the provisions of the American Indian Religious Freedom Act of 1978 (Doc. 63), Congress attempted to remedy some of the problems relating to the use of peyote by Native Americans for religious purposes through amendments.

An Act to amend the American Indian Religious Freedom Act to provide for the traditional use of peyote by Indians for religious purposes, and for other purposes. . . .

SECTION 1. SHORT TITLE.

This Act may be cited as the "American Indian Religious Freedom Act Amendments of 1994."

SEC. 2. TRADITIONAL INDIAN RELIGIOUS USE OF THE PEYOTE SACRAMENT.

The Act of August 11, 1978 (42 U.S.C. 1996), commonly referred to as the "American Indian Religious Freedom Act," is amended by adding at the end thereof the following new section:

"SEC. 3. The Congress finds and declares that for many Indian people, the traditional ceremonial use of the peyote cactus as a religious sacrament has for centuries been integral to a way of life, and significant in perpetuating Indian tribes and cultures; since 1965, this ceremonial use of peyote by Indians has been protected by Federal regulation; while at least 28 States have enacted laws which are similar to, or are in conformance with, the Federal regulation which protects the ceremonial use of peyote by Indian religious practitioners, 22 States have not done so, and this lack of uniformity has created hardship for Indian people who participate in such religious ceremonies; the Supreme Court of the United States, in the case of *Employment Division v. Smith*, 494 U.S. 872 (1990), held that the First Amendment does not protect Indian practitioners who use peyote in Indian religious ceremonies, and also raised uncertainty whether this religious practice would be protected under the compelling State interest standard; and the lack of adequate and clear legal protection for the religious use of peyote by Indians may serve to stigmatize and marginalize Indian tribes and cultures, and increase the risk that they will be exposed to discriminatory treatment.

Notwithstanding any other provision of law, the use, possession, or transportation of peyote by an Indian for bona fide traditional ceremonial purposes in connection with the practice of a traditional Indian religion is lawful, and shall not be prohibited by the United States or any State. No Indian shall be penalized or discriminated against on the basis of such use, possession or transportation, including, but not limited to, denial of otherwise applicable benefits under public assistance programs.

This section does not prohibit such reasonable regulation and registration by the Drug Enforcement Administration of those persons who cultivate, harvest, or distribute peyote as may be consistent with the purposes of this Act.

This section does not prohibit application of the provisions of section 481.111 of Vernon's Texas Health and Safety Code Annotated, in effect on the date of enactment of this section, insofar as those provisions pertain to the cultivation, harvest, and distribution of peyote.

Nothing in this section shall prohibit any Federal department or agency, in carrying out its statutory responsibilities and functions, from promulgating regulations establishing reasonable limitations on the use or ingestion of peyote prior to or during the performance of duties by sworn law enforcement officers or personnel directly involved in public transportation or any other safety-sensitive positions where the performance of such duties may be adversely affected by such use or ingestion. Such regulations shall be adopted only after consultation with representatives of traditional Indian religions for which the sacramental use of peyote is integral to their practice. Any regulation promulgated pursuant to this section shall be subject to the balancing test set forth in section 3 of the Religious Freedom Restoration Act (Public Law 103-141; 42 U.S.C. 2000bb-1).

This section shall not be construed as requiring prison authorities to permit, nor shall it be construed to prohibit prison authorities from permitting, access to peyote by Indians while incarcerated within Federal or State prison facilities.

Subject to the provisions of the Religious Freedom Restoration Act (Public Law 103-141; 42 U.S.C. 2000bb-1), this section shall not be construed to prohibit States from enacting or enforcing reasonable traffic safety laws or regulations.

Subject to the provisions of the Religious Freedom Restoration Act (Public Law 103-141; 42 USC 2000bb-1), this section does not prohibit the Secretary of Defense from promulgating regulations establishing reasonable limitations on the use, possession, transportation, or distribution of peyote to promote military readiness, safety, or compliance with international law or laws of other countries. Such regulations shall be adopted only after consultation with representatives of traditional Indian religions for which the sacramental use of peyote is integral to their practice.

For purposes of this section—

—the term 'Indian' means a member of an Indian tribe;
—the term 'Indian tribe' means any tribe, band, nation, pueblo, or other organized group or community of Indians, including any Alaska Native village (as defined in, or established pursuant to, the Alaska Native Claims Settlement Act (43 U.S.C. 1601 et seq.)), which is recognized as eligible for the special programs and services provided by the United States to Indians because of their status as Indians;
—the term 'Indian religion' means any religion which is practiced by Indians; and the origin and interpretation of which is from within a traditional Indian culture or community; and
—the term 'State' means any State of the United States and any political subdivision thereof.

Nothing in this section shall be construed as abrogating, diminishing, or otherwise affecting the inherent rights of any Indian tribe; the rights, express or implicit, of any Indian tribe which exist under treaties, Executive orders, and laws of the United States; the inherent right of Indians to practice their religions; and the right of Indians to practice their religions under any Federal or State law."

Approved October 6, 1994.

Source: *U.S Statutes at Large*, 108:3124.

68 Bureau of Indian Affairs Apology, September 8, 2000

In September 2000 Assistant Secretary for Indian Affairs Kevin Gover (Pawnee) apologized on behalf of the Bureau of Indian Affairs for the systematic genocide and ethnocide practiced by the bureau since its inception in 1824.

In March 1824, President James Monroe established the Office of Indian Affairs in the Department of War. Its mission was to conduct the nation's business with regard to Indian affairs. We have come together today to mark the first 175 years of the institution now known as the Bureau of Indian Affairs.

It is appropriate that we do so in the first year of a new century and a new millennium, a time when our leaders are reflecting on what lies ahead and preparing for those challenges. Before looking ahead, though, this institution must first look back and reflect on what it has wrought and by doing so, come to know that this is no occasion for celebration; rather it is time for reflection and contemplation, a time for sorrowful truths to be spoken, a time for contrition.

We must first reconcile ourselves to the fact that the works of this agency have at various times profoundly harmed the communities it was meant to serve. From the very beginning, the Office of Indian Affairs was an instrument by which the United States enforced its ambition against the Indian nations and Indian people who stood in its path. And so, the first mission of this institution was to execute the removal of the southeastern tribal nations. By threat, deceit, and force, these great tribal nations were made to march 1,000 miles to the west, leaving thousands of their old, their young and their infirm in hasty graves along the Trail of Tears.

As the nation looked to the West for more land, this agency participated in the ethnic cleansing that befell the western tribes. War necessarily begets tragedy; the war for the West was no exception. Yet in these more enlightened times, it must be acknowledged that the deliberate spread of disease, the decimation of the mighty bison herds, the use of the poison alcohol to destroy mind and body and the cowardly killing of women and children made for tragedy on a scale so ghastly that it cannot be dismissed as merely the inevitable consequence of the clash of competing ways of life. This agency and the good people in it failed in the mission to prevent the devastation. And so great nations of patriot warriors fell. We will never push aside the memory of unnecessary and violent death at places such as Sand Creek, the banks of the Washita River and Wounded Knee.

Nor did the consequences of war have to include the futile and destructive efforts to annihilate Indian cultures. After the devastation of tribal economies and the deliberate creation of tribal dependence on the services provided by this agency, this agency set out to destroy all things Indian.

This agency forbade the speaking of Indian languages, prohibited the conduct of traditional religious activities, outlawed traditional government and made Indian people ashamed of who they were. Worst of all, the Bureau of Indian Affairs committed these acts against the children entrusted to its boarding schools, brutalizing them emotionally, psychologically, physically and spiritually. Even in this era of self-determination, when the Bureau of Indian Affairs is at long last serving as an advocate for Indian people in an atmosphere of mutual respect, the legacy of these misdeeds haunts us. The trauma of shame, fear and anger has passed from one generation to the next, and manifests itself in the rampant alcoholism, drug abuse, and domestic violence that plague Indian country. Many of our people live lives of unrelenting tragedy as Indian families suffer the ruin of lives by alcoholism, suicides made of shame and despair and violent death at the hands of one another. So many of the maladies suffered today in Indian country result from the failures of this agency. Poverty, ignorance and disease have been the product of this agency's work.

And so today I stand before you as the leader of an institution that in the past has committed acts so terrible that they infect, diminish and destroy the lives of Indian people decades later, generations later. These things occurred despite the efforts of many good people with good hearts who sought to prevent them. These wrongs must be acknowledged if the healing is to begin.

I do not speak today for the United States. That is the province of the nation's elected leaders and I would not presume to speak on their behalf. I am empowered, however, to speak on behalf of this agency, the Bureau of Indian Affairs and I am quite certain that the words that follow reflect the hearts of its 10,000 employees.

Let us begin by expressing our profound sorrow for what this agency has done in the past. Just like you, when we think of these misdeeds and their tragic consequences, our hearts break and our grief is as pure and complete as yours. We desperately wish that we could change this history, but of course we cannot. On behalf of the Bureau of Indian Affairs, I extend this formal apology to Indian people for the historical conduct of this agency.

And while the BIA employees of today did not commit these wrongs, we acknowledge that the institution we serve did. We accept this inheritance, this legacy of racism and inhumanity. And by accepting this legacy, we accept also the moral responsibility of putting things right.

We therefore begin this important work anew and make a new commitment to the people and communities that we serve, a commitment born of the dedication we share with you to the cause of renewed hope and prosperity for Indian country. Never again will this agency stand silent when hate and violence are committed against Indians. Never again will we allow policy to proceed from the assumption that Indians possess less human genius than the other races. Never again will we be complicit in the theft of Indian property. Never again will we appoint false leaders who serve purposes other than those of the tribes. Never again will we allow unflattering and stereotypical images of Indian people to deface the halls of government or lead the American people to shallow and ignorant beliefs about Indians.

Never again will we attack your religions, your languages, your rituals, or any of your tribal ways. Never again will we seize your children, nor teach them to be ashamed of who they are. Never again.

We cannot yet ask your forgiveness, not while the burdens of this agency's history weigh so heavily on tribal communities. What we do ask is that, together, we allow the healing to begin: As you return to your homes and as you talk with your people, please tell them that time of dying is at its end. Tell your children that the time of shame and fear is over. Tell your young men and women to replace their anger with hope and love for their people. Together, we must wipe the tears of seven generations.

Together, we must allow our broken hearts to mend. Together, we will face a challenging world with confidence and trust. Together, let us resolve that when our future leaders gather to discuss the history of this institution, it will be time to celebrate the rebirth of joy, freedom and progress for the Indian Nations. The Bureau of Indian Affairs was born in 1824 in a time of war on Indian people. May it live in the year 2000 and beyond as an instrument of their prosperity.

Source: Bureau of Indian Affairs, press release on the 175th anniversary of the establishment of the Bureau of Indian Affairs, September 8, 2000, available at http://www.doi.gov/bia/as-ia/175gover.htm.

Appendices

List of Cases

The following legal cases are cited in the text. An asterisk indicates that the case is reprinted in part or in whole in the Documents section. See the index for page references.

Antoine v. Washington, 420 U.S. 194 (1975)
Arizona Public Service Company v. Environmental Protection Agency, 211 F.3d 1280 (D.C. Cir. 2000)
Arizona v. California, 373 U.S. 546 (1963)
Backcountry Against Dumps v. Environmental Protection Agency, 100 F.3d 147 (D.C. Cir. 1996)
Blue Legs v. Bureau of Indian Affairs, 867 F.2d 1094 (8th Cir. 1979)
Bottomly v. Passamoquoddy Tribe, 599 F.2d 1061 (1st Cir. 1979)
Brendale v. Confederated Tribes and Bands of the Yakima Indian Nation, 492 U.S. 408 (1989)
Buster v. Wright, 135 F.947 (8th Cir. 1905)
Cabazon Band of Mission Indians v. California, 480 U.S. 202 (1987)
California ex rel. Department of Fish and Game v. Quechan Tribe of Indians, 595 F.2d 1153 (9th Cir. 1979)
California v. Cabazon Band of Mission Indians, 480 U.S. 202 (1987)
Carpenter v. Shaw, 280 U.S. 363 (1930)
Cherokee Nation v. Georgia, 30 U.S. 1 (1831)*
Chevron, U.S.A., Inc. v. Natural Resources Defense Council, Inc., 467 U.S. 837 (1984)
City of Albuquerque v. Browner, 97 F.3d 415 (10th Cir. 1996)
Colville Confederated Tribe v. Walton, 460 F.Supp. 1320 (E.D. Wash. 1978); 647 F.2d 42 (9th Cir. 1981)
Confederated Tribes of the Colville Indian Reservation v. Washington, 412 F.Supp. 651 (E.D. Wash. 1976)
Confederated Tribes of the Umatilla Reservation v. Alexander, 440 F.Supp. 533 (Dist. Ct. Ore. 1977)
Conrad Investment Co. v. United States, 161 F.2d 829 (1908)
Cortez v. Wilson, S07851 (1998)
Cotton Petroleum v. New Mexico, 490 U.S. 163 (1989)
County of Oneida v. Oneida Indian Nation, 470 U.S. 226 (1985)

County of Yakima v. Confederated Tribes and Bands of Yakima Nation, 502 U.S. 251 (1992)
Davis v. United States, 192 F.3d 951 (10th Cir. 1999)
Duncan v. United States, 229 Ct. Cl. 120 (1981)
Elk v. Wilkins, 112 U.S. 94 (1884)*
Employment Division, Department of Human Resources of Oregon v. Smith, 485 U.S. 660 (1988)
Employment Division, Department of Human Resources of Oregon v. Smith, 494 U.S. 872 (1990)
Evans v. McKay, 869 F.2d 1341 (9th Cir. 1989)
Ex Parte Crow Dog, 109 U.S. 556 (1883)*
Fletcher v. Peck, 10 U.S. 87 (1810)
Goat v. United States, 224 U.S. 458 (1912)
Hatahley v. United States, 351 U.S. 173 (1956)
Hodel v. Irving, 481 U.S. 704 (1987)
Hotel Employees and Restaurant Employees International Union v. Wilson, S074850 (1999)
Iowa Mutual Insurance Co. v. LaPlante, 480 U.S. 9 (1987)
Johnson and Graham's Lessee v. William McIntosh, 21 U.S. (8 Wheat.) 543 (1823)*
Jones v. Meehan, 175 U.S. 1 (1889)
Kansas v. Colorado, 206 U.S. 46 (1907)
Leech Lake Band of Chippewa Indians v. Herbst, 344 F.Supp. 101 (D.Minn 1971)
Lone Wolf v. Hitchcock, 187 U.S. 553 (1903)*
Lyng v. Northwest Indian Cemetery Protective Association, 485 U.S. 439 (1988)*
Marbury v. Madison, 5 U.S. (1 Cr.) 137 (1803)
Menominee Tribe v. United States, 391 U.S. 404 (1968)
Merrion v. Jicarilla Apache Tribe, 455 U.S. 130 (1982)
Mississippi Band of Choctaw Indians v. Holyfield, 490 U.S. 30 (1989)
Moe v. Confederated Salish and Kootenai Tribes, 425 U.S. 463 (1976)
Montana v. Environmental Protection Agency, 137 F.3d 1135 (9th Cir. 1998)
Morton v. Mancari, 417 U.S. 535 (1974)
Nance v. Environmental Protection Agency, 645 F.2d. 701 (9th Cir. 1981)
National Farmers Union v. Crow Tribe, 471 U.S. 845 (1985)
Native American Church v. Navajo Tribal Council, 272 F.2d 131 (1959)*
Oklahoma Tax Commission v. Citizen Band Potawatomi Indian Tribe, 498 U.S. 505 (1991)
Oliphant v. Suquamish, 435 U.S. 191 (1978)
Pan American Co. v. Sycuan Band of Mission Indians, 884 F.2d 416 (9th Cir. 1989)
People v. LeBlanc, 248 N.W.2d 199 (1976)
Puget Sound Gilnetters Association v. United States District Court, 573 F.2d 1123 (9th Cir. 1978)
Puyallup Tribe v. Department of Game of Washington, 391 U.S. 392 (1968)
Puyallup Tribe v. Department of Game of Washington, 414 U.S. 44 (1973)
Puyallup Tribe v. Department of Game of Washington, 433 U.S. 165 (1977)
Rice v. Cayetano, 528 U.S. 495 (2000)
Santa Clara Pueblo v. Martinez, 436 U.S. 49 (1978)
Seminole Nation of Oklahoma v. Acting Director, Office of Trial Service, Bureau of Indian Affairs, 24 BIA 209 (1993)
Seminole Nation of Oklahoma v. Gale Norton, Civ. Action No. 00-2384 (CKK), U.S.D.C.D.C., Mem. Opin. Sept. 27, 2001
Seminole Nation v. United States, 78 Ct. Cl. 455 (1933)
Seminole Nation v. United States, 90 Ct. Cl. 151 (1940)
Seminole Tribe of Florida v. Butterworth, 491 F.Supp. 1015 (S.D.Fla. 1980), aff'd, 658 F.2d 310 (5th Cir. 1981), cert. den., 455 U.S. 1020 (1982)
Seminole Tribe of Florida v. Florida, 517 U.S. 44 (1996)
Skeem v. United States, 273 F.2d 93 (1921)
Smith v. Bonifer, 132 Fed. 889 (1907)
South Dakota v. Yankton Sioux Tribe, 522 U.S. 329 (1998)
Stephens v. Cherokee Nation, 174 U.S. 445 (1899)*
Strate v. A-1 Contractors, 520 U.S. 438 (1997)
Talton v. Mayes, 163 U.S. 376 (1896)
Tee-Hit-Ton Indians v. United States, 348 U.S. 272 (1955)
Three Affiliated Tribes v. Wold Engineering, 476 U.S. 877 (1986)

Tillie Hardwick v. United States, U.S. District Court for the Northern District of California, No. C-79-1710-SW (1983)

Trans-Canada Enterprises, Ltd. v. Muckleshoot Indian Tribe, 634 F.2d 474 (9th Cir. 1980)

Tulee v. Washington, 315 U.S. 681 (1942)

United States ex rel. Standing Bear v. Crook, 5 Dill. 453 (1879)*

United States v. Aanerud, 893 F.2d 956 (8th Cir. 1990)

United States v. Cappaert, 375 F.Supp. 456 (Nev. 1974)

United States v. Kagama, 118 U.S. 375 (1886)*

United States v. McBratney, 104 U.S. 621 (1881)

United States v. Michigan, 471 F.Supp. 192 (W.D. Mich. 1979)

United States v. Montana, 450 U.S. 544 (1981)

United States v. Mottaz, 476 U.S. 834 (1986)

United States v. Percheman, 32 U.S. 51 (1833)

United States v. Sandoval, 231 U.S. 28 (1913)

United States v. The Seminole Indians, 180 Ct. Cl. 375 (1967)

United States v. Washington, 384 F.Supp. 343 (1974)

United States v. Wheeler, 435 U.S. 313 (1978)

United States v. Winans, 198 U.S. 371 (1905)

Wall v. Williamson, 8 Ala. 48 (1945)

Ward v. Race Horse, 163 U.S. 504 (1896)

Washington Department of Ecology v. Environmental Protection Agency, 752 F.2d 1465 (9th Cir. 1985)

Washington v. Washington State Passenger Fishing Vessel Association, 443 U.S. 658 (1979)

Wells v. Philbrick, 486 F.Supp 807 (DSD 1980)

Winters v. United States, 143 F.2d 743 (1906)

Winters v. United States, 207 U.S. 564 (1908)

Wisconsin v. Gurnoe, 53 Wis. 2d 390, 192 N.W. 2d 892 (Wis. 1972)

Worcester v. Georgia, 31 U.S. 551 (1832)*

List of Statutes

The following statutes are discussed or cited in the text. An asterisk indicates that the law is reprinted in part or in whole in the Documents section. See the index for page references.

Abolition of Treaty Making, 1871*
Unilaterally forbade further federal treaty making with American Indians, changing the process of treaty making in the Senate to the negotiation of "executive agreements" ratified by both houses of Congress. The law was passed by the House of Representatives.

Act for Governance and Protection of Indians, 1850
Extended federal powers onto reservations in matters concerning Indian affairs.

Alaska Native Claims Settlement Act, 1971*
Authorized the enrollment of Alaskan Natives so the federal government could settle Alaskan Native land claims following the discovery of oil in the state. The act created regional native corporations, conveyed lands to the various corporations, and deposited monies in the Alaska Native Fund.

American Indian Religious Freedom Act, 1978*
Intended to grant religious freedom to Native Americans. The Supreme Court would strike down most of its provisions in the 1980s and early 1990s.

American Indian Religious Freedom Act Amendments, 1994*
Attempted to remedy some of the problems related to the use of peyote by Native Americans for religious purposes. Congress passed the measure after the Supreme Court struck down many of the provisions of the American Indian Religious Freedom Act of 1978.

Antiquities Act, 1906
Classified funerary objects in Indian graves on reservations and federal lands as cultural resources belonging to the United States.

Blue Lake Lands Return to Taos Pueblo, 1970*

Provided for the return of the Blue Lake lands to the Taos Pueblo in New Mexico. In 1906 President Theodore Roosevelt had declared the lands part of what is now Carson National Forest, restricting American Indians' exclusive use of the land, which they considered sacred.

Burke Act, 1906*

Allowed the federal government to lengthen the trust period over Indian lands at its discretion. It also stipulated that citizenship for Native Americans agreeing to allotment would be granted at the end of the trust period rather than at the beginning as previously provided.

Civilization Fund Act, 1819*

Intended to promote the education of American Indian children. The act was passed as Native American contacts with white settlers increased and benevolent societies became interested in educating Native Americans. Congress established a "civilization fund" to promote the policy.

Commissioner of Indian Affairs Authorization, 1832*

Authorized the creation of the office of commissioner of Indian affairs and delegated the management and direction of Indian affairs to it. The new commissioner replaced the head of the Indian office created in the War Department in 1824.

Curtis Act, 1898*

Required the established and regulation of town sites and issued new provisions for management of mineral rights leases. Its stipulations circumscribed various aspects of Indian life, destroying Native American tribal governments and courts in Indian Territory (present-day Oklahoma).

Elementary and Secondary Education Act, 1972

Created the Office of Indian Education and the National Advisory Council on Indian Education to improve the quality of public education for Native Americans.

Establishment of the War Department, 1789*

Placed implementation of Indian affairs and policies under the jurisdiction of the War Department, where it would remain until the creation of the Department of the Interior in 1849.

General Allotment Act (Dawes Act), 1887*

Empowered the president to divide reservations into family farms, replacing Native American communal landholdings with Euro-American agriculture and capitalism. Native American recipients of allotments automatically became U.S. citizens.

General Allotment Act Amendment, 1891*

Allowed equal allotments to all Native Americans and the leasing of allotments.

House Concurrent Resolution 108, 1953*

Removed federal supervision of Native Americans by abolishing treaties with certain Indian nations and subjecting American Indian individuals to the same privileges, responsibilities, and laws extended to other U.S. citizens. After passage of the resolution, the federal government began to "terminate" its relations with selected Native American nations with which it had treaties.

Indian Child Welfare Act, 1978*

Sought to redress some of the problems created by federal policies involving Native American ethnocide, including the removal of American Indian children from their families and tribes and placement with non-Indian families.

Indian Citizenship Act, 1924*

Unilaterally made citizens of all Native Americans born in the United States who had not been granted citizenship under previous legislative provisions.

Indian Civil Rights Act, 1968*
Stipulated the application of the Bill of Rights to Native Americans in federal-tribal relations, the creation of a code for courts of Indian offenses, and the requirement of obtaining Native American consent for states to assume jurisdiction over reservations.

Indian Claims Commission Act, 1946*
Created the Indian Claims Commission to hear Native American grievances.

Indian Crimes Act, 1976
Amended the Major Crimes Act of 1885, adding provisions concerning charges of assault. In such cases, it brought treatment of American Indians into line with that of non-Indian citizens.

Indian Gaming Regulatory Act, 1988
Set forth regulations for gambling operations in Indian country and stipulated the necessity of compacts with state governments where gaming ventures sought to operate.

Indian Health Services Transfer, 1954*
Transferred health care for Native Americans from the Bureau of Indian Affairs to the Public Health Service of the U.S. Department of Health, Education, and Welfare. The move was part of the federal policy of termination.

Indian Homestead Act, 1875
Granted Indians the right to homestead federal lands, a right provided non-Indians under the Homestead Act of 1862.

Indian Peace Commission Authorization, 1867*
Created the Indian Peace Commission to examine why there were so many conflicts on the Great Plains during and after the Civil War. The commission was also empowered to negotiate treaties and create reservations.

Indian Removal Act, 1830*
Empowered President Andrew Jackson to negotiate removal treaties with American Indian nations east of the Mississippi River. Native American nations were to exchange lands in the East for lands in the trans-Mississippi West.

Indian Reorganization Act (Wheeler-Howard Act), 1934*
Brought a halt to the allotment of reservation lands and sought to sustain American Indian tribal organizations.

Indian Self-Determination and Education Assistance Act, 1975
Asserted that in the past government paternalism had retarded Indian self-determination and promised henceforth to work with tribes to improve governmental self-determination, especially in education. It also provided for Indian preference in hiring for all federal contracts relating to Indian tribes.

Johnson-O'Malley Act, 1934*
Provided for federal contracts with states to pay for educational, medical, and other services delivered by the states to Native Americans.

Lacey Act, 1907*
Extended Congress's power over communal trust funds and provided for the allotment of tribal funds to certain classes of American Indians.

Major Crimes Act, 1885*
Gave federal courts jurisdiction over seven crimes when committed by one Native American against another while on a reservation.

Menominee Indians Termination, 1954*
Terminated the Menominee as a federally recognized Native American nation.

Menominee Restoration Act, 1973*
Repealed the termination act of June 17, 1954, thus restoring the Menominee to the status of a federally recognized tribe.

National Museum of the American Indian Act, 1989
Created the National Museum of the American Indian as part of the Smithsonian Institution. The act also sought to settle reburial issues with Native Americans to facilitate cooperation with Indian communities in the planning, development, and maintenance of the museum.

Native American Graves Protection and Repatriation Act, 1990*
Facilitated the return to tribes of hundreds of thousands of Native American human remains deposited in federal agencies.

Public Law 83-280, 1953*
Authorized state jurisdiction over offenses committed against or by Native Americans on certain reservations, dramatically abridging the self-determination of Native American societies and their relations with the federal government.

Rancheria Act, 1958
Provided congressional authorization for the termination of federal trust responsibility and divided the assets of California Indian tribes among individual members. The act also required that state standards for water, sanitation, and health be met by California before trust status was discontinued.

Trade and Intercourse Act, 1790*
Sought to facilitate and enforce various treaties in frontier areas against the objections of many white settlers.

Trade and Intercourse Act, 1802*
Comprehensively restated the Trade and Intercourse Acts of 1790, 1796, and 1799. It was the fundamental legislation governing Indian affairs until 1834.

Treaties and Trade Regulations Authorization, 1824*
Empowered the president to negotiate treaties with Indian nations west of the Mississippi River. The law was passed after frontier violence on the Missouri River caused fur traders to demand government protection.

1 Indian Land Cessations, 1784–1809

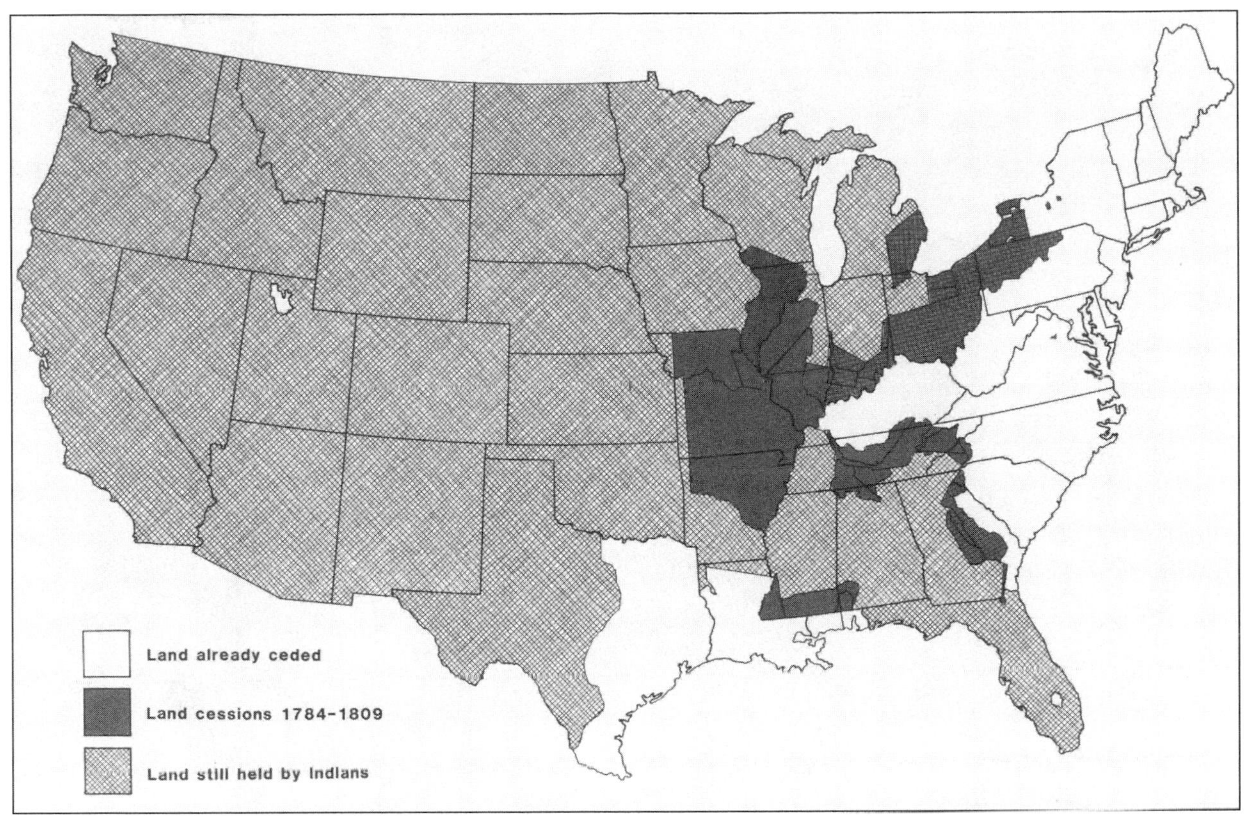

Source: Francis Paul Prucha, *Atlas of American Indian Affairs* (Lincoln: University of Nebraska Press, 1990).

2 Indian Land Cessations, 1820–1829

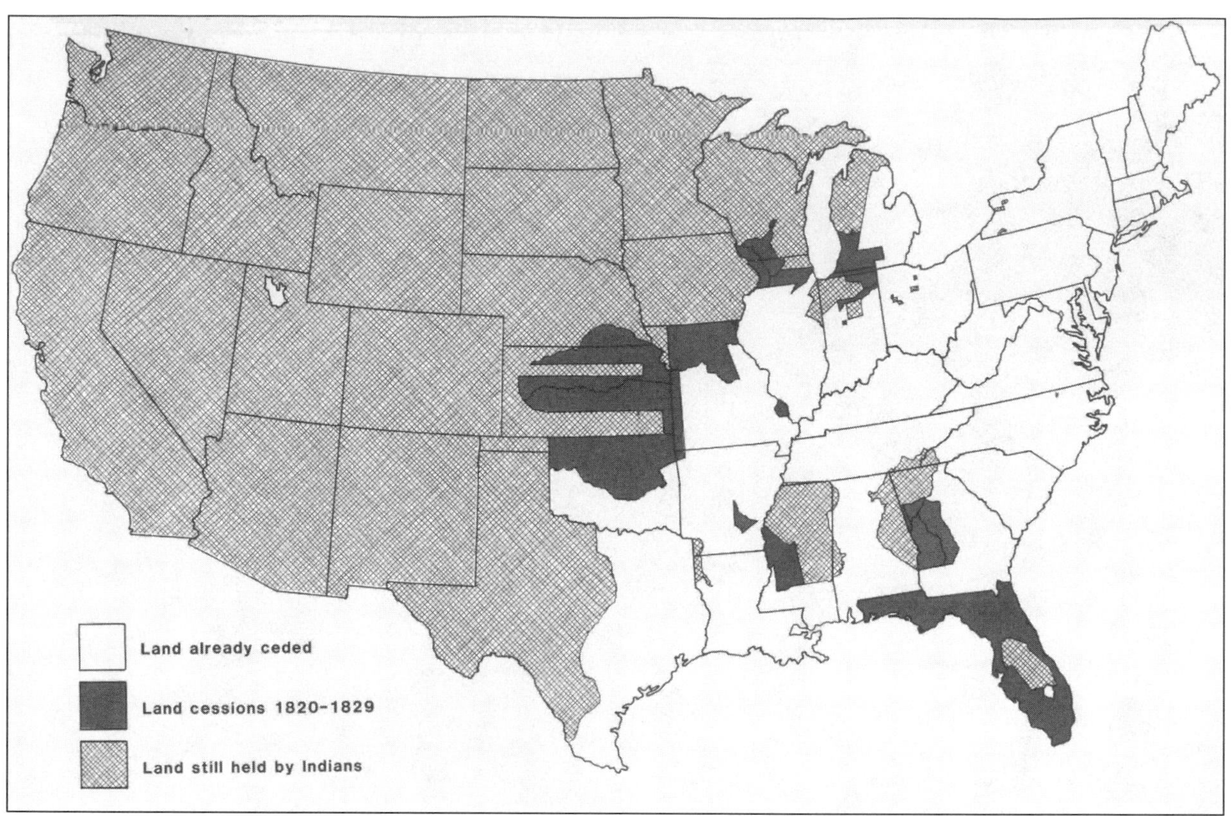

Source: Francis Paul Prucha, *Atlas of American Indian Affairs* (Lincoln: University of Nebraska Press, 1990).

3 Indian Land Cessations, 1860–1869

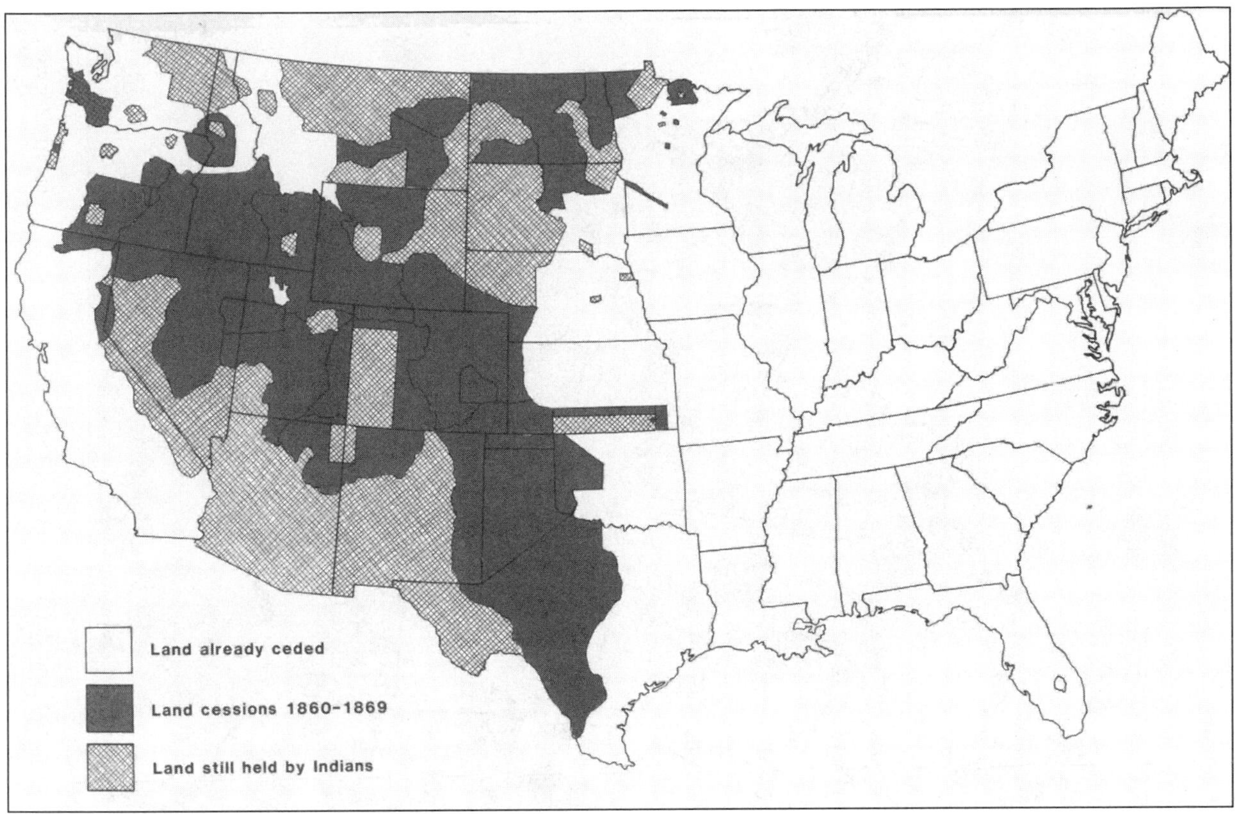

Source: Francis Paul Prucha, *Atlas of American Indian Affairs* (Lincoln: University of Nebraska Press, 1990).

4 Indian Reservations in the Continental United States, 2002

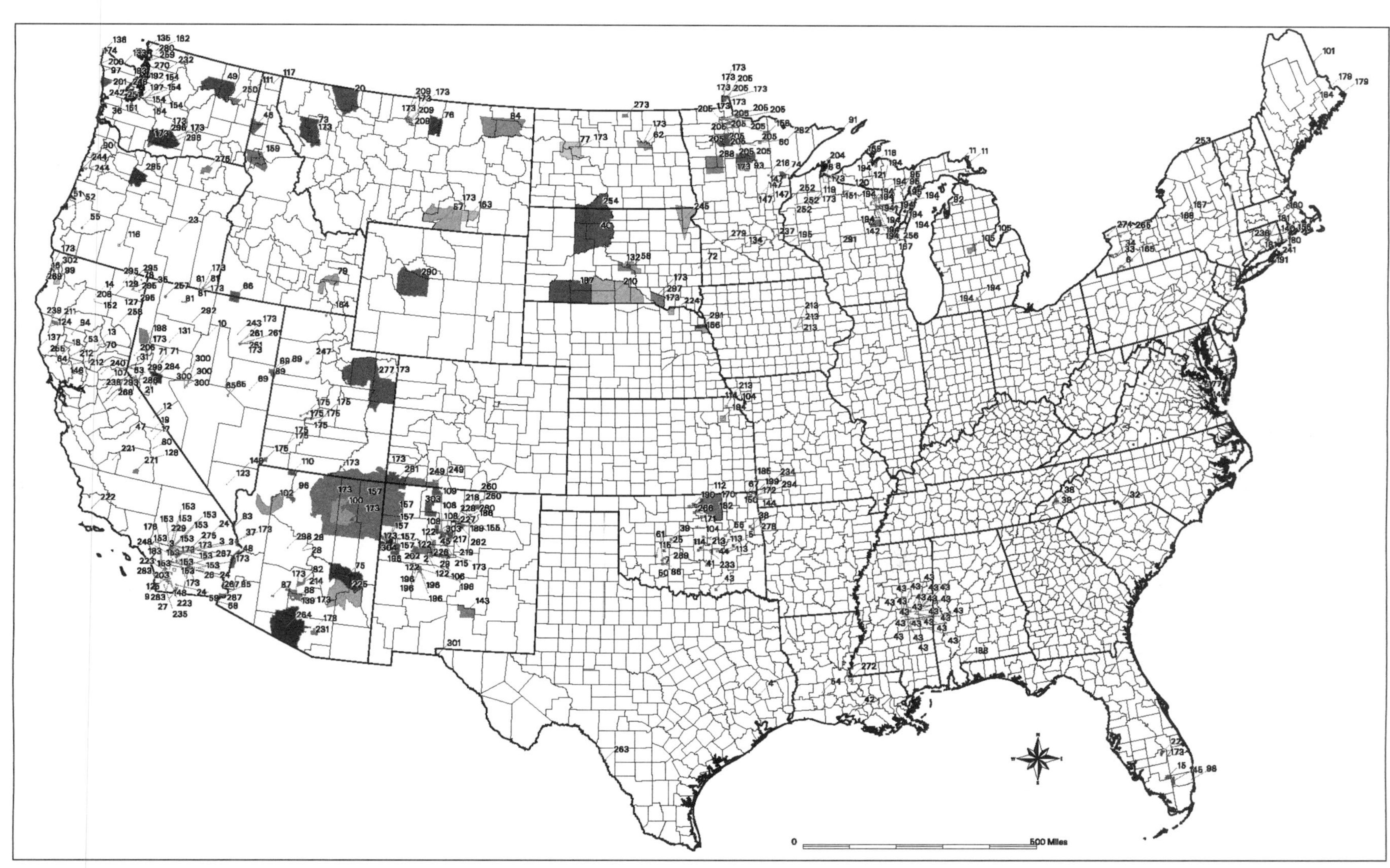

Source: Bureau of Indian Affairs and the National Park Service. For additional information and detailed views of reservation locations, go to http://www.cr.nps.gov/nagpra/nacd/namap-2.htm.

Key: Indian Reservations in the Continental United States

There are 562 federally recognized Indian tribes. Of these, 337 are in the continental United States. They do not all have reservations. Trust lands are not included in this map. Spellings may differ from those in the text.

1 Absentee Shawnee*
2 Acoma
3 Agua Caliente
4 Alabama-Coushatta
5 Alabama-Quassarte Creeks*
6 Allegany
7 Apache*
8 Bad River
9 Barona Ranch
10 Battle Mountain
11 Bay Mills
12 Benton Paiute
13 Berry Creek
14 Big Bend
15 Big Cypress
16 Big Lagoon
17 Big Pine
18 Big Valley
19 Bishop
20 Blackfeet
21 Bridgeport
22 Brighton
23 Burns Paiute Colony
24 Cabezon
25 Caddo*
26 Cahuilla
27 Campo
28 Camp Verde
29 Canoncito
30 Capitan Grande
31 Carson
32 Catawba
33 Cattaraugus
34 Cayuga*
35 Cedarville
36 Chehalis
37 Chemehuevi
38 Cherokee[a]
39 Cheyenne-Arapahoe*
40 Cheyenne River
41 Chickasaw*
42 Chitimacha
43 Choctaw[b]
44 Citizen Band of Potawatomi*
45 Cochiti
46 Coeur d'Alene
47 Cold Springs
48 Colorado River
49 Colville
50 Comanche*
51 Coos, Lower Umpqua, and Siuslaw
52 Coquille*
53 Cortina
54 Coushatta
55 Cow Creek
56 Creek*
57 Crow
58 Crow Creek
59 Cuyapaipe
60 Deer Creek
61 Delaware*
62 Devils Lake
63 Dresslerville Colony
64 Dry Creek
65 Duckwater
66 Duck Valley
67 Eastern Shawnee*
68 East Cocopah
69 Ely Colony
70 Enterprise
71 Fallon
72 Flandreau Indian School
73 Flathead
74 Fond du Lac
75 Fort Apache
76 Fort Belknap
77 Fort Berthold
78 Fort Bidwell
79 Fort Hall
80 Fort Independence
81 Fort McDermitt
82 Fort McDowell
83 Fort Mohave
84 Fort Peck
85 Fort Yuma
86 Fort Sill Apache*
87 Gila Bend
88 Gila River
89 Goshute
90 Grande Ronde
91 Grand Portage
92 Grand Traverse
93 Greater Leech Lake
94 Grindstone
95 Hannahville
96 Havasupai
97 Hoh
98 Hollywood
99 Hoopa Valley
100 Hopi
101 Houlton Maliseets
102 Hualapai
103 Inaja
104 Iowa*
105 Isabella
106 Isleta
107 Jackson
108 Jemez
109 Jicarilla
110 Kaibab
111 Kalispel
112 Kaw*
113 Kialegee Creek*
114 Kickapoo*
115 Kiowa*
116 Klamath*
117 Kootenai
118 L'Anse
119 Lac Courte Oreilles
120 Lac du Flambeau
121 Lac Vieux Desert
122 Laguna
123 Las Vegas
124 Laytonville
125 La Jolla
126 La Posta
127 Likely
128 Lone Pine
129 Lookout
130 Los Coyotes
131 Lovelock Colony
132 Lower Brule
133 Lower Elwah
134 Lower Sioux
135 Lummi
136 Makah
137 Manchester
138 Manzanita
139 Maricopa
140 Mashantucket Pequot
141 Mattaponi†
142 Menominee
143 Mescalero
144 Miami*
145 Miccosukee
146 Middletown
147 Mille Lacs
148 Mission
149 Moapa
150 Modoc*
151 Mole Lake
152 Montgomery Creek
153 Morongo
154 Muckleshoot
155 Nambe
156 Narragansett
157 Navajo
158 Nett Lake
159 Nez Perce
160 Nipmoc-Hassanamisco†
161 Nisqually
162 Nooksack
163 Northern Cheyenne
164 Northwestern Shoshone
165 Oil Springs
166 Omaha
167 Oneida[c]
168 Onondaga
169 Ontonagon
170 Osage
171 Otoe-Missouri*
172 Ottawa*
173 Out
174 Ozette
175 Paiute
176 Pala
177 Pamunkey†
178 Pascua Yaqui
179 Passamaquoddy
180 Paucatauk Pequot†
181 Paugusett†
182 Pawnee*
183 Pechanga
184 Penobscot
185 Peoria*
186 Picuris
187 Pine Ridge
188 Poarch Creek
189 Pojoaque
190 Ponca*
191 Poosepatuck†
192 Port Gamble
193 Port Madison
194 Potawatomi[d]
195 Prairie Isle
196 Puertocito
197 Puyallup
198 Pyramid Lake
199 Quapaw*
200 Quillayute
201 Quinault
202 Ramah
203 Ramona
204 Red Cliff
205 Red Lake
206 Reno-Sparks
207 Rincon
208 Roaring Creek
209 Rocky Boys
210 Rosebud

211 Round Valley
212 Rumsey
213 Sac and Fox[e]
214 Salt River
215 Sandia
216 Sandy Lake
217 Santa Ana
218 Santa Clara
219 Santa Domingo
220 Santa Rosa
221 Santa Rosa (North)
222 Santa Ynez
223 Santa Ysabel
224 Santee
225 San Carlos
226 San Felipe
227 San Ildefonso
228 San Juan
229 San Manual
230 San Pasqual
231 San Xavier
232 Sauk Suiattle
233 Seminole*
234 Seneca-Cayuga*
235 Sequan
236 Shagticoke†
237 Shakopee
238 Sheep Ranch
239 Sherwood Valley
240 Shingle Spring
241 Shinnecock†
242 Shoalwater
243 Shoshone
244 Siletz
245 Sisseton
246 Skokomish
247 Skull Valley
248 Soboba
249 Southern Ute
250 Spokane
251 Squaxon Island
252 St. Croix
253 St. Regis
254 Standing Rock
255 Stewarts Point
256 Stockbridge Munsee
257 Summit Lake
258 Susanville
259 Swinomish
260 Taos
261 Te-Moak
262 Tesuque
263 Texas Kickapoo
264 Tohono O'odham
265 Tonawanda
266 Tonikawa*
267 Torres Martinez
268 Toulumne
269 Trindad
270 Tulalip
271 Tule River
272 Tunica-Biloxi
273 Turtle Mountains
274 Tuscarora
275 Twenty-nine Palms
276 Umatilla
277 Unitah and Ouray
278 United Keetoowah Band of Cherokee*
279 Upper Sioux
280 Upper Skagit
281 Ute Mountain
282 Vermilion Lake
283 Viejas
284 Walker River
285 Warm Springs
286 Washoe
287 West Cocopah
288 White Earth
289 Wichita*
290 Wind River
291 Winnebago[f]
292 Winnemucca
293 Woodford Indian Community
294 Wyandotte*
295 XL Ranch
296 Yakama
297 Yankton
298 Yavapai
299 Yerington
300 Yomba
301 Ysleta Del Sur
302 Yurok
303 Zia
304 Zuni

Notes

* Do not have federal reservations. The tribal office is in the location indicated.

† Do not have federal reservations. The state reservation is in the location indicated.

[a] 38 Cherokee: The eastern band of Cherokee in North Carolina has a federal reservation; the Cherokee nation in Oklahoma does not have a federal reservation.

[b] 43 Choctaw: The Mississippi Choctaw in Mississippi have a federal reservation; the Choctaw nation in Oklahoma does not have a federal reservation.

[c] 167 Oneida: The Oneida nation of New York has a federal reservation; the Oneida tribe in Wisconsin also has a federal reservation.

[d] 194 Potawatomi: Two Potawatomi groups in Wisconsin have state reservations; the rest have federal reservations.

[e] 213 Sac and Fox: The Sac and Fox tribe of the Mississippi in Iowa have a federal reservation; the Sac and Fox nation in Kansas and Nebraska has a federal reservation; and the Sac and Fox nation of Oklahoma does not have a federal reservation.

[f] 291 Winnebago: The Winnebago tribe of Nebraska has a federal reservation; the Ho-Chunk nation, formerly known as the Wisconsin Winnebago, has a federal reservation in Wisconsin

Contributors

Ward Churchill (Keetowah Cherokee), Professor of American Indian Studies, University of Colorado, Boulder

Joely De La Torre (Luiseno), Associate Professor of American Indian Studies, San Francisco State University

Vine Deloria Jr. (Standing Rock Sioux), Emeritus Professor of History, Religion, and American Indian Studies, University of Colorado, Boulder

Philip L. Fetzer, Professor of Political Science, California Polytechnic State University, San Luis Obispo

Carole Goldberg, Professor of Law, UCLA School of Law

Donald A. Grinde Jr. (Yamasee), Professor of History and ALANA/Ethnic Studies, University of Vermont

Larry W. Gross (White Earth Chippewa), Assistant Professor of Religious Studies and American Indian Studies, Iowa State University

M. A. Jaimes-Guerrero (Yaqui/Juaneno), Associate Professor of Women's Studies, San Francisco State University

Bruce E. Johansen, James T. Reilly Professor of Communication and Native American Studies, University of Nebraska, Omaha

Stacy L. Leeds (Cherokee), Assistant Professor of Law, and Director, Northern Plains Indian Law Center, University of North Dakota

Carol A. Markstrom, Associate Professor of Child Development and Family Studies, West Virginia University

Jack Norton (Hupa/Cherokee/Yurok), Emeritus Professor of Native American Studies, Humboldt State University

James Riding In (Pawnee), Professor of Justice Studies, Arizona State University

Natsu Taylor Saito, Professor of Law, College of Law, Georgia State University

Dean B. Suagee (Cherokee), Director, First Nations Environmental Law Program and Assistant Professor of Law, Vermont Law School

David E. Wilkins (Lumbee), Associate Professor of American Indian Studies, Political Science, and Law, University of Minnesota

Index

Page numbers in italics indicate references to the Documents section, starting on page 191.